Corporate Governance 3.0

Karl George
Simon Osborne
Alexander Van de Putte

One Victoria Square
Birmingham
B1 1BD

www.thegovernanceforum.com

September 2021

CONTENTS

FOREWORD vi
Mervyn King SC

INTRODUCTION x
Karl George, Simon Osborne & Alexander Van de Putte

1. Introducing Corporate Governance 3.0 – The History of Corporate Governance 3
Karl George

2. World-wide Good Governance is our History, Present and Future 25
Jeffrey Ridley

3. Board Leadership 45
Simon Haslam & Alexander Van de Putte

4. Director Duties and Their Implications 67
Sharon Constançon

5. The Pivotal Role of the Company Secretary 85
Simon Osborne

6. Board Diversity – A Historical Perspective 105
Ann Holder

7. The Gen 3.0 Broader Context of Diversity 137
Karl George, Helen Higginbotham & Tom Proverbs-Garbett

8. The Board's Role in Strategy 155
Alexander Van de Putte & Simon Haslam

9. Providing Financial Stewardship of Companies 173
Jean Pousson

10. The Governance of Big Tech	193
Simon Osborne	
11. The Governance of Large Private Companies	217
Kenneth Olisa	
12. An Australian Perspective	239
Julie Garland-McLellan	
13. A Central Asian Perspective	261
Kairat Kelimbetov & Alexander Van de Putte	
14. A MENA Perspective	283
Ashraf Gamal El Din	
15. A South African Perspective	301
Sharon Constançon & Simon Osborne	
16. The Governance of Asian Family Businesses – The Second Generation Growth and Sustainability Imperatives	321
Ser-Keng Ang & Alexander Van de Putte	
17. The Dynamics of Corporate Reporting	343
George Littlejohn & Alexander Van de Putte	
18. Is Corporate Governance 4.0 Emerging?	363
Alexander Van de Putte	
ABOUT THE AUTHORS	387
ENDORSEMENTS	398

FOREWORD

In the last half of 2020 and the beginning of 2021 there was incredible movement among framework providers in the ESG space. Apparently driven by the extraordinary collaboration in finding a vaccine against the Corona virus, the aforesaid framework providers started collaborating instead of seeing one another as competitors.

The result of this collaboration has led the International Financial Reporting Standards (IFRS) Foundation to expand its mandate and to establish a Sustainability Standards Board (SSB) which will have lessons learned from the other collaborators built into the standards. There is every indication that the standards will be looked at through an enterprise value creation lens rather than a civil society one.

The more informed corporate reporting is, the more transparent is the board's accountability but sustainability standards need to be as reliable, consistent and rigorous as are financial reporting standards. The intent is for the SSB to lie alongside the International Accounting Standards Board (IASB) both under the oversight of the IFRS.

Reporting does influence corporate behaviour and consequently it is timely to have a book setting out the history of corporate governance and some of its current critical features. This is what the authors Karl George, Simon Osborne and Alexander Van de Putte have set out to do in their new book, Corporate Governance 3.0. They have dealt with the history of corporate governance, talking about the period prior to the Cadbury Report in 1992; the computer age from 1991 to 2010 and then what has happened in the last decade of the 21st century where the corporate world has changed from focusing on the primacy of the shareholder to value creation in a sustainable manner because of the resource constraints of planet earth.

In this changing corporate world the authors deal with the question of trust, integrity and openness where the focus is no longer on increasing the wealth of shareholders but rather ensuring that the collective business judgment calls made by a board will add value to society. This connotes that boards, individually and as a collective, have to make decisions in the long term best interests of the health of the company but take account of the needs, interests and expectations of all the stakeholders, accepting that in making decisions in the best interests of the company there would invariably be tradeoffs between the various stakeholder groupings.

Consequently, corporate leaders at the top have to endeavour to ensure that the perception of external stakeholders is that they are steering the company as effective leaders, that there are adequate and effective internal controls, that there is trust and confidence in the company by the community where the company operates and that the company is seen to be a responsible corporate citizen.

The above depends on the quality of board leadership and the authors deal with this in some detail. The collective decisions made by a board should be in the long term best interests of the health of the company but taking account of the needs, interests and expectations of all the company's stakeholders.

The diversity of boards has become a critical issue especially intergenerational diversity and the authors have dealt with the various kinds of diversity in some detail.

The board is the steward of the company's assets and finalizes and approves management's proposals on strategy. The collective mind of the board has to be applied to the long term issues which will impact on the company. Corporate leaders have, in the first decade of the 21st century, focused on the impacts of the company's activities and its product on the three critical dimensions for sustainable development, namely the economy, society and the environment. In the second decade of the 21st century there was a focus on the impacts which these three critical dimensions had on the limited liability company. For example, the collapse of Lehman Brothers impacted adversely on companies. From a societal point of view the pandemic is having an adverse impact on companies. From an environmental point of view, climate change is the critical risk factor of businesses in the 21st century. The authors correctly deal with the question of stewardship and that companies will be governed in the context of the fourth industrial revolution.

They deal with what is happening in Australia and Asia in regard to governance. From this discussion it will be seen that the drive to try and create a global comprehensive corporate reporting system must be the end game for a resource constrained planet which cannot sustain infinite growth with finite assets.

The company secretary is critical in bringing together management reports on risk, internal controls and compliance while drafting the pack for the board to make business judgment calls. The company secretary is absolutely pivotal in ensuring the quality of information placed before a board. This aspect of corporate governance is also dealt with in the book.

The corporate reporting landscape has changed and is changing dramatically. This is having an impact not only on listed companies but also unlisted companies, particularly in the supply chain of large listed companies. Corporate leaders have learned that if something adverse, such as the use of child labour by a major supplier is taking place, it has an adverse impact on the market capitalisation of the consumer company listed on a Stock Exchange.

The authors have also done a comparative study of the approach to corporate governance in different jurisdictions and have referred, inter alia, to the King IV Report.

A rules based corporate governance model which is mandated is not the pathway to quality governance. It becomes a mindless, checklist exercise. What has to happen is a mindful, outcomes based approach to governance. This fits in with the corporate reporting narrative which has become outcomes based such as set out in the Integrated Reporting Framework, as well as the Sustainable Development Goals. In this context shouldn't governance be outcomes based?

The conclusion of the authors is that the way companies are governed is more inclusive as opposed to the exclusive approach to focus on shareholders and has to be sustainable and resilient in our resource constrained world. The test for success will be the benefit to society of the company's activities, product or services.

The book is to be welcomed at a time when there is such change in the corporate reporting world to have a SSB operative in 144 jurisdictions sitting alongside the IASB under the oversight of the IFRS. This change will rid a large part of the world of the clutter and confusion for preparers and users in the ESG space as a result of the proliferation of framework providers.

It is said that to understand what is happening now one has to have knowledge of that which has happened in the past. To have an understanding of the current expeditious changes taking place in corporate reporting and governance the book written by the three authors is timeous.

Prof. Mervyn King SC

INTRODUCTION

Following a series of occasional meetings which the three of us had in 2020, at first in person and then via Zoom, Alexander enthused us with the idea of producing and publishing a book about the progressive development of corporate governance and the future for good governance with the onset of what Professor Klaus Schwab, the Founder and Executive Chairman of the World Economic Forum, has called the Fourth Industrial Revolution. Governance is too often considered as an end in itself without regard to its historical development and, particularly, the three generations of modern corporate governance.

Modern governance has involved a journey through three levels of maturity. From Governance 1.0, in which the successful operation of governance was held back by dominance hierarchy (e.g., the Robert Maxwell saga); through Governance 2.0, in which the successful application of governance principles was held back by corporate scandals and failures (e.g. Enron); and through to Governance 3.0, in which governance has taken advantage of new technology, new ways of collaborative working and has had necessarily to make room for Generations Y and Z.

Governance 3.0 has displayed the potential to help all types of organisation successfully to navigate fast-changing, uncertain, ambiguous and disruptive environments. At the time of publication, we consider that the era of Governance 3.0 is drawing to a close to be succeeded by a fourth generation of governance, Governance 4.0. That fourth generation of governance seems to us to coincide more or less with the onset of the Fourth Industrial Revolution, or 4IR. It promises to be an interesting journey

You may not find explicit reference to Governance 3.0 in every chapter but, in determining the content of the book, we wanted to provide an international perspective and to explain the approaches to governance taken in different parts of the world which have developed their own distinctive approach – Asia, Australia, MENA (but particularly Dubai), South Africa and South-East Asia. Governance principles are in a perpetual state of development so we wanted in conclusion to highlight some of the major governance challenges which lie ahead, particularly the governance of Big

Tech; the inevitable challenges thrown up by 4IR; the complexity of tackling demographic changes and diversity; and the increasing importance of ESG and sustainability reporting.

We are immensely grateful to the team of authors who have worked with us and who have endured with good humour our demands about deadlines, house styles and word count. Each of the authors whom we invited to contribute to this book has made a significant impact on its development and the final publication. We want to thank all of them and in particular two of our authors, Ann Holder and Tom Proverbs-Garbett, who have contributed also to the task of editing. We extend our appreciation and grateful thanks to all of them.

We wish also to express our grateful thanks to Professor Mervyn King SC for writing the foreword to this book. It is a matter of immense pride to us that such an eminent jurist and governance expert as Dr. King should have agreed to contribute to the book in this significant way.

In conclusion, we hope that you will find this book interesting, even stimulating. If there are any errors or omissions, they are the responsibility of the three of us.

Karl George
Simon Osborne
Alexander Van de Putte

CHAPTER 1. INTRODUCING GOVERNANCE 3.0 – THE HISTORY OF CORPORATE GOVERNANCE

Karl George, Managing Director, The Governance Forum

Introduction

In a fast paced, increasingly complex business environment, we need to ensure there are mechanisms in place to help us measure and monitor how well organisations are performing in order to prevent failure.[1] For over 15 years I have been working with organisations across the private, public and voluntary sectors to help raise the standards of governance. What I have found is that governance can sometimes be seen as something done to tick the box.[2] When we talk about a robust governance framework, or good governance, it means different things to different people.[3]

Good governance is much more than a compliance issue. It is about how we ensure that an organisation's purpose, strategy, values and culture have a golden thread that aligns them.[4,5] It is the intertwining and linking of

---

[1] Askarany D. (2011), 'Factors Affecting Organizational Performance', Paradigms: A Research Journal of Commerce, Economics and Social Sciences, vol. 5, no. 1, pp. 14-31.
[2] Lee S. (2017), 'Saving Governance: Beyond the Tick-box', 22 May, HR Magazine, available online: <https://www.hrmagazine.co.uk/content/insights/saving-governance-beyond-the-tick-box> (accessed 14 May 2021).
[3] L'huillier B. (2014), 'What Does "Corporate Governance" Actually Mean?', Corporate Governance International Journal of Business in Society, vol. 14, no. 3, pp. 300-319.
[4] Financial Reporting Council (2018), The UK Corporate Governance Code, available online < https://www.frc.org.uk/getattachment/88bd8c45-50ea-4841-95b0-d2f4f48069a2/2018-UK-Corporate-Governance-Code-FINAL.PDF> (accessed 14 May 2021);

strategy and policy, oversight and disclosure. It's about running the organisation well. The better the governance, the better and more sustainable the organisation.[6] Oversight and foresight are necessary but promoting success is more than satisfying profit objectives or the needs of one stakeholder group.[7] It generates positive outcomes for business, the economy and the environment.[8]

In these changing times, it is important to recognise how governance has moved from being compliance based and responding to corporate failure (first generation); to generative – trying to anticipate failure (second generation); and then to where we are today, where the rate and pace of change require a new approach to good governance (third generation).[9] It is time to think about a methodology which responds to this rapidly changing technological environment and which considers the interest and influence of stakeholders, environmental issues such as climate change and social issues such as globalisation.

In this environment, we must consider questions such as: what are the major forces that shape societies around the world and are likely to influence the future of business and how it is run? As Yuval Noah Harrari puts it: "*…a global world puts unprecedented pressure on our personal conduct and morality.*"[10]

Governance does not exist in a vacuum. We should consider how the workforce and customers experience a new world and develop a new way of working as a result. Preparing for the future means considering the impact of disruptive technologies. But rather than just responding to or

---

[5] See, for example, Principle B: "The board should establish the company's purpose, values and strategy, and satisfy itself that these and its culture are aligned. All directors must act with integrity, lead by example and promote the desired culture."
[6] MacAvoy P. and Millstein I. (2003), The Recurrent Crisis in Corporate Governance, London: Palgrave McMillan.
[7] Williams R. (2012), 'Enlightened Shareholder Value in UK Company Law', UNSW Law Journal, vol. 35, no. 1, pp. 360-377.
[8] Neville-Rolfe L. (Baroness) (2015), 'The Importance of Corporate Governance', speech, available online: <https://www.gov.uk/government/speeches/the-importance-of-corporate-governance> (accessed 14 May 2021).
[9] Gordon J. (2018), 'Is Corporate Governance a First-order Cause of the Current Malaise?', Journal of the British Academy, vol. 6, no. 1, pp. 405–436.
[10] Harari Y.N. (2018), 21 Lessons for the 21st Century, London: Penguin Random House.

anticipating disruption, a good governance framework should help to create, innovate, influence change and improve long-term, sustainable success.

We may not be able to predict or prevent failure but we should have governance standards that are relevant across all sectors (regardless of size) and jurisdictions, whose insightful application will give assurance that the risk and impact of failure are minimised so far as practicable. This is why I believe it is time for us to consider *The Governance Framework* as **Governance 3.0 – The Third Generation**.

In order to interpret, discuss or evaluate what we mean by poor and good governance it makes sense to offer a working model of the governance framework. An investigation that spreads across three generations and covers a period of 50 years must be robust enough to deal with the different types of governing models over time, the different sectors that organisations operate in and the different stages of business maturity that these organisations go through.

This chapter concludes with a principles-based approach to considering what good governance looks like. As we consider each generation, we will examine the following:

– the demographics of the boardrooms in that generation and leadership styles
– the technology and information flow
– high profile corporate successes and failures over that time

1. Generation 1.0

Generation 1.0 started in what I call 'pre-history' and take us up to 1992.

Governance stretches back to early civilisation because, for societies to function effectively, there has to be a governance regime of some sort or anarchy will prevail. In the Bible narrative, Moses was advised by his father-in-law, Jethro, to organise people and to appoint trustworthy chiefs over thousands, hundreds, fifties and tens with appropriate delegations of authority for resolving issues.[11] It is only in the 1980s and 1990s, however, that we first hear the term corporate governance.[12]

The boardrooms of Generation 1.0 were dominated by what is known as the Silent Generation.[13] Born between 1927 and 1946, they were the generation who were seen and not heard. It makes sense, then, that boardrooms did not experience the challenge and scrutiny that we have come to expect.[14]

Generation 1.0 was characterised by Dominance Hierarchy tendencies[15] So if the choices confronting a group are simple, and a leader needs cohesion for effective and smooth implementation, command and control works well. Dominant leaders who don't tolerate challenge will flourish, as was demonstrated by the late Robert Maxwell. In certain circumstances, this type of command and control leadership can even make for good governance. A UK Department of Trade and Industry report in 2001 described Maxwell thus:

> *"he was a bully and domineering personality but could be charming on occasions".* [16]

This style of leadership does not work, however, where there are many complicated and inter-related dynamics with which to contend; nor does it work where the advantage of utilising the myriad skills and experience of board members to achieve competitive advantage is lost.[17]

---

[11] Exodus 18:21-23
[12] Cheffins B. (2015), 'Corporate Governance since the Managerial Capitalism Era', History Review, vol. 89, no. 4, pp. 717-744.
[13] See <https://aboutgenerations.com/silent-generation/> (accessed 14 May 2021).
[14] Cheffins B. (2015), 'The Rise of Corporate Governance in the UK: When and Why' Current Legal Problems, vol. 68, no. 1, pp. 387–429.
[15] Lahn B. (2020), 'Social Dominance Hierarchy: Toward a Genetic and Evolutionary Understanding' Cell Research, vol. 30, pp. 560–561.
[16] Department of Trade and Industry (2001), 'Investigation under Sections 432(2) and 442 of the Companies Act 1985 of Mirror Group Newspapers plc', available online: < https://webarchive.national archives.gov.uk/20060213225148/http://www.dti.gov.uk/cld/mirrorgroup/index.htm> (accessed 14 May 2021), p. 319.
[17] Ryan L. (2016), 'Command-And-Control Management Is For Dinosaurs, Forbes, 26 February, available online:

The Cadbury Code, published in 1992, had recommended that no single individual should have unfettered powers of decision-making; that non-executive directors (NEDs) should be introduced to boards; and the roles of the chair and chief executive officer (CEO) should be split.[18] Generation 1.0 governance, developed in the 1990s, encouraged the appointment of independent directors and the establishment of fully functioning and independent audit committees.[19]

Generation 1.0 governance then was predicated on shareholder primacy and directors' attention was focused on increasing shareholder value. Companies had to protect themselves from hostile takeovers and cater to institutional investors, producing better information about performance and longer-term strategy.[20]

In this generation, information was paper-based and reporting was constrained by labour intensive systems and processes which had not been able fully to embrace the full potential of computers. The mass use of computers with the introduction of the mini-computer in the late 1960s wouldn't see mass acceleration until the 1990s, that is during Governance 2.0. The computer age and its true potential had not established itself as far as corporate governance was concerned in Generation 1.0, so manual interpretation of data and unsophisticated data management meant that reporting was within the control of those reporting, with transparency limited to what they decided should be disclosed.

Carrying out a non-executive role in this era meant getting assurance from powerful executive directors and needed powerful NEDs to require the checks and balances that provided the relevant assurance.[21]

<https://www.forbes.com/sites/lizryan/2016/02/26/command-and-control-management-is-for-dinosaurs/?sh=4482731b24ed> (accessed 14 May 2021).

[18] 'Report of The Committee on the Financial Aspects of Corporate Governance' (1992) available online: <https://www.icaew.com/-/media/corporate/files/library/subjects/corporate-governance/financial-aspects-of-corporate-governance.ashx?la=en> (accessed 14 May 2021).

[19] Cheffins (note 14).

[20] Keay A. (2010), 'Shareholder Primacy in Corporate Law: Can it Survive? Should it Survive?', European Company and Financial Law Review, vol. 7, no. 3, pp. 369–413.

[21] Tricker R. (2020), 'The Evolution of Corporate Governance', Cambridge University Press, Cambridge.

<u>Case Studies around corporate failure</u>
Maxwell, Polly Peck, BCCI

<u>Growth Businesses of the era</u>
IBM, Kodak, Nokia

2. Generation 2.0

Generation 2.0 starts where Generation 1.0 ends, but there is some overlap as you would expect. The 1992 Cadbury report was a seminal piece of work so it is a logical place at which to note a distinction. We run now from about 1992 until about 2010.

It is over the period of Generation 2.0 that governance became more formalised and structured, with comprehensive models developed, applied and interpreted around the world. The launch of the Cadbury Code principles in 1992,[22] the King Report I in South Africa in 1994[23] and the OECD principles in 1998[24] was complemented by a rigorous rules based approach introduced by Sarbanes-Oxley in 2001-2.[25] This generation can rightly be considered to be the growth era for corporate governance.

The boardrooms of Generation 2.0 were now dominated by Baby Boomers born between 1946 and 1964.[26] In 2021 they would be aged in their 70s and coming to the end of their board careers but in Generation 2.0 they were in their prime. The computer generation was fully established and, although the Baby Boomers didn't grow up with the rapid change in technology driven by the internet, they had to embrace technological change relatively late in their careers. It wasn't until 1993 that the first Microsoft Windows browser was released and Hotmail went live in 1996 before Google in 1998.

The Baby Boomers would not have benefitted from technology to aid governance. Nowadays, the corporate world has fully embraced the

---

[22] Note 18.
[23] < https://www.iodsa.co.za/page/kingIII> (accessed 14 May 2021).
[24] < https://www.oecd.org/corporate/principles-corporate-governance/> (accessed 14 May 2021).
[25] Sarbanes-Oxley Act 2002 < https://www.govinfo.gov/content/pkg/COMPS-1883/pdf/COMPS-1883.pdf> (accessed 14 May 2021).
[26] See <https://aboutgenerations.com/baby-boomers/> (accessed 14 May 2021).

potential afforded by the use of technology.[27] When you consider the preoccupation during that period with the 'Millennium bug', use of Facebook (2004) and Twitter (2006) was going to be more comfortable for the next generation In this era, it is difficult to excuse a lack of openness and transparency since real time reporting and snapshot reports, complex data management and big data became increasingly common. The ability to scrutinise and monitor performance was enhanced and the more inquisitive and confident Baby Boomers engaged in more challenging interactions at board level.

Although the Sarbanes-Oxley legislation with its rules-based approach was seen as the antidote in the United States to the corporate failures of the early 2000s, the UK has maintained faith in a principles-based approach.[28] There was a common requirement for governance through this period to ensure that, no matter how complex organisations might be, there should always be an acceptance of certain governance precepts and standards and a more transparent disclosure of information.

Investors, stakeholders and regulators should be able to interpret through integrated reporting what was happening over and above profit, including any impact on the environment and employees.[29] The company's efforts in the areas of corporate social responsibility (CSR) were examined through reporting on environmental, social and governance factors (ESG).[30]

Generation 2.0 had developed sophisticated and comprehensive ways of analysing information and data, but it was primarily historic information that was considered through an array of key performance indicators and dashboards. Tackling future sustainability would start to have a well needed focus in Generation 3.0.

Boards in Generation 2.0 are more independent in their composition, unlike

---

[27] Financial Reporting Council (2020), 'A Matter of Principles: The Future of Corporate Reporting', available online: <https://www.frc.org.uk/getattachment/cf85af97-4bd2-4780-a1ec-dc03b6b91fbf/Future-of-Corporate-Reporting-FINAL.pdf> (accessed 14 May 2021).
[28] Cheffins, notes 12 and 14.
[29] Williams, note 7.
[30] Drake S. (2020), 'ESG in the Spotlight', Chartered Governance Institute Blog, available online: < https://www.cgi.org.uk/blog/esg-spotlight-blog> (accessed 14 May 2021).

the early Generation 1.0 boards. They are starting to become more diverse in terms of functional and professional skills, but have some way to go in other aspects of diversity.[31]

Generation 2.0 developed sophisticated and comprehensive ways of analysing information and data, but it was primarily historic information that was considered through an array of key performance indicators and dashboards.

In Generation 2.0 we would expect to see a balance of finance, legal, human resources and governance skills and, by the first decade of the 2000s, boards begin to consider what the impact of gender diversity. It is not until Generation 3.0, however, that we see a concentrated effort to address gender diversity and, more recently, ethnic and age diversity in the boardroom, with the stage set to consider cognitive diversity.

Generation 3.0 governance is poised too to take the stage to address a more complex but enlightened stakeholder theory and reporting environment.

Case Studies of corporate failure
UK: Marconi, Railtrack, Laming Inquiry 2003,
International: Australia HIH Insurance, Italy Parmalat, U.S. Enron 2001, WorldCom 2002, Lehman 2008

Growth businesses in Generation 2
Walmart, Google.

3. Generation 3.0

Two world events provide the timeline for generation 3.0. The 9/11 attack on the World Trade Center in 2001 ('9/11') sees the launch of Generation 3.0 while the onset of the COVID-19 pandemic marks its end.

It is the era in which we see paper board packs becoming less common as

---

[31] For example, the Parker Review on Ethnic Diversity and updates, available online: <https://www.gov.uk/government/publications/ethnic-diversity-of-uk-boards-the-parker-review> (accessed 14 May 2021).

Introducing Governance 3.0 – The History of Corporate Governance

directors have information provided to them electronically[32] and the advent of the 4th Industrial Revolution threatening to change the way we work, live and play.

In the boardroom we begin to see Generation X coming through into senior roles. They were born between 1965 and 1980.[33] They are aged 40 to 55 and are making more of a mark in the boardroom. A large proportion of boards are led still by and populated by Baby Boomers but, for the first time, there is potential for Generation Y to begin to make a mark as they are aged now between 25 and 40.[34] At the time of writing this potential has not been maximised and unfortunately there is a preponderance of board members who are not fully aligned with the digital age of business.

We live in a world where technology is developing at lightning speed, causing exciting opportunities and massive disruption, and creating big challenges for boards in organisations of every size and across every sector. Are we fully capitalising on the benefits of the latest digital developments in the boardroom or are board members:

- being left behind because they don't appreciate the technology?
- leaving their organisations vulnerable to cyber-attack?
- missing out on valuable opportunities to rise to new heights of performance?

Science fiction is becoming science 'fact'.. Ongoing revolutions in bio- and info-tech are game-changers and buzz words like 'globalisation', 'virtual and augmented reality', 'machine learning', 'cyborgs' and 'networked algorithms' are central to the vocabulary of this new world.[35]

Augmented reality glasses or headsets are rumoured to be in the

---

[32] Chartered Governance Institute (2018), Effective Board Reporting, available online: <https://www.cgi.org.uk/knowledge/effective-board-reporting> (accessed 14 May 2021).
[33] See <https://aboutgenerations.com/generation-x/> (accessed 14 May 2021).
[34] See <https://aboutgenerations.com/generation-y/> (accessed 14 May 2021).
[35] Financial Reporting Lab (2021), 'Virtual and Augmented Reality in Corporate Reporting: Digital Future of Corporate Reporting', available online: <https://www.frc.org.uk/getattachment/e1e6befb-d635-4284-a022-2354a04d5873/VR-and-AR-in-corporate-reporting-1702.pdf> (accessed 14 May 2021).

development pipeline of tech giant Apple, moving us ever nearer to the fantasy worlds portrayed in the Marvel comics. Are we really that far away from the *Iron Man* helmet, developed by the fictional Stark Industries, which allows its wearer to see data overlaying the people and places in its line of sight?

Professor Klaus Schwab, founder and executive chair of the World Economic Forum, calls the era in which we are living: 'The Fourth Industrial Revolution characterised by a range of new technologies that are fusing the physical, digital and biological worlds, impacting all disciplines, economies and industries, and even challenging ideas about what it means to be human.'[36]

In order to have productive discussions at board level there needs to be enough understanding and knowledge of the digital world, but many boards do not have the necessary expertise.[37] We currently recruit to ensure that boards have collective and individual expertise around finance, law and human resources, but is it time to ensure that the same focus is given to expertise in areas such as IT, data security, social media, cyber risk and emerging technologies?[38] Although there may be expertise at executive level, is there an argument for board representation in this area to be more robust with at least one board member with up to date and sector-relevant technology expertise[39]?

Here are just three examples of recent corporate failures. Please reflect on these high-profile cases, and the role of the board, and consider whether

---

[36] Schwab K. 'The Fourth Industrial Revolution', available online: <https://www.weforum.org/about/the-fourth-industrial-revolution-by-klaus-schwab> (accessed 14 May 2021).
[37] Ismail N. (2018), 'The Lack of Digital Skills at Board Level is Hurting Organisations', Information Age, 3 April, available online: <https://www.information-age.com/lack-digital-skills-board-level-hurting-organisations-123471303/> (accessed 14 May 2021).
[38] ibid.
[39] One lesson to emerge from the regulator's investigation into the workings of Australia's Commonwealth Bank was the board's lack of skills in technology and a perceived lack of hands-on experience in this area on the part of NEDs. The regulator considered that the ability of the board critically to challenge senior bank executives, who themselves were highly literate in technology, in a constructive manner could lead to a failure to ask the right question or offer the right level of challenge. A director cannot be all things and possess all skills, but how much knowledge and skill in technology is enough for a competent and fully informed director?

they were sufficiently informed and knowledgeable?

- **IT and systems** - As reported in The Times, on June 22, 2018, TSB did not test its new IT system adequately before embarking on its ill-fated migration of customers that left thousands unable to access their accounts, according to IBM. The board got its assurance from Sabis, a subsidiary of the holding company, and its CEO, Paul Pester, said the evidence it received was 'instrumental' in the board's decision-making.[40]

- **Social media** – In April 2017, a passenger was forcibly removed from a United Airlines flight ahead of take-off. In an initial statement, CEO Oscar Munoz backed the behaviour of the airline, but after a video of the incident went viral the airline was forced to reconsider its position. As a result of the outrage across social media, politicians expressed concern and called for an official investigation. U.S. President Donald Trump criticised United Airlines, calling the treatment of its customer 'horrible'.[41]

- **Data security** – Imagine you were a board member of British Airways: would you understand the wider IT security issues around some 380,000 credit and debit cards potentially compromised as a result of a data breach between August 21 and September 5, 2018? Hackers were able to steal the details of customers who booked flights on the airline's website during this two-week period, apparently by injecting malicious code into the payments section of the British Airways' website.[42]

What inventions should we be understanding and embracing? Putting aside the dangers of the new digital landscape for a moment, in this generation boards will be exposed if they fail to maximise the benefits and opportunities that technology offers.

---

[40] Griffiths K. (2018), 'TSB 'Failed to Test New System Properly Before IT Meltdown', available online: <https://www.thetimes.co.uk/article/tsb-failed-to-test-new-system-properly-before-it-meltdown-95djq59qw> (accessed 14 May 2021).

[41] Shugerman E. (2017), 'United Airlines Reverses Plans to Make CEO Oscar Munoz Chairman After Passenger Dragging Scandal', The Independent, 21 April, available online: < https://www.independent.co.uk/news/world/americas/united-airlines-david-dao-ceo-oscar-munoz-not-promoted-dragging-scandal-a7696266.html> (accessed 14 May 2021).

[42] Bevan K. (2018), ' BA Promises to Compensate Customers After Data Breach', Which, available online: <https://www.which.co.uk/news/2018/09/ba-promises-to-compensate-customers-after-data-breach/> (accessed 14 May 2021).

Generation 3.0 must have some predictive ability. Expressions such as 'black swan' come to the fore after Taleb's book[43] and acronyms such as 'VUCA' describe or reflect on the volatility, uncertainty, complexity and ambiguity of general conditions and situations affecting strategy. The importance of the stakeholder has a greater degree of emphasis and large, unlisted businesses have a growing impact on society when they fail (See also chapters 8 and 18 for an in-depth discussion on how to deal with disruptive risks)

A review of the circumstances leading to the demise of the world's largest travel company, Thomas Cook, illustrates how Generation 3.0 is now emerging. The company had been trading for 178 years before its collapse in September 2019. It was the victim of a perfect storm: climate change resulting in hotter summers in the UK; more customers booking directly, enabled by the growth of the internet; and the death of a holidaymaker's child, that was badly mismanaged by the company, being spread quickly across social media.[44] These factors on top of repeated financial restructuring meant the business just could not cope.

Boards of Generation 3.0 need to be functionally diverse and gender diverse and drawn from different backgrounds so that they are able to tackle not one 'black swan' event but several 'black swan' events occurring simultaneously.

Cognitive diversity and greater generative governance are the order of the day. Technology is having a real impact on Generation 3.0 with boards needing to embrace the use of artificial intelligence (AI), big data and the merging of bio and info technology.

Chait, Ryan and Taylor[45] posit that type 1 governance is the fiduciary mode or stewardship of assets, type 2 the strategic mode or creating a strategic

---

[43] Talab N.N. (2007), The Black Swan: The Impact of the Highly Improbable, Allen Lane: London.
[44] Collinson P. (2019), 'Why did Thomas Cook Collapse After 178 Years in Business?', The Guardian, 23 September, available online: <https://www.theguardian.com/business/2019/sep/23/thomas-cook-as-the-world-turned-the-sun-ceased-to-shine-on-venerable-tour-operator> (accessed 14 May 2021).
[45] Chait R.P., Ryan W.P. and Taylor B.E. (2011), Governance as Leadership, Reframing the Work of Non-Profit Boards, John Wiley & Sons: London.

partnership with management, then finally type 3 generative model or governance as leadership.

Baby Boomer and Generation X board members are reducing in number and a different skillset is required to manage real time manipulation of information and the navigation of a disruptive, rapidly changing and truly global business environment.

This generation has seen B2B shifting from bricks and mortar to e-commerce, emergence of social media networks, the impact of big data, companies have to consider now sustainability, environmental and social impact, a more informed global consumer base.[46]

What is not so clear is what exactly boards need to look like in terms of structure, composition and activity to create a framework that provides confidence in this rapidly changing business environment. What is clear is they will have to adapt as being adaptable and resilient is just as important as were the structural and functional responsibilities of Generation 1.0 and Generation 2.0.

In conclusion, here are three areas to consider in Governance 3.0:

– there is the need for an appropriate governance structure which is more adaptable than in previous generations;
– strong leadership through a cognitively diverse team, having independent board members and functional diversity, is not enough - all aspects of diversity are crucial; and
– the will and capacity to make timely and swift decisions and act on them.

Let's examine these three areas in turn:

The *first* area involves the governance structure and the importance of everyone having clear roles and responsibilities and understanding the boundaries. The CEO has oversight and a strategic role and should develop a core team of executives. The frequency of board and committee meetings may have to change as well as the terms of reference.

---

[46] Stafford B. and Schindlinger D. (2019), Governance in the Digital Age, Wiley: London.

An example of flexible and proactive governance structures is the UK Government's emergency COBRA meetings. COBRA stands for Cabinet Office Briefing Room A, which is where these meetings usually take place. As well as the Prime Minister, who usually chairs the meetings, they are attended by a cross-departmental range of senior ministers, security officials, military chiefs, emergency services leaders and civil servants. The attendees change according to the nature of the crisis. Medical and scientific experts have been brought in for coronavirus meetings.

Similarly, in a business or organisation you need to develop an extended team that can be brought in for specific responses. We typically ask the board to stay strategic, to challenge the executive, be ambassadors to all stakeholders and get to grips with the key risks. In Governance 3.0 there will a greater need to exercise all of those roles, but it is even more important to take a more collaborative approach than is normally expected. The board may need to dig a little bit deeper than normal when providing support and advice, but it is important to get the balance right so as not to interfere in day to day management. NEDs may be required to join a particular 'task and finish' group and serve the organisation with their specialist skills.

Secondly, consider the need for strong, flexible and visible leadership. Boards need to support the management in stressful and uncertain times. The leadership must be positive, forward-looking, well-informed but decisive and focus on getting people on the same page. It is much more sophisticated than Generation 1.0 or dominance hierarchy, more flexible than Generation 2.0 that sensitive balance with powerful executive directors. A strong leadership will be thinking about the post-crisis strategy even in the midst of the crisis in order to provide the necessary confidence for management about technological disruption before it manifests itself. A diverse board will anticipate, innovate and care enough about sustainability to act before it is forced to act by factors outside their control.

Boards governing in the era of Governance 3.0 will understand the importance of adaptability and helping people get through change, to reassure them and give them the right perspective. To ensure that boards have the right mix of skills and capabilities to address all of the challenges that may arise in a crisis, for example, directors should ask themselves different questions. Has anyone on the board been through a crisis, epidemic, pandemic; such as 9/11 or the global financial crisis in 2008-09? What can we learn from their expertise? Equally, how many have recent and relevant experience of the digital landscape and what that means for our business now?

In his book, Good to Great, Jim Collins creates a memorable metaphor by comparing a business to a bus and its leader as the bus driver. He says you must always start by getting the right people on the bus, the wrong people off the bus, and the right people in the right seats.

In Governance 3.0, there is no room for hangers-on. Everyone needs to step up and be in alignment. We need to make the best use of the talent that we have, ensuring that we avoid the temptation to work only with the people with whom we are most comfortable. Neither group-think nor conflict is wanted. There should be healthy collaborative tension. The governance structure, mentioned as the first step, may not have all of the current leaders operating in their normal capacity. In this new era of governance there will be key individuals who step up to the plate, from different disciplines or backgrounds. It is imperative that bureaucracy, or overly-rigid governance structures, don't stop employees at all levels from being empowered to carry out their roles. Embracing the talent of Generation Y whether through shadow boards or other means is a business imperative.

Thirdly, it is important for the board of a Governance 3.0 organisation to be open, authentic and accountable for their decisions. The board is the highest decision-making authority in the organisation and they need to listen first, take everyone's views and all the facts into account and then exercise good judgment to make an unequivocal decision and ensure agreed actions are implemented within agreed timescales by an accountable executive.

A good board will stand by their decisions, however difficult they are and however unpalatable they may be to others. In times of crisis, of the proportion of the current pandemic, where post-crisis factors may not be the same again, decisions need to be made about the business model and whether it is still fit for purpose.

Considering the impact of virtual board meetings may lead to reduction in the requirement for office space or changes to business travel changing the way work is carried out.

Adaptability, resilience and effective decisions made in a structured manner once all the relevant timely information has been gathered will be the hallmark of successfully run organisations.

Case Studies of corporate failure
UK - Francis Inquiry 2013 Kids Company 2015 , Grenfell 2017, Carillion 2018, , Thomas Cook 2019
International - Deepwater Horizon Oil Spill 2010, Etihad Etisalat, Mobily 2015, Abraaj 2018, NMC Health 2020

Growth business in generation 3
Amazon , Apple, Tesla

4. Conclusion

Governance 3.0 reviews and analyses good and poor governance over the past 30 years or so. It recognises the shifts in the culture of businesses and boardrooms over this period and the influence of technology, the composition of the board room and the changing emphasis of what contributes to the long-term sustainability of an enterprise.

It is hoped that by examining the structure, composition and the activity of boards, organisations can be better prepared for, and even anticipate, crisis and disruption. The development of appropriate governance frameworks to suit the contextual, cultural, generational and legal influences of the day will help organisations to respond positively to opportunities that arise from the interaction of the Fourth Industrial Revolution, globalisation, cognitively diverse boards and a wider stakeholder approach to understanding purpose and mission.

Governance is much more than compliance. Outdated perceptions of mere control and supervision, that constrained previous generations, need no longer hinder what should always be evolving and developing – the pursuit and application of high quality governance across the private, public and voluntary sectors.

Appendix

Having summarised the history of governance since the early 1990s to the present day, and a methodology to measure the components of governance, what does Governance 3.0 look like using the 12 principles from a study of different codes of governance from across sectors and geographic jurisdictions[47].

Resources

Principle 1: The board should have a clear purpose and the right resources and structures.

- Generation 1 - Structures are complicated. Vision and objectives are very generic.
- Generation 2 - Structures are streamlined and simple. Purpose and objectives are well documented and there is a strategic alignment in line with the organisation's values.
- Generation 3 - Structures are dynamic and flexible - there is a well-documented corporate plan and alignment with the purpose, values, strategy aligned with culture across all documentation.

Principle 2: 'The board should have access to the right reports and information.

- Generation 1 - Reports, minutes are overly simplistic - receive dated and historic information. Board reports are paper based. Disclosure is poor.
- Generation 2 - Reports are overly complicated and lack transparency. Complicated KPIs, but boards do receive up to date and relevant information. Board Reports Portal based. Disclosure is compliance based and all regulatory reporting is completed well.

---

[47] Principles of Good Governance tgf in association with the Chartered Governance Institute Nov 2019. http://www.thegovernanceforum.com/wp-content/uploads/2019/12/tgf-governance-code.pdf Readers are recommended to review the 12 principles in full so as to gain a better understanding of the comparative review which follows.

- Generation 3 - There is concise information received in real time. Board reports include real-time interactive analysis. Disclosure reporting is based on providing outcome-based understanding over and above statutory reporting. Papers are summarised with key information, using technology to update in real time and robotics to highlight and answer queries.

Principle 3: The board should have the right documentation in place.

- Generation 1 - There is a lack of a strategic policy framework and review schedule.

- Generation 2 - The strategic policy framework is well thought through and monitored regularly in line with a strict checklist.

- Generation 3 - The strategic policy framework is monitored electronically and is updated in real time and approved through a dynamic review cycle.

Principle 4: The board's roles and responsibilities should be clearly defined.

- Generation 1 - Roles and responsibilities between the board and executive are blurred and there is no real comprehensive delegated authority schedule.

- Generation 2 - Roles and responsibilities are clarified with a properly documented suite of documents to outline these, including financial and other delegated authorities although they may not be well rehearsed across the board.

- Generation 3 - There are clear but flexible responsibilities with a governing framework that allows the structure and personnel to be adapted for various projects, a crisis or using specific expertise.

Competency

Principle 5: The board should be diverse and balanced.

- Generation 1 - Lack of diversity - silent generation dominates - suspicious of technology and its use in the board room in supporting skills.

- Generation 2 - Functionally diverse i.e. mainly skills based particularly finance, with some legal and human resources, and tackling gender diversity. Baby boomers dominate - technology complements traditional board activity.

- Generation 3 - The board is independent and functionally diverse tackling age, gender, ethnic and other diversity but focused on being cognitively diverse - Generations X and Y dominate the composition. The board use technology to enhance board skills, including robotics and AI.

Principle 6: The board should conduct themselves appropriately.

- Generation 1 - Boards are quite poor in demonstrating independence and behaving appropriately.

- Generation 2 - Boards are able to demonstrate independence, and upholding the law and probity standards but struggle sometimes with appropriate ethical behaviour.

- Generation 3 - Board members are clear about their role on the board and their duty to the wide group of stakeholders and evidence this with their behaviours.

Principle 7: The board should have clear processes for appointment, induction and training.

- Generation 1 - The appointment and induction processes are weak and training and development are non-existent combined with a reluctance to carry out appraisal activity. No succession strategy.

- Generation 2 - Appointment and induction processes are improving. Training and development amongst board members is generally but not universally accepted and appraisal activity is tolerated. Basic succession strategy is in place.

- Generation 3 - Appointment and induction processes are seen as crucial in developing high performing boards. There is a real appetite for training and development with a number of virtual and personalised programmes. Appraisal is welcomed with a well thought through succession strategy and plans well underway.

Principle 8: The board should have effective processes for evaluation.

- Generation 1 - There is no real appraisal or evaluation process and those that are in place are tick box exercises.
- Generation 2 - Evaluation becomes comprehensive and better structured. Outcomes form detailed action plans and follow a rigid process of implementation.
- Generation 3 - Appraisal activity is real time and makes use of technology with outcome focused objectives being identified.

Execution

Principle 9: The board should make informed decisions that take risk into account.

- Generation 1 - No real decision making framework is in place and the chair is dominant . Risk setting and monitoring are cumbersome and poor.
- Generation 2 - Good decision making processes. Risk management is robust with clear risk plans and strategies for mitigation and regular review at the right level.
- Generation 3 - Sophisticated technology based using robotics and big data for decision making protocols linked to assurance levels to predict and mitigate crises. Risk mapping and monitoring are enhanced by the use of technology and machine learning to prompt discussion and decision making by the board.

Principle 10: The board should be able to evidence challenge and debate.

- Generation 1 - Inappropriate or non-existent challenge at face to face board meetings, while technology is non-existent or seen as a barrier to board debate and assurance. There is an oversight focus.
- Generation 2 - Good challenge, with face to face and conference calling for board meetings. Technology supports board debate and assurance. There is a foresight focus.
- Generation 3 - There is healthy tension in board meetings and virtual board meetings are used to best effect. Technology enhances board

debate and assurance Gaining insight is the focus rather than oversight and foresight.

Principle 11: The board should be stewards of the vision and culture of the organisation.

- Generation 1 - Monitoring is highly operational.
- Generation 2 - Monitoring is more strategic.
- Generation 3 - There is monitoring to ensure real alignment with the purpose, values, strategy and culture.

Principle 12: The board should demonstrate effective engagement with stakeholders.

- Generation 1 - Communication with one main stakeholder.
- Generation 2 - Inform a wide group of stakeholders and consult extensively with some groups .
- Generation 3 - There is full two-way engagement with all stakeholders which influences strategic direction and policy and clear engagement with all stakeholders beyond mere consultation.

CHAPTER 2. WORLD-WIDE GOOD GOVERNANCE IS OUR HISTORY, PRESENT AND FUTURE

Jeffrey Ridley, Visiting Professor, London South Bank University, University of Lincoln and Birmingham City University

Introduction

> *'What will you do about restoring trust in our leaders and the quality of governance...?'[1]*

The 130[2] year history of The Chartered Governance Institute (CGI) shows that its Royal Charter[3] objective of "...effective governance and efficient administration of commerce, industry and public affairs..." has consistently

---

[1] Question asked by Bob Garratt to the reader in the Preface of his latest book Stop the Rot (2017)

[2] Thomas Brown founded the London-based Institute of Secretaries in 1891 to represent the interests of corporation secretaries who had emerged to govern the administration of joint stock companies following the introduction of limited liability in 1855. The Royal Charter was granted in 1902. In 1970, the Institute of Secretaries merged with the Corporation of Secretaries becoming the Institute of Chartered Secretaries and Administrators (ICSA) in 1971. To demonstrate the broadening of the professional support it provides to all those in governance roles its name was changed to The Chartered Governance Institute when the Royal Charter was amended in September 2019.
https://en.wikipedia.org/wiki/Institute_of_Chartered_Secretaries_and_Administrators (accessed 9 February 2021).

[3] The Charter in its current form refers to the Royal Charter of 22 June 1966 and the Supplemental Charter of 10 September 1971 as amended under article 21 by Order of the Privy Council dated 5 March 2014

been its aim; improving and maintaining the effectiveness of boards of directors, not just in companies and organisations across all sectors in the United Kingdom but also in its many "…divisions, branches and other local organisations.", across "…the Commonwealth and elsewhere.". Since its foundation, achieving the fundamental principles of good governance in all sectors has been the Institute's objective.

In 1962 I became an overseas student member of the Institute of Chartered Secretaries[4]. After qualifying I was elected as an Associate member in 1967, followed by Fellowship. Sixty three years later I am a Fellow of The Chartered Governance Institute (CGI). My journey as a chartered secretary is a small part of the history of worldwide good governance, as seen today in its three main principles of accountability, integrity and openness: leading us all as stakeholders into what has to be a trust in each other, in the societies we live in and in the organisations which serve and provide for our wellbeing. That trust is the outcome achieved by good governance in the 'direction and control' of many organisations and will always be its outcome in the future, nationally and internationally for all organisations.

1. Worldwide Good Governance

ICSA[5] influenced my thinking on worldwide good governance when in 1979 it published a series of papers on corporate governance and accountability by distinguished contributors from industry and academia, introducing these with:

> *"In recent years, public debate has ranged over industrial democracy, audit committees, the duties and responsibilities of company directors, disclosure of information, accounting standards and other subjects but there has been little new thought about more fundamental aspects - the 'why'; and 'how' of corporate governance."*

---

[4] It became the Institute of Chartered Secretaries and Administrators (ICSA) in 1970 after merging with the Corporation of Secretaries; and in 2019 it became the Chartered Governance Institute

[5] The Aims And Objectives Of Corporate Bodies (979), Sir Arthur Knight; and To Whom Should The Board Be Accountable….And For What? (1979), Dr. K. Midgley, Institute of Chartered Secretaries and Administrators, London, England.

Two of the contributors examined boardroom responsibilities, listing the claims of various groups of which management need to take account in their decision making. These lists included most of the groups currently referred to as an organisation's "stakeholders". In ranking these groups they identified consumers as "Customers come first; ...". They did not at that time see other groups (stakeholders) as customers! In listing groups with claims on an organisation, they both predated the current wide definition of 'stakeholder'. Conclusions reached by both contributors placed accountability clearly at the door of directors and profitability still the most reliable guide to management efficiency. Profitability alone is being challenged today by many.

In 1992 Sir Adrian Cadbury[6] stated simply 'governance is the system by which companies are directed and controlled.' defining it as:

> "... being the structures, systems and policies in an organisation, designed and established to direct and control all operations and relationships on a continuing basis, in an honest and caring manner, taking into account the interests of all stakeholders and compliance with all applicable laws and regulatory requirements."

The principles on which his committee's recommended code of best practice for organisations were based were "... those of openness, integrity and accountability going together". These principles and their related best practices are today reported publicly by all sizes of organisation across all sectors. Such reports vary in content, but all demonstrate a commitment to trust which was the setting for the Cadbury report "Bringing greater clarity to the respective responsibilities of directors, shareholders and auditors ...".

Cadbury travelled worldwide making presentations on his committee's corporate governance principles and code of best practice. Later, just before his death, he contributed to a history of the Cadbury Committee, researched by Spira and Slinn,[7] writing in his foreword:

---

[6] The Financial Implications of Corporate Governance (1992), Sir Adrian Cadbury, Financial Reporting Council, London, England.
[7] The Cadbury Committee – A History (2015), L.F. Spira and J. Slinn, Oxford University Press, Oxford, England.

"I saw it as my task after publication of the Report and Code to respond to invitations to discuss the Committee's findings and to help to overcome misunderstandings as to their purpose. I wanted to explain how the Committee had arrived at its conclusions and the reasoning that lay behind the recommendations of the Code. What was unexpected was the international interest in the Committee's work, which led to invitations to visit individual countries and to participate in corporate governance discussions with bodies such as the World Bank and the OECD."

ICSA was an acknowledged contributor to the Cadbury Committee Report and Code. What is little known today, is the acknowledged contribution made by ICSA to the first worldwide corporate governance code[8] published in 1999 by the Commonwealth Association for its member countries: its corporate governance principles embraced not only the Cadbury 1992 principles of openness, integrity and accountability but referenced into codes of governance and related reports in 10 countries. Its content covered all of what is seen today as best practice board effectiveness, culture, stakeholder engagement and assurance; even introducing each of the themes in today's concept of ESG, with many references to global and national economies.

"Reports and communications must be made in the context that society now demands transparency and greater accountability from corporations in regards to their non-financial affairs, for example, their workers and environmental issues. In reports to all stakeholders matters such as the following should be addressed employment; environmental matters; social responsibility; customer interest matters; and supplier interest matters."[9]

---

[8] Principles for Corporate Governance In the Commonwealth – Towards global competitiveness and economic accountability (1999), published by Commonwealth Association for Corporate Governance (CACG) established in April 1998 in response to the Edinburgh Declaration of the Commonwealth Heads of Government meeting in 1997 to promote excellence in corporate governance in the Commonwealth. Following its title is 'The proper governance of companies will become as crucial to the world economy as the proper governing of countries.' James D. Wolfensohn, President of the World Bank . https://www.governance.co.uk/resources/commonwealth-cacg-guidelines-principles-for-corporate-governance-in-the-commonwealth/ (accessed 14 February 2021). In its Introduction acknowledgement is given to support in its preparation from ICSA. .

[9] Note the similarity to the duty of a director to promote the success of a company in section 172 of the UK Companies Act 2006.

In 2012 the Commonwealth Association published an agreed charter[10] embracing all of the themes in the above paragraph adopted by its 52 country member governments and establishing "For the first time in its 64 year history …..a single document setting out the core values of the organisation and the aspiration of its members." For good governance it states:

> *"We reiterate our commitment to promote good governance through the rule of law, to ensure transparency and accountability and to root out, both at national and international levels, systemic and systematic corruption."*

For values, it affirms a commitment to the values and principles of the Commonwealth Association.

Before and since Cadbury the unitary board of directors had been the adopted governing body for companies and other organisations in the UK and most other countries across the world.[11] Yet its effectiveness and efficiency has always been in question. Cadbury questioned it: "Our proposals aim to strengthen the unitary board system and increase its effectiveness, not to replace it": one strength recommended was the challenge of a "strong and independent element on the board, with a recognised senior member": that independent element to include "…non-executive directors of sufficient calibre and number for their views to carry sufficient weight in board decisions." Cadbury also linked effectiveness into the economy of companies in their governance processes. Effectiveness and efficiency are two different achievements. Effectiveness is "doing the right things" to achieve a company's purpose. Efficiency is about quality, "doing things right" first time always. Both are needed to achieve good governance.[12]

---

[10] The Commonwealth Charter (2012), Commonwealth Association, London, England. https://thecommonwealth.org/sites/default/files/page/documents/CharteroftheCommonwealth.pdf (accessed 14 February 2021).

[11] There are exceptions to this in the legal two-tier board system recommended by the European Union and adopted by many companies in other European countries: though rejected for listed companies in the United Kingdom yet adopted for its National Health Service.

[12] Why all audit committees should be concerned about quality (2017), Professor Jeffrey Ridley and Professor John Oakland, Quality World July 2017, Journal of the Chartered Quality Institute, London, England.

2. Key Themes for Today and Tomorrow's Worldwide Good Governance

In my two books of this century[13] I have written on the progress worldwide which good governance has made in its legal and regulatory requirements and guidance for board effectiveness, culture, stakeholder engagement and assurance at both board and independent auditor levels. I am convinced the following four themes are key for today and tomorrow's trust in good governance; that all are needed for that goodness to be good:

- **Board effectiveness** – "…challenge from non-executive directors as an essential aspect of good governance."[14] both with themselves and with their executive team

- **Culture** – "… the board sets the correct "tone from the top".[15] of good conduct and behaviour in all its four levels – Board: Executive: Workforce: Stakeholder

- **Stakeholder engagement** – "Responsive and responsible leadership at board level"[16] in environmental, social, governance direction and control

- **Integrated Assurance** – All reported "… metrics should be capable of verification and assurance, to enhance transparency and alignment among corporations, investors and all stakeholders."[17]

---

[13] Cutting Edge Internal Auditing (2008), J. Ridley, John Wiley & Sons, Chichester, England and Creative and Innovative Auditing (2018), Routledge, Abingdon, England and Nework, United States.
[14] Guidance on Board Effectiveness (2018), Financial Reporting Council, London, England
[15] Corporate Culture and the Role of Boards (2016), Financial Reporting Council, London, England.
[16] 2017 Article by Klaus Schwab, Founder and Executive Chair, World Economic Forum https://www.weforum.org/agenda/2017/01/a-call-for-responsive-and-responsible-leadership/ (accessed 9 February 21).
[17] Measuring Stakeholder Capitalism Towards Common Metrics And Consistent Reporting Of Sustainable Value Creation (2020), World Economic Forum, Geneva, Switzerland.

A. Board effectiveness

*"Well-informed and high-quality decision making –
one of the hallmarks of an effective board does not happen by accident."*[18]

The unitary board of today in every sector and nation is governed by laws for which all its directors are separately and collectively responsible. These laws require directors to be effective and caring in the duties they perform. For directors in registered companies in the United Kingdom, these duties are now set out clearly in the Companies Act 2006 (sections 171-177), supplemented by other enactments related to their duties. However, I believe today's board is no longer unitary; it is divided in its governance responsibilities between those who are executive directors and non-executive directors (and those who are independent and those not). The spirit of directors' legal duties is also seen in the principles of good governance in the UK governance code and associated board effectiveness guidance; if not also by other nations in their codes and board guidance. These codes and their guidance divide the unitary board into one of legal and governance.

There is also a growing and important governance third division of the unitary board's committees and their members' responsibilities, now being publicly reported on by their chair annually and assessed by their stakeholders for board effectiveness. Already on one of these committees – audit – there is a trend to appoint independent specialist members/advisers who are not board members. This development is likely to spread to other board committees in the future.

To be effective a board must be led by an effective chair. This is now a basic principle for all organisations and governance codes:

- The chair leads the board and is responsible for its overall effectiveness[19]

---

[18] Review of the Higgs Guidance on behalf of the FRC – Improving Board Effectiveness (2010), Institute of Chartered Secretaries and Administrators (now Chartered Governance Institute), London, England.

[19] The UK Corporate Governance Code (2018), Financial Reporting Council, London, England.

- The governing body should elect an independent non-executive member as chair to lead the governing body in the objective and effective discharge of its governance role and responsibilities.[20]
- Every company should be headed by an effective board that is collectively responsible for the long-term success of the company. The chair is responsible for leadership of the board[21]
- The chair of the board, who will normally be the lead minister, will maintain a high standard of discussion and debate, helping to steer the department by facilitating collective working and ensuring that systems are in place to provide board members with the support they need to carry out their role effectively.[22]
- The chair is responsible for leadership of the board of directors and the council of governors, ensuring their effectiveness on all aspects of their role and leading on setting the agenda for meetings.[23]

The UK code requires "formal and rigorous" annual evaluations of the performance of the board, its committees, the chair and individual directors'. These can be by the board itself, by external consultants and a mixture of both. Similar evaluations are required by most governance codes worldwide. The practice, results and actions are required to be publicly reported on annually. The UK Code recommends boards having an annual external evaluation '…at least every three years'. There is little overall evidence of today's quality of external board evaluations, though recently BEIS[24] noted in a statement on 'Insolvency and Corporate Governance' consultation paper, published in August 2018:

> *"Several respondents, particularly institutional investors, suggested that the market for independent board evaluations should be reviewed with a view to introducing*

---

[20] Report on Corporate Governance for South Africa (King IV) (2016), Institute of Directors Southern Africa, Cape Town, South Africa.
[21] Corporate Governance for main Market and Aim Companies (2012, London Stock Exchange, London, England.
[22] Corporate governance in central government departments: code of good practice (2017). Cabinet Office, UK Government, London, England.
[23] The NHS Foundation Trust Code of Governance (2016) Monitor, London, England.
[24] Insolvency and Corporate Governance Government Response (2018), Department of Business, Energy and Industrial Strategy, UK Government, London, England.

minimum standards… Respondents argued that whilst many companies are embracing best practice in dealing with issues identified in evaluations, some do not. Additionally, some respondents pointed out that the standards or thoroughness of these evaluations can vary significantly."

This is of concern in the achievement of board effectiveness and good governance. BEIS invited ICSA "…to identify further ways of improving the quality and effectiveness of board evaluations including the development of a code of practice…" Results from ICSA's[25] review have been reported to BEIS concluding "there is scope for broader adoption of good practice and greater transparency on the part of both board reviewers and companies using their services." **Board effectiveness will always be a key part of saving the planet, a worldwide must for the achievement of good governance of every organisation.**

B. Culture

"…more needs to be done to bring ethics into the boardroom."[26]

Cadbury in 1992 did not refer to culture in an organisation but to its behaviour and with it, the importance of his underlying principle of integrity. "At the heart of the Committee's recommendations is a Code of Best Practice designed to achieve the necessary high standards of corporate behaviour" and:

"The way forward is through clear definitions of responsibility and an acceptance by all involved that the highest standards of efficiency and integrity are expected of them. Expectations of corporate behaviours are continually rising and a corresponding response is looked for from shareholders, directors and auditors."

These expectations had been rising for some time, addressed by

---

[25] Review of the effectiveness of independent board evaluation in the UK listed sector (2021), Institute of Chartered Secretaries and Administrators, London, England.
[26] Embedding Business Ethics: 2020 report on corporate ethics policies and programmes (2020), Institute of Business Ethics, London, England.

management gurus, government commissions and, in 1977, a White Paper on the Conduct of Directors[27], stating their responsibilities to act with *"care and skill"* in the exercise of their legal duties. Integrity is not mentioned in this government statement but can be seen in the White Paper's intent.

The Institute of Business Ethics (IBE) was established in 1986 "…to promote high standards of business behaviour based on ethical values." IBE is listed as a contributor to the Cadbury committee considerations. Its mission is to promote the importance of a culture of integrity:

> *"All organisations need to demonstrate they are trustworthy in order to operate effectively and sustainably. Reputations are not based solely on the delivery of products and services, but on how an organisation values its stakeholders. Having a reputation for acting with honesty and integrity not only differentiates an organisation, it makes it more successful."*[28]

In 1995, a public sector commission led by Lord Nolan developed seven principles of conduct in public life, which still are applied today across all organisations in the public sector. Although these principles were not addressed to listed companies at the time, the Cadbury governance principles can be seen in them. All seven can also be seen in later regulatory governance codes across all sectors and in the values and codes of conduct adopted by most if not all listed companies and other sector organisations today. Today, Lord Evans chairs the Committee for Standards in Public Life and in 2021 blogs[29] about what should also be in the culture of all organisations worldwide:

> *"How decisions are made – in the public interest – is ultimately what the 7 Principles of Public Life are about. Honesty, Integrity, Accountability, Objectivity, Openness, Selflessness and Leadership are the values that those serving the public, in whatever capacity, should demonstrate. High standards are a public good. They improve predictability and promote better outcomes for society, increasing public trust and understanding, and the functioning of the economy."*

The Financial Reporting Council's (FRC) first corporate governance code (2003) questioned whether a company's "… culture, code of conduct,

---

[27] The conduct of company directors (Cmnd.7037) Paperback – Import, January 1, 1977
[28] https://www.ibe.org.uk/about-ibe/what-we-do.html (accessed 18 January 2021).
[29] https://cspl.blog.gov.uk/2021/01/14/cspls-year-ahead/ (accessed 9 February 2021).

human resource policies and performance reward systems support the business objectives and risk management and internal control system." Sir Winfried Bischoff, FRC chair in 2016[30] introduced its first report on the importance of integrity in a company's culture:

> *"There needs to be a concerted effort to improve trust in the motivations and integrity of business. Rules and sanctions clearly have their place, but will not on their own deliver productive behaviours over the long-term. This report looks at the increasing importance which corporate culture plays in delivering long-term business and economic success."*

This message has been repeated since in guidance by the FRC, government and all organisations regulating and advising on responsible leadership, business practices and good governance: not only in the UK but by international organisations and national governments worldwide, in law, regulations, standards and behaviour. **Culture will always be a key part of saving the planet, a worldwide must for the achievement of good governance of every organisation.**

C. Stakeholder engagement

> *"…most companies and their boards also recognise that effective engagement with key stakeholders – which may include employees, suppliers, customers, third sector organisations and regulators – is a key component of long-term sustainability and success."* [31]

Company engagement was seen as only a concern for shareholders for most of the life of private registered companies over the past two centuries (and still is in some companies today!). For a few philanthropic companies this extended to the concerns of their workforce and to communities in which they operated. Management gurus and thought leaders like Fayol, Humble,

---

[30] Corporate Culture and the Role of Boards (2014), Financial Reporting Council, London, England.
[31] The Stakeholder Voice in Board Decision Making: Strengthening the business, promoting long-term success (2017), Institute of Chartered Secretaries and Administrators (now Chartered Governance Institute) and Investment Managers Association, London, England.

Drucker, and Handy,[32] amongst many others in the 19th, 20th and 21st centuries,[33] have all published on aspects of stakeholder engagement for the success of companies and the wellbeing of society. Professor Edward Freeman[34] in the United States in the 1980s created his now well-known stakeholder theory: well-known at least to academics and students, if not some responsible management practitioners and today's regulators of governance processes and practices. At the time Freeman saw his stakeholder engagement theory to be important for the achievement of worldwide good governance and the long term success of an organisation:

> *"... customers, employees, suppliers, political action groups, environmental groups, local communities, the media, financial institutions, governmental groups, and more. This view paints the corporate environment as an ecosystem of related groups, all of whom need to be considered and satisfied to keep the company healthy and successful in the long term."*

In the past 50 years the importance of companies and organisations across all sectors engaging with the concerns of their different stakeholders has grown globally across all civil societies; driven by thought leaders, governments, international organisations, professions, agitators and demands from civil societies. Yet stakeholder engagement in many civil societies and the reporting of its practices is still at an early stage in its development for business purpose and good governance. Stakeholder engagement has many movements and standards driven by social responsibilities: industrial democracy; Business in the Community; Investors in People; ISO 14000 Environmental Standards; Corporate Social Responsibility; SA8000 Social Certification Programmes; AccountAbility 1000 Assurance Standards; United Nations Declarations of Human Rights, Principles of Responsible Investment and Sustainable Development Goals; ISO 26000 Guidance on Social Responsibility; BSI Organisation Resilience Framework; and other movements.

---

[32] Henri Fayol 1841-1925; John Humble 1925-2011; Peter Drucker 1909-2005; Charles Handy 1932 -

[33] See RSA published article by Bob Garratt What are company boards for now? (2020). https://medium.com/@thersa/what-are-company-boards-for-now-8b6993ed901c (accessed 10 December 2020)

[34] Strategic Management- A Stakeholder Approach (1984), R.E. Freeman, Cambridge University Press reproduction (2010), Cambridge, England.

These have all influenced each other over time and the content of many corporate governance codes published across the globe today.

At the beginning of this century the Institute of Environmental and Social Ethics, in its AccountAbility 1000 Exposure Draft 1999,[35] set a global requirement for stakeholder engagement. Its introduction and subsequent revisions have led to its latest sustainability principles which embrace its stakeholder engagement principles[36], introducing and defining ESG:

> *"Environmental, social and governance (ESG) refers to the three central factors in measuring the sustainability and ethical performance of an organisation: recognising and working with its '… stakeholder engagement guidelines, other international, national, sectoral and/or topic-driven sustainability-related standards and frameworks.' and an external assurance process."*

Today ESG considerations are discussed in businesses worldwide and addressed in corporate governance codes, driven by the 17 Sustainable Development Goals and 169 targets in the United Nations 2030 Agenda for Sustainable Development[37] and statements by other international organisations and governments. There are many national and global definitions of ESG, but I like the following from the United States[38] which broadens its meaning and embraces many stakeholder engagements:

> *"For many, the term "ESG" brings to mind environmental issues like climate change and resource scarcity. These form an element of ESG—and an important one—but the term means much more. It covers social issues like a company's labour practices, talent management, product safety and data security. It covers governance matters like board diversity, executive pay and business ethics."*

---

[35] AccountAbility 1000 (AA1000) framework Standards, guidelines and professional qualification Exposure draft (1999), The Institute of Social and Ethical AccountAbility, London, England.
[36] AA1000 Accountability Principles (2018) https://www.accountability.org/ (accessed 15th February 2021).
[37] Transforming our World: The 2030 Agenda for Sustainable Development (2015), United Nations, New York, United States.
[38] https://www.pwc.com/us/en/services/governance-insights-center/library/esg-environmental-social-governance-reporting.html (accessed 19 January 2021).

ESG is also the international movement today for 'impact investment' with the Impact Investment Institute's 2019 mission[39]:

> "...to accelerate the growth and improve the effectiveness of the impact investing market in the UK and internationally. We want to see more capital contributing to the well-being of people and the planet – as set out in the United Nation's Sustainable Development Goals."

This mission also brings into stakeholder engagement and ESG the important quality of economic performance: as Professor Freeman wrote in his stakeholder theory culture in 1984 'to keep the company healthy and successful in the long term'.

In 2020 the World Economic Forum (WEF) launched its Davos Manifesto[40] with the following definition of the purpose of company: an excellent quality benchmark for all organisations today and tomorrow for 'board effectiveness and efficiency'; 'culture and conduct'; and, 'stakeholder leadership and engagement':

> "The purpose of a company is to engage all its stakeholders in shared and sustained value creation. In creating such value, a company serves not only its shareholders, but all its stakeholders – employees, customers, suppliers, local communities and society at large. The best way to understand and harmonize the divergent interests of all stakeholders is through a shared commitment to policies and decisions that strengthen the long-term prosperity of a company."

Adding:

> "A company serves society at large through its activities, supports the communities in which it works, and pays its fair share of taxes. It ensures the safe, ethical and efficient use of data. It acts as a steward of the environmental and material universe for future generations. It consciously protects our biosphere and champions a circular, shared and regenerative economy. It continuously expands the frontiers of knowledge, innovation and technology to improve people's well-being."

Involvement of stakeholders in the performance of all of a company's activities is now seen as essential for its long term success. It is already an

---

[39] https://www.impactinvest.org.uk/about-us/ (accessed January 2021).
[40] https://www.weforum.org/agenda/2019/12/davos-manifesto-2020-the-universal-purpose-of-a-company-in-the-fourth-industrial-revolution (accessed 19 January 2021).

essential contributor to the quality of good governance in the economic performance of every organisation worldwide. Professor Klaus Schwab[41], founder of WEF, writes today on "...the need for a new social contract with shared responsibility', introducing us to 'stakeholder capitalism' as a contrast to 'shareholder capitalism and state capitalism", both of which "..,. have led to rising inequalities of income, wealth and opportunity, increased tensions between the haves and have-nots and above all, a mass degradation of the environment." His well known dedication to stakeholder interests driving the economies of all countries embraces not just the individual but civil societies at large. His followers are many both at government and institutional levels. The UK Government[42] in its 2018 new civil society strategy sets out a national plan including much of the concept of stakeholder capitalism. In the same year stakeholder engagement in the achievement of good governance has now been required in the FRC (2018) UK Code of Governance and guidance for Board Effectiveness "... a company's culture should promote integrity and openness, value diversity and be responsive to the views of shareholders and wider stakeholders." **Stakeholder engagement will always be a key part of saving the planet, a worldwide must for the achievement of good governance of every organisation (See also chapter 18).**

D. Integrated Assurance

"All auditors should be searching for and achieving Excellence in the assurance products and services they provide to organisations across all levels – board, executive and operations." [43]

Integrated assurance "...promotes shared risk intelligence and accountability with a common goal to strengthen the organisation's risk

---

[41] Stakeholder Capitalism (2021), Klaus Schwab and Peter Vanham, John Wiley & Sons Inc., Hoboken, New Jersey, United States.
[42] Civil Society Strategy: Building a Future that Works for Everyone (2018), Cabinet Office, UK Government, London, England.
[43] Creative and Innovative Auditing (2018), Jeffrey Ridley, Routledge, Abingdon, England, New York, United States.

management and oversight."[44] For all organisations the independence of all assurances of board and executive ESG decision-making, practices and reporting must be questioned. That assurance starts first at board level because "... the calibre of the non-executive members of the board is of special importance in setting and maintaining standards of corporate governance"[45], as well as the independent challenge they should provide at board level and in the audit committee[46] supplemented by independent and objective internal auditing[47]. This extends outside the board and organisation to the independent assurance received from both financial and operational auditors and consultants[48].

Independent challenge, scepticism and assurance are fundamental aspects of good governance at all levels in an organisation. Today, boards of all organisations seek independent financial and operational assurances to measure the quality of their performance, some through their management and executive leadership teams; and some independently from internal and external auditors and consultants.

Whatever the source and assurance, they are essential contributors to the continuous quality improvement needed by boards to ensure they are learning from their past performance: understanding, controlling and managing the risks in their current performance and making changes to manage and improve their future performance. Assurance mapping[49] is now an essential part of the integration of assessment and management of risk in

---

[44] Integrated Assurance – Risk Governance Beyond Boundaries (2014), Vicky Kubitscheck, Gower Publishing Limited, Farnham, England.
[45] Cadbury (1992) followed by successive similar statements in reviews into board performance and governance codes.
[46] See model terms of reference for the audit committee (2020), Institute of Chartered Secretaries and Administrators, London, England.
[47] Internal auditing has grown as a profession since 1941 across the globe with its own International Professional Practices Framework and Qualifications, researched and directed by The Chartered Institute of Internal Auditors Inc. Its definition of internal auditing is - Internal auditing is an independent, objective assurance and consulting activity designed to add value and improve an organisation's operations. It helps an organisation accomplish its objectives by bringing a systematic, disciplined approach to evaluate and improve the effectiveness of risk management, control, and governance processes. https://global.theiia.org/Pages/globaliiaHome.aspx (accessed January 2021).
[48] The IIA's Three Lines Model - An Update of The Three Lines of Defense (2020), The Institute of Internal Auditors *Global*, Florida, USA. www.globaliia.org
[49] https://www.icaew.com/technical/audit-and-assurance/assurance/assurance-mapping (accessed 10th February 2021).

all organisations. Today, more than ever before, and in the future, the quality of assurances are dependent on the creativity and innovation assurance providers display in their approach to the challenges boards face. These challenges will continue to grow from the ESG risks and issues of today and what will be for tomorrow.

However, there is much more to consider when addressing quality in independent assurances than the auditing of financial statements. Every independent assurance given to a board and its executive team must consider the openness, integrity and accountability of published non-financial information. This consideration has ESG relevance with legal, regulatory and auditing standard requirements; all of which will become more important in the future. The WEF purpose of a company mentioned earlier is followed by recommended internationally consistent metrics in the reporting by organisations on their ESG strategies and achievement in addressing the United Nations Sustainable Development Goals[50] "…a set of universal material ESG metrics and recommended disclosures…" "…capable of verification and assurance…". These metrics use four pillars – Principles of Governance: Planet: People: Prosperity – not to be seen in isolation of each other. Governance is seen as the foundation for purpose: "Without good governance companies lack the supportive context within which to make ESG progress on the other three pillars.". The newly formed Impact Institute[51] also supports ESG in its first report published January 2021:

> *"The coronavirus pandemic has shown that we need truly resilient and sustainable systems that support our societies and economies so they can weather the effects of future ecological, social, and financial shocks. The need to address both the consequences of climate change and the social impact of a transition to a net-zero economy has never been more apparent."*

Debate on the quality and scope of independent assurances which companies receive has been around for a long time with many questions being asked by government commissions and professions on how these can

---

[50] Measuring Stakeholder Capitalism = Towards Common Metrics and Consistent Reporting of Sustainable Value Creation – White Paper (2020), World Economic Forum, Geneva, Switzerland.
[51] Impact Report 2019-20 (2021). Impact Investing Institute, London, England.

be guaranteed. Current proposals by BEIS[52] for the regulation of financial audit in listed companies require boards to publish an audit and assurance policy explaining "...their approach to internal audit and assurance and what improvements they might propose to this in the light of lessons learned, as well as to set out what policies the company might have in relation to the appointment of the company auditor." Such a policy should focus boards' attention on all the assurances they receive and how these integrate to mitigate the risks they face in the achievement of their purpose. **Integrated assurance will always be a key part of saving the planet, a worldwide must for the achievement of good governance of every organisation (See also chapter 17).**

3. Conclusion

In 2017, on reaching my 50th year as a Chartered Secretary I wrote an article for CGI's journal titled "The Times are still changing"[53]. I ended the article with this message:

> *"Faster communications and digital networking beyond our imaginations today are already here and more are appearing on the horizon. We are already seeing this happen in and across all continents. As my last career comes to an end changing times will never end for Chartered Secretaries'*

Since then, climate control and a worldwide pandemic have increased the need for improved worldwide good governance beyond our imaginations. Action for good governance in all organisations is needed now more than ever before. The United Nations Sustainable and Development Goals Agenda mentioned earlier "...is a plan of action for people, planet and prosperity." It requires implementation by "All countries and all stakeholders acting in collaborative partnership ... to free the human race from tyranny of poverty and want and to heal and secure our planet." It envisages:

---

[52] Restoring trust in audit and corporate governance – Consultation on the government's proposals (2021), Department of Business Energy and Industrial Strategy, London, England.

[53] https://www.icsa.org.uk/knowledge/governance-and-compliance/careers/july-2017-the-times-are-still-changing (accessed 9 February 2021)

*"…a world in which every country enjoys sustained, inclusive and sustainable economic growth and decent work for all. A world in which consumption and production patterns and use of all natural resources from air to land, from rivers, lakes and aquifers to oceans and seas are sustainable. One in which democracy, good **governance and the rule of law**, as well as an enabling environment at the national and international levels are essential for sustainable development, including sustained and inclusive economic growth, social development, environmental protection and the eradication of poverty and hunger. One in which development and the application of technology are climate sensitive, respect biodiversity and are resilient."*

"Good governance and the rule of law" worldwide will always require independently assured measures of quality in board effectiveness, culture, stakeholder engagement and integrated assurance: measures whose requirements will keep changing. Today, all organisations, governments and regulators must recognise this basic principle. Do all board members, executives and their stakeholders? They should if there is to be any achievement of the United Nations Sustainable Development Goals by 2030 and maintenance of these afterwards during this century for the benefit of all civil societies and their populations.

CHAPTER 3. BOARD LEADERSHIP

Simon Haslam, Programme Lead for Strategy, Institute of Directors, and Visiting Professor, Durham Business School

Alexander Van de Putte, Professor of Strategic Foresight, IE Business School and Chairman of Corporate Governance & Stewardship, AIFC

Introduction

Back in the 1992 Cadbury Report, leadership was already emphasised as one of the four responsibilities of the board alongside setting strategic aims, supervising management and reporting to shareholders. Several corporate scandals have, however, emphasised that board leadership, behaviours of individual board members and board dynamics have contributed significantly to these detrimental outcomes.

Therefore, in this chapter, we argue that board leadership is essential for the proper functioning of the board and for individual directors to discharge their duties. From a corporate governance vantage point, leadership relates to the behaviour of the board and of individual directors.

1. Leadership in context: the board's role

There are many definitions of leadership; most business textbooks and reference sources will carry their preferred ones. Common factors across definitions are that leadership is about being influential over a group of people and also facilitating the achievement of things that otherwise would not have happened. In short, leaders make a difference, and leadership adds value to an organisation.

At the director level, the leadership task carries the gravity of top-level responsibility. Here is a selection of senior leaders expressing the task in their own words:[1]

> *"Leadership is about helping others realise their potential and inspiring them to work with you to achieve a shared vision for the future." Kathy Mazzarelli, CEO, Graybar.*
>
> *"Leadership is helping people succeed, inspiring and uniting people behind a common purpose and then being accountable." Paul Polman, former CEO, Unilever.*
>
> *"Leadership is showing up and stepping up at a time when people need you and doing the right thing, no matter how hard it is. I remember a former boss said to me that there's a right thing to do and an easy thing to do, and very rarely is the right thing to do the easy thing to do." Keith Barr, CEO, InterContinental Hotels Group.*
>
> *"Leadership is about the ability to drive results, set the vision and share it, create an environment of success, and remove obstacles." Judy Marks, CEO, Otis Elevator.*

There are many board and director duties which relate to leadership, such as promoting the success of the company, exercising independent judgement, exercising reasonable care and skill, and avoiding conflicts of interests. But the above emphasise that at a governance level, the importance of vision clarity, responsibility and accountability, and pro-activity loom large as leadership qualities.

A. The governance leadership arena

At a governance level, the leadership domain is capably represented by a

---

[1] https://medium.com/jacob-morgan/14-top-ceos-share-their-definition-of-leadership-whats-yours-2b89a58576a6.

combination of short- and long-term considerations, along with internal and external vistas. Hence, board leadership perspectives can be summarised as follows:

— *Long term – external*

Connecting with the trends and dynamics of the external world and markets, helping the organisation to be aware and prepared, plus keeping the organisation's vision relevant. Linking with external stakeholders, such as institutional investors, in the shaping and governance of collaborative ventures.

— *Long term – internal*

Considering and refining the organisation's vision and its values. Using these as the 'north star' of the formulation of its strategic journey. Continually reflecting on insight from external and internal sources to think about and shape strategy.

— *Short term – external*

Ensuring compliance with external imperatives (e.g. regulators). Stepping forward in extraordinary circumstances such as crisis.

— *Short term – internal*

Living and breathing the organisation's values, being a role model and leading by example. Working to ensure the organisation has the resources and guidance it needs to deliver the vision. Taking responsibility for the conduct of the organisation.

A board's ability to know where its focus should be and to make sound judgement sits across these domains. Sometimes judgement can be clouded by short-term pressures or emotional considerations such as relationships. To help with focus and objectivity, the 'successor question' can be useful. If a director or board is ever in doubt about what course to follow, ask the question: what choice would my successor have wished me to make? The points are that keeping long-term ambition front and centre remains vital, even when faced with immense short-term pressures, and leadership is not a popularity contest. As the US military and political leader Colin Powell said, the responsibility of leadership involves sometimes pissing people off.[2]

B. The board, as a leadership context

The composition of boards varies from organisation to organisation, though there are several characteristics that distinguish boards from other teams or groups. Appreciating these characteristics can help a director make a strong contribution to a board.

Strong-willed people – people working at board level usually demonstrate an appetite for the role and for senior responsibility, in addition to their other abilities. Boards often comprise more strong-willed people than other teams.

Multiple interests – it is not usual for directors to have other responsibilities other than that for the overall organisation. Even if this duty to the organisation is enshrined in law, it does not make reconciling this an easy task, when some of the conflicting pressures are considered. Directors might have executive duties, might be nominee appointments from a shareholding group, represent family interests, or have director responsibilities at a subsidiary or parent company level.

Varying degrees of knowledge – this is not only apparent in the difference between executive and non-executive roles with respect to how the organisation 'works', but also presents itself across the subjects discussed at board level (e.g. finance, law, strategy).

Less familiarity (and perhaps trust) – this particularly impacts independent and non-executive directors. Executive leaders are more likely to have contact with their peers in the normal course of work, but when a director's connection with peers is limited to a handful of meetings a year it is harder to build relationships and trust.

Cultural differences and, hopefully, cognitive diversity – multi-sited

---

[2] Colin Powell, On Leadership, https://www.goodreads.com/quotes/113574-being-responsible-sometimes-means-pissing-people-off.

organisations, and those that straddle geographical boundaries, potentially benefit from cognitive diversity. Progressive enterprises often strengthen cognitive diversity at board level to help avoid narrow perspectives and groupthink. But a strong team needs to have an ability to harness the value of individual differences, not to be limited by it.

The term 'lean in', popularised by Sheryl Sandberg[3], points out that leaders have a personal choice of how they contribute to the performance of the board as a leadership team. The context might be challenging for the reasons mentioned above, but the responsibility and duty to help a board lead an organisation well rests with each director not just the board chair. A skilled director knows when to 'lean in' and also how to lean in. For example, the Thomas-Kilmann conflict mode instrument[4] encourages individual leaders to know when to assert a position, when to accommodate the views and wishes of others, when a collaborative win-win solution should be sought and compromise is the most pragmatic order of the day, and when not to wade in.

2. The personal nature of leadership

Anyone can lead, with one proviso: that they want to lead. Leadership is different to management in this respect. A manager can be appointed, and that appointment gives them positional power and in turn influence. The willingness to lead is very much an intrinsic quality that comes from within the director. The leader's power comes not from her or his rank in the organisation but from the ability to be influential.

As the title of this section suggests, there's a strong link between leadership style and personality. Different people will lead in different ways – personability being a combination of our unique DNA (nature) and our shaping through experience (nurture). There is no single way to lead and no perfect recipe. However, being able to use influence and adopt an appropriate leadership style sits at the core of effectiveness.

---

[3] See Sheryl Sandberg's 2013 book, *Lean in: Women, Work and the Will to Lead* (New York: Random House).
[4] See https://kilmanndiagnostics.com.

A. Power through influence

In leadership, the power to affect change comes from the ability to be influential. Much is written on influence. Embracing the subject, the techniques and their application is a task that stays with us through our working lives.

The following summarises some of the ways leaders generate power to effect change through influencing skills and some of the things that have helped them.

- Prepare the information (data, examples, cases, reasoned choice).
- Allow people to work out their own conclusions from the data.
- Get friendly stakeholders on board (especially powerful ones).
- Pitch your arguments to appeal to authority (where the decision-making power sits).
- Build the trust of others – be authentic, credible, reliable and not self-interested.
- Be prepared and open to consulting experts (e.g. cybersecurity, digital technology).
- Walk, act and communicate with authority (which usually means confidence and grace).
- Frame your messages to relate to your target audience.
- Listen to people and seek to build common ground.
- Be enthusiastic about whatever you're proposing.
- Explore the consequences of not adopting a proposed course of action.
- Allow others to 'save face', give them a way out of otherwise entrenched positions.
- If it is a big challenge people are facing, create the opportunities for them to experience small wins quickly to help build confidence.

B. The balcony and the dance floor

The ability for senior leaders to work across the arena necessitates the ability to change vantage points. To demonstrate what is now known as adaptive leadership, Heifetz and Linsky[5] likened this to shifts between the balcony and the dance floor.

— *Your balcony view*

The balcony affords the overview and breadth of vision. This is the big picture, and very much linked with the longer-term view. Too little time on the balcony can mean a director gets caught up in organisational issues and loses sight of the overall raison d'être, whereas too much time on the balcony can see the leader become viewed as disconnected and remote.

— *Your dance floor view*

The dance floor has a buzz, many leaders find this energy appealing and may even gravitate towards it. The dance floor enables a director to 'walk the talk' and be a demonstrable leader: leading by presence and actions not just words. However, the dance floor carries the allure of dragging the leader too far into operational issues and mechanics and possibly the risk of micromanaging.

Both the balcony and the dance floor viewpoints are important. From a governance perspective, they remind leaders to be skilled in working in both and to know the value and limitations of time in each.

C. Being 'ambidextrous'

Related to the distinction between the balcony and the dancefloor is knowing the difference between when to be 'explorative' and when to be 'exploitative'. When an organisation can be 'ambidextrous'[6] it can work in both domains simultaneously. It can simultaneously work on the exploitation of current organisational capabilities, delivering value for

---

[5] Ronald Heifetz and Marty Linsky, "A survival guide for leaders", *Harvard Business Review*, 2002.
[6] The term 'ambidextrous leadership' is a relatively new one. See, for example, Kathrin Rosing, Michael Frese, and Andreas Bausch, "Explaining the heterogeneity of the leadership-innovation relationship: Ambidextrous leadership", *The Leadership Quarterly* 22(5): 956-974, 2011.

customers, while also exploring future opportunities and ideas.

The sense is that ambidextrous organisations tend to be better not only at innovation but the translation of fresh thinking into commercial reality. If this is understood at a governance level, the board is more likely to be able to contribute to the organisation's sustainability and ongoing relevance in uncertain times.

3. Understanding yourself and others

Understanding yourself is the basis of emotional intelligence and understanding others is the platform for being able to use emotional intelligence. Emotional intelligence helps gives leaders the insight of how to lead and what to do in any situation.

D. The emotionally intelligent leader

Effective leaders are often emotionally intelligent leaders. Unlike raw intellect, where a leader needs only sufficient reasoning ability for their role, a common reflection is that a leader cannot have too much emotional intelligence.

Emotional intelligence, or EQ, is the ability to recognise one's own emotions and the emotions of other people. And for a person to use this emotional information to guide their thinking, and behaviour. This can make the difference between a leader being able to 'connect' with others or not.

For leaders at any level, including board directors, a valuable characteristic of EQ is that it's developable. A director is not limited by their current emotional intelligence capabilities. We can all build on our current EQ quotient. Below, we explore the means by which leaders can further strengthen their emotional intelligence.

E. Spiritual intelligence, or the moral compass

If emotional intelligence underpins what effective leaders are able do, a higher- order intelligence – 'spiritual intelligence'[7] – serves to guide their endeavour. The point here is that a person may possess well-developed leadership skills but not necessarily apply them in a wholesome way.

Contemporary governance, as we have seen, has its focus clearly on the sustainability agenda. So the assumption here is the organisation's values and its spiritual intelligence (SQ) are encompassed by good ethical principles and the sustainable development goals. It can be helpful to consider spiritual intelligence as being akin to a moral compass.

At the board level, a strong hope is that all board members have what is called 'values congruency', i.e. their personal values are in tune with those prized by the organisation. Without this, a director is less able to be the embodiment of the organisation's values and less able to communicate with stakeholders (internal and external) in ways that are helpful to the organisation. A lack of values congruency may also lead to the director feeling more disconnected from the organisation, and feeling not 'at home'.

Where a director doesn't feel comfortable with the values of the organisation they share the responsibility for, the one option not to take is to 'do nothing'.

F. Applying and developing emotional intelligence

With emotional intelligence sitting at the heart of effective leadership, there are some routes that senior leaders can use to help develop their self-understanding, EQ and leadership skill. Here are several examples.

---

[7] The first noted reference to 'spiritual intelligence' belongs to Australian author Ken O'Donnell in 1997. Various definitions of spiritual intelligence exist. Cindy Wigglesworth expressed it as "the ability to act with wisdom and compassion, while maintaining inner and outer peace, regardless of the circumstances" in "Why Spiritual Intelligence is Essential to Mature Leadership", *Integral Leadership Review* 6(3): 1–17, 2006.

Coaching/mentoring. In the field of elite sport, the top teams and sportspeople vie for the attention of the world's top coaches. It has taken some time, but the world of business and organisational leadership is beginning to get the message. Senior leaders looking to further advance their skillset now benefit from coaches and mentors.

Psychometric profiling. In the hands of skilled practitioners, psychometric profiling can help a leader hold up a mirror on themselves. She or he can have the privilege of reflecting on their natural disposition and preferences. This 'detached' view is empowering to leaders who see the benefit of modifying their approaches across their different stakeholders. While the leader's values and principles hopefully remain the unshakable core, emotional intelligence stimulated by greater self-awareness underpins consistent effectiveness across differing contexts.

Formal stakeholder survey processes, such as 360-degree assessment, provide senior leaders with a potential additional insight into the way they are perceived by others. Handled in a developmental manner, with the focus on reflection and change, like the other methods mentioned above, formal feedback provides the leader with the appetite for learning and an energised journey along the road to even greater proficiency.

In addition to the formal methods, many directors draw on less structured approaches to reflecting on their ability to contribute to their organisations. Solo reflection – through activities like mindfulness, yoga, walking and aerobic exercise – can meld with more informal feedback from significant others, trusted colleagues and critical friends. Whatever the method, the onus rests with the leader at the centre of this focus and her or his willingness to use this insight to excellent effect.

4. The role of the board in leading the organisation and defining the culture

Though it's debated whether management theorist Peter Drucker actually said "culture eats strategy for breakfast", very few people disagree with the sentiment; an organisation's culture is that important. [8] The board should consider culture like any other essential function in an organisation – be that of finance or operations – a critical cog which requires constant attention, maintained over time with persistent and focused effort.

It is hard to find a universal definition of organisational culture as many aspects of culture are intangible and multifaceted. Put simply: "it is the way we do things around here" as Marvin Bower of McKinsey & Company explained over five decades ago in his 1966 book *The Will to Manage*.[9]

A. 'Leading' culture – the tone from the top

Every organisation has a culture, or what is commonly referred to as: 'a way doing things around here'. Leadership expert Simon Sinek famously said that most organisations end up with a culture by accident rather than design. Clearly, that is far from optimal. The board's role with respect to culture involves setting the tone (agreeing the organisation's values), then leading with these values by example. Directors and boards influence their organisation's culture by pretty much every thought, word and deed. Netflix co-founder Reed Hasting and former Chief Talent Officer Patty McCord created a means by which culture could be designed and curated – the Netflix Culture Deck.[10] Sheryl Sandberg, Facebook's COO at the time, called it one of the most important documents ever to come out of Silicon Valley. The example hopefully emphasises the importance that corporate governance involves being serious and deliberate when it comes to culture.

B. The echo from the bottom

Culture specialists Mostly Consulting propose a three stage process: Assess, Define and Develop – ADD Culture – to help directors and boards lead

---

[8] Many have searched, but no one has found a robust reference for this Drucker quote. It came to prominence mainly through a 2006 interview with Ford Motor Company senior executive Mark Fields, who mentioned this quote was one of his favourites.
[9] Marvin Bower, *The Will to Manage: Corporate Success Through Programmed Management*, McGraw Hill, 1966.
[10] For more information see, for example, https://libertymind.co.uk/what-is-behind-the-magic-of-netflix-company-culture.

culture effectively.[11] The model reminds leaders that whatever the cultural tone from the top of the organisation might be, there is always an echo from the bottom. Ideally, the echo chimes in unison with the 'the way the organisation would like things done around here', but the only way to know that is to go and find out. Informal methods such as spending time on the dance floor will help. But culture is perhaps too important an organisational resource not to treat with greater prudency. The question for directors and boards is around how they know with confidence what their organisation's cultural echo from the bottom is.

5. Developing leadership talent and succession planning

Ensuring proper succession planning in both the organisation and at the board is critical to contribute to the organisation's sustainable long-term success. Talent development provides a critical lever to ensure this.

Some companies have adopted a talent development model that is based on 'grow your own' combined with 'continuous coaching and feedback'. McKinsey provides a good example where this has been applied for almost 100 years. This has the added benefit that a single culture based on shared and deeply embedded values prevails in the organisation. In private organisations such as McKinsey, the board is composed of the partners who are the organisation's senior members. In publicly-traded organisations, however, this is not acceptable in most countries because of the independence criteria required to satisfy the regulator and shareholders.

In Section 1, the metaphor that leaders, including board members, should at times pivot between the balcony and the dance floor was introduced. This helps with the identification and development of future leaders. It also results in at least three benefits: accelerated development of executive talent, higher motivation through empowerment, and it keeps leaders from falling into the busy trap.[12]

A talent development philosophy based on continuous coaching and

---

[11] See https://mostly.consulting.
[12] It is easy to be busy, but more difficult to be productive. Pivoting between the balcony and the dance floor helps leaders to remain productive.

feedback has the additional benefit that staff, and board members alike, always know what their development needs are and what their prospects are for growth and continued employment. In other words, the turkeys know that they are turkeys.[13]

In the US, although executive sessions were introduced as part of the board's risk oversight process following the Enron scandal, they also serve an important purpose in succession planning. Executive sessions are different from regular board meetings as they allow the independent directors to meet without the presence of management.[14] CEO and other senior executive succession matters are frequently discussed during executive sessions. These sessions are usually led by the non-executive chair or, when the role of the chair and chief executive are combined, the lead independent director.

Board diversity needs to be seriously considered in succession planning. Diverse boards, when well designed, are better at risk oversight, including ESG oversight. Although diversity comes in many forms, typically the following four are considered: gender, ethnic, experience, and age diversity.

Several studies conducted by McKinsey[15] and Harvard Business School[16] illustrate that gender diversity leads to improved business performance, less extreme risk-taking, and enhanced governance. Ethnic diversity at the board level has contributed to more consideration of the wider societal aspects in and the implications of strategic decisions. Similarly, younger board members tend to challenge decisions that would adversely affect future generations, therefore ensuring that risk-taking is better aligned with the company's risk appetite, which in turn contributes to improved long-term performance.

In general, board diversity reduces potential bias in decision-making. The risk of unconscious bias – the potential prejudice against a particular group or decision – is largely reduced in more diverse boards where the various

---

[13] Classroom quotations from Jack Welch. https://www.nbcnews.com/id/wbna15242623.
[14] In the UK, 'executive sessions' are referred to as 'non-executive directors' meetings'.
[15] Vivian Hunt, Sara Prince, Sundiatu Dixon-Fyle, and Lareina Yee, "Delivering through diversity", McKinsey & Company, January 2018.
[16] Stephen Turban, Dan Wu, and Letian Zhang, "When gender diversity makes firms more productive", *Harvard Business Review*, February 2019.

issues, risks, and societal perspectives are constructively debated before a decision is made. Similarly, more diverse boards tend to suffer less from over-confidence and confirmation bias. These forms of biases have often led to excessive risk-taking by boards with often devastating outcomes. A good example is Lehman Brothers, whose largely 'stale and male' board of directors allowed it to take excessive risks. By 2008 the bank's financial leverage ratio exceeded 30, making it highly vulnerable to changes in the value of real estate[17] and the 161-year-old firm collapsed.

The perceived wisdom of both investors and other stakeholders is that 'diversity is good', especially as there is evidence that it can reduce the likelihood of groupthink. There is also strong evidence that diverse boards tend to contribute better to the long-term sustainable success of the company. Board diversity is extensively discussed in Chapters 6 and 7.

Term limits for directors are increasingly common and a good way to refresh the thinking in the boardroom. Board succession planning needs to be an early and ongoing process, typically managed through the nomination committee. Effective board succession planning includes all of the following:[18]

- The competences and behaviours needed to effectively lead the company drive the search for new director profiles and candidates.
- Board succession planning is an ongoing process to avoid having gaps in skills and board composition.
- The annual director and board evaluation process provides excellent insights about where the skill and experience gaps in the board are or may be emerging.
- The nomination committee considers not only present but also future skills needed. This is particularly important now that many companies are experiencing a digital transformation and directors need to be conversant with the concepts and challenges of the digital economy.
- Planned changes to the board's composition are properly timed to avoid a loss of institutional memory.

[17] Mark Williams, *Uncontrolled Risk*, McGraw-Hill Education, 2010.
[18] https://www.spencerstuart.com/research-and-insight/boardroom-best-practice-chapter-5.

6. The board induction process and practices

Upon joining the board, all directors should receive induction to allow them to function optimally as a board member. The induction process includes providing access to relevant information, conducting site visits, organising meetings with management and other directors, and when needed, training.[19]

Although conducted under the board chair's leadership, the company secretary plays an important role in arranging and facilitating the induction process. The role of the company secretary in both the director induction and development programme cannot be underestimated. After all, the company secretary is often the only full-time governance professional in a company who is highly skilled in matters of corporate governance, ethics, and compliance.

The 2003 Higgs Report[20] suggests that the director induction process should aim for the following:

- Building an understanding of the nature of the company, its business, and the markets in which it operates. This includes the company's articles of association, board procedures, matters reserved for the board, the company's products and services, the company's risk profile, and potential regulatory constraints.
- Building a link with the people of the organisation. This includes senior management, company site managers and staff, other non-executive directors, and working relationships away from the formal setting of the boardroom.
- Building an understanding of the company's main relationships, including major customers, suppliers and shareholders, as well as the organisation's auditors.

A properly designed induction programme has some of the following characteristics:

---

[19] ICSA: The Chartered Governance Institute, Guidance note: Induction of directors, 2015.
[20] Derek Higgs, Review of the role and effectiveness of non-executive directors, 2003.

- Comprehensive and time-consuming and may take up to 12 months to complete.
- Tailored to the organisation's specific needs and the director in question.
- Diverse in the way information is delivered to the director, from reading materials, meetings, site visits, presentations, etc.
- Includes a relevant training and development programme based on the needs of the director and the organisation.

The induction process is an integral part of a structured process to ensure that the new director gets up to speed quickly on board matters, is well equipped to discharge his or her duties, and can contribute to the organisation's sustainable long-term success.

7. Board dynamics and behaviour for effective decision-making

Jeremy Cross (2019) defines boardroom dynamics as "[t]he interaction between board members individually and collectively in the boardroom."[21] Given the board's importance in making judgements that contribute to the company's sustainable long-term success, the board is similar to a 'high-performing team', which Katzenbach and Smith (1993) define as "[a] small group of people with complementary skills who are committed to a common purpose, performance goals, and approach for which they hold themselves mutually accountable."[22]

Metaphorically, the board can be referred to as an orchestra; the board members are the musicians and the chair functions as the conductor. Each musician brings his or her unique yet complementary skills to the performance, while the conductor's primary responsibilities are to unify musicians, set the tempo, listen critically, and ensure the timely entry of the musicians.

---

[21] Jeremy Cross, *Boardroom dynamics*, ICSA Publishing, 2019.
[22] Jon Katzenbach and Douglas Smith, *The Wisdom of Teams*, Harvard Business School Press, 1993.

The board chair in close consultation with the chief executive is responsible for developing the board agenda and decides which board matters require discussion and engagement from the independent directors and what decisions need to be made. During the discussion, the chair acts as a facilitator, decides who has the floor and solicits input from directors. In a diverse board, the chances are bigger that the major issues are being looked at from different angles and perspectives before a decision is reached. The best chairs keep their opinions to the end in order not to force fit their judgement on other directors and the board.[23]

Another responsibility of the chair is to implement a common policy for board papers to ensure that the board has timely access (i.e. typically one week before the meeting) to relevant reports, data and information to allow directors to prepare themselves for the board meeting. Ideally, reports are succinct, include an executive summary, and are presented in an easily recognisable format.

Meeting locations, often away from company headquarters, further contribute to the dynamics and the behaviour of directors during board meetings. Increasingly, there is a tendency to hold these at or close to a major operation of the organisation – a plant, a service centre, an R&D centre, etc. After all, a visible board is a strong morale booster for employees.

8. Stakeholder management

The first step when eliciting information from a large number of internal and external stakeholders is to conduct a stakeholder identification and mapping exercise. This is to assess the relative importance of stakeholder groups and their potential impact on the company with regards to risks.

The two dimensions of the stakeholder map are influence and level of interest. Based on these two dimensions, mapping stakeholders gives the following combinations: 1) stakeholders with low influence and interest, the board monitors; 2) stakeholders with low interest and high power need to

---

[23] Lorin Letendre and Ann James, "Board dynamics: How to get results from your board and committees", National Association of Corporate Directors (NACD), 2012.

be kept satisfied; 3) stakeholders with high interest and low influence need to be acknowledged and kept informed; and 4) stakeholders those with both high interest and influence need to be involved and managed closely. It is especially this latter group that requires timely engagement by both the board and management.

In addition to the stakeholder identification and mapping exercise, a variety of consultation options with external stakeholders are conducted, including surveys, workshops, focus groups, and public meetings. Pandemic-related travel restrictions mean boards can also make use of online forums, press articles, and social media groups. Sometimes, and on material issues such as ESG, combined internal/external stakeholder workshops have proven to be effective. Not only to understand stakeholder concerns but also to brainstorm effective mitigation solutions.

Values need to be lived and reflected in the company's culture. As a board member, it is appropriate to spend time with top management, outside of board meetings, and with employees to have a feel whether there is a good understanding of the organisation's purpose, whether the right risks and ESG issues are being addressed, and how individual employees can contribute to the organisation's sustainable long-term success.

Stakeholder management also forms an integral part of the organisation's strategy. As discussed in Chapter 8, strategic options need to be acceptable to a broad group of stakeholders, including shareholders, employees, and customers.

9. Risk and crisis leadership

Following the global financial crisis, boards of financial institutions in both the UK and the US were required to have a separate risk committee. While risk management was typically the responsibility of the audit committee, it became apparent that in a fast-paced and changing environment, forward-looking risks are important matters for the board to consider. We would argue that forward-looking risks, managed by a separate risk committee, should be considered by any board of any organisation. Its role is to identify the potential disruptive risks and their implications for the organisation's strategy. Chapter 8 (The board's role in strategy) discusses the various types of risks – black swans, grey rhinos, and white elephants – and how these can be identified and mitigated.

There are times, however, that a crisis not envisioned by the board materialises. This is a fact of life. Examples include the 1982 Johnson & Johnson Tylenol capsules crisis when eight people died from cyanide poisoning, and the 1986 Gerber[24] baby food glass scare, when glass was discovered inside baby food jars in more than 30 US states. Johnson & Johnson's response was multi-faced, broad, and rapid: products were immediately, and voluntary removed from the shelves and the company reached out to the public to stop using its Tylenol capsules. Its chairman took a leadership role and the board worked in close collaboration with the regulator to design tamper-resistant packaging. Gerber, on the other hand, resisted product recall demands, avoided stakeholder engagement, defended its actions, and even sued the governor of the state of Maryland and other officials for banning the sale of some of its baby food products and creating a 'climate of fear and confusion'. These two crisis situations clearly demonstrate different styles when dealing with key stakeholders. And although both were deemed legal, the Johnson & Johnson response meets a higher ethical standard.

During times of a crisis, an organisation's stakeholder map can potentially change. Stakeholders with low influence and interest may suddenly become high influence and interest stakeholders. Consider the Gerber baby food glass scare. Before the crisis, Maryland's state government had limited influence and was not that interested in Gerber's products and activities. But after glass was found inside baby food jars, the government had to step in and act in the best interest of its citizens by banning the sale of Gerber's peaches. If Gerber would have updated its stakeholder map during the crisis, its response to the crisis and to the state of Maryland would likely have been different.

10. Leading in the external environment

An organisation does not operate in a vacuum and the actions of the board

---

[24] Gerber Products Company, a subsidiary of Nestlé, is the world's largest baby foods company.

could significantly impact society – either positively or negatively. Corporate social responsibility, or CSR, should therefore be taken very seriously by directors and the entire board. There are various ways that directors can lead by example in the external environment.

The first way is to properly define the organisation's purpose, values, and culture.[25] The next step includes stakeholder mapping (see Section 8 above) with the objective to understand how the organisation's purpose, values and culture are perceived by external stakeholders. Then, decide how you want to engage the relevant stakeholders on sensitive matters with the objective to have a positive influence on the wider community.

The following example illustrates that although Shell was doing the right thing from an environmental perspective, decisions can potentially misfire in the external environment because of a lack of understanding and improper engagement with an external stakeholder. In 1991 Shell UK decided to decommission Brent Spar, an oil storage buoy, and sink it as reef in the deep Atlantic Ocean, 250 kilometres west of Scotland. Greenpeace, a non-governmental environmental organisation, criticised Shell's decision and campaigned against the company. Greenpeace's actions changed public opinion against Shell and resulted in a boycott of its products. Under pressure from the German government, Shell decided that they were no longer going to sink Brent Spar but instead dismantle it in Norway. The moral of the story is that both Shell and Greenpeace later agreed that sinking Brent Spar was the best environmentally responsible option, but the reason why Shell failed to initially convince Greenpeace was because 'Shell provided an engineering answer to an emotional problem.'[26]

Later in Chapter 18 (Is corporate governance 4.0 emerging?), the importance for organisations to build a sustainable, inclusive, and resilient business in a fast-changing and ambiguous competitive landscape will be explored.

---

[25] See also Chapter 8: The board's role in strategy.
[26] Quoted from a conversation between Sir Mark Moody-Stuart and Alexander Van de Putte in 2004.

Conclusion

There are two concluding messages. First, a key message in this book is the shift in corporate governance from the protection/compliance perspective to one of organisational performance and sustainability. Governance is now very much about the organisation being the best it can be. Second, leaders and leadership make a difference. In this chapter we have explored how. So given the duties and responsibilities that people in governance positions carry, it makes perfect sense to learn how to lead well and lead effectively.

Corporate Governance 3.0

CHAPTER 4. DIRECTOR DUTIES AND THEIR IMPLICATIONS

Sharon Constançon, CEO, Genius Boards and Chair of the South African Chamber of Commerce in the UK

Introduction

Boards of directors have had to transition from the profit and bottom-line focus which was in vogue twenty years ago to the purpose driven focus of today,[1] underpinned in the UK by the UK Corporate Governance Code 2018 and by the Companies Act 2006.[2]

Today's directors are required to be 'agile', 'resilient', open to 'transformation' and 'digitally savvy'. In today's digital age, referred to in Chapter 1 as Governance: Generation 3.0 and the 'Digital Age', the board is compelled to have access to the knowledge and talent that will protect them from what, to most, is the 'unknown unknown'. It is essential to ask the right questions to ensure that transformation from legacy risk is successful and engagement in addressing external cyber risk occurs.

What we see now, since the global financial crisis and in a period of

---

[1] See Principle B: https://www.frc.org.uk/getattachment/88bd8c45-50ea-4841-95b0-d2f4f48069a2/2018-UK-Corporate-Governance-Code-FINAL.pdf (Financial Reporting Council, FRC).
[2] UK government legislation website: https://www.legislation.gov.uk/ukpga/2006/46/contents.

unprecedented technological change, are companies experiencing more of the influence of the Millennials (currently aged 25–40 years) who are coming into senior roles within organisations. They bring with them a different sense of personal expectation, access to information, purpose, work/life balance and engaging with the 'gig economy'.[3] Boards need to be mindful of the impact all of this will have on board demographics.

Millennials, in comparison to their parents who were mostly born between 1965 and 1980, are likely to be more digitally agile and savvy and these are the skills which boards need; the challenge being that boards populated with baby-boomers (born 1946–1964), who are likely to be resistant to change, are limited in technical skills and challenged by the current degree of transparency required by stakeholders.

In the UK, directors are 'governed' by the Companies Act 2006, the UK Corporate Governance Code 2018, its related guidance and industry focused governance codes. In this chapter we shall not focus on directors' general legal duties but address instead the implications upon them in terms of responsibilities as well as some of the consequences to them personally and their organisation of ineffective discharge of their duties and related responsibilities.

1. Introduction to UK board governance and the unitary board

UK registered companies have a unitary board structure and good practice requires the board to have more independent non-executive directors that the sum of the chair and the executive and non-independent non-executive directors. All directors, executive and non-executive, are equal in terms of their fiduciary and other statutory duties. Essentially, a director is a director.

Key aspects of the role of the non-executive director on a unitary board involve scrutinising executive management and achieving consensus where possible on decisions taken by the board. All are involved in the oversight

---

[3] Lebowitz A, and Akhtar A., "14 things millennials do completely different from their parents," 21 November 2019, https://www.businessinsider.com/millennials-habits-different-from-baby-boomers-2018-3?r=US&IR=T.

of all aspects of the business, from strategy to governance and key business decisions.

One deviation from equal accountability of all directors is seen in the financial services sector. The Senior Managers and Certification Regime (SM&CR) prescribes different accountabilities for key executive, managerial and certain board roles.[4,5] SM&CR will apply eventually to all Financial Services and Markets Act 2000 (FSMA) authorised firms, including banks, building societies, asset managers, investment firms, insurers, mortgage providers, consumer credit firms and sole traders. It includes the chair, executive directors, and most committee chairs and key executive heads of function.

Executive and non-executive directors have different levels of insight and information about the day-to-day activities of the business. The governance requirements are such that directors should receive quality and timely information in board papers usually delivered via an online board portal.

2. Directors' general duties under the Companies Act 2006

Sections 171 to 177 set out the key general duties of a director.[6] These are duties to abide by the company's constitution and exercise powers only for purposes for which they were conferred; to promote the success of the company (we return to this below); to exercise independent judgment; to exercise reasonable care, skill and diligence; to avoid conflicts of interest and duty; not to accept benefits from third parties by reason of being a director or doing (or not doing) anything as a director; and to declare any interest in transactions or arrangements. These are fairly obvious requirements for a director operating in good faith, so following and

---

[4] FCA's guide for solo-regulated firms (https://www.fca.org.uk/publication/policy/guide-for-fca-solo-regulated-firms.pdf), applicability for dual-regulated firms (https://www.fca.org.uk/firms/senior-managers-certification-regime/dual-regulated-firms), and guidance on responsibilities (https://www.fca.org.uk/publication/finalised-guidance/fg19-02.pdf).

[5] See SM&CR announcement (https://www.fca.org.uk/firms/senior-managers-certification-regime) and an overview for solo-regulated firms (https://www.farrer.co.uk/news-and-insights/overview-of-the-senior-managers--certification-regime-for-fca-solo-regulated-firms/).

[6] https://www.legislation.gov.uk/ukpga/2006/46/part/10/chapter/2/crossheading/the-general-duties

adhering to these duties should be second nature. However, rather than set out what these duties entail (the details may be found in the 2006 Act or in a variety of readily available books and guidance notes), I wish instead to focus on the wider implications of being a director of, particularly, a publicly quoted company. As stated by Albert Camus, the French philosopher, author and journalist who won the Nobel Prize in Literature in 1957: 'Yes, everything is simple. It's people who complicate things'!

Challenges that boards experience include varying expectations, abilities and personal agendas, differing degrees of alignment with the company's purpose, and the focus of the management and being a complementary personality to the collective team.

A. Reporting against section 172: Duty to promote the success of the company

Reporting against this section in the company's strategic report is mandated by the Companies (Miscellaneous Reporting) Regulations 2018, which provide that the company must explain how the directors have had regard to these matters when carrying out their duties.

Every entity to which the regulations apply must define the issues, factors and stakeholders the directors consider relevant and how they have formed that opinion. They must identify the principal methods the directors have used to engage with stakeholders and understand the issues to which they must have regard; and how that information impacts the company's decisions and strategies.[7]

Concerning how detailed it should be, 'companies will need to judge what is appropriate, but the statement should be meaningful and informative for shareholders, shed light on matters that are of strategic importance, and be consistent with the size and complexity of the business.'[8]

These new reporting requirements represented a challenge for many

---

[7] Dept for Business, Energy & Industrial Strategy, "Corporate Governance: The Companies (Miscellaneous Reporting) Regulations 2018 Q&A," November 2018, p. 8.
[8] Ibid.

companies. Research in 2019 by Baker McKenzie found that almost three-quarters (72%) of firms surveyed would have difficulty compiling/verifying the information necessary to comply, over half (56%) lacked a clear corporate governance framework, and a third (32%) lacked the resources to comply with the new legislation. But most (80%) indicated that good corporate governance is a board priority.[9]

B. Annual reporting

Directors need to focus in some detail on how the business generates long-term value and how decisions take cognisance of the strategic longer-term value and the long-term consequences of capital allocation and dividend policy decisions.

Given the critical importance of the internal stakeholder, directors need also to focus on talent or the workforce as an asset of the business and the organisation's related development strategy. These are topics which, typically, are not as well covered as some others. Another key stakeholder concern relates to the supply chain, including issues of anti-bribery, sustainability, and engagement with the various stakeholders in the supply chain.

Today's boards cannot escape reporting on the required environmental disclosures in respect of various sites and communities, the actions being taken, the impacts expected and targets, measures and related culture. The annual report needs to include information about embedding of the culture into the management and throughout the organisation; how this is achieved and measured whilst ensuring fair access to information and addressing asymmetry of information dissemination.

Further information is to be provided on other areas of governance effectiveness including, inter alia, about the role of the chair, strategy, information, policies and practices, and training such that the board can delegate, empower, mitigate and assess the embedding of culture.

---

[9] https://www.globalcompliancenews.com/2019/05/15/more-than-half-uks-very-large-private-companies-lack-clear-corporate-governance-framework-20190319/

C. Individual director's sense of responsibility

While statutes and regulations set out the letter of a director's duties, one must look to governance codes and associated guidance to shed light on what is entailed in being an *effective* director. Even then, and notwithstanding all the governance codes and principles in the world, it is ultimately up to each individual – their character, style, knowledge, capabilities, competencies – being a team player; having a balance of IQ, EQ and AQ; being aligned to the purpose and the culture of the organisation; having the business outcomes front of mind; being challenging, strategic, engaging and visible; and working constructively with the chair, executives, company secretary and non-executives.

It is important, therefore, to ensure that prospective and current directors will be a good fit within the culture, both as to competencies and character. They also need to respond well to leadership, engage effectively with the team, communicate with clarity and be visible and proactive in performing their duties.

If a director has the right ethical compass and personal integrity and considers the strategic needs of the long-term business success as a team member, the board will be a more effective vehicle to deliver oversight of the business.

3. UK Corporate Governance Code and related guidance

A. The UK Corporate Governance Code 2018

The Code has evolved over almost three decades since the original Cadbury Report 1992,[10] the most recent version being the governance code published in 2018. The aim of these reforms is to build trust in business. This is being driven by a reformist mindset, seeking improved stakeholder engagement which, in itself, is key to a company's long-term success.

Directors need to be mindful of the focus of the code whose precepts are

---

[10] "Report of the Committee on the Financial Aspects of Corporate Governance" (1992) chaired by Sir Adrian Cadbury,
https://ecgi.global/sites/default/files//codes/documents/cadbury.pdf.

additional, and directly complementary to, their fiduciary and other legal duties. A quick guide for directors, to help them embed this into their 'DNA', is found in the key responsibilities filtered from the first five governance principles in the UK code, which address board leadership and company purpose:

- In Principle A it is mandated that 'a company is led by an effective and entrepreneurial board, whose role is to promote the long-term sustainable success of the company, generating value for shareholders and contributing to wider society'.
- In Principle B, whilst leading by example and acting with integrity, the board must establish the company's purpose, values and strategy and be satisfied that these and the company's culture are aligned.
- In Principle C the board is mandated to ensure the business is resourced to meet objectives and measure performance; and 'establish a framework of prudent and effective controls, which enable risk to be assessed and managed'.
- In Principle D the board is asked to ensure effective engagement with, and encourage participation from, all shareholders and stakeholders.
- In Principle E the board is required to 'ensure that workforce policies and practices are consistent with company values and support its long-term sustainable success'; and there is the ability for the workforce should be able to raise any matters of concerns.

Directors also need to be mindful of other code principles: considering good governance, working to support an effective chair, delivering independence in decision-making, and understanding the importance of the nominations committee, which needs to consider the capacity of each director and the appointment processes to deliver diversity and optimum composition.

Other principles cover the evaluation of the board, the efficacy of the audit, risk and internal control functions, and the balance of the remuneration policies.

Stakeholders wish to understand how code principles have been applied by each company, not just as a mere compliance statement, but rather discerning how governance, relationships and decision-making come together and work for the benefit of the company. Thus, it is an outcomes-based code, with the beneficial outcomes being embodied within a business which operates, therefore, with transparency and integrity.

B. Guidance on Board Effectiveness 2018

The related Guidance on Board Effectiveness issued by the FRC augments the code.[11] It follows the same section structure as the code, giving insights and suggesting applications whilst defining what is considered good practice.

A good example of added information in the guidance which may stimulate boards' thinking may be seen in paragraph 13 of the guidance, which states:

> *'A sound understanding at board level of how value is created over time is key in steering strategies and business models towards a sustainable future. This is not limited to value that is found in the financial statements. An understanding of how intangible sources of value are developed, managed and sustained – for example a highly trained workforce, intellectual property or brand recognition – is increasingly relevant to an understanding of the company's performance and the impact of its activity. These are important considerations for boards when setting corporate strategy.'*

The guidance also has helpful question sections to help boards and directors to identify ways of being more effective. An example of a question, related directly to Principle A mentioned above, and which identifies something that is often overlooked by boards, is:

> *'Is sufficient board time allocated to idea generation, opportunity identification and innovation?'* [12]

Boards can be so busy 'doing' or 'overseeing' that time to think may often be forgotten outside the board meeting or the board's annual calendar. An analogy is of those on the bridge of a ship who have a different mindset

---

[11] See the FRC's 2018-Guidance-on-Board-Effectiveness-final.pdf.
[12] Ibid., p. 4.

and focus to those who are ensuring its forward momentum, docking or dealing with cargo and people. Those on the bridge (the board) should be plotting course, considering risks, looking at external influences, taking time to think innovatively, and identifying appropriate opportunities.

Demonstrating the value of the guidance to boards and individual directors, the section on monitoring culture has helpful breakout boxes which support a board's focus on the challenges, behaviours, and outcomes of a board and executive team:[13]

- Common attributes of a healthy culture: honesty, openness, respect, adaptability, reliability, recognition, acceptance of challenge, accountability and a sense of shared purpose.
- Signs of possible culture problems: including inter alia – silo thinking, dominance of the CEO, leadership arrogance, pressure to meet the numbers/overambitious targets, lack of access to information, low levels of meaningful engagement between leadership and employees, lack of openness to challenge, tolerance of regulatory or code of ethics breaches, short-term focus and misaligned incentives.
- A culture insights breakout box identifies sources of culture problem indicators (e.g. turnover/absenteeism rates, exit interviews) and the actions which businesses can take to pick up emerging problems (e.g. board interaction with senior management and workforce, prompt payment to suppliers).

The framework offered by the guidance provides a sound and valuable structure for supporting board development strategies and is a 'must read' for all directors to ensure that they deliver on their fiduciary duties.

4. Changing demands on and expectations of a board

A. Change

Some may consider that changed demands on boards have been brought about solely by the global COVID-19 pandemic, but others recognise that years of focusing on key long-term issues are finally producing a greater

---

[13] Ibid., pp. 6–7.

understanding among directors of the importance of sustainability and leading to eventual acceptance by boards.

It has been a journey along the Kübler-Ross Change Curve[14] which has been adapted to many 'change and acceptance' situations such as the rise of the climate change agenda. Developed by psychiatrist Dr. Elisabeth Kübler-Ross in the 1960s to explain five distinct stages of grief experienced after we lose a loved one, her model has been the basis for extensions into organisational change research.[15]

'The event' – where the change agent occurs, and which often includes a degree of 'shock' – triggers the five stages:[16]

- Denial: We resist, deny, and ignore the changes being demanded, as they involve a new mindset, cost, and transparency.
- Anger: There is a realisation of the impact of the event which can engender anger and the desire to blame.
- Bargaining: We think of ways out of the inevitable or at least to postpone or compromise.
- Depression: The common feelings are regret, fear, sadness, guilt, trapped, failure, and indifference or lack of ownership of the outcome.
- Acceptance: There is a resignation to, and acceptance of, the inevitable that they cannot prevent happening. The fight stops but happiness is not necessarily the leading emotion. They then own the situation and take control, delivering positive emotions and ultimately outcomes.

Let me illustrate my point with two examples: one business related and the other at a current human level.

---

[14] 'Understanding the Kübler-Ross Change Curve', https://www.cleverism.com/understanding-kubler-ross-change-curve/.
[15] See e.g. Zell D., "Organizational change as a process of death, dying, and rebirth," *The Journal of Applied Behavioral Science* 39(1): 73-96, 2003; or Kauppinen J-P., Hannu K. and Talvinen J., "Committing to organizational change in IT industry," *International Journal of Social and Organizational Dynamics in IT* 1(4): 1–17, 2011.
[16] NB Movement along the Kübler-Ross change curve is not necessarily in a linear or step-by-step manner.

Example 1: Business – Regulation change

The Financial Conduct Authority (FCA) regulatory changes that focused on the customer, customer care, and the evolution of customer-centric boards caused some boards to go into denial and determine that no change was needed as they already considered the customer.

Anger arose when boards were advised internally or via external specialists that this regulation demanded a completely new journey and that it needed to be embraced. Boards first bargained, challenged and hoped that management had this sorted. Boards felt frustrated not fully understanding the challenge but knowing it would take time, money and effort. Also, not everyone was on the journey. So a struggle to implement the change was foreseen.

The final stage – acceptance – was reached when directors embraced the changes and expertise was engaged to deliver the right and required outcomes.

Example 2: Personal – COVID-19 vaccination

The vaccinations are available and you are invited to be vaccinated. But your thoughts include 'I am not that old, I am not vulnerable, this is for others, not me.' Mounting restrictions on travel freedom and access to hospitality venues and public places, and 'test and trace', leads to anger that this does indeed now include you and cannot be avoided, even if you have personal safety concerns.

You share your views with your doctor, family, even specialists; you read about blood clots; you deploy all the tactics to justify why you are legitimately and safely able to be excluded. As time moves on, there is mounting advice and evidence forcing your hand even though you are concerned about a physical health reaction to the vaccination components. Eventually, you realise that the risks of COVID-19 to your safety are much higher than the risks of the vaccine so you capitulate and book your appointment.

Keeping those illustrations in mind, stakeholders are demanding real action, not lip service, from businesses. There are some key topics which boards should have on their horizon, agendas, strategies and action plans.

B. Stakeholders

The organisation needs to define its purpose that is supported by vision, mission and values and includes sustainability, long-term considerations in decision-making, the green agenda, ESG (environmental, social, and governance factors) and, specifically, climate change and what the business is doing to address its own impacts.

Stakeholder capitalism has demanded recognition of all stakeholder groups, from internal to external: the people within the organisations, the customers, the supply chains, investors, and communities. No longer does investor short-term behaviour alone drive board decision-making.

The internal stakeholder profile has risen during COVID-19 with considerations around pay, incentive schemes, wage stagnation, wage gaps, gender gaps, health and safety, and a genuine concern for their welfare and the related issues of furlough, safe return to work, flexible working, and adaptability for different workers' needs.

For directors, important issues include board composition, board refresh, role of the nominations committee and the company secretary, known diversities, cognitive diversities, holding management accountable, board and management transparency, and the growing need for organisations to embrace cultural and digital transformation.

Within the broad board agenda, some of the key internal focus areas brought about by the COVID-19 pandemic should remain on boards' agendas, including working norms, staff safety, and staff well-being. A prevalent topic is the impact of change on staff welfare at an emotional level. Boards need to determine how they recognise and respond when teams are showing strain, understand why individuals are responding to various stress factors, and decide what plans will be implemented to support the individuals and teams.

Another challenge is the integration of those working remotely or furloughed and, importantly, retraining for changes in roles. Many companies have engaged new people without meeting them in person and need to ensure induction is robust to mitigate risks (including control risks) arising. Accountability of mixed working styles needs clarity and education for both leaders and team members.

C. Board priorities today

Ongoing assessment is needed of the market factors, customer and competitor behaviour and changed needs, new themes, and different expectations.

Increasing demands are still being made of directors, who have necessarily participated in many more board and committee meetings than before the pandemic and have given time to address issues arising from the crisis. This is potentially the new norm.

This is an important time, therefore, to seek to embed growing risk awareness that has improved across the globe because boards are now more mindful of the importance of risk planning than ever before.

Below are shared board priorities as identified by three different market participants.

— EY, a Big Four accounting firm, defines board priorities as the following: overseeing strategy to create long-term value; promoting enterprise resiliency in the face of uncertainty; focusing on workforce transformation and new ways of working; leading on diversity, equity and inclusion; guiding an ESG strategy that drives stakeholder engagement and value; and challenging board composition and effectiveness.[17]

— Russell Reynolds, a lead executive search firm, believes boards should focus on these areas: climate change risk; diversity, equity and inclusion

---

[17] EY, "Six priorities for boards in 2021," https://assets.ey.com/content/dam/ey-sites/ey-com/en_us/topics/cbm/ey-cbm-six-priorities-for-boards-in-2021.pdf.

(DEI); convergence of sustainability reporting standards; human capital management; return of activism and increased capital markets activity; and dealing with virtual board and shareholder meetings, an element of which will remain.[18]

- ISS, a leading workplace and facility management company, considers board focus of the future to include the following: board diversity; board oversight of material environmental and social risk; virtual shareholder meetings; workplace proposals; and practical issues. These practical issues include racial/ethnic and gender self-identity, ESG, sustainability and embracing, whilst being mindful of risk, the virtual meeting.[19]

What we learn from these three sources is that there are a few common themes: ESG and related agendas, diversity perspectives, human capital and talent focus.

5. Consequences of not being an effective director

There are consequences of not being an effective director, the most obvious being losing the role on that board. Regarding the Companies Act, the director could also be sued for damages, declared delinquent, held liable for losses, incur monetary penalties, and suffer reputational damage.

In terms of the UK code and codes for various industries, the director may also suffer the impact of investors being less mindful to invest in that business. Activist shareholders could seek to remove the director, customers may not engage with a business that fails to follow good governance practices, and the company may struggle to attract the right talent.

---

[18] Russell Reynolds, "2021 Global and Regional Trends in Corporate Governance," https://www.russellreynolds.com/insights/thought-leadership/2021-global-and-regional-trends-in-corporate-governance.

[19] "ISS Policy Changes for 2021: Increased Expectations for Diversity and Accountability," https://www.fenwick.com/insights/publications/iss-policy-changes-for-2021-increased-expectations-for-diversity-and-accountability.

It is the fiduciary duty of the board of directors to consider the company first. Most directors do intend to deliver on this requirement but collectively this is not always the universal outcome.

Well-known examples include:

Example 1: Co-operative Bank

Co-operatives and friendly societies tend, though less so now as time passes, to have large boards with long-serving directors having low levels of relevant business expertise.

The lack of banking expertise and modern banking products resulted in poor strategic planning and weak risk management leading to a £1.5 billion capital shortfall.

The capital failure was a result of changed regulation, ineffective management of the merger with the Britannia Building Society in 2009, and inadequate focus and understanding by the board and executive team. There was no culture of accountability, challenge or financial expertise to address the decisions and the ownership of the issues at stake. In an independent review of this debacle, Sir Christopher Kelly said: 'This report tells a sorry story of failings in management and governance on many levels.'[20]

The directors failed in their duties, particularly that of long-term sustainability.

Example 2: Carillion

The key governance failing at construction group Carillion was at the apex of the company.

Poor leadership, ineffective board oversight of executive decision-making and a lack of accountability on the part of the executive, poorly negotiated contracts, and excessive reliance on external consultants compounded its problems. In a parliamentary inquiry report, the board was described as

---

[20] https://www.co-operative.coop/investors/kelly-review

'either negligently ignorant of the rotten culture at Carillion or complicit in it'.[21]

The chair was overly optimistic, dividend payouts exceeded cash generated and the pension deficit was growing, yet the board collectively did not take professional advice or action to consider the long-term sustainability of the company, which collapsed into insolvency in January 2018.

The directors individually and collectively did not deliver under their duties, particularly in showing due care, skill and diligence and the UK Insolvency Service has launched disqualification proceedings against the former directors. Auditor KPMG is expected to settle with the FRC after the regulator uncovered breaches of auditing standards in KPMG's audit of Carillion.

Example 3: Patisserie Valerie

In 2018 this UK cafe chain collapsed after a £40 million black hole, which forensic accounts later determined was £94 million, in its accounts was discovered. The key factor in the company's failure was an accounting fraud. That caused follow-on failures and led eventually to the company's demise.

Failings identified included poor governance, lack of effective internal controls and quality of the external audit. The level of false entries, accounting manipulation and lack of insights from internal audit should have been sensed by at least some of the directors if they had been performing their roles effectively and challenging the numbers – for example, the above-market operating profits.

Poor governance and accountability should have alerted all directors and changes brought to bear through the audit committee.

---

[21] https://publications.parliament.uk/pa/cm201719/cmselect/cmworpen/769/76908.htm#_idTextAnchor175

6. Conclusion

The ability to call for an evaluation of the board is one way to identify ineffectiveness at board and individual director levels and the recommendations, if adopted and followed, can help the chair lead the board to adopt and display more effective behaviours.

The unitary board and board directors are regulated by the Companies Act and in the event of misfeasance (and, certainly, malfeasance) will suffer personal joint and several liability and possible disqualification. In many cases also risk the loss of a good reputation, whether or not such reputation loss was deserved.

Collectively if the chair and the directors are ineffective, then short of removing them all from the board there are staged actions which the company or stakeholders can take. In these circumstances, the removal of the chair would begin the process of a systematic refresh of the board.

The core duties of directors[22] emphasise the significant personal responsibilities to be assumed by a company director.

As the former Master of the Rolls, Lord Woolf, remarked over 20 years ago: 'It is of the greatest importance that any individual who undertakes the statutory and fiduciary obligations of being a company director should realise that these are inescapable personal responsibilities.'[23] This statement preceded the codification of directors' general duties by eight years.

The law reflects the essentially professional nature of directorship where directors acquire and maintain sufficient knowledge and understanding of the business and the principal business risks which it faces. That obliges directors to properly supervise the discharge of delegated functions and not to regard delegation as a means of self-exculpation should things go wrong.

A study project, Business Judgment and the Courts[24], by a team from

---

[22] Duties arise also under e.g. Listing, Disclosure and Transparency Rules, see FCA's Disclosure Guidance and Transparency Rules sourcebook (May 2021), https://www.handbook.fca.org.uk.
[23] In *Secretary of State for Trade and Industry v Griffiths and Others*, re: Westmid Packing Services Ltd (1997), https://www.casemine.com/judgement/uk/5a938b4060d03e5f6b82bccc.
[24] Business Judgment and the Courts: End of Project Report,

University of Leeds School of Law and University of Liverpool Management School reported in 2018 three particularly relevant findings in relation to the Companies Act 2006[25]:

— Directors were generally not conversant with their general duties.

— Section 172 was a matter of significant concern to directors.

— Generally, a low level of awareness of section 174 – the duty to act with reasonable care and skill.

These findings suggest that directors are not receiving or absorbing instruction about their fundamental responsibilities as directors. This argues that board chairs, supported by their company secretary, should give greater focus to director induction and regular board training which, in financial services, is common practice. One particular error is a common assumption that a newly appointed executive director knows about directors' duties and does not need to be taken through them as part of their induction.

Historically, the law has focused on the care, diligence and skill of individual directors; many recent examples suggest systemic failure by the board as a whole, often due to the collective culture. With growing emphasis on stakeholder governance and the expectations of the societies in which companies operate, the inexorable increase in regulation as a reaction to corporate failures and the erosion of trust in business going back at least to the banking crisis of 2008, if not earlier, the demands for greater transparency, and the growth in reporting obligations have all contributed in different ways to the idea of directors' collective responsibility.

While some may challenge the notion of a collective director responsibility in law, directors should recognise that failure laid at the door of a board colleague will taint the reputation and good standing of every director on the board. This is the kind of 'mud' which tends to stick.

---

www.law.leeds.ac.uk/research/projects-business-judgment-and-the-courts
[25] Ibid. p.3

CHAPTER 5. THE PIVOTAL ROLE OF THE COMPANY SECRETARY

Simon Osborne, Chartered Governance Consultant and Former Chief Executive, The Chartered Governance Institute UK & Ireland

Introduction

This chapter considers how the company secretary's role has evolved and identifies some of the characteristics and responsibilities of this important, wide-ranging and complex, but oft misunderstood, role. In particular it will highlight behaviours, qualities and skills which company secretaries contribute to the delivery of good governance and well-governed organisations. Despite the statutory duty on UK public companies to appoint a company secretary,[1] the role has never been clearly defined in UK company law, nor has it been widely understood.[2] Life as a company secretary will vary significantly between employers and across sectors according to the size, operations and stage of development of the organisation involved.

---

[1] Companies Act 2006, section 271.
[2] The International Finance Corporation has published a helpful handbook which gives an international perspective on the role - (2016), *The Corporate Secretary: The Governance Professional*, Washington: World Bank, available online:
<https://www.ifc.org/wps/wcm/connect/4b96fc61-80da-4508-98f7-8a3641e8178c/CG_CoSec_June_2016.pdf?MOD=AJPERES&CVID=llo4tQ-> (accessed 1 July 2021).

However, it is increasingly clear, as the era of Governance 3.0[3] draws to a close and we stand on the cusp of Governance 4.0,[4] that the role is growing in importance and is benefitting from a better understanding and growing recognition on the part of board directors, particularly board chairs. Nowadays many company secretaries occupy a unique and privileged position at the top of their organisations.

1. History and background

In England, the Latin term *secretarius* was used in the Middle Ages to denote, for example, a member of the monarch's council.[5] Later the title became associated with the keeper of the monarch's signet.[6] From the Renaissance to the late nineteenth century, those involved in the daily affairs and activities of the powerful assumed the title of Secretary.[7]

Yet despite this illustrious history there had a been a long-standing perception that the role of company secretary, perhaps because of its administrative nature, was low in status and without influence. In 1887 in a decision of the Court of Appeal, it was said that "a secretary is a mere servant; his position is that he is to do what he is told, and no person can assume that he has any authority to represent anything at all".[8] In a 1902 decision of the House of Lords Appellate Committee, it was opined that the duties of a secretary were "of a limited and of a somewhat humble character."[9]

By 1971, the role was gaining in importance and appreciation. In another Court of Appeal decision, it was said that "a company secretary is a much more important person now than he was in 1887. He is the chief administrative officer of the company with extensive duties and responsibilities ... he regularly makes representations on behalf of the

---

[3] See chapter 1: Introducing Governance 3.0 – The history of corporate governance
[4] See chapter 18: Is Corporate Governance 4.0 Emerging?
[5] Dibben, L. (1910), 'Secretaries in the thirteenth and fourteenth centuries', *The English Historical Review*, vol. 25, no. 99, pp. 430-444.
[6] Ibid.
[7] Biow, D. (2002), *Doctors, Ambassadors, Secretaries: Humanism and Professions in Renaissance Italy*, Chicago: University of Chicago Press.
[8] Barnett, Hoares & Co v. South London Tramways Co (1887) 18 QBD 815.
[9] George Whitechurch Ltd v. Cavenagh [1902] AC 117.

company and enters into contracts on its behalf which come within the day to day running of his business".[10]

Notwithstanding this judicial recognition of the importance of the role, there was a growing trend from the early 1980s and into the 2000s, through the eras of Governance 1.0 and 2.0,[11] for the role of the company secretary to be combined with that of the general counsel. This approach reinforced the belief that the role of the secretary was somehow of less importance. Thus in larger companies the secretariat was headed by a deputy company secretary or head of secretariat, usually reporting to the general counsel. Whatever their skills, attributes and in-house company experience, I know from my own experience that a lawyer's training did not equip me to be a practitioner of good governance. In smaller companies, the general counsel may concentrate on the company's legal affairs with much less focus being given to the responsibilities of the secretariat. When I was first appointed to a combined role of company secretary and general counsel, it was said that there were at least 400 different criminal offences for which a company secretary could be prosecuted. While these were mostly regulatory, rather than genuinely criminal, in nature, this range of personal liability illustrates the relative significance of the office of the company secretary.

Although bigger companies seem to have moved away from combining the two roles, there are smaller companies which combine the role, including with that of finance director or financial controller.[12]

2. The company secretary in private companies

Further demonstrating the misperception of the potential value and contribution of the company secretary was the repeal in the Companies Act 2006 of the requirement to appoint a company secretary for private companies. This repeal did not preclude the appointment of a company secretary, but it ignored the needs of private companies (some operate significant businesses) for effective board management and good

---

[10] Panorama Developments (Guildford) Ltd v Fidelis Furnishing Fabrics Ltd [1971] 2 QB 711.
[11] See chapter 1.
[12] Note 23 129

governance. The repeal was justified by the UK's Company Law Review Committee as deregulatory, but none of the statutory duties attaching to the office was repealed.[13]

3. Emerging corporate governance

With the growing focus throughout the Governance 2.0 era on the importance of companies practising high quality governance, the skills and contribution of an experienced company secretary began increasingly to be recognised. Starting with *The Cadbury Report* in 1992,[14] each successive edition of what has become the *UK Corporate Governance Code,* together with increased scrutiny from institutional investors on the quality of their investees' governance standards, has imposed much greater focus on companies' board procedures, decision-making and governance frameworks. The office holder providing the desired level of support for the board, and particularly for the chair, is the company secretary.

This shift was recognised first in *The Cadbury Report*[15] and later by a report commissioned by the All Party Parliamentary Corporate Governance Group (APPCGG), which drew attention to the independence and impartiality that company secretaries need to have and display to be effective in this wider, advisory role. It stated that:

> *"The breadth and importance of the role of the company secretary has increased markedly over the past five years. It is a unique role as the company secretary is often neither part of 'line management' nor a member of the board itself. There are endeavours to move the profession beyond that of being the 'administrative servant of the board' to one which encompasses the broader role of board adviser".*[16]

---

[13] Company Law Review Steering Group. (2000), *Modern Company Law for a Competitive Economy, Developing the Framework (URN 00/656),* London: Department of Trade and Industry, chapters 6 and 7, available online:
<https://webarchive.nationalarchives.gov.uk/20100304135036/http://www.berr.gov.uk/whatwedo/businesslaw/co-act-2006/clr-review/page25086.html> (accessed 1 July 2021).
[14] Cadbury, A. et al. (1992), *Report of The Committee on the Financial Aspects of Corporate Governance*, available online: <https://www.icaew.com/-/media/corporate/files/library/subjects/corporate-governance/financial-aspects-of-corporate-governance.ashx?la=en> (accessed 1 July 2021).
[15] Ibid.
[16] (2016), 'Elevating the role of the Company Secretary: Lessons from the FTSE All Share', All Party Parliamentary Corporate Governance Group website, available online:

Interestingly, this significant change in the fortunes of the role was envisaged by David Jackson, the former company secretary of BP p.l.c., in a chapter contributed to *The Business Case for Corporate Governance*.[17] He wrote:

> *"I believe that the enhanced focus on governance and performance presents a major challenge to the company secretary but also an opportunity. Whatever the views of chairmen now, the role of the board will come under increasing scrutiny in the coming years. There is an increasing interest in what business does and in what is the role of corporations in society... shareholders will, over time, become more demanding in their engagement with company's and more searching in their desire to understand companies' explanations for non-compliance with governance provisions ... boards will need to rise and meet these challenges. The company secretary will need to move into this space."*[18]

In his concluding paragraph, David Jackson put out this challenge:

> *"The opportunity is there. Company secretaries can again play the pivotal role that they performed in the past. Governance and board performance lie at the heart of all that they should be focusing on in the future. It's up to them to walk into that space."*[19]

Have company secretaries risen to that challenge? I believe that they have and with great success.

4. The current position

The description of the company secretary in the APPCGG's report as 'board adviser' is prescient.[20] Because of its history, the role has developed as a hybrid, combining responsibility for company administration and regulatory compliance - requiring technical knowledge and managerial expertise - with responsibility for shaping the organisation's governance framework and putting it into practice - which requires the ability to

---

<https://www.appcgg.co.uk/elevating-the-role-of-the-company-secretary-lessons-from-the-ftse-all-share-may-2012/> (accessed 1 July 2021).
[17] Jackson, D. (2008), 'The role of the company secretary' in Rushton, K. (ed.), *The Business Case for Corporate Governance*, Cambridge: Cambridge University Press, 67-80.
[18] Ibid, 79.
[19] Ibid, 80.
[20] Note16.

negotiate, mentor and manage board relationships through formal and informal means. This is a demanding skillset.

As the one person in the boardroom who truly works for the board, the company secretary occupies a unique position as an honest broker. With access to all members of the board, the company secretary has evolved to become the 'bridge' between the non-executives and the executive leadership team, facilitating strategic alignment and enabling constructive decision-making. This can be challenging when tension may escalate into boardroom conflict. As pointed out in a report of 2017:

> *"The company secretary's role is to advise the chairman when tension is positive and when it is likely to escalate into conflict. The company secretary should also facilitate conversations and build trust with all parties."*[21]

5. Role, responsibilities and relationships

The Companies Act 2006 (section 271) requires public companies to appoint a company secretary. The various qualifications for appointment are listed in section 273, but the Act does not specify how the secretary should be appointed or to whom they should report. For the last 25 years or so, various iterations of what is now the *UK Corporate Governance Code 2018* have stated that the appointment and removal of the company secretary should be a matter for the board as whole; yet reporting lines remain unclear and vary according to the size of the organisation and how the role is perceived.[22] In larger corporates, the company secretary tends to report to the chair but this is by no means always the case. Some report to the chief executive or sometimes the chief financial officer, while others may have split reporting lines for specific aspects of the role. Whatever the structure, boards should be aware of the impact of the reporting line on the execution of the role.

---

[21] The Chartered Governance Institute and Henley Business School. (2017), *Conflict and Tension in the Boardroom: How Managing Disagreement Improves Board Dynamics*, available online: <://www.cgi.org.uk/knowledge/research/the-conflict-and-tension-in-the-boardroom-report> (accessed 1 July 2021 – (free) log in required), 36.
[22] Financial Reporting Council. (2018), *UK Corporate Governance Code*, available online: <https://www.frc.org.uk/getattachment/88bd8c45-50ea-4841-95b0-d2f4f48069a2/2018-UK-Corporate-Governance-Code-FINAL.PDF> (accessed 1 July 2021).

The Pivotal Role of the Company Secretary

A major challenge that a company secretary can face is that directors and senior colleagues may not understand the significance of the job title because the role is difficult to define neatly. Each organisation and board is unique so the role becomes a matter of context, taking account of the individual's background and skillset and the company's own way of doing things. In smaller organisations, company secretaries often have broader responsibilities which may include managing data protection, the compliance function, the risk register, the pension scheme, insurance and even property management; in addition to all the statutory requirements laid down in company legislation relating to filings, statutory forms and registers and a wide range of other functions.

In a larger organisation, the role may be more defined and narrower in its scope. Responsibilities will likely include:

- organising board and board committee meetings (including drafting agendas and organising the circulation of board papers) and ensuring compliance with board procedures and regulation;
- induction of new directors, director development and being the point of contact for the non-executive directors;
- keeping the board chair up to date on governance matters and keeping the governance framework under review;
- facilitating the evaluation of the board, its main committees and individual directors;
- coordinating the annual general meeting and ensuring that it complies with current legislation and the company's own procedures;
- listed company compliance and relations with major shareholders and other stakeholders;
- overseeing the production of the annual report with specific responsibility for sections within the report;
- accountability for other statutory and regulatory compliance.

The fundamental point is that there is no 'one size fits all' approach to defining the role of the company secretary but an effective individual will build and define the role in their image.

Because of the nature of the role, the company secretary needs to have good relationships at some level with each member of the board. Some directors will be easier to get on with than others but it is essential that the company secretary should gain the trust of and build a sound relationship with each member of the board, whether or not they are likeable as individuals. The principal relationship to be developed is with the board chair. As Sir Adrian Cadbury stated:

> *"At the chairman's right hand at board meetings is the company secretary. Company secretaries are responsible for board administration, whether or not they are full members of the board. Professional company secretaries who anticipate problems and who draft well make life a great deal easier for their chairman."*[23]

He continued:

> *"The company secretary has a key role to play in ensuring that board procedures are followed and regularly reviewed. Chairmen will look to company secretaries for guidance on their legal responsibilities and duties. The company secretary should be in a position to give objective professional advice to the chairman and to other members of the board. Arguably, company secretaries are better placed to give this kind of impartial guidance if they are not themselves board members. Chairmen will also be in close touch with their company secretaries over the range of regulations and official demands for information which apply, to a varying extent, to companies of all sizes... in handling all the complex legal regulations which affect companies, board secretaries are the chairman's and the company's first line of defence."*[24]

That extract goes to the heart of the role. To enable the smooth operation at the top of organisations, company secretaries must have access to the chair, chief executive and the board, together with good knowledge of and insight into the key external and internal issues. As a pivotal point of contact between the chief executive, chief financial officer, the senior independent director and other non-executive directors, the company secretary is also their link to the chair. The role is truly a leadership position because the company secretary often provides a bridge between the

---

[23] Cadbury A. (2002), *Corporate Governance and Chairmanship: A Personal View*, Oxford: Oxford University Press.
[24] Ibid,128.

executive leadership team and the non-executive directors who make up the rest of the board - the majority in the case of a publicly quoted company.

But to act in the company's best interests, they must have and preserve an independent view. As one company secretary put it:

> *"What matters is that you stand alone as an independent person, servicing a board, company, shareholders and every other constituent you have."*[25]

That need for independence, and not being under the influence of the chair, another director or senior management, is well illustrated by the company secretary's role as 'the conscience of the company'; advising individual directors and the full board on what the right thing is to do. This aspect of the role goes beyond law and regulation into the realm of business ethics and can sometimes add to the loneliness of the role. Asking, 'Should we be doing this?', can be challenging and requires courage when the executive and perhaps the full board are enthusing about a proposal which may be legal but is at variance with the company's stated values.

6. The company secretary's role in corporate governance

The Cadbury Report[26] set out, perhaps for the first time, an unequivocal and non-statutory statement in support of the governance role played by the company secretary. Paragraph 4.25 states:

> *"The company secretary has a key role to play in ensuring that board procedures are both followed and regularly reviewed. The chairman and the board will look to the company secretary for guidance on what their responsibilities are under the rules and regulations to which they are subject and on how those responsibilities should be discharged. All directors should have access to the advice and services of the company secretary and should recognise that the chairman is entitled to the strong and positive support of the company secretary in ensuring the effective functioning of the board. It should be standard practice of the company secretary to administer, attend and prepare minutes of board proceedings."*

---

[25] Note 21, 32.
[26] Note 14.

Para 4.26 refers to directors' statutory duty to appoint as secretary someone who is capable of carrying out the duties which the post entails. It goes on:

> *"The responsibility for ensuring that the secretary remains capable, and any question of the secretary's removal should be a matter for the board as a whole."*

Para 4.27 adds that:

> *"The company secretary will be a source of advice to the chairman and to the board on the implementation of the Code of Best Practice."*

The *Combined Code* 1998[27] did not repeat the ringing endorsements of the governance role of the company secretary found in *The Cadbury Report*, but it did acknowledge the status and access that the secretary needs to be effective in the role. These principles were retained in the 2003 edition of the *Combined Code*, which had rather more to say about the company secretary's role in board effectiveness, emphasising the secretary's contribution to board information flows and professional development. It stipulated too that 'the company secretary should be responsible for advising the board through the chairman on all governance matters.'[28]

In the 2018 edition of the *UK Corporate Governance Code*, Principle I states:

> *"The board, supported by the company secretary, should ensure that it has the policies, processes, information, time and resources it needs in order to function effectively and efficiently."*[29]

Provision 16, which supplements Principle I, states:

---

[27] Committee on Corporate Governance. (2003), *The Combined Code on Corporate Governance*, available online: <https://www.frc.org.uk/getattachment/53db5ec9-810b-4e22-9ca2-99b116c3bc49/Combined-Code-1998.pdf> (accessed 1 July 2021); Provision A.1.4 stated that: "All directors should have access to the advice and services of the company secretary who is responsible to the board for ensuring that board procedures are followed and that applicable rules and regulations are complied with. Any question of the removal of the company secretary should be a matter for the board as a whole.'
[28] Financial Reporting Council (2003), *The Combined Code on Corporate Governance*, available online: <https://www.frc.org.uk/getattachment/edce667b-16ea-41f4-a6c7-9c30db75bb0c/Combined-Code-2003.pdf> (accessed 1 July 2021).
[29] Note 22.

The Pivotal Role of the Company Secretary

"All directors should have access to the advice of the company secretary, who is responsible for advising the board on all governance matters. Both the appointment and removal of the company secretary should be a matter for the whole board."[30]

The wording of Principle I and Provision 16, taken together, mark an enhanced recognition of the role of the company secretary and their need to have access to, and a close relationship with, all members of the board on all governance matters and without having to go through the chair.

However it is in the companion to the Code, the *Guidance on Board Effectiveness*, that we see a real step change in the official recognition given to key aspects of the role of the company secretary.[31] Paragraphs 79 to 85 identify several key functions and responsibilities:

— The company secretary should report to the chair on all board governance matters;

— The company secretary's remuneration should be determined by the remuneration committee;

— The company secretary has responsibility for ensuring board procedures are complied with, advising the board on all governance matters, supporting the chair and helping the board and its committees to function efficiently;

— Under the chair's direction, the secretary will ensure good information flows within the board and its committees and between senior management and non-executive directors;

— The company secretary is expected to facilitate induction, arrange board training and assist with professional development, as required.

— The company secretary should arrange for the necessary resources to be made available to develop and update directors' knowledge and capabilities;

— It is the company secretary's responsibility to ensure that directors, especially non-executive directors, have access to independent

---

[30] Ibid.
[31] Financial Reporting Council. (2018), *Guidance on Board Effectiveness*, available online: <https://www.frc.org.uk/getattachment/61232f60-a338-471b-ba5a-bfed25219147/2018-Guidance-on-Board-Effectiveness-FINAL.PDF> (accessed 1 July 2021).

- professional advice at the company's expense where they judge it necessary to discharge their responsibilities as directors;

- Provision of assistance to the chair in establishing policies and processes which the board needs in order to function properly is described as "a core part of the company secretary's role";

- The chair and the company secretary should periodically review whether the board and the company's governance processes are fit for purpose; and

- Lastly, and certainly not least, it is said that the company secretary's effectiveness can be enhanced by building relationships and mutual trust with the chair, the senior independent director and the non-executive directors while maintaining the confidence of executive director colleagues because "they are in a unique position between the executive and the board and well placed to take responsibilities for concerns raised by the workforce about conduct, financial improprieties or other matters".[32]

While it is encouraging to see this level of recognition by the regulator, it is faintly depressing that it has taken over 25 years from publication of *The Cadbury Report*, which showed such confidence in the role, for its importance to be acknowledged. It is encouraging also to see how company secretaries themselves have risen to the challenge presented by investors and stakeholders who seek improvements in the standards of governance applied by companies in the delivery of their business purpose and the values by which that purpose is to be accomplished.

7. The pivotal role of the company secretary

Building relationships with the members of the board and acting as a bridge between the non-executive directors and the executive leadership team amply demonstrate that an effective company secretary must, in addition to mastering the technical and regulatory landscape, be a conciliator, an influencer, a negotiator and, above all, a leader.[33]

---

[32] Ibid, 22-23.
[33] The London Business School Leadership Institute offers an interesting definition of leadership, which can be appropriately applied to the role of the company secretary:

The Pivotal Role of the Company Secretary

In 2014, The Chartered Governance Institute UK & Ireland published *The Company Secretary: Building trust through governance,* a collaborative study with Henley Business School.[34] The research focused on the role of the company secretary and examined 'the expectations of stakeholders, board dynamics, the interactions of other board members and their views, identifying evidence of high performance and the characteristics of best practice'. The report's authors sought views from FTSE, small and medium enterprises, private, not for profit and public sector board level stakeholders in the UK, the Republic of Ireland and internationally. Its findings, conclusions and recommendations are as relevant now as they were at the point of publication in 2014. Here are the findings:

1. The role of the company secretary is much more than just administrative. At its best, it delivers strategic leadership, acting as a vital bridge between the executive management and the board and facilitating the delivery of organisational objectives.

2. Company secretaries are ideally placed to align the interests of different parties around a boardroom table, facilitate dialogue, gather and assimilate relevant information, and enable effective decision-making. They are often the only people to know first-hand how the decisions made have been reached.

3. The skills and attributes of the best company secretaries are closest to those of the chairman: humanity, humility, high intelligence, understanding of agendas, negotiation and resilience.

4. It is vital that company secretaries have both direct and informal access to board members – executive and non-executive directors (NEDs), CEOs and chairmen

5. Maximising effectiveness requires that the company secretary's direct reporting line should be to the chairman, and there should be parity of esteem and good teamworking between the 'triumvirate at the top' – the chairman, the company secretary and the CEO.

'Leadership is about having the courage to be yourself, the willingness to put yourself at risk when you are needed by your group, and the ability to harness your position, power, relationships and insights in order to increase the positive impact of your group'

[34] Available online: <https://www.cgi.org.uk/knowledge/research/the-company-secretary-report> (accessed 1 July 2021 – (free) log in required).

6. The role is changing: it is increasingly outward-focused (incorporating investor engagement and corporate communications), and not just about internal administration.

7. ICSA-qualified company secretaries deliver a more rounded governance and board member service than those who have come to the role via other professional routes.

8. There is a conflict of interest in the combined 'Head of Legal (or General Counsel) and Company Secretary' role. The roles should be separate, as they can be incompatible.

9. Board members often have a lack of awareness of the ways in which the company secretary supports an organisation in its decision-making. Boards may miss out on making full use of the skills, knowledge and experience at their disposal.

10. Company secretaries are often the longest-serving members present at board meetings, and so are a vital repository of company history and culture, and a guarantor of continuity.

11. Company secretaries are embedded in the process of making boards more effective; they contribute by observing boards in action and advising on any skills gaps that need filling.

12. The breadth of the company secretarial role includes additional responsibilities such as being an officer of the company, chief of staff to the chairman and adviser to the board on governance. Consequently, the secretariat needs to retain independence to rebalance power as required and demonstrate accountability.[35]

The research demonstrates that company secretaries across all sectors are playing that pivotal role and doing so in ways that could not be envisaged when David Jackson put out his challenge in 2008.[36] Let us explore that thought in relation to some of the key findings:

— Finding 1 - The sheer volume of governance requirements and the level of challenge and advice which the company secretary has now to give the chair, executive team, and non-executive directors exceeds significantly what was expected of company secretaries in 2008.

---

[35] Ibid, 7.
[36] Note 17.

- Finding 2 confirms what company secretaries have been doing for years, often informally. The effective company secretary realises that comments and suggestions made in discreet one-on-one discussions may be repeated by the other parties to the conversation as their own. Attributes of an effective company secretary are a lack of ego and a willingness to have one's ideas 'stolen'. A good chair will know the probable source of a governance-related suggestion made by an executive or non-executive director!

- Finding 3, that the skills and attributes of the best company secretaries are closest to those of the chair, breaks new ground. Only time will tell if this finding is taken on board by nomination committees and search consultants. One can but hope.

- Finding 5 challenges the orthodoxy that the three most knowledgeable people in the boardroom are the chair, chief executive and chief financial officer. The study demonstrated that, in reality, this 'triumvirate at the top' comprises the chair, chief executive and company secretary.

- Finding 7 confirms the view of Sir Adrian Cadbury that "...a legal rather than an accountancy training, combined with professional corporate secretarial qualifications, has become the preferred background for a company secretary".[37] A bespoke qualification which encompasses, *inter alia*, an in-depth study of boardroom dynamics, corporate governance, risk management and the development of strategy will provide the company secretary of the future with a more effective springboard to becoming the company secretary of the best organisations.

- Finding 8 suggests that there is a conflict of interest in the combined general counsel and company secretary role. While I would dispute that there is a *conflict* of interest, there can certainly be a *misalignment* of interests; particularly if the general counsel aspect of the role involves detailed transactional work subject to pressurised time limits. If the general counsel role is high-level advisory in nature rather than transactional, any misalignment will be more manageable. Nonetheless there seems to be a growing realisation that the separation of roles is a better outcome.

---

[37] Note 23, 129.

- Finding 9 comes as little surprise. A board chair is quoted by Sir Adrian Cadbury as saying: "the most underestimated people are the company secretaries" to which Sir Adrian Cadbury responded: "I agree".[38]

- Finding 12 harks back to Finding 5 and the proposition that the company secretary's direct reporting line should be to the chair rather than to a main board executive director such as the chief executive or the chief financial officer. That independence should be reinforced by the organisation's remuneration committee being responsible for all aspects of the company secretary's compensation and benefits.

While Finding 3 identifies the skills and personal qualities that company secretaries need to perform effectively in the role, the report also highlights that in some senses, company secretaries operate in an isolated role and may feel lonely at times, particularly when they have to assert the necessary independence of thought and action in order to sustain the integrity of the board.

When levels of trust between executive directors and non-executive directors are variable and there are issues which one or other group may be unwilling to air in the presence of the other, the company secretary may need to step in and facilitate conversations - including in a formal discussion at board meetings - to ensure that the board faces up collectively to its responsibilities to promote the success of the company and to act in the best interests of shareholders and other stakeholders.

Amplifying this point, Baroness Virginia Bottomley, a non-executive director and the chair of the Board Practice of the search firm Odgers Berndtson, highlighted in a short video in September 2020 several attributes which are needed by a good company secretary, namely discretion, judgment, independence, courage ("but in a quiet way"), tenacity and excellent relationship management.[39]

While technology has been widely adopted, for example using apps to

---

[38] Ibid.
[39] Available online: <https://www.linkedin.com/posts/alexhamiltonbaily_companysecretary-companysecretaries-governance-activity-6707205573135400960-hz8c> (accessed 1 July 2021).

circulate board packs electronically, the COVID-19 pandemic has driven rapid technological change to enable virtual governance with board meetings and AGMs being held online.[40] The immediate and proactive responses of company secretaries to facilitate remote meetings and AGMs, and to keep the wheels of good governance turning, are strong evidence of the worth and value of company secretaries. Good company secretaries are genuinely comfortable with the uncomfortable as their responses to the impact of COVID-19 have amply demonstrated.

As the volume of governance requirements, and the expectations of governments, investors, media, regulators, stakeholders and society at large, have grown, it is encouraging to see how company secretaries of larger companies have responded. The challenge now is for smaller listed companies, and larger private companies, to recognise their need to engage an appropriately qualified governance professional as their company secretary.

8. Future of the company secretary

The company secretary is a critical component of effective boards so it is vital for companies not to view the secretariat purely as a cost centre and a burden on the business. But how much interest do boards *really* take in the calibre and value of their company secretary and the strength on the bench among the rest of the team? How do the secretariat and the governance teams identify the value that governance adds to the business?

Secretariats need to be properly resourced and all board members, particularly chairs, need to reflect on the level of support being given to them. Companies and their directors are being subjected to increasing levels of scrutiny, not just from regulators, activist shareholders and stakeholders but the public too.

More fundamentally, boards need to reflect on how the composition of the secretariat can affect board effectiveness and ensure that their business is recruiting the appropriate mix of skills, experience and qualifications to suit their context. Alongside the increased reporting and compliance demands

---

[40] See chapter 7.

being made on the secretariat, the shift for the company secretary personally to key board adviser requires strategic leadership, influencing and relationship-building skills, resilience and independence.

I asked David Jackson for his thoughts on what company secretaries (by whatever name) will be doing in 2021 and beyond:

> "I believe that the role has not fundamentally changed and that the relationship with the chair remains at the heart of the company secretary's ability to operate and to add value to the board's work.
>
> So the answer to the question is probably having the interest, having the capacity and having the time to think about the role of the board and to be constantly alert to ways that the board adds value to the company in carrying out its tasks. What has struck me recently… is that many of the issues around governance that were surfacing [when I retired from BP] are still current and indeed have become more focused. This has been given extra oxygen by the pandemic.
>
> The role of the company, the role of the board and the duties of directors remain central to this. Is there a need to re-write 'the social contract' around the purpose of the company? Is section 172 [of the Companies Act 2006] enough? Does section 172 encompass purpose? It is not clear where the answers to these questions are going to come from. In many ways, the world is less rather than more certain in these days. I agree that the law and the regulation have not changed; that said, there are evolving societal expectations.
>
> This is an example of where the company secretary has to have a breadth of thought and inquisitiveness. So, the answer in many ways is to be ready technically and intellectually to address the challenges which will come forward. Be ready to be challenged and have the confidence to be innovative."[41]

So IQ, EQ and well-honed 'political' instincts (PQ) will continue to be a must for the modern company secretary. Additionally, as the era of Governance 3.0 draws to a close and we face the huge challenges posed by the fourth industrial revolution[42] or 4IR (described as 'a fusion of advances in artificial intelligence, robotics, the Internet of Things, genetic engineering,

---

[41] Personal communication with the author.
[42] Schwab, K. (2017), *The Fourth Industrial Revolution*, New York: Penguin. Professor Klaus Schwab is the founder and executive chairman of the World Economic Forum. He labelled today's advances as a new revolution.

quantum computing, and more'[43]), all round agility (AQ) will need to be displayed too.

The role of the company secretary is pivotal, as many companies discovered during the COVID-19 pandemic. That will not change during 4IR and the looming era of Governance 4.0. Increasingly it will be a leadership role, which can be lonely.[44] For the right people, however, the pivotal role of the company secretary promises to give an influential and rewarding career and the opportunity to exercise real influence and power, tempered always with good judgment and discretion.

---

[43] McGinnis, D. (2020), 'What is the Fourth Industrial Revolution?', *The 360 Blog*, available online: <https://www.salesforce.com/blog/what-is-the-fourth-industrial-revolution-4ir/> (accessed 1 July 2021).
[44] Ashkenas, R. (2017), 'How to overcome executive isolation', *Harvard Business Review*, available online: <https://hbr.org/2017/02/how-to-overcome-executive-isolation> (accessed 1 July 2021).

CHAPTER 6. BOARD DIVERSITY – A HISTORICAL PERSPECTIVE

Ann Holder, Chief Editor, Sustainable Foresight Institute

Introduction

In a 2010 TED talk, creativity and education expert the late Sir Ken Robinson said that "human communities depend upon a diversity of talent, not a singular conception of ability."[1] A diverse talent pool can accomplish the seemingly impossible. In March 2021, Dr Özlem Türeci, co-founder of German company BioNTech, recognised the role of gender diversity in their rapid vaccine development: "At BioNTech, women make up 54% of our total workforce and 45% of top management. We like to think that being a gender-balanced team has been critical to making the seemingly impossible possible – developing a Covid-19 vaccine within 11 months without shortcuts."[2] The power of diversity lies in embracing our differences as strengths instead of considering them to be insurmountable barriers.

Over the years, the UK's Financial Reporting Council (FRC) continued to fine-tune the UK corporate governance code, but we had to wait for the 2012 edition for diversity, including gender diversity, any measurable

---

[1] https://www.ted.com/talks/sir_ken_robinson_bring_on_the_learning_revolution
[2] https://theguardian.com/world/2021/mar/08/biontech-co-founder-says-gender-equality-made-vaccine-possible

objectives set for implementing the policy, and progress towards the objectives to be reflected in the code. This is to some degree not surprising given that boards in the US, UK, Canada, Australia and European countries tend to be comprised of male, white and older individuals. Although board diversity is gradually improving, the transformation of corporate boards is an on-going process. This chapter touches on several topics about board diversity (in mainly the UK and US): diversity defined, some recent developments, diversity and board performance, ways to increase board diversity and two examples of different approaches to it.

1. Changing societies

By 2050 there will be no clear racial or ethnic majority in the US. Immigrants and their children will continue to account for most (83%) of the growth in the US labour force while nearly a fifth of Americans will be born outside the country.[3] In the UK, about 14% of the working-age population have a Black, Asian and minority ethnic background, and by 2030 this will be about 20%.[4] Between 2004–2019, the largest employment rate increases were in the combined Pakistani and Bangladeshi ethnic group (from 44–56%) and the white other ethnic group (from 71– 83%).[5] In 2018, a record 10 million people over 50 years-old made up a third of the UK workforce.[6] With half the population 40 or under, ethnic and age diversity is also changing the face of the UK workforce.

The late Katherine Phillips of Columbia Business School said that just hearing the word diversity often made people "a little nervous" although organisations now realise that if they can capture the benefits of diversity – not always an easy task – they can gain a competitive advantage; the challenge is reconciling the "promise of diversity" with the "reality of

---

[3] Vanessa Cárdenas, Julie Ajinkya and Daniella Gibbs Léger, "Progress 2050: New ideas for a diverse America", Center for American Progress, 2011.
[4] CIPD, "Addressing the barrier to BAME employee career progression to the top", December 2017.
[5] "White other" was defined as any white background other than English, Welsh, Scottish, Northern Irish, British, Irish, Gypsy or Traveller. https://www.ethnicity-facts-figures.service.gov.uk/work-pay-and-benefits/employment/employment/latest.
[6] https://www.ageing-better.org.uk/news/number-over-50s-uk-workforce-10-million

diversity".[7] According to research,[8] the main benefits of workplace diversity include: varied perspectives help build better innovation teams; enhanced problem-solving and decision-making opportunities; more engaged employees; higher employee retention; more reputational capital; more insight into stakeholders; and higher profits.

According to McKinsey & Company, companies with high levels of racial and cultural diversity are 33–35% more likely to financially outperform their industry peers, while those with high levels of gender diversity are 15–21% more likely. As stated in their *Delivering through Diversity* report, despite the connection between diversity and financial performance – "gender and ethnic diversity are clearly correlated with profitability" – women and people of colour remain under-represented in corporate roles, especially in top leadership positions.[9]

Diversity is also important to employees on a personal level. A lack of diversity and inclusion can stifle a positive corporate culture. A 2019 Society for Human Resource Management (SHRM) study found that half (49%) of US workers have considered leaving their current employer, one in five has left a job within the last five years because of a toxic workplace culture, and one in four dreads even going to work. This translates into a 5-year turnover cost of over $223 billion.[10] At the same time, companies that are intentional about diversity and inclusion show different results. For instance, a global PwC survey found that most CEOs whose companies have a formal diversity and inclusiveness strategy think it has improved their bottom-line (85%) and competitiveness (56%).[11] When board diversity becomes a strategic imperative for an organisation, then measurable targets, goals and objectives can be developed, monitored, and adjusted as

---

[7] https://www8.gsb.columbia.edu/video/videos/vice-dean-katherine-phillips-benefits-diversity

[8] See, for example, Katherine Phillips, "How diversity makes us smarter", *Scientific American* 311(4): 43-47, 2014; Sylvia Hewlett, Melinda Marshall and Laura Sherbin, "How diversity can drive innovation", *Harvard Business Review* 91(12): 30, 2013; Hershey Friedman, Linda Friedman and Chaya Leverton, "Increase diversity to boost creativity and enhance problem solving", *Psychosociological Issues in Human Resource Management* 4(2): 7–33, 2016.

[9] Vivian Hunt, Lareina Yee, Sara Prince and Sundiatu Dixon-Fyle, "Delivering through diversity", *McKinsey & Company* 231, 2018, 3.

[10] SHRM High cost of a toxic workplace culture report 2019.pdf

[11] https://www.pwc.com/gx/en/ceo-survey/2015/assets/pwc-18th-annual-global-ceo-survey-jan-2015.pdf

necessary. And as the saying goes: what gets measured, gets done.

As social diversity increases, traditional notions of culture and leadership are also evolving. Some companies, like Unilever, are anchoring diversity and inclusion to the core of their business model to evolve in a way that respects and embraces the changing social landscape, in a way that encourages everyone to thrive. Generation Z (born after 1996) – the first "digital natives" and sustainability-focused generation – is also the most racially and ethnically diverse: almost half of Gen Z are people of colour.[12] They expect to be able to thrive in an inclusive world that reflects this diversity. They also represent future colleagues, customers, shareholders, stakeholders, and board members. So there is a need to be intentional in creating inclusive company cultures and eliminating barriers to career advancement (e.g. a lack of mentor/sponsorships and role modelling). More diverse talent in company leadership is the future and it's unfolding now.

Communities – government, corporate and civil society – are confronting a world that requires a new vocabulary around issues of diversity and inclusion with terms such as unconscious/implicit bias, microaggressions, privilege and intersectionality.[13] There are (potentially) transformative discussions taking place about diversity in the workplace right now (e.g. how companies can embed diversity in different ways such as by using diverse suppliers – money managers, legal services, PR). How companies decide to proceed will affect everyone, from the entry-level positions to those in the boardroom.

2. Board diversity defined

A. What is diversity?

Diversity is defined through many lenses and is a term that continues to evolve. Today we use terms like diversity, equity and inclusion. Equity is to

---

[12] https://www.pewresearch.org/social-trends/2018/11/15/early-benchmarks-show-post-millennials-on-track-to-be-most-diverse-best-educated-generation-yet/psdt-11-15-18_postmillennials-00-00/. While "people of colour" is a term used to describe "non-white" people, it's not necessarily how people describe themselves.
[13] For example, the Diversity Style Guide (www.diversitystyleguide.com).

ensure fairness, justice and equal access to information and resources. Inclusion builds a culture of belonging by actively inviting everyone's contribution and participation.[14] Board leadership is key to promoting policies/practices that facilitate diversity and inclusion. Diversity Council Australia notes that inclusion happens "when a diversity of people are respected, connected, progressing and contributing to organisational success".[15] In other words, as Netflix's VP of inclusion strategy Vernā Myers puts it: "Diversity is being invited to the party. Inclusion is being asked to dance."

Broadly, diversity speaks to how we differ from one another. This can manifest in many dimensions including: ethnicity, race or cultural background; gender; age; sexual orientation; religion or belief system; geography; disability status; language and accent; neurodiversity (e.g. people with dyslexia, autism); experience; expertise; and what Columbia Business School's Paul Ingram calls the "forgotten dimension" – social class.[16] Increasingly, companies are trying to attract neurodivergent candidates and look beyond the neurotypical talent pool. Harvard Business School's Gary Pisano describes neurodiversity as a competitive advantage[17] (see also Chapter 7).

B. Some types of diversity

In their survey of 40 years of management research, Wiliams and O'Reilly (1998) noted that diversity results from any attribute that we use to tell ourselves that somebody else is different.[18] Mannix and Neale (2005) define it as "variation based on any attribute people use to tell themselves that

---

[14] Ford Foundation, *Diversity, Equity and Inclusion: Annual Report 2020*. Inclusion can also imply a power dynamic; it can signal that someone is including "you" in "their" professional organisation, company or board of directors, for instance. https://www.fordfoundation.org/media/5533/2019-dei-update.pdf
[15] https://www.dca.org.au/inclusion-at-work-index
[16] Paul Ingram, "The forgotten dimension of diversity", *Harvard Business Review*, January–February 2021.
[17] Gary Pisano, "Neurodiversity as a competitive advantage", *Harvard Business Review*, May–June 2017.
[18] Katherine Williams and Charles O'Reilly, "The complexity of diversity: A review of forty years of research", *Research in Organizational Behavior* 21: 77–140, 1998.

another person is different."[19] Some authors refer to factors such as gender, ethnicity and age as "visible or observable diversity"[20] and others "surface-level diversity".[21] Diversity includes a broad spectrum of individual differences.[22]

A concept that is also relevant here is "intersectionality". Intersectionality is the idea that people experience discrimination differently depending on their overlapping identities (e.g. gender, race, social class) and how they intersect.[23] It resonates with something that US feminist writer and civil right activist Audre Lorde once said: "There is no such thing as a single-issue struggle because we do not live single-issue lives."

3. A recent history of board diversity

A. What is board diversity?

At the board level, diversity can manifest in boards that reflect demographic, functional and neural or cognitive diversity (see Chapter 3). While diversity can be defined in different ways, our current understanding is that it is more complex, dynamic and intersectional than previous conceptions (e.g. nonbinary gender identities, self-identifying as multiracial). Companies and boards are moving to better understand cognitive diversity

---

[19] Elizabeth Mannix and Margaret Neale, "What differences make a difference? The promise and reality of diverse teams in organizations", *Psychological Science in the Public Interest*, 6(2):31–55, 2005.
[20] For example, Sébastien Point and Val Singh, "Defining and dimensionalising diversity: Evidence from corporate websites across Europe", *European Management Journal* 21(6): 750–761, 2003.
[21] For example, Myrtle Bell, "Anti-blackness, surface-level diversity continues to matter: What must we do?" *Equality, Diversity and Inclusion: An International Journal* 39(7): 749-759, 2020; Jie Wu, Orlando Richard, Xine Zhang, and Craig Macaulay, "Top management team surface-level diversity, strategic change, and long-term firm performance", *Journal of Leadership & Organizational Studies* 26(3): 304–318, 2019.
[22] This chapter references mainly gender, racial/ethnic and age diversity as they are commonly used to describe differences and most board diversity research focuses on their influence. For example, Maretno Harjoto, Indrarini Laksmana and Robert Lee, "Board diversity and corporate social responsibility", *Journal of Business Ethics* 132: 641–660, 2015; Toyah Miller and María Del Carmen Triana, "Demographic diversity in the boardroom: Mediators of the board diversity-firm performance relationship", *Journal of Management Studies* 46(5): 755–786, 2009.
[23] Columbia University/UCLA law professor Kimberlé Crenshaw conceptualized and coined the term "intersectionality" in 1989.

or diversity of thought processes. Cognitive diversity refers to differences in our knowledge and perspectives; how we process and interpret information; and our approaches to problems-solving. Improving cognitive diversity in the boardroom can enhance board performance (e.g. improved decision-making). Kent Business School's Moorad Choudhry says:[24]

> *"It doesn't necessarily produce tangible benefits if a company's executive committee or board contains a diverse mix of people, but all of them think in more or less the same way ... What is needed is diversity of thought. The key point here is that visual diversity is not necessarily any guarantee of this."*

EY managing partner Alison Kay echoed this in her foreword to the 2020 *Female FTSE Board Report*: "If you have a board that largely looks and thinks the same, with similar experience, it will have a narrow view on a world that is changing fast, regardless of how talented its members are." Boards should strive for a mix of functional, cognitive, demographic and generational diversity to benefit from a more holistic conception of diversity.

B. Waves of diversity

The first wave of diversity focussed on gender diversity as more women joined the corporate world and advanced to middle and upper management positions. As women's participation in the workforce increased in the mid-20th century, the face of the business sectors throughout industrialised economies began to change. Eventually, women began to earn seats in the previously all-male boardrooms.

Women still remain somewhat of a rarity in the boardroom despite a growing body of literature that supports the potential benefits of gender board diversity.[25] Directorships held by women in 2018 were highest in Norway (41%), France (37%) and Sweden (33%) and lowest in South

---

[24] Moorad Choudhry, "Managing through a stress event: Why diversity of thought is important", *The International Banker*, Autumn 2020, 19
[25] For example, McKinsey & Co., "Woman Matter 2010: Moving Women to the Top: McKinsey Global Survey Results," https://www.mckinsey.com/business-functions/organization/our-insights/moving-women-to-the-top-mckinsey-global-survey-results; Nada Kakabdse et al., "Gender Diversity and Board Performance: Women's Experiences and Perspectives," *Human Resource Management* 54(2): 265–281, 2015; McKinsey & Co., Women Matter: Time to Accelerate, 2017.

Korea (2%), Saudi Arabia and Qatar (less than 1% each). Women held 30% or more of the board seats in only six countries, five European – Norway, Belgium France, Finland, Sweden – plus New Zealand (three with binding quotas and three without). The UK fared better than the US with 23% and 18%, respectively. There were also almost three times as many women CFOs as CEOs globally (13% versus 4%).[26] In companies with a female CEO, women held 29% of board seats versus only 17% in those with a male CEO.

The pace of change is, however, sluggish. The Alliance for Board Diversity's (ABD's)[27] latest *Missing Pieces Report* estimates it will take until 2074 before the number of Fortune 500 board seats held by historically under-represented groups reaches their aspirational 40% representation rate. And while women and people of colour gained more board representation in the Fortune 500 between 2016–2020 than between 2010–2016, the average growth for minority board representation since 2004 (when data was first collected) is less than 0.5% per year. Fortune 500 board representation for women and people of colour continues to climb, up from 34% (1,929 board seats) in 2018 to 38.3% (2,253 board seats) in 2020. Since 2010, the number of companies with greater than 40% diversity has nearly quadrupled.

The pace of progress has been slow, though; some might say "glacial". Egon Zehnder's 2018 *Mind the Gap* report on female leadership noted that with just 24, women accounted for under 5% of Fortune 500 CEOs. In October 2020, women's leadership organisation C200, non-profit research group Catalyst, and the Women's Business Collaborative released a first-of-its-kind report tracking women CEOs across public and private companies, including Fortune 500, S&P 500 and Russell 3000 firms. *Women CEOs in America* found that:

– Women constitute 8% of Fortune 500 CEOs, 6% of S&P 500 CEOs, and 5% of Russell 3000 CEOs (as of Sept. 2020).

---

[26] Deloitte Global Center for Corporate Governance, *Women in the boardroom: A global perspective*, 2019.
[27] The ABD comprises four US leadership organisations: Catalyst, the Executive Leadership Council, the Hispanic Association on Corporate Responsibility, and LEAP.

- The number of women CEOs in Fortune 500 and S&P companies has increased by more than 54% and 25%, respectively, since 2018.
- Companies with at least 30% women executives are more likely to outperform other companies.

Thirty percent female board representation is considered a key marker towards gender parity. In 2011 the Thirty Percent Coalition was formed in the US to help companies meet this goal as well as stimulate increased racial/ethnic board diversity. It represents over $7 trillion assets under management and currently works with 500+ companies.

At the board level, women are still under-represented globally. Deloitte Global's *Women in the Boardroom Report* (2019) showed that women held only 17% of board seats globally, up almost 2% from last report (2017). Chair Sharon Thorne observed: [28]

> *"If the global trend continues at its current rate of an approximately 1% increase per year, we will be waiting more than 30 years to achieve global gender parity at the board level. And even then, actual parity is likely to be concentrated to the few countries that are currently making concerted efforts to overcome this issue, leaving several regions lagging behind."*

Thirty years is quite long to wait for global (inconsistent) board gender parity. But there has been progress. For example, the share of women joining S&P 500 boards more than doubled in the past decade from 21% to 47% between 2010 and 2020.[29] At the same time, new minority director representation increased to 22% in 2020 – where women's representation was a decade ago. Of the 413 new independent S&P 500 directors in 2020:

- almost half were women (47% versus 53% men)
- less than a quarter (22%) were minorities (10% men, 12% women)

Spencer Stuart's 2021 tracking shows that almost half (47%) of new S&P

---

[28] https://www2.deloitte.com/id/en/pages/risk/articles/women-in-the-boardroom-report-highlights-slow-progress-for-gender-diversity-pr.html
[29] Spencer Stuart, *Board Diversity Snapshot: Six recommendations for becoming a more diverse and inclusive board*, 2020. https://www.spencerstuart.com/research-and-insight/board-diversity-snapshot

directors are from historically under-represented groups, a third of all new independent directors are Black/African American (three times more than in 2020), and over 40% are women.[30]

Conversely, MSCI reported a slowdown in women's representation on MSCI-listed company boards and estimates that it will take until 2029 for women to comprise 30% of these boards and until 2045 to make up half of them.[31]

Despite movement in some areas, Bank of America research estimates that it will take over two centuries – 257 years – to close the still-increasing gender pay gap. Since 2000, another $10 trillion (£7.3 trillion) in wages and benefits could have been generated by closing the gap. Similarly, while the World Economic Forum's (WEF) 2020 *Global Gender Gap Report* showed that it would take almost a century (99.5 years) to achieve gender parity globally, the 2021 edition now estimates closing this gap in 135.6 years.[32] Gender parity would bring a 34% boost to global GDP, but the rate of progress has slowed.

In the UK, gender parity on FTSE350 boards arrives only in 2036 according to the *Women Count 2021* report. In the meantime, UK companies with less than 33% women on their executive committee are missing out on extra £123 billion in pre-tax profits versus their more gender diverse peers.[33] Women represent 5% of CEOs and 17% of CFOs in FTSE350 companies.

In a second diversity wave, more people from historically under-represented groups begin to claim space in the corporate world but progress has also been slow. While female representation among new S&P 500 directors more than doubled recently, new minority director representation increased to just 22% in 2020 — the same level women

---

[30] https://www.spencerstuart.com/research-and-insight/2021-sp-500-board-diversity-snapshot
[31] https://www.msci.com/www/women-on-boards-2020/women-on-boards-2020-progress/02212172407
[32] There are also great regional disparities. Western Europe could close its gender gap first (52.1 years) followed by North America (61.5 years) while Sub-Saharan Africa is the first century-plus region (121.7 years) that ends with South Asia (194.5 years). Global Gender Gap Report 2021 WEF.pdf
[33] The Pipeline, *Women Count 2021*. Women-Count-2021-Report.pdf

reached 10 years ago. While a tenth (11%) of MSCI's institutional investors believe that industry diversity has improved, the vast majority (86%) admit that more still remains to be done.[34]

C. Missing diverse voices

While companies continue to publicise and affirm their efforts to include diverse voices in senior leadership, the numbers tell a different story. According to *Fortune*, since the Fortune 500 list was first published in 1955, there have been only 19 Black/African American CEOs out of 1,800 CEOs, or 1%. Only four have been Black women, two of whom took the helm in 2021. Currently, there are five African American Fortune 500 CEOs and 4% of Russell 3000 directors are Black. According to Equilar, a leadership data clearinghouse, over a quarter of S&P 500 companies lack at least one Black director. At the same time, Black people represent about 13% of the US population. Recently though, 148 Black/African American directors were appointed to S&P 500 boards during a period of 12 months (as of May 2021), or 33% of all new directors.

A record-high 41 women CEOs lead 8% of the Fortune 500 (as of May 2021); and women hold 29 (6%) of S&P 500 CEO positions, according to Catalyst. When you consider all C-Suite leaders today, 21% are women and just 1% are Black women. Mellody Hobson is the only African American women to currently chair a Fortune 500 company, Starbucks.

Latino/x directors are missing in corporate boardrooms. According to the Latino Corporate Directors Association (LCDA), there are only sixteen Hispanic S&P 500 CEOs. The Latino Board Tracker indicates that almost three-quarters of 2020 Fortune 1000 companies lack a single Latino/x board director.[35] Less than a quarter of Fortune 1000 companies have at least one Latino/x director. But 7% of new S&P 500 directors were Hispanic/Latino (versus 3% in 2020).

---

[34] MSCI Investment Insights 2021. https://www.msci.com/our-clients/asset-owners/investment-insights-report

[35] https://mms.latinocorporatedirectors.org/members/directory/search_board_lcda.php?org_id=LCDA

Asian voices are also missing in the boardroom. KPMG's Board Leadership Center and Ascend Pinnacle analysed Asian representation on Fortune 1000 boards in 2020 and found that almost three-quarters (72%) have no Asian directors. The same is true for two-thirds of Fortune 500 and over half (58%) of Fortune 100 companies. Of the 332 Asian Fortune 1000 directors, a quarter (24%) serve on tech company boards, most (60%) are in their 50s or younger (versus 32% for all Fortune 1000 directors) and most (64%) serve on only one board (versus 58% of all Fortune 1000 directors).[36] In 2021, just 7% of the new S&P 500 directors were Asian. The vast majority of Fortune 500 CEOs are still white men (Table 6.1).

Table 6.1: Board diversity in the UK
Source: Missing Pieces Report: The 2020 Board Diversity Census[37]

Group	Fortune 500 board seats	US Population
White	80.7%	55.8%
Black/African American	8.6%	13.4%
Hispanic/Latino	3.8%	18.3%
Asian/Pacific Islander	3.7%	5.9%

In the UK, progress was beginning to reverse itself when the Green Park Business Leaders Index 2021 revealed in 2021 that there were no Black CEOs, CFOs or board chairs in the FTSE 100 for the first time since 2014. Green Park's research also found that only ten of 297 (3%) leaders in the top three roles have ethnic minority backgrounds, the same proportion as when Green Park started its yearly FTSE analysis in 2014.

4. Diversity and board performance

Diversity brings several benefits to corporate governance including having a wide range of perspectives during board meetings, less cognitive bias, a

---

[36] asian-representation-fortune-1000-boards.pdf
[37] Alliance for Board Diversity, missing-pieces-fortune-500-board-diversity-study-6th-edition.pdf

reduced risk of groupthink (but more constructive debate), increased understanding of the company, and a better external perception of the company.

Board diversity reduces potential bias in decision-making, specifically the risk of implicit bias (or unconscious bias), i.e. prejudices we might have of which we are unaware (e.g. classism).[38] Harvard University psychology professor Mahzarin Banaji calls them "mind bugs". We all have implicit biases and these mind bugs creep into our thinking. There is often a misalignment between our implicit biases and our stated beliefs that can affect our relationships with others and have real-world consequences. Didier Cossin, founder of IMD's Global Board Center, identifies nine mental biases that can mask risk, thereby impacting a board's ability to accurately perform its risk governance duties: groupthink, optimism, overconfidence, Dunning-Kruger effect, belief perseverance, confirmation bias, hindsight bias, anchoring and representativeness.[39] While there are other implicit biases, here are some of the most common cognitive biases that can affect boardroom dynamics:[40]

- Confirmation bias: When people seek evidence to confirm their pre-existing ideas while discounting opposing viewpoints that might lead to a better understanding of the problem, and more informed decision-making.
- Groupthink/herd mentality: When you abandon your own beliefs and information and follow the group in decision-making.
- Authority bias: The tendency to attribute greater accuracy to the opinion of an expert; directors can be too influenced by that one opinion.
- Status quo bias: Maintaining the familiar due to loss aversion (see below). It can have serious consequences when boards must deal with

---

[38] In contract to those biases of which we are aware – our explicit biases.
[39] Didier Cossin, "Inside the boardroom: 9 mental biases that mask risk", *CEOWORLD Magazine*, July 2020. https://ceoworld.biz/2020/07/22/inside-the-boardroom-9-mental-biases-that-mask-risk/ https://boardandfraud.com/2020/05/11/board-overconfidence-an-often-unrecognized-risk/
[40] See footnote 41, and PwC, Unpacking board culture: How behavioral psychology might explain what's holding boards back, February 2021;

"black swans" or wildcards, the "unknown unknowns" (e.g. a pandemic).[41]

- Anchoring: An over-reliance on the first piece of information you get when making a decision.
- Hindsight bias: The tendency to view a past unpredictable event and believe it was easily predictable, the so-called I-knew-it-all-along phenomenon.
- Representativeness: Making judgements and decisions based on mental patterns without considering significant differences between the two situations (e.g. a pandemic) that disrupt patterns.
- Loss aversion: The tendency to prefer avoiding losses than acquiring equal gains, which may drive boards to take less risk and "leave value on the table").[42]
- Belief bias (Tolstoy effect): The tendency to only accept information that agrees with what you believe.
- Optimism bias: The tendency to overestimate the chance of experiencing positive future outcomes (and underestimating the chance of negative ones).
- Dunning Kruger effect and overconfidence: When people fail to recognise their own incompetence (and the potential consequences). The so-called not-knowing-what-you-don't-know phenomenon.

In an increasingly digitised world, another boardroom bias that directors need to be cognisant of is algorithmic bias in AI systems (e.g. gender bias, racial prejudice). While public concerns about AI bias continue to mount, Princeton University computer science professor Olga Russakovsky points out that "debiasing humans is harder than debiasing AI systems": AI can be re-engineered from the ground up to produce more accurate results, but the process is dependent on human training (and the [biased] training data). A recent Columbia University study found that more diverse engineering

---

[41] Chapter 8 (The board's role in strategy) and chapter 18 (Is corporate governance 4.0 emerging?) for a discussion of the risks and opportunities that arise from black swans, grey rhinos and white elephants.
[42] https://knowledge.insead.edu/blog/insead-blog/intelligent-boards-know-their-limits-5321

teams reduce the chance for algorithmic biases.[43] This illustrates the complex challenge of the AI bias problem and how decision-making and problem-solving by diverse teams can mitigate some of its effects.[44] Boards are ultimately responsible for the algorithms – rules put into computer programs – that a company's AI uses (e.g. Amazon's gender-biased recruitment AI).

Another benefit of diversity is that a variety of ideas and ways of thinking can make boards less vulnerable to *groupthink* (see above). Groupthink is a psychological phenomenon in which people strive for consensus and harmony within a group at the expense of critical reasoning or evaluation of alternative viewpoints. Groupthink is based on a common desire to maintain the group balance: the so-called don't-rock-the-boat phenomenon. It can be benign at best, and lethal at worst (e.g. a genocide).[45]

While strong cohesion inside the boardroom does not necessarily mean that board effectiveness will be compromised, groupthink has contributed to several corporate scandals: Enron's collapse (2001), the Olympus accounting fraud (2011) and Volkswagen's 'dieselgate' (2015).

In their *Board Guide*, which gives Singapore-listed company directors practical guidance on discharging their duties and responsibilities, the SID states: "Diversity avoids groupthink and provides fresh and multiple perspectives that enhance decision making. A diverse Board is more likely to challenge management, and to help the Board understand and appreciate the perspectives of different stakeholders."[46] Similarly, the FRC's *Guidance on Board Effectiveness* (2018) also states that board diversity drives board

---

[43] Bo Cowgill, Fabrizio Dell'Acqua, Samuel, Deng, Daniel Hsu, Nakul Verma and Augustin Chaintreau, "Biased Programmers? Or biased data? A field experiment in operationalizing AI ethics", 34th conference on neural information processing systems (NeurIPS 2020).

[44] See Will Knight, "AI is biased: Here's how scientists are trying to fix it," *Wired*, 19 December 2019; and Steve Nouri, "The role of bias in artificial intelligence", *Forbes*, 4 February 2021,

[45] Irving Janis, 'Groupthink', *Psychology Today* (reprint), Ziff-Davis Publishing Co., 1971: 84–90.

[46] SID, *Board Guide: Corporate governance guides for boards in Singapore* (Singapore: Write Editions, 2017), p. 108. Other country corporate governance codes contain similar language about diversity (e.g. Malaysian Code on Corporate Governance 2021, mccg2021_1.pdf).

effectiveness and helps weaken a tendency towards groupthink.[47] Diverse viewpoints improve decision-making which is particularly important at the board level.

Myers et al. (2012) argue that to effect emergent change – unplanned, spontaneous change that suggests organisations are constantly evolving – organisations must stimulate new forms of social interaction. To do this, companies should "maximize the diversity in decision-making, so that different viewpoints and ways of thinking have space to exist, and fresh ideas surface."[48] Arayssi, Dah and Jizi (2016) showed that diverse work groups produce more cognitive processing and more exchange of information.[49] Diversity brings in new ideas, experiences and perspectives that leads to better problem-solving.

Working in diverse teams opens dialogue and promotes creativity. "Diverse perspectives and points of view make the team better: they expand the talent pool," says John Rogers Jr, Nike board member and founder of Ariel Investments, the largest Black-owned US mutual fund. Managing diverse teams can sometimes be challenging but the benefits to the team – and the board – can have significant ripple effects throughout the organisation. Moreover, Chebbi et al. (2020) found that board gender diversity enhances environmental sustainability reporting and ESG disclosures.[50]

Diverse teams can be more innovative, and innovation is critical to a company's sustainable success. Innovation gives companies a competitive edge; it means creating what the International Innovation Summit calls a 'moonshot culture': one that encourages taking bold and creative leaps in thinking, inspires people to do their best and go beyond what they think

---

[47] https://www.frc.org.uk/getattachment/61232f60-a338-471b-ba5a-bfed25219147/2018-Guidance-on-Board-Effectiveness-FINAL.PDF. Other country corporate governance codes contain similar language about diversity (e.g. Malaysian Code on Corporate Governance 2021, mccg2021_1.pdf).

[48] Piers Myers, Sally Hulks and Liz Wiggins, *Organizational Change: Perspectives on Theory and Practice* (Oxford: Oxford University Press, 2012), p. 221.

[49] Mahmoud Arayssi, Mustafa Dah and Mohammad Jizi, "Women on boards, sustainability reporting and firm performance," *Sustainability Accounting, Management and Policy Journal* 7(3): 376–401, 2016.

[50] Kaouther Chebbi, Meqbel Aliedan and Abdulaziz Alsahlawi, "Women on the Board and Environmental Sustainability Reporting: Evidence from France," *Creativity and Innovation Management*, 2020.

they can achieve, and has imaginative yet achievable goals.[51] Better services, business models, company performance, and ways of adapting to change (e.g. developing resilience) can be the result. Boards can help facilitate this process.

A board that reflects a company's stated commitment to diversity sends a different message to employees, customers, and the public than one that does not.

Boards define the organisational culture and set the tone for the rest of the organisation's stakeholders, internal and external. Leading by example and modelling ethical behaviour is a critical part of this process; it starts with board leadership. As Mellody Hobson, co-CEO and president of Ariel Investments and Starbucks chair says:[52]

> *"Starting with a diverse board, you can see where the intention is for the company because they selected those people to come in and be fiduciaries for the shareholders ... I believe that's very, very important. And it's not just a belief, the data backs me up. There's a saying, 'math has no opinion'. The math is very clear: companies that have more diverse boards have had better outcomes in terms of shareholder appreciation. As board members, we're there to enhance shareholder value."*

5. Improving board diversity

A. Gender quotas

Several countries established quotas to redress the structural imbalance and accelerate board diversity. After encouraging voluntary board gender diversity for more than 25 years, Norway became the first country to legally impose a 40% gender quota for corporate boards in December 2005.[53]

Companies failing to comply within two years faced a severe sanction: dissolution. Women accounted for just 5% of board directors on Norwegian public limited companies (PLCs) in 2001 and 16% in 2005. But

---

[51] https://innosummit.org/
[52] Mellody Hobson, "Leading from the chair: How the board sets the tone", Heidrick & Struggels, January 2021.
[53] https://www.ilo.org/dyn/natlex/docs/WEBTEXT/12790/64813/E78NOR01

by 2008 this had more than doubled to 41% with almost all PLCs (98%) in compliance in Norway.[54]

Other European countries soon followed with binding quotas to increase board gender balance: Belgium (33%), France (40%) Germany (30%), Iceland (40%) and Italy (33%). Others implemented 'soft' quotas (or 'targets'):[55] e.g. Austria (30%), Denmark, Finland, Greece, Ireland, the Netherlands, Poland, Portugal (33%), Spain (40%), Sweden, Switzerland (30%), and the UK (33%).[56] In 2017 Sweden rejected legislation to sanction listed companies failing to reach a 40% minimum target for women directors, but women held almost half (48%) of Sweden's jobs and a third (32%) of board positions (above the 23% EU average but below the EU's 2020 goal of 40% for NEDs) at the time.[57]

Non-compliance is not sanctioned in Spain, the Netherlands (until 2020) or Iceland, while the other countries have some form (or combination) of sanctions including fines (Italy), non-payment of directors (Belgium), nullification of board appointments (France) and liquidation (Norway).[58] When its soft quota failed, the Netherlands implemented a compulsory quota: companies under the 30% threshold could only appoint a woman to a vacant board position; if proposed nominees did not lower the gap towards compliance, such appointments would be annulled (the "empty chair"). German researchers found that a gender quota combined with tough sanctions (France) significantly increased gender diversity in decision-making bodies while weaker sanctions (Germany's "empty chair") were relatively ineffective.

Critics suggest that voluntary measures are more effective and just need more time to take effect. They claim that quotas result in tokenism, box-

---

[54] Knut Nygaard, "Forced board changes: Evidence from Norway", Discussion Paper Series in Economics 5/2011, Norwegian School of Economics, Dept of Economics, 2011.
[55] Soft quotas are without sanctions or only applicable to public companies, for example.
[56] Paula Arndt and Katharina Wrohlich, "Gender quotas in a European comparison: Tough sanctions most effective", DIW Berlin Weekly Report, 9(38): 337-344, 2019; EWoB-Gender-Diversity-Index-2020.pdf
[57] https://www.theguardian.com/world/2017/jan/12/sweden-rejects-quotas-women-boardroom-listed-companies
[58] Ruth Mateos de Cabo, Siri Terjesen, Lorenzo Escot and Ricardo Gimeno, "Do 'soft law' board gender quotas work? Evidence from a natural experiment," *European Management Journal* 37(5): 611-24, 2019.

ticking, virtue signalling and selecting unqualified people, perhaps diluting the board's effectiveness.[59] IMD's Bettina Büchel says that "quotas are not enough to improve board diversity" and companies must focus on integrating these new directors onto their boards to benefit from the diversity they bring.[60] When voluntary efforts to diversify boards fail, quotas can compel companies and shareholders to focus on enhancing board composition and development processes (e.g. recruitment, tenure policies, training).

Nasdaq is also shifting the demographics of its listed companies. In December 2020 it proposed listing rule changes to the SEC: all listed companies to have at least two diverse directors, one who self-identifies as female and one who self-identifies as either an under-represented minority or LGBTQ+. Companies would also disclose board diversity statistics to aid transparency. Gradually board diversity is increasing: US publicly listed firms more than quadrupled the number of Latino directors to 82 from 19 in 2021; and women hold about a third of S&P 500 board positions.[61] Nasdaq's board diversity proposal follows similar legislation in California (US).

California's quota approach is two-phased: requiring public companies to appoint at least one female director by end-2019 and at least one director from an under-represented community by end-2021. Several other US states have introduced similar legislation.

B. Shadow boards

Corporate boards tend to be composed of older individuals. The average age of a FTSE100 board chair is 65; the average NED is 60; independent directors are on average 63, according to Spencer Stuart. However, the

---

[59] For example, see https://calmatters.org/economy/2018/11/california-women-boardroom-law-faces-legal-challenges/
[60] https://www.imd.org/research-knowledge/articles/why-quotas-are-not-enough-to-improve-boardroom-diversity/
[61] https://www.bloomberg.com/news/articles/2021-05-14/boards-are-adding-more-women-and-minorities-ahead-of-nasdaq-rule

typical unicorn founder started their business at age 34.[62] A 2019 Conference Board study found that only 10% of Russell 3000 directors are under 50 while about 20% are over 70.[63] Combined with an average director tenure of a decade or longer (in Russell 3000s), board seats are not often vacant and when they are, an experienced director rather than a first-time new director usually fills it. Board refreshment continues to be a challenge and makes promoting board-level age diversity tougher for companies. Governance expert Prof. Mervyn King observed that intergenerational diversity is the most important type and is often forgotten in diversity discussions.[64]

Typically, younger employees have less business experience and would rarely be able to influence senior company leaders in their strategic decision-making. But a "shadow" (or "mirror") board is a way for companies to bridge the intergenerational leadership gap, get a fresh take on the business, and drive innovation. Shadow boards have tackled business-model reinvention (Accor hotels), process redesign (Stora Enso paper) and organisational transformation (media GroupM).[65] Shadow board members – millennials and soon Gen Z – are more engaged, are upskilled and get more visibility while top managers benefit from their new, diverse perspectives. Two-way mentoring occurs between the shadow board and top management/directors and companies develop a diverse pool of future directors. A well-managed and inclusive process engages shadow boards in real-world problem-solving, an invaluable experience.

IMD's Jennifer Jordan and Michael Sorrell define a successful shadow board as a CEO-sponsored programme that casts a wide net, looking beyond the known 'high potentials' to create a more diverse cohort and

---

[62] https://www.cnbc.com/2021/05/27/super-founders-median-age-of-billion-startup-founders-over-15-years.html
[63] https://www.conference-board.org/press/news/index.cfm?id=49831&mod=article_inline
[64] Comments made during the "Is corporate governance 4.0 emerging?" panel, Astana Finance Days conference, 2 July 2021.
[65] Other examples include Interbrand's Horizon Board, Beazley's NexCo, and Chime's Innovate Board.

uncover 'hidden gems'.[66] It should also mirror the actual board in size and roles/positions to truly reflect and engage its members.

Establishing shadow boards might be more challenging, however, in cultures with strong patriarchal systems or where a premium is placed on age and tradition.[67] For instance, in Japan almost all (99%) CEOs are men, NEDs are closer to 70 years-old, and under 2% of boards are at least 30% female.[68] Certain sectors might also initially be less responsive to them, but savvy, forward-thinking companies realise their benefits. Shadow boards could be considered as a transition phase until greater diversity is hardwired into corporate governance.

Many, including Simon Osborne, former chief executive of The Chartered Governance Institute, believe that most boards are more focussed on looking backwards than forwards, and that the average director age is too high. One solution, instead of shadow boards, is for companies to recruit directors with less board experience. Spencer Stuart finds that chairs are increasingly open to recruiting "next-gen" talent to get specific skills and competencies (e.g. cybersecurity), have more diverse perspectives around the table or shift the focus of debate. [69]

C. Investor's push

Institutional investors and proxy advisers are increasingly pushing for more diverse boards. BlackRock, the world's largest investment fund (about $9.5 trillion), is a global leader on this issue. CEO Larry Fink's annual letter to CEOs outlines the issues important to BlackRock. The fund may vote against directors on the nomination committee (NC)/governance

---

[66] https://hbr.org/2019/06/why-you-should-create-a-shadow-board-of-younger-employees.
[67] In cultures where gender equality is still lacking, for example, this could be particularly challenging.
[68] https://www.spencerstuart.com/research-and-insight/international-comparison-chart#foreign.
[69] https://www.spencerstuart.com/research-and-insight/how-next-generation-board-directors-are-having-an-impact

committee if the board is insufficiently diverse.[70] State Street Global Advisors (about $3.6 trillion), also outlines its voting agenda to companies. In 2021, State Street will vote against the NC chairs at S&P 500 and FTSE100 companies who fail to disclose the board's racial/ethnic diversity; in 2022, they will vote against them for failing to have at least one director from an under-represented community and against compensation committee chairs who fail to disclose demographic.[71]

For the UK's largest institutional investor, Legal & General Investment Management (LGIM) (£25.2 billion), diversity is a financially material issue. As of 2022 they will vote against NC chairs who fail to meet their expectations of board ethnic diversity by end-2021.[72] NBIM manages Norway's sovereign wealth fund, the world's largest ($1.3 trillion), and owns about 1.5% of all listed stocks. It also practices active ownership.

Regulators are also calling for change. A decade after Hong Kong introduced voluntary disclosure of company diversity policies, a 2020 report showed that only 14% of Hong Kong listed company directors are women (ranging from 0–33%). About a third of all companies had no female directors, 38% had one – 70% had one or zero. Hong Kong's companies have yet to tap into the wider pool of potential directors. With 30% of the companies having 2–6 female directors, some boards have made more progress than others. While most of Hong Kong's listed companies are family-controlled businesses, the optics of this imbalance – especially for a major financial centre – were not good. Instead of implementing quotas, they set targets for gender diversity: 25% by 2025 and 30% by 2030. The UK's Financial Conduct Authority (FCA) recently called for changes too, i.e. women should hold at least 40% of board seats and at least one senior board position (chair, CEO, DFO or senior independent director). Companies will need to 'comply or explain'. Australia, New Zealand and

---

[70] BlackRock, Proxy voting guidelines for US securities (as of Jan. 2021), blk-responsible-investment-guidelines-us.pdf . BlackRock voted against 1,862 directors and 975 companies globally because of concerns about board diversity during the 2020/21 proxy voting year. https://esgclarity.com/board-diversity-tops-list-of-concerns-for-blackrock-investment-stewardship/

[71] https://www.ssga.com/us/en/institutional/ic/insights/ceo-letter-2021-proxy-voting-agenda

[72] In 2020 LGIM voted against 208 directors globally because of concerns about board diversity. active-ownership-report-2020.pdf

South Africa have also used targets instead of quotas.

Increasing awareness and tracking board diversity is another step towards improving board diversity. Numerous indicies have been created for this, including: the Singapore Board Diversity Index benchmarks primary-listed companies on the Singapore Exchange against eight diversity parameters; the Governance Institute of Australia's index tracks five areas; European Women on Boards (EWoB) publishes a gender diversity index; and The Boardroom Africa (TBA) is mapping gender diversity across the 50+ African countries with country-specific reports.[73]

In the US, the Human Rights Campaign Foundation publishes an index to drive workplace equity for LGBTQ+ people;[74] Disability:IN tracks workplace inclusion with their disability equality index (DEI).[75] While all Fortune 1000 companies and the largest 200 US law firms (Am Law 200) can participate, only 319 companies were part of the 2021 DEI. The results showed that only a tenth of companies have a senior executive who identifies as a person with a disability while few employees (5%) disclosed their disability to employers.[76] There is also a lack of disclosure among FTSE100 leaders: an analysis of 2020 annual reports showed that no senior executives or senior managers disclosed having a disability. Again, few employees (3%) disclosed a disability; only 20 companies gave all employees the chance to disclose disabilities; and just 12 publicly reported the number reported as disabled.[77]

Board observer programmes offer another pathway for aspiring directors. Some companies start small like insurance group HCI ($242 million revenues, 2019) in Florida, US. Its Kenyan-born Indian founder, Paresh Patel, and his senior leadership team "wanted to embrace the change they wanted" and allocated resources to create a board observer programme to develop board diversity from within. Launched in 2018, this programme is

---

[73] TBA reports to date: Nigeria, South Africa, Kenya, Ghana, Morocco, Egypt, Tanzania, Uganda, Zambia, Côte D'Ivoire and Rwanda.
[74] https://www.hrc.org/resources/corporate-equality-index
[75] https://disabilityin-bulk.s3.amazonaws.com/2021/2021-DEI-Report+-+FINAL_508.pdf
[76] According to the WHO, about 1 billion people are living with disabilities, representing the world's largest minority group. WHO_NMH_VIP_11.01_eng.pdf
[77] https://www.peoplemanagement.co.uk/news/articles/no-ftse-100-executives-or-senior-managers-have-disclosed-a-disability#gref

unique for US publicly held companies: two board observers per year can actively participate in all meetings (without voting) for one year; they receive $50,000 (half of the annual remuneration for HCI's full board members). HCI searches for candidates from under-represented groups and while full board membership is not guaranteed after the programme, participants gain invaluable knowledge and experience about corporate governance and how boards operate. Importantly, participants are better prepared for their next board role. HCI developed an intentional, targeted, and sustainable way to drive board diversity and expand the board's talent pool.[78] Companies are also partnering with non-profit organisations such as Board Apprentice to increase board diversity.

6. Independent reviews on diversity

Several UK government-backed initiatives have explored gender and ethnic and cultural diversity in company leadership. A 2011 Equality and Human Rights Commission (EHRC) report about women's progress to the UK's top positions of power and influence noted a "waxing and waning" trend versus one of "constant upwards movement".[79] The report noted that of over 5,000 women "missing" from the top jobs, 1,232 were missing from the 3,042 board seats in FTSE350 companies. It also highlighted an alarming statistic: gender-balanced UK boardrooms would only arrive in 2080.[80]

A. Gender diversity

The *Female FTSE Board Report* has tracked the women's progress on corporate boards since 1999. A decade ago, the 2010 edition noted that the 12.5% female directors represented a three-year plateau.[81] Board gender diversity appeared to be stagnating. The 2011 *Women on Boards* review by

---

[78] Business Observer, "Insurance firm years ahead of boardroom diversity trend", 12 Feb. 2021. https://www.businessobserverfl.com
[79] EHRC, *Sex and Power 2011*. sex_and_power_2011_gb_2_.pdf
[80] Ibid, 10. "Missing" is defined as half (i.e. women are half of the UK population) of the positions minus the number already held by women.
[81] Susan Vinnicombe, Ruth Sealy, Jacey Graham and Elena Doldor, *The Female FTSE Board Report 2010*, Cranfield School of Management, 2010.

Board Diversity – A Historical Perspective

Lord Davies stated that better decision-making boards include many voices and this "mix of voices must include women." To improve women's board representation, the review recommended: [82]

- A minimum of 25% female directors on FTSE100 boards by 2015. FTSE350 boards should announce their aspirational targets for 2013 and 2015.
- FTSE companies should be required to disclose gender diversity data.
- The UK corporate governance code should require companies to establish board diversity policies.
- Transparent and meaningful annual reporting about the NC and board recruitment process.
- Investors should pay attention to these recommendations.
- Companies should advertise NED positions to expand the applicant pool.
- Executive search firms need a voluntary code of conduct addressing gender diversity.

The report encouraged a voluntary (versus quotas) data-led approach for companies, although quotas could be introduced if the business-led approach failed. The 5-year summary review (2015) revealed that women's representation on FTSE100 boards more than doubled from 2011 to 26.1% and to 19.6% on FTSE250 boards. The 21 all-male FTSE100 boards had disappeared while the 131 in the FTSE250 had dropped to 15.[83] The representation of women on FTSE100 boards had cleared the 25% threshold.

The Hampton-Alexander Review (2016) aimed to boost the number of women on boards and in senior leadership across the FTSE350. It recommended a 2020 target of 33% women on FTSE350 boards and two

---

[82] The Davies Review, *Women on Boards*, February 2011. 18–21, 11-745-women-on-boards.pdf.
[83] Davies Review, *Women on Boards*, 2015, Appendix A. Improving the Gender Balance on British Boards.pdf

leadership layers below, excoms and their direct reports.[84] It also recommended a revised UK corporate governance code that includes these disclosures. This was a signal to FTSE companies to address board gender imbalance – again voluntarily. The 2021 final report shows that although progress was made, success was mixed:

- FTSE100s exceeded (36%) and FTSE250s met (33%) the target for women directors but both fell short with combined excoms and direct reports. Men received the most (64–66%) leadership roles.[85]
- FTSE350 all-male boards disappeared as of January 2021.

Efforts to end board gender imbalances continue as most (65–70%) FTSE board and leadership positions are held by men. The so-called gender say gap – the invisibility of women's voices – remains significant. These reviews failed to capture ethnicity and social class background data on women directors, but the UK's next review of FTSE350 boards would examine this.

B. Ethnic diversity

The Parker Review (2017) aimed to improve ethnic diversity on UK company boards. It set a target for FTSE100 companies to have at least one director of colour by end-2021 and the same for FTSE250 companies by end-2024. NCs should require their internal/external recruiters to identify and present qualified board candidates of colour for vacancies. The report also looked at career development and progression (including mentoring) to build a pipeline of diverse talent and plan for succession. By early 2021, 74 FTSE100 companies had met that goal, while 21 boards still lacked such representation.[86]

---

[84] The Hampton-Alexander Review, *FTSE Women Leaders*, 2016. Hampton-Alexander Review – November 2016.pdf
[85] The Hampton-Alexander Review, *FTSE Women Leaders*, 2021. HA-REPORT-2021_FINAL.pdf
[86] Three FTSE100s did not respond and two submitted no data. parker-review-appendix.pdf

C. 2018 UK Corporate Governance Code

In July 2018 the FRC published an updated UK Corporate Governance Code that reflects more recent thinking about diversity: "[a] company's culture should promote integrity and openness, value diversity and be responsive to the views of shareholders and wider stakeholders."[87] It noted the role of diversity in board composition, succession planning and annual reporting. It recommends that diversity – gender, ethnic, cognitive, functional etc. – also be considered when companies are looking for qualified board and succession candidates. Board evaluations should also consider board diversity and companies should report on their diversity and inclusion policies (including objectives and progress on achieving them). A September 2018 analysis of compliance with the FRC's new board diversity reporting recommendations showed:[88]

- 15% of FTSE100 companies fully complied while 20% partially complied
- 6% of FTSE250 companies fully complied while 8% partially complied
- FTSE350 approaches ranged from "a sophisticated understanding of diversity as the best utilisation of talent and a significant strategic issue … to a minimalistic, 'tick-box' approach."

Until more companies, and particularly those charged with leading them, appreciate the strategic imperative of diversity, it will be difficult for companies to reap the benefits of a diverse workplace in a fast-changing and increasingly diverse world.

7. Lessons from Uber and Unilever

A. Uber's governance failure

In April 2021, Uber was valued at over $106 billion but also known for

---

[87] FRC, *The UK Corporate Governance Code, 2018*. 2018-UK-Corporate-Governance-Code-FINAL.pdf
[88] University of Exeter Business School and FRC. *Board diversity Reporting, 2018*. Board-Diversity-Reporting-September-2018.pdf

having a toxic culture[89] and lack of board diversity. In February 2017, former Uber engineer Susan Fowler shared a blogpost about her experiences with sexism and retaliation at the company. Things quickly unraveled for Uber. By June, several top executives resigned, including the CEO, and over 20 employees were fired over claims of sexual harassment and discrimination. Former US attorney general Eric Holder's law firm released a scathing report that identified four themes in Uber's failures: "tone at the top, trust, transformation, and accountability."[90] A lack of diversity, especially at the top levels, was also cited as a big problem. The report recommended that Uber basically rebuild its leadership team from scratch, strengthen board oversight, and enhance diversity and inclusion at all levels among other things. Uber hired new executive leaders and added four new independent directors to the board.[91] In an April 2019 SEC filing, Uber stated that their leadership team "sought to reform our culture fundamentally by improving our governance structure, strengthening our compliance program, creating and embracing new cultural norms, committing to diversity and inclusion, and rebuilding our relationships with employees, Drivers, consumers, cities, and regulators".[92]

B. Unilever's governance success

In March 2020, London-based Unilever announced that it has achieved gender balance across management globally, [93] a year earlier than expected. The company is closing the gender gap with 50% women at management level globally and a non-executive board of 45% women. Women made progress in departments where they have been historically under-represented: finance (50%), operations/tech (47%), and supply chain (40%).

---

[89] Uber also received about 6,000 allegations of serious sexual assault in the US during a two-year period (2017–2018) with victims including customers, drivers and third parties. https://www.uber.com/us/en/about/reports/us-safety-report/

[90] Covington Recommendations.pdf

[91] They were former Xerox CEO Ursula Burns, the first Black female Fortune 500 CEO; Nestlé EVP Wan Ling Martello; former Northrop Grumman CEO Ronald Sugar; and former Merrill Lynch CEO John Thain.

[92] Uber's US SEC Amendment No. 1 to Form S-1 Registration Statement filed on 26 April 2019. https://d18rn0p25nwr6d.cloudfront.net/CIK-0001543151/f0dcd9ae-31ea-40c2-ac8b-36d85158c8a2.pdf

[93] "Unilever achieves gender balance across management globally", Unilever press release, 3 March 2020.

Unilever's gender balance milestone follows a long commitment to drive workplace gender equality. Their Diversity & Inclusion team has implemented several initiatives including: a Global Diversity Board that reports monthly to executive leadership; a network of over 200 DI champions; an online coaching programme for women leaders run by INSEAD; an agile working policy for new parents; gender neutral pay structures; and advocating for racial and ethnic board diversity through Change the Race Ratio, a coalition of 75 FTSE100 companies. Tools are also being used to drive gender equity in recruitment (e.g. gender-balanced interview requirements). Diversity and inclusion is part of who Unilever is.

8. Conclusion

Research shows that diversity increases creativity and innovation, promotes higher quality decisions, and enhances economic growth. More diverse organisations tend to make better strategic decisions, show superior growth and innovation, and exhibit lower risk. Companies that make diversity and inclusion a strategic imperative will be better positioned to tap the benefits from an increasingly diverse talent pool. Companies should explore and continue to dismantle the barriers to boardroom access that still impact candidates from under-represented background. Inclusive board leadership can facilitate this process. Boards should be proactive and intentional about board diversity, embedding it in their organisational leadership, pathways to the boardroom, and training programs. Harnessing a greater talent pool benefits everyone. Greater board diversity and is not just a social or moral imperative, it's also great for a company's sustainable long-term success.

Appendix A: Diverse board talent development organisations/initiatives

Organisations working to identify and develop diverse board talent.

- **theBoardlist**: founded in 2016 by Silicon Valley tech executive Sukhinder Singh Cassidy to address the need for gender parity in the boardroom. The company launched with a database of 1,000 board-ready women recommended by Silicon Valley's most prominent directors, CEOs and founders in February 2016; their first board placement was in October 2016.[94] As of early 2021, with a candidate pool of over 8,000 and about 18,000 members (C-suite executives, board directors and emerging talent), theBoardlist has helped over 2,000 companies find directors. Connecting exceptional diverse talent with global board opportunities, they are "debunking the pipeline problem myth" at the same time.[95]

- **The Board Challenge (TBC)**: is a movement to improve the representation of Black directors in the US boardrooms. **Pledge partners c**ommit to add a Black director to their board within the next year (e.g. online real estate company Zillow). **Charter partners and supporters,** with at least one Black director already, pledge to continue to accelerate board diversity representation (e.g. sustainability non-profit Ceres, Nasdaq). Co-founded by three Silicon Valley tech leaders, including theBoardlist's Sukhinder Singh Cassidy.

- **Women on Boards (WOB) Project**: launched a partnership with leading private equity firms and an inaugural group of 20 companies to increase gender diversity and inclusion on consumer company boards. Women on Boards (WOB) Project was created in 2020 by industry leaders to increase the number of women serving on boards while also expanding diversity including race, ethnicity, age, socio-economic status, and sexual orientation, gender fluidity.

---

[94] https://site.theboardlist.com/about-us
[95] https://site.theboardlist.com/about-u

Board Diversity – A Historical Perspective

Examples of programmes driving the pipeline of diverse young talent in the UK and the US:

- **10,000 Black Interns**:[96] a UK programme to offer 10,000 internships over 5 years, across 24 sectors, in 700+ companies, to Black students/recent graduates. Sectors include banking, education, health data research, law, finance and tech.

- **Equate Scotland**:[97] the UK's only network for women STEM students to support, train and champion them as they are often one of few in typically male-dominated STEM environments.

- **10K by 2025**:[98] an initiative of the US National Society of Black Engineers (NSBE) to diversify the engineering pipeline and produce 10,000 new Black engineers annually by 2025. Focusses on multiple STEM pipeline programmes, including career academies, university scholarships, conferences, and summer engineering camps for 9–12-year-olds. They have strategic partnerships with the US department of energy's (DOE) renewable energy office, Engineers Without Borders/CE Corps and MindEdge, among others.

- **50K Coalition**:[99] over 40 organisations working to create a US pool of engineering talent. The goal is to graduate 50,000 diverse engineers in the US annually by 2025. Created in 2016 by the top diverse engineering organisations – NSBE, the American Indian Science and Engineering Society (AISES), the Society of Hispanic Professional Engineers (SHPE) and SWE – it serves over 85,000 pre/university and professional members.

---

[96] www.10000blackinterns.com
[97] www.equatescotland.org.uk
[98] www.nsbe.org
[99] www.50kcoalition.org

CHAPTER 7. THE GEN 3.0 BROADER CONTEXT OF DIVERSITY

Karl George, Managing Director, The Governance Forum
Helen Higginbotham, Corporate Solicitor, Harrison Clark Rickerbys Limited
Tom Proverbs-Garbett, Corporate Lawyer, Pinsent Masons LLP

Introduction

We saw in chapter 6 that diversity as a concept is complex. Seeking to create a board that is diverse in terms of social-category without having a clear idea of the purpose and goals of an organisation and, perhaps even more pressingly, its values, may result in negative effects on decision making. We also saw the successes of looking at board diversity in terms of exploration rather than exploitation. The idea of expecting diversity to contribute positively to board behaviour because this gives a broader suite of individual skills and viewpoints to requisition, gives way to the view that a heterogeneous group is more able to, collectively, explore an issue by way of considering different points of view and approaches.[1]

---

[1] Mannix, E. and Neale, M. (2005) "What Differences Make a Difference? The Promise and Reality of Diverse Teams in Organizations", *Psychological Science in the Public Interest*, vol. 6.2, pp. 31-55.

This is a subtle but important point which, as we have seen, suggests that quotas are only a very small part of the solution. The positions recommended by, for example, the Davies,[2] Hampton-Alexander[3] and Parker[4] reviews and subsumed in some cases into the UK Corporate Governance Code issued in 2018 need to be considered alongside the move towards purposive business and board responsibility for strategy exemplified in that code and elsewhere.[5] Only with an established and shared vision for the future direction of the business can a board access its diversity effectively. This is entirely compatible with the aims of those publications, their quotas being in place as a minimum acceptable level of participation (even if at this stage that tends to remain aspirational).

In this chapter we will consider some of the same issues through a different lens. We begin by considering neural or cognitive diversity and consider how we might identify and recruit those who think differently to incumbent board members. We will then go on to look at how, in addition to variegated thought, further advantages pertain when an organisation and particularly the board, is open to functional diversity. We use this term to capture the idea that variation and development of the *processes* by which a board acts and by which its meetings take place or are run, together with encouraging a variation in types of interactions between board members, can lead to better ways of working and increased diversity in all senses. In the context of those two strands, we will move on to think about the advent of the virtual boardroom, brought to the fore as a result of 2020's Covid pandemic but in genesis long before, and the views of the next generation, X and Y.

Our aim is to consider, heuristically, the many and differentiated ways

---

[2] (2011-2021) *Women on Boards – Collected Reports*, available online: <https://www.gov.uk/government/collections/women-on-boards-reports> (accessed 25 May 2011).
[3] (2016-2021) *FTSE Women Leaders: Improving Gender Balance*, available online: <https://www.gov.uk/government/publications/ftse-women-leaders-hampton-alexander-review> (accessed 25 May 2021).
[4] (2017-2021) *Ethnic Diversity of UK Boards*, available online: <https://www.gov.uk/government/publications/ethnic-diversity-of-uk-boards-the-parker-review> (accessed 25 May 2021).
[5] Available online: <https://www.frc.org.uk/getattachment/88bd8c45-50ea-4841-95b0-d2f4f48069a2/2018-UK-Corporate-Governance-Code-FINAL.PDF> (accessed 25 May 2021).

practitioners are considering these issues in their governance practices in this third generation of corporate governance.

1. Neural Diversity

The concept of neural or cognitive diversity stems from the underlying principle that in order for a boardroom to be effective, it needs to be a forum in which meaningful debate is encouraged and multiple perspectives are welcomed, enabling new initiatives to be explored. The FRC's *Guidance on Board Effectiveness* (2018) refers to the principle of avoiding *"a tendency towards 'group think'"* by ensuring that the group consists of a collection of individuals with different skills, backgrounds and strengths.[6] How can this be achieved? The Corporate Governance Institute similarly asks in its *Building a Balanced Board* publication (2019) *"how can an organisation that doesn't take advantage of the skills of a significant percentage of society....really be getting the 'best' candidates to lead it?"*[7] This question provides, albeit obliquely, the answer. In order to have a neutrally diverse board, the objectives must be to establish (1) clear, fair and objective recruitment processes to ensure that appointments are based on merit and skills without discrimination and (2) boards which reflect the demographic they serve. Indeed, both principles have been codified in *The UK Corporate Governance Code* (2018)[8] which requires appointments to boards and senior management positions to be based on *"merit and objective criteria"* which, it states, should in turn promote *"diversity of gender, social and ethnic backgrounds, cognitive and personal strengths"*.[9] Further, it is a fundamental principle of UK company law: the Companies Act 2006 requires directors to promote the success of the company, taking into account the interests of stakeholders including employees.[10] Is a board which does not reflect the demographic of its workforce able to fully

---

[6] Available online: <https://www.frc.org.uk/getattachment/61232f60-a338-471b-ba5a-bfed25219147/2018-Guidance-on-Board-Effectiveness-FINAL.PDF> (accessed 4 February 2021), p.4.
[7] CGI: ICSA and Diligent (2019) *Building a Balanced Board*, available online: <https://diligent.com/en-gb/resources/building-a-balanced-board-thoughts-on-the-challenges-of-boardcomposition/?utm_source=ICSA&utm_medium=sponsoredcontent&utm_content=whitepaper&utm_campaign=ICSAEffective Boards> (accessed 4 February 2021 – requires free registration).
[8] Note 5
[9] Principle J.
[10] Section 172 Companies Act 2006.

comply with its duty to take into account their interests?

Diversity on boards has been discussed commonly in the context of gender and ethnic diversity, and although the principle of cognitive diversity has not been in the spotlight in the same way, there are synergies between the discussions and the objective of ensuring all voices are heard. It is therefore useful to consider the topical focus on gender and race diversity in the boardroom and ask how this can act to improve neural diversity.

A. Gender Diversity

Dialogues have focussed on the inequality of women in the workplace, from under-representation of women on boards[11] to the introduction of gender pay gap reporting requirements by The Equality Act 2010 (Gender Pay Gap Information) Regulations 2017. The 2019 update to the Hampton-Alexander Review acknowledged that *"improving gender diversity in positions of power and decision-making....[is] recognised as a key pillar in improving women's economic empowerment and setting a path towards gender equality"*.[12] Lord Davies' report, *Women on Boards* (2011)[13] and its subsequent updates[14] focused on the significant under-representation of women on boards starting from the bald statistic that in 2010, women accounted for only 12.5% of the members of the boards of FTSE 100 companies.[15] This was followed by the Hampton-Alexander Review[16] and its updates[17] which sought to redress the balance and improve company performance by implementing a minimum target of 33% for women on FTSE 350 boards

---

[11] Notes 2 and 3.
[12] Hampton-Alexander Review (2019) *FTSE Women Leaders: Improving gender balance in FTSE Leadership November 2019*, available online: <https://ftsewomenleaders.com/wp-content/uploads/2019/11/HA-Review-Report-2019.pdf> (accessed 25 May 2021).
[13] Davies, E. (2011) *Women on Boards*, available online: <https://assets.publishing.service.gov.uk/government/uploads/> (accessed 25 May 2021).
[14] Note 2.
[15] Davies, note 13, p.3.
[16] Hampton-Alexander Review (2016) *FTSE Women Leaders: Improving gender balance in FTSE Leadership November 2016*, available online <https://assets.publishing.service.gov.uk/government/uploads/system/uploads/attachment_data/file/613085/ftse-women-leaders-hampton-alexander-review.pdf> (accessed 25 May 2021).
[17] Note 3.

including two layers of leadership below the board by the end of 2020.[18] Its 2019 update shows progress and anticipates that if this is sustained until the end of 2020, the targets set in 2016 will have been met.[19] However, the report also acknowledges that there is still more to be done in working towards equity in the boardroom, the positions of chair and CEO still predominantly occupied by men.[20]

How does gender diversity improve cognitive diversity? The aforementioned reviews aver that greater representation of women on boards is linked to improved financial performance of businesses. Lord Davies states *"Corporate boards perform better when they include the best people who come from a range of perspectives and backgrounds"* and *"it is clear that boards make better decisions where a range of voices, drawing on different life experiences, can be heard"*.[21] While acknowledging that a variety of perspectives is important, it is useful to pause to consider what is meant by gender diversity. The focus of the above studies and reporting requirements relate solely to representation of women on boards. However, this view of gender may soon become outdated as it neglects to recognise that gender is fluid and thus may have the inadvertent effect of marginalising sections of society. True cognitive diversity can only be achieved if there is recognition of all gender identities (including transgender and non-binary) in the boardroom and, in the third generation of governance, a true reflection of the ethnicity of a company's stakeholders.

B. Ethnic Diversity

As with the reviews into gender representation on boards, reviews into race representation have tended to set quotas. The Parker Review of 2017 recommended that each FTSE 100 board should have at least one director of colour by 2021 and each FTSE 250 board should have at least one

---

[18] Hampton Alexander Review, note 16, p.10.
[19] Note 12.
[20] Note 12, p.28.
[21] Davies, note 13, pp.2-3.

director of colour by 2024.[22] The 2020 update to the review found that although progress had been made, 59% of companies reviewed had not met the target of having at least one director of colour on their board.[23] Progress towards equal representation of black people and ethnic minorities in the boardroom is, at best, slow.

The Black Lives Matter movement which achieved prominence on social media in 2020, highlighted discrimination against black people by the police with the use of fatal force. In these instances, it was suggested, the perspective of the police was that of a perceived threat of violence from the black victims which necessitated deadly force raising the question: would their view have been the same if the incidents involved white suspects? Answering such a question is beyond the reach of this chapter, but the movement and the questions arising from it both demonstrate the frustration felt by wider society and, pertinent for present purposes, the issue of unconscious bias.

The McGregor-Smith Review (2017)[24] provided a number of recommendations for businesses to address the issue of unconscious bias – the idea that, as the review puts it, "*[w]e all find it easier to relate to those who are most like ourselves or who come from similar backgrounds*"[25] – including undertaking a review of recruitment processes, entry requirements and language used in the job adverts. Further, in order to identify and prevent barriers to entry, people from ethnic minorities should be mentored and supported; And barriers there are.

---

[22] Parker, J. (2017) *A Report into the Ethnic Diversity of UK Boards*, available online: <https://assets.ey.com/content/dam/ey-sites/ey-com/en_uk/news/2020/02/ey-parker-review-2017-report-final.pdf> (accessed 4 February 2021), recommendation 1.1.

[23] Parker, J. (2020) *Ethnic Diversity Enriching Business Leadership: An Update Report from The Parker Review*, available online: <https://assets.ey.com/content/dam/ey-sites/ey-com/en_uk/news/2020/02/ey-parker-review-2020-report-final.pdf> (accessed 4 February 2021), p.16.

[24] McGregor-Smith, R. (2017) *Race in the Workplace: The McGregor Smith Review*, available online: <https://assets.publishing.service.gov.uk/government/uploads/system/uploads/attachment_data/file/594336/race-in-workplace-mcgregor-smith-review.pdf> (accessed 4 February 2021).

[25] Note 24, p.18.

UK Government statistics show that the biggest increase in entry rates into higher (post-secondary) education between 2006 and 2019 was among black pupils compared with other ethnic groups,[26] whereas between 2004 and 2018 the percentage of workers in "elementary" jobs (the lowest skilled type of occupation) was highest in black people.[27] These statistics suggest that there are clear impediments to black people being recruited to senior professional roles and onwards onto boards and management teams. It further illustrates the inherent disparity between the socio-economic environments of different ethnic groups and the potential barriers to entry to the boardroom which McGregor-Smith seeks to redress.

The examples of gender and race diversity provide an insight into how businesses benefit from the participation of people from different backgrounds and with different skill sets when given the opportunity to sit at the table and be heard. Boards need to ensure that they have clear and fair policies which encourage diversity at recruitment and progression pathways, and that the full spectrum of diversity is explored to ensure that businesses have the benefit of specialist skills and training, but also life experiences and perspectives. The first generation of corporate governance focussed on incorporating independent board members; the second, on ensuring some level of diversity. The third generation will enthusiastically recruit board members in light of their backgrounds and cognitive diversity in order to benefit in this way.

2. Functional Diversity

As we will see later in this chapter, the virtual boardroom has become a reality. But there are many other ways in which the functioning of the board can be reassessed in order that diversity is privileged and allowed to flourish. It has been demonstrated that diverse boards tend to be more

---

[26] Universities and Colleges Admissions Service. (2020) *Entry Rates into Higher Education*, available online: <https://www.ethnicity-facts-figures.service.gov.uk/education-skills-and-training/higher-education/entry-rates-into-higher-education/latest#by-ethnicity> (accessed 4 February 2021).

[27] Office for National Statistics. (2020) *Employment by Occupation*, available online: <https://www.ethnicity-facts-figures.service.gov.uk/work-pay-and-benefits/employment/employment-by-occupation/latest> (accessed 4 February 2021).

innovative;[28] arguably, this is a reciprocal relationship and an innovative board is more likely to be diverse. Innovation does not need to mean wholesale changes to the business or ideas for major disruption. Innovation is often most effective when it is incremental and regular, especially in the face of complexity.[29] It is in this way that a board can demonstrate its commitment to both innovation and diversity by considering its own processes. A board might consider the frequency and timing of board meetings, the way in which agendas are set, the active performance of the board, and the willingness of its members to explore different ideas and points of view that have emerged (ideally as a result of the newly diverse board investigated in previous chapters).

A. Calendar planning, timetabling and agendas

Let us start with the idea of timetabling. It is common to set an annual calendar at the beginning of the year and to repeat the calendar, with minor amendments, from the year before. Meetings might be monthly or quarterly, but they will follow a pattern and be held at similar times of day. Immediately, there is likely to be an impact on diversity – this rigidity of process will not be flexible enough for someone, for example, who needs to consider childcare. What about carers? What about those within the business for whom this is an unsustainable time, whether because of shift patterns or otherwise? Planning the calendar, giving it serious thought rather than delegating to a board assistant, is a small but powerful change that will provide immediate easy wins.

This is an important aspect of diversity – not just an administrative task. Being willing to make changes and to think deeply about structural issues will help promote a more diverse board and is the first example of what we are calling functional diversity. Process can be a key perpetuating factor in inequality, particularly through use of committees. If the procedures of the

---

[28] Cook, A. and Glass, C. (2015), "Do Minority Leaders Affect Corporate Practice? Analyzing the Effect of Leadership Composition on Governance and Product Development", *Strategic Organization*, vol.13(2), pp.117-140.
[29] Rupietta, C. and Backes-Gellner, U. (2019) "Combining Knowledge Stock and Knowledge Flow to Generate Superior Incremental Innovation Performance — Evidence from Swiss Manufacturing", *Journal of Business Research*, vol.94, pp. 209-222.

board and its committees are systemically incomplete, unfair or skewed – deliberately or otherwise – then increased diversity will only ever be an unrealised goal. Procedural justice requires that participants are judged fairly and treated equally. Providing clear procedure is more likely, it has been argued, to cut through resistance to diversity than the distributive justice quotas are intended to supply.[30] And an easy way to begin is to establish an equitable board and committee calendar. If nothing else, it sets the right tone and encourages board members from the outset to think in this way.

What about agenda setting? It is tempting to take the same items in the same order on the same annual cycle. But is this the most efficient way of looking at the material?

The responsibility of the board has evolved from – at least on the non-executive side – a source of independent critical challenge of management to leading on strategy.[31] Strategy is now a headline of the UK Corporate Governance Code, Principle B reading: "*The board should establish the company's purpose, values and strategy, and satisfy itself that these and its culture are aligned. All directors must act with integrity, lead by example and promote the desired culture.*"[32] In ensuring that proper and significant thought is given to strategically important aspects of a board meeting, why is it so often the case that those items are relegated to the second half of a board meeting after standard business? Instead of having boilerplate, business as usual material upfront with the result that everyone is dead-eyed by the end of the first hour, why not open with the strategically important items which will require serious consideration? It might even help to have a sub-committee of the board whose role is to look critically at the agenda, regularly mixing up the approach to avoid the blindness of repetition, while remaining informed and alert to usual business so that nothing is overlooked.[33]

---

[30] Gröschl, S. and Takagi, J. (2012) *Diversity Quotas, Diverse Perspectives: The Case of Gender*, Ebook: Taylor & Francis Group.
[31] Pugliese, A., Bezemer, P., Zattoni, A., Huse, M., Van den Bosch, F., and Volberda, H. (2009), "Boards of Directors' Contribution to Strategy: A Literature Review and Research Agenda", *Corporate Governance: An International Review*, vol. 17.3, pp. 292-306.
[32] Note 5.
[33] Board Administrator (2020), "Agenda-setting Committee Builds Board Trust", *Board Administrator*, vol. 36.7, p. 2.

Developing the agenda will have real impact on the way meetings are run, where the focus of the board's time will be and where collective energies are spent. Attention to the agenda can even enhance voices. What if, for example, the agenda calls on everybody to speak early on, perhaps giving a report of just a minute or two on their individual circumstances and/or their respective departments? Those in the room or on the (video) call hear their voices at this early stage which, as we know from experience helps to encourage contributions on substantive matters later on. Doing this will trigger those innovative and diverse voices the board has worked hard to ensure are present, meaning functional diversity has a direct impact on broader diversity. If a board begins with these significant but relatively easily dealt with procedural points then it will be well on the way to being functionally diverse.

B. New methods

Use of technology, of course, is going to play a huge role in any process work done, both as a testament to the board's willingness to be diverse and innovative and as a way of assisting the promotion of wider diversity goals. We will talk about the virtual boardroom in more detail, including commenting on its spectacular rise during the pandemic, below. For present purposes, it is worth focusing on the ways in which willingness to look for and, importantly, adopt simple technological adjustments can help to assist the board in becoming more diverse. For example, a board might consider using different presentation technologies which will appeal to the future generation of governance professionals, so-called "digital natives". Collaborative document suites; board pack software; app-based voting – all of these new ways of working will encourage the board to reflect not only on its visible diversity but also on its preparedness to be diverse, so closely related to the diversity of thought that we explored above.

Indeed, reflection and reflexivity are two often overlooked aspects of functional diversity. If the point of diversity, in addition perhaps to reflecting the communities of a company's stakeholders, is to make better decisions, then working out how best to make those decisions and tracking whether they are in fact being made is crucial.[34] The board needs to consider its ability to reflect, reflexively, on both the ideas generated and *the ways in which* ideas are generated and used by the board. Part of generating those ideas is having the right people around the table and a sufficiently diverse group of thinkers. But it is also about making sure that the board is acting optimally.

To that end, board self-assessment and external assessment should be welcomed and regular. The UK Corporate Governance Code requires premium listed companies to have externally facilitated evaluations every three years (Provision 21) and should assess itself every year (Principle L).[35] The code is the gold standard for corporate governance and is written with listed companies in mind, but that does not mean other organisations should be happy with lesser governance. In reflecting and thinking reflexively about the board's performance – of the whole and for each director considering their individual contribution – the board will, inherently and necessarily, increase its functional diversity. Are there different ways the board could approach problems? Are there different ways in which it could delegate? Are there different ways in which individual directors could approach meetings or papers? The list is endless. Treating an area of governance best practice as an opportunity to facilitate learning will foster an arena where diversity of thought, diversity of approach and diversity of gender and race will thrive and be welcomed. And that is, after all, the overarching aim.

Linked very closely to self-assessment is the capturing of ideas. All too often, however diverse the board is in terms of its constitution, it will nevertheless focus (sometimes by necessity) on immediate problems, or it finds itself so caught up with operational matters that time for strategic thinking is lost. Functional diversity assists with this. For example, the board might investigate different ways of brainstorming strategically. This could be by meeting more regularly in subgroups, rather than formal committees, and subsequently reporting back with ideas for the full board to consider. Or it could use online platforms – virtual whiteboards or the

---

[34] Phillips, K., Northcraft, G., and Neale, M., (2006), "Surface-Level Diversity and Decision-Making in Groups: When Does Deep-Level Similarity Help?", *Group Processes & Intergroup Relations*, vol 9.4, pp. 467–482.

[35] Note 5.

like – allowing members to comment in real time without interrupting a presentation or discussion on virtual post-it notes and "stick" them up as thoughts occur. Would that be useful for capturing ideas at speed, without the deafening silence of the open board call for suggestions, resulting in genuine innovation?

Clearly, there are limits to the board's foresight and pursuing strategy beyond the three to five year term is unlikely (and, depending on the sector, it may be considerably less), but recall that this is about having a diversity of process. Shaping arrangements so that they are as fluid as possible is much more likely to provide those moments of inspiration and insight than a rigid adherence to the approaches of last year. A board that operates in that way is primed to continue to increase its diversity in every sense – including considering their backgrounds and cognitive diversity, demonstrating third generation governance.

3. The Virtual Boardroom

In 2020, the Covid-19 pandemic saw the introduction of regulations to "stay at home" and businesses being forced to find new ways of working with urgency. Boards faced unprecedented challenges to adapt how business is conducted and decisions are made. Modern technology has facilitated the transition of video calls and virtual meetings, now considered to be the "new normal". But what is a "virtual boardroom"? What has been learned by the implementation of these new systems of working and communicating, and what is there still to learn in this ever-changing technological landscape?

For companies incorporated in the UK, the starting point will be their articles of association. This will be a bespoke document, but the Model Articles for private limited companies[36] provide that in order for directors to make decisions, either agreement is required from all directors by way of written resolution or the agreement of the majority present at a meeting is

---

[36] Available online: <https://www.gov.uk/government/publications/model-articles-for-private-companies-limited-by-shares>.

needed.[37] Resolutions may be signed electronically and therefore during a global "lockdown" a written resolution may be a simple solution. However, this method of decision-making does not allow for debate and discussion amongst the board, which may not be appropriate unless the matter is of a simple nature. A meeting allows for discussion, questions and challenge. New ideas can be shared. A meeting in some form is therefore likely to be more appropriate, more often, for the majority of matters to be considered by the board.

Unless the articles of association of a company expressly exclude the ability of the board to meet using electronic means, it appears that it is generally accepted that meetings can be held in this manner;[38] participants do not all need to be in the same place or using the same form of communication. However, in such a situation the choice of communication and clear instructions will be vital to running an effective meeting.[39] The advent of live video calls has further enabled meetings to be held by way of a virtual platform so that participants can dial-in from a range of locations. All of this means that boards have been able to conduct meetings through the various national lockdowns caused by the pandemic, using email to share board papers, and virtual platforms to hold meetings and keep recordings. In fact, technology and companies' willingness to embrace new ways of working, particularly as regards virtual shareholders' meetings, has out-paced legislative reform.[40]

The Corporate Governance and Insolvency Act 2020 briefly redressed the balance by expressly permitting general meetings to be held virtually and

---

[37] Articles 7 and 8 of the *Model Articles for Private Companies Limited by Shares*, available online: <https://www.gov.uk/government/publications/model-articles-for-private-companies-limited-by-shares/model-articles-for-private-companies-limited-by-shares#unanimous> (accessed 4 February 2021).
[38] Topham, A. (ed). (2014) *Palmer's Company Law*, vol. 2, paragraph 8.2128.
[39] CGI:ICSA and Lorraine Young Board Advisory Services. (2020) *Good Practice for Virtual Board and Committee Meetings*, available online: <https://www.icsa.org.uk/assets/files/pdfs/guidance/good-practice-for-virtual-board-and-committee-meetings-web1-002(1).pdf> (accessed 4 February 2021).
[40] There is legal uncertainty over whether a company can validly hold a general meeting on an entirely virtual basis – see Financial Reporting Council. (2020) *Corporate Governance AGMs: An Opportunity for Change*, available online: <https://www.frc.org.uk/getattachment/48c4ee08-b7be-4b7c-8f19-bcaf3d44e441/Corporate-Governance-AGM.pdf> (accessed 4 February 2021), p.8.

ratifying any previous meetings held in apparent contravention of the preceding legislation, but the question of whether virtual shareholder meetings are permitted remains a live issue.[41]

This shift in meeting etiquette has brought additional advantages. The reduction of travel time between meetings has been of assistance to, for example, working parents and those board members from different geographical locations. This may increase the ability of the board to attract a wider section of society with different skills and experiences, and thus increase the neural diversity of the board.

The use of virtual meetings has also required boards to reappraise their boardroom practices; the Corporate Governance Institute suggests that virtual meetings should be structured more simply than face to face meetings.[42] Company secretaries and governance professionals have reported anecdotally that they have experienced shorter, more focused and more efficient board meetings held electronically compared with physical meetings. The use of software can also aid with information sharing, with virtual boardrooms accessing features such as shared presentation screens, poll voting options and enhanced security. Board members can easily invite speakers from different countries.

With such advantages, it is difficult not to believe that electronic meetings – in some form – will not be here to stay, a "new normal" for board meetings after the pandemic. However, boards should be mindful that a tailored approach may be required – certain meetings may be best conducted in person or on location. Companies need to be aware that not all members of the board may have access to a reliable internet connection or computer equipment, and more support may be required to ensure that all board members have access to meetings. It will be important for policies to be implemented to deal with such eventualities, so that companies do not inadvertently discriminate against any board member. It is anticipated that practice may coalesce around "hybrid" meetings (where some attendees are present in person and others use electronic means to communicate) as national lockdowns ease and a more flexible working environment is

---

[41] At the time of writing, this flexibility terminated on 31 March 2021.
[42] Note 39.

established. With further technological advances, it is likely that development in this area will be fast-paced, and caution may be required to ensure adequate policies and support systems are put in place ahead of implementation.

4. Generation X & Y

The governance professionals of Generation X, the cohort born approximately between 1966 and 1980, and Generation Y, born between 1981 and 1995, enter the profession with a markedly different approach to both the role and to diversity.[43]

The Chartered Governance Institute carried out research in 2018 which described how these generations put more value on the moral positioning of the organisation they join – *"[y]ounger company secretaries see a stronger connection between these pervasive social issues and the governance landscape of the future."*[44] Social representation and social well-being were as important as job prospects, with the expectation that organisations took action in the social interest before being compelled to do so by regulatory means. This backing away from the "play to the whistle" mentality that, arguably, characterised the world before Governance 3.0 is something that boards will need to really understand as that generation progress to middle and senior positions.

There are several things current boards could do to prepare for these issues and, again, they involve process. Giving less experienced but talented colleagues the opportunity to impact on the direction, strategy and culture of an organisation can be done simply by creating or fully utilising consultative fora. There may be the space for an influencer board, a junior forum which feeds specific ideas into the main board. Certainly, as investor focus on ESG[45] increases – see, for example, the requirements of the

---

[43] Rowe, K. (2010) *Managing Across Generations*, American Society for Training and Development.
[44] Bradley, L. (2018) *ICSA: Next Generation Governance*, available online: <https://www.icsa.org.uk/assets/files/ICSA%20Next%20Generation%20Governance%20Report%20web.pdf> (accessed 4 February 2021), p.28.
[45] Environmental, social and governance issues.

revised Stewardship Code for 2020[46] – such an in-house think-tank, in tune with the prevailing views, may be of significant assistance.

In order to fully understand the pace of change and to make their businesses attractive to top talent, it must be uncontroversial to suggest that the board will need to understand the needs and wants of the new generations of professionals. Inviting younger people on to the board or, at the very least, supporting them so that they can be in a position to join the board at some point in the near future is the obvious solution. This means that succession planning and appropriate staffing of subsidiary boards with those who need experience should be borne in mind. Mentorships from non-executive directors to those future board members is also a hugely useful, and rewarding, way of preparing the next generation and also bringing another stakeholder voice directly into the boardroom.[47]

To return to functional diversity for a moment, it is not, whatever the name might suggest, about collecting more information and data. Instead, it is about having processes in place to enable the thinking around problems because of a sufficient depth of challenge and ideas generation such that opportunities and solutions can be found. Generation X and Y board members, children of the digital age and the app generation, will expect information to be provided in a different way. There is already a reaction against 1000-page board packs, which do not make clear what decisions need to be made and in what context, the wood being obscured for the trees.[48] People who prepare board papers, therefore, will need to think in a different way about how they present proposals for decision to boards and this is where a diverse range of options presents itself. Infographics, app-based voting, the provision of bite-sized headlines where high-level information is provided through an app with directors able to click through

---

[46] Financial Reporting Council. (2020) *The UK Stewardship Code*, available online: <https://www.frc.org.uk/getattachment/5aae591d-d9d3-4cf4-814a-d14e156a1d87/Stewardship-Code_Dec-19-Final-Corrected.pdf> (accessed 4 February 2021).

[47] CGI:ICSA and The Investment Association. (2017) *The Stakeholder Voice in Board Decision Making: Strengthening the Business, Promoting Long-term Success*, available online: <https://www.icsa.org.uk/assets/files/free-guidance-notes/the-stakeholder-voice-in-Board-Decision-Making-09-2017.pdf> (accessed 4 February 2021).

[48] ICAEW. (n.d) *Are Board Packs too Long?*, available online: <https://www.icaew.com/technical/business-resources/are-board-packs-too-long> (accessed 4 February 2021).

examine issues in greater detail. There is also the ever-present idea of the blockchain which might assist in, for example, ensuring supply arrangements are a lot less opaque. Board members might receive assurance at the click of a button that the procedures they have put in place are reacting as planned, meaning that their operational overview becomes truly strategic.

There is a lot of uncertainty here. Yet change of any kind will require the board to move out of its comfort zone – something cognitive and functional diversity encourages – contributing to the diversity that is expected by Generation X and Y, a marked change that is the hallmark of Governance 3.0.

5. Conclusion

The concept of corporate governance encapsulates the manner in which companies are governed to achieve their purpose.[49] This chapter has explored the ways in which a board, which dictates the manner in which a company is governed with a view to achieving a particular end, can be made more diverse and how diversity, technology and generational drivers for change shape discussions in the boardroom. Directors must, if nothing else, consider carefully their statutory duties. Can the duty to promote the success of the company be fulfilled without a deep understanding of the interests of all stakeholders?[50] And will they be complying with their duty to exercise reasonable care and skill if, due to a lack of diversity, their collective decision-making powers are impaired?[51]

It is likely that social and cultural drivers will continue to influence the expectations of organisations and their boards in answering these questions. It will therefore be important for boards, senior management teams, company secretaries and other corporate governance professionals to develop policies and procedures that promote equality and diversity and help shape a positive and inclusive future for governance. If, as argued,

---

[49] Coyle, B. and Hill, T. (2017) *ICSA Study Text: Corporate Governance*, 6th ed., London: ICSA Publishing Limited.
[50] Note 10.
[51] Section 174 Companies Act 2006.

diversity in the boardroom can be traced over three generations, the third generation is – in addition to ideas of independence (first) and age and gender diversity (second) – demonstrated in this recent and increasing pressure to answer such questions, to consider the backgrounds of board members and the contribution they make to the board's overall cognitive diversity, both as simple good business sense and as an expectation of society.

CHAPTER 8. THE BOARD'S ROLE IN STRATEGY

Alexander Van de Putte, Professor of Strategic Foresight, IE Business School and Chairman of Corporate Governance & Stewardship, AIFC

Simon Haslam, Programme Lead for Strategy, Institute of Directors, and Visiting Professor, Durham Business School

Introduction

In unified boards, the board collectively develops strategy proposals then delegates its implementation to management and holds management accountable. An annual survey conducted by the Sustainable Foresight Institute identifies five characteristics of companies that are better at weathering discontinuities in the external environment than others.[1] These factors include:

- Having a set of deeply ingrained and shared values that are a guide to action. Values are the beliefs, the guiding principles and philosophies that drive behaviour in an organisation. This implies that throughout

---

[1] Annual survey, 2008-2020, "What drives corporate longevity", the Sustainable Foresight Institute.

the world, one would find a single set of corporate values and these values would be reflected in the decisions that staff make. The board plays an important role in articulating these values and ensuring that they are communicated and understood by staff.

- Being increasingly purpose driven. Purpose-driven organisations recognise the need to create value for all stakeholders, including society at large. This factor only emerged as a critical factor during the 2016 survey and it has since risen in prominence.

- Being skilled at spotting discontinuities in the external environment. Day and Schoemaker (2005) argue that executives tend to ignore weak signals because they do not scan the periphery.[2] Relevant weak signals tend to foretell discontinuities in the external environment and by spotting them early, companies can avoid being blindsided. In a fast-paced environment where disruption can occur even from the outside, it is therefore crucial for the board to have an understanding about the forces that are shaping industries, companies and even society. In the current environment, only by scanning the periphery for relevant weak signals will companies be able to articulate strategic options that allow them to navigate uncertainty.[3]

- Having an experimental mindset at the fringes of their market. Companies need to generate value today and ensure that they articulate a portfolio of strategic options to allow them to compete and create value in the future. By making decisions whether to exercise strategic options in the face of uncertainty, boards will be able to contribute to the sustainable long-term success of the company.[4]

- Being financially conservative. Debt is cheaper than equity because the interest payments are tax deductible and because debt providers (i.e., banks) are risk averse. This logic only holds to a point though because companies need to be able to service debt and pay back its principal. Therefore, long-lived companies tend to be financed conservatively to allow them under a variety of scenarios not to become insolvent.[5]

---

[2] George Day and Paul Schoemaker, "Scanning the Periphery", *Harvard Business Review*, November 2005.
[3] Alexander Van de Putte, "The evolution of scenario planning: A perspective from a capital intensive, slow clock-speed industry", unpublished PhD thesis, University of Cambridge, 2012.
[4] Ibid.
[5] Alexander Van de Putte, "The value of strategic flexibility: A real options approach", unpublished PhD thesis, University of London, 2001.

These characteristics form an integral part of the strategic planning process and therefore the board plays a crucial role in ensuring that these factors are addressed during board discussions. Later in this chapter, these characteristics are examined in detail.

This chapter discusses the various aspects of strategy formulation at board level: articulating the company's vision, mission and values; strategy's meaning and purpose; the strategic planning process; avoiding being blindsided; strategic options thinking and; the board's role in developing strategy proposals.

1. The board's role in articulating the company's vision, mission and values

In most Commonwealth nations and the United States (US), unified boards composed of both executive and non-executive directors are the norm. In these board settings, the board collectively articulates the company's vision, mission and values. In addition, the board also defines the risk appetite of the company and ensures that it is aligned with its vision, mission and values. Vision, mission, values and risk appetite provide the context to develop strategy proposals and is the focus of this chapter.

A good company **vision** should be succinct and articulates what the company wants to achieve in the longer term. Therefore, a vision needs to be specific enough to provide direction, yet open enough to allow initiative.

A **mission,** on the other hand, articulates why a company exists. It's a declaration of its purpose. For example, Tesla's mission is to accelerate the world's transition to sustainable energy, which is broader than just building electric vehicles.[6]

Values are the norms that drive behaviour in organisations. They epitomise the culture the organisation is seeking to create. For example, Tesla's headline core values are:

> *"Always do your best*
> *No forecast is perfect, but try anyway*
> *Respect and encourage people*
> *Always be learning*
> *Respect the environment"*[7]

---

[6] https://www.tesla.com/en_GB/blog/mission-tesla (accessed 15 April 2021)
[7] https://www.teslaforecast.com/about-tesla (accessed 15 April 2021)

The board's role here is to take the lead on the curation of the values. To be the exemplars and set the tone. This implies that an organisation's existing values (its 'actual' values) might be different to the values it promotes ('espoused' values) or indeed the values it desires or aspires to. This places a leadership role for every board member and senior executive to make sure that the appropriate values are 'lived' and not just 'listed'.

The link between strategy and leadership is a close one, and organisations with effective strategies usual have highly competent board-level leadership. The point we are making here is that boards can determine the line of sight for the organisation (vision/mission/values) and take the leading in communicating this.

Different organisations approach this in different ways. For example, some organisations have a very clear and precise vision that acts as a beacon of light on the horizon and a destination. Other organisations are guided more by principles and values. They choose to carry the light on their journey, using this to illuminate opportunities and threats along the way. Either way, a key duty is one of communication and for senior leaders to recognise their role as articulators, promoters and demonstrators of their organisation's overall purpose and direction.

A final thought in this section should go the work of Simon Sinek who in 2009 amplified the importance of organisations explaining their rationale. He called this 'start with why'.[8] Up until this point, much of the communication of vision/mission/values was around the 'what', namely leaders trying to be clear on points they were saying. This remains important but Sinek's encouragement for leaders to treat the question of 'why' seriously plays to the point that people are curious, and can offer different levels of commitment depending on their appetite for the issue. Terms such as people feeling 'passionate' or 'committed' are emotional considerations which will govern the degree of buy-in or enfranchisement. To communicate the 'what' is still necessary, but strong strategic leadership also appreciates that the 'why' is perhaps an essential accompaniment.

2. The meaning and purpose of strategy

Historically, strategy was concerned with allocating resources – both human and capital – with the objective to maximise shareholder value. While the shareholder as the provider of risk capital remains a very important

---

[8] Simon Sinek, "Start with why: How great leaders inspire everyone to take action", Penguin, 1999.

stakeholder of the company, strategy these days is concerned with contributing to the sustainable long-term success of the company. Experienced leaders understand that no static market or industry position is 'sustainable' and the task of helping an organisation sustain success is one of constant vigilance. Directors therefore have to make judgements and decisions within the context of the company's vision, mission and risk appetite. From a strategic governance perspective, organisations need both a compass and a radar.[9] The compass provides it with strategic direction while the radar gives it peripheral vision. This foresight enables it to become sensitised to discontinuities and dynamics in the external environment and within the organisation.

Great strategy involves being able to make the best judgement at any point in time, with reference to the organisation's vision, mission and values, in the context of an ever-changing world. Irrespective of short-term pressure and priorities, strategic eyes never lose sight of the long-term prize. In some parts of the world, there's an obligation for larger organisations to make public their strategic statement. This need to not be lengthy but it offers a synopsis of the organisation's strategic position and its view of future opportunities and challenges. Whereas such a statement does not guarantee great strategic thinking, it does help remind all senior leaders of the importance of being strategically diligent. Failure to do strategy well can leave an organisation making decisions without an underpinning logic blowing in the breeze, totally at the mercy of the market and the moves of competitors. Worse still, the lack of strategic thinking and decisions can see organisations clinging to progressively outmoded thinking and becoming increasingly entrenched and immobile. The corporate sector is littered with casualties of both types. The situation is further complicated by 'clock speed', the rate at which things happen. Change is now a constant and external clock speed – market, technology, innovation are accelerating.

There are many elements to directors and boards being able to demonstrate strategic thinking and strategic ability, and the following hopefully presents a useful summary.

- **Direction and purpose** – as highlighted in the previous session, the vision, mission and values for the organisation provide reference points for any strategic decisions the board should take.

---

[9] A quote by Alexander Van de Putte based on an interview with Charles Orton-Jones and published in a special edition of the Economist Publication, 2016.
http://shapingthefuture.economist.com/redefining-corporate-success-surviving-the-profit-motive

- **The business model** – how the organisation generates value and remains relevant in the eyes of its stakeholders. This includes its position in the supply/value chain, the degree of vertical integration and the scope of operations, and its interdependence on its immediate eco-system.

- **Horizon scanning** – helping connect with the future that's unfolding. This involves appreciating the direction of travel of the main trends and forces potentially impacting on the organisation and exploring the implications.

- **Reputation** – is perhaps the most value organisational asset. Today's reputation is tomorrow's income. Strong strategy values corporate reputation and frames options with this in mind.

- **Stakeholder liaison** – an organisation can be considered as a collection of stakeholder interests, therefore the logic of stakeholder considerations being part of the strategic conversation is clear.

- **Risk appetite** – the degree to which an organisation wishes to speculate is a necessary strategic consideration. An organisation's strategy is its logic for generating value from uncertainty. The degree to which risk is to be embraced should be a key strategy and governance consideration.

- **Resource allocation** – despite a changing world, the allocation and prioritisation of resources remains a major strategic consideration. Resources are often scarce, so prioritising and the consequences of such decisions is very importance. Not all of them have strategic value in the form they are in, and most resources can be transformed into other forms, for example money into capability.

- **Strategic performance** – all organisations are works in progress, and strategy is akin to steering a ship having boarded it while it is in motion. Cognisance of the current trajectory and relative performance is often a very useful starting point when looking at strategy.

The above suggest that effective strategy is born out of a series of deliberations and considerations. To help manage this in a governance context, some form of process should be considered as useful. The next section looks at how the ingredients of strategic thinking can be brought together

3. The strategic planning process

Strategic planning has evolved. In the beginning, the planning process was dominated by financial considerations, primarily around the allocation of resources. With eyes towards the future, financial planning and resource allocation benefited from the use of forecasts. In the third evolutionary stage, the planning process embraced external perspectives more strongly and took greater cognisance of the forces of change. And as strategic planning continues to evolve it is moving from seeing strategy as a noun, i.e. something that is created, towards strategy as a verb, something the organisation does. The value in strategic planning lies in the process not the resultant strategy. Strategy evolves.

Within the strategic planning process there are a number of considerations that help some organisations manage strategy better than others.

- **Cover the right things**: a) make sure the process considers the three elements of strategic space (purpose, resources/capabilities, external environment/changes), b) encourage the process to generate strategic options, thus giving decision-makers the opportunity to decide, c) have an acid test to help sense-check proposed strategies – for example 'suitability, acceptability, feasibility analysis'.

- **Get the right people in the room**: consider how a sufficiently broad stakeholder voice and cognitive diversity can be incorporated in the process to prevent blinkered perspectives, and be upfront about the scope of people's involvement – participating in discussions and consultation doesn't mean democratic decision-making (the optimum number of people to make a decision is lower than the desired number of stakeholders inputting into the process).

- **Avoid being 'asleep at the wheel'**: it is easy for the governance level to be complacent around strategy. Current results are an endowment of previous decisions and no testament to the strengths of a current strategy – often when the results are the best, strategic thinking is the weakest. Organisations become 'path dependent' and unnecessarily constrained by previous investments, current areas of focus and culture, and without diligent challenge an organisation's history can constrain its potential future.

- **Change the pace**: the world's complexity discriminates against organisations whose strategic planning has a single pace. Good strategic governance involves being sufficiently immersed in the subject in conjunction with the ability to change gear. Organisations with strong strategic planning often appreciate the merits of 'feasting' on strategy with periodic deep-dives, and regular 'snacking' by digesting frequent bite-sized chunks. And recognising that strategy discussions need not go hand in hand with strategy decisions can enable boards to see strategy deliberation as a delicious slow-cooked meal, rather as a shallow conversation pressured by the need make a decision.

- **Decide how and when to decide**: linked to the above, changing the pace of the strategy process in line with circumstances helps organisations makes decisions around strategy when they ought to be made, and not when a pre-determined calendar says they should be made.

Jeanne Liedtka's[10] work around strategic thinking provides a good steer on what a strong strategic planning process should embrace: maintain a focus on the intent/vision/goal; grasp the 'big picture' and see the ecosystem; understand how things work – it's the only way to evaluate – and appreciate insight from 'little pictures'; be prepared to challenge current thinking and assumptions; and avoid being hampered by previous decision – when the world changes, so does the landscape and opportunities for every organisation.

4. Avoid being blindsided: the need to internalise externalities

A company does not operate in a vacuum. Instead, there are changes in the external environment that company executives and the board need to internalise with the objective to avoid being blindsided. To avoid being

---

[10] Jeanne Liedtka, "Strategic thinking: Can it be taught?", *Long Range Planning* 31(1): 120–129, 1998.

blindsided, companies and their boards need to be skilled at scanning for weak signals that are relevant for the business.

Unfortunately, when trying to process and interpret information in the external environment, directors are often affected by errors when making sound judgements and decisions that concern the company. This bias, which is referred to as cognitive bias,[11] is particularly important when trying to make these judgements in the face of uncertainty and affects decision-making in most boardrooms. Priest argues that when directors become aware of their own cognitive biases through introspection, chances are that they will be able to make better judgements.[12] In addition, foresight tools (such as scenario planning) can help directors address deep-seated cognitive biases and improve decision-making.[13]

A distinction needs to be made between 'black swans,' 'grey rhinos' and 'white elephants,' three concepts that are part of the strategic foresight practitioner's toolkit.

Black swans or wildcards (or the unknown unknowns) were specified as a phenomenon by Herman Khan (1960s) and Pierre Wack (1970s).[14] It was however, Nassim Taleb who popularised the term 'black swan', which he describes as having three characteristics: 1) low probability, 2) big impact, and 3) can only be logically explained after the facts.[15] Taleb's definition is incomplete, however, and has been developed from the perspective of a mathematician, who approaches future events from a purely probabilistic perspective.

For example, he describes the global financial crisis as a black swan and argues that COVID-19 is not. In fact, it is the other way around. A key

---

[11] Daniel Kahneman, *Thinking Fast and Slow*, Penguin, 2011.
[12] Henry Priest, *Biases & Heuristics: The Complete Collection of Cognitive Biases and Heuristics That Impair Decisions in Banking, Finance and Everything Else*, Amazon Digital Services, 2019.
[13] Drew Erdmann, Bernardo Sichel, and Luk Yeung, "Overcoming obstacles to effective scenario planning", *McKinsey on Finance* 55, Summer 2015.
[14] In 1697, Willem de Vlamingh was the first European to record seeing an actual black swan in its native Australian habitat. Later in 1843, the philosopher John Stuart Mill later wrote in A System of Logic: "No amount of observations of white swans can allow the inference that all swans are white, but the observation of a single black swan is sufficient to refute that conclusion."
[15] Nassim Taleb, *The Black Swan: The impact of the highly improbable*, Random House, 2010.

characteristic of a black swan is that the event in question cannot be anticipated, either in time or in space.[16] In addition, black swans emerge suddenly, without any early warning.[7] Examples of black swans are therefore COVID-19, the Fukushima triple disaster (i.e., earthquake, tsunami, and nuclear meltdown), and the 2010 BP Macondo oil spill. None of these events were anticipated, by anybody, neither in time, nor in space. It is still important for boards as part of their risk practices to try to anticipate 'possible' future black swans, although they cannot be anticipated neither in time, nor in space. The benefit for companies to anticipate possible future black swans is to be operationally ready to mitigate an event, in case that disaster would strike. Thus, it would be possible for companies to mitigate most of the severe consequences of black swan events.[17]

Niall Ferguson (2021) puts it as follows: *"Disasters are inherently hard to predict. Pandemics, like earthquakes, and wars, are not normally distributed; there is no cycle of history to help us anticipate the next catastrophe. But when catastrophe strikes, we ought to be better prepared than the Romans were when Vesuvius erupted or medieval Italians when the Black Death struck."*[18]

Grey rhinos (or the known unknowns) are different in that they are driven by an event or a combination of events that can be reasonably anticipated based on cause and effect. They also tend to emerge gradually and therefore weak signals provide early indications of what is about to unfold.[7,19] Examples of grey rhinos include global climate change, the global financial crisis, and the emergence of driverless vehicles. Scenario planning – plausible, divergent and internally consistent views of the future – is a useful tool to anticipate how the future could unfold and, when combined with strategic options thinking and strategic early warning, helps companies remain competitive in a changing, complex and uncertain environment.[7]

Finally, white elephants (or the known knowns) pose potential existential

---

[16] See footnote 3.
[17] While a good attempt to classify potential disruptive risks, James Lam in his 2019 article fails to convince. Similar to Taleb, his article lacks critical thinking. James Lam, "An animal kingdom of disruptive risks: How boards can oversee black swans, gray rhinos, and white elephants", NACD, January/February 2019.
[18] Niall Ferguson, *Doom: The Politics of Catastrophe*, Penguin, 2021.
[19] Michele Wucker, *The Gray Rhino: How to Recognize and Act on the Obvious Dangers We Ignore*, St. Martin's Press, 2016.

risks to the company. A well-documented example of a white elephant is that although Kodak invented digital photography, the board was unwilling to cannibalise its existing chemical photography business until it was too late. Proper succession planning and board diversity are ways to avoid complacency and from white elephants.[20] Table 8.1 summarises the various strategic foresight concepts and their potential strategic response.

Table 8.1 Various foresight tools and their use
Source: Sustainable Foresight Institute, 2004[21]

	Black Swans "unknown unknowns"	**Grey Rhinos** "known unknowns"	**White Elephants** "known knowns"
Characteristics	– Cannot be accurately anticipated nor in time nor in space	– An event or series of events that can be reasonably anticipated based on cause and effect	– The writing is on the wall
Manifestation	– Abruptly (no early warning)	– Gradually (early warning signs)	– Already omnipresent
Examples	– Pandemics, natural disasters	– Financial crises	– Complacency, lack of vision & risk taking
Mitigation tool	– Contingency planning	– Scenario planning driven peripheral vision	– Internal peripheral vision
Objective	– Operational readiness & rapid response	– Avoid being blindsided or being disrupted	– Avoid becoming obsolete

---

[20] Succession planning and board diversity are discussed in Chapters x and y, respectively.
[21] Taken from a report that I wrote when transitioning from Shell International to the World Economic Forum. Alexander Van de Putte, "Actionable foresight – Identifying disruptive forces that shape companies, industries, countries and the future of competition", Sustainable Foresight Institute, 2004

Over time, what was initially a black swan becomes a grey rhino and when it becomes clear which scenario is unfolding, a grey rhino becomes a white elephant.[7] Consider the current pandemic.

Given that COVID-19 is a black swan, some companies (e.g., Swiss Re) had only identified 'generic' pandemics as part of their risk assessment, not knowing when and where or how hard a possible pandemic could hit. However, once it became apparent that a pandemic was upon us (i.e., a grey rhino), several companies, consulting firms and think tanks started to develop scenarios to explore how the pandemic could unfold. Fast forward to today, when it becomes clear(er) which scenario is unfolding (i.e., a white elephant), companies can accelerate the scaling of previously identified strategic options.

Similarly, consider global climate change. Thirty or even twenty years ago, global climate change was considered a grey rhino. Therefore, companies and countries that could be negatively affected by the potential disruptive effects of global climate change developed scenarios to understand how they would be affected and as the context to generate strategic options. Now that it is understood that global climate change poses a potential existential threat, a white elephant, companies are exercising previously identified strategic options to mitigate the risks of global climate change and to capture value upside from more sustainable products and services.

To put this another way: *"A trend is a trend until it bends."*[22]

Understanding the trends and spotting the discontinuities is inherently hard because humans tend to have biases when making decisions. Cognitive biases, which originate from psychological needs and wants, and logical fallacies often impair a leader's ability to make rational and informed decisions. In addition, Kahneman demonstrates that in the face of uncertainty, decision-makers rely on rules of thumb and mental shortcuts to oversimplify decisions, but this often has devasting effects.

---

[22] A statement made by Van de Putte (see footnote 10) that while it is easy to spot trends, it is far more difficult to spot the discontinuities in the external environment.

5. Strategic options thinking

Strategic options thinking is a way for boards and companies to plan for an uncertain future given a variety of options. When considering strategy in the face of uncertainty, it is critical to make the distinction between endogenous versus exogenous uncertainty.[23] Endogenous uncertainty is technical or project related, such as the uncertainty inherent in research and development (R&D). Exogenous uncertainty, on the other hand, is economic or market related, such as the formation of market prices.[24] This distinction is important because endogenous uncertainty can only be resolved by actually undertaking the project, while exogenous uncertainty is resolved over time through waiting and observing. Figure 8.1 below contrasts endogenous with exogenous uncertainty.

Figure 8.1 Endogenous versus exogenous uncertainty
Source: Van de Putte (2001)[25]

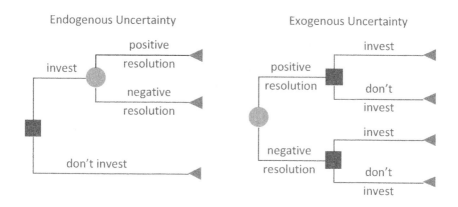

An option is the right but not the obligation. Therefore, a strategic option is the right but not the obligation to implement or terminate a strategic proposal based on certain conditions, often changes in the external environment or the inability of the R&D department to address the

---

[23] See footnote 5.
[24] Peter Cornelius, Alexander Van de Putte, and Mattia Romani, "Three decades of scenario planning in Shell", *California Management Review*, 48(1): 92–109, 2005.
[25] See footnote 5. In a decision tree, a square denotes a decision, a circle denotes an uncertainty, and a triangle denotes an end state.

endogenous uncertainty. During times of uncertainty, strategic options thinking provides a powerful alternative to traditional strategic thinking. Strategic options as an alternative to traditional strategic thinking requires us to understand the nature and degree of endogenous and exogenous uncertainty of the envisioned strategic options and what that implies for decision-making.

As mentioned, strategic options that face endogenous uncertainty can only be resolved by actually undertaking the project. These irreversible decisions are referred to by Van de Putte (2012)[26] as 'proactive strategic options' and by McGrath (2019) as 'Type 1 decisions'.[27] Given the potential significant risks associated with resolving endogenous uncertainties, boards need to link these decisions back to the company's risk appetite and individual directors need to apply independent judgement before embarking on any Type 1 decision.

Given that exogenous uncertainties are resolved through waiting and observing, strategic options that face significant exogenous uncertainties have embedded flexibility to be exercised or not. These so-called 'flexible strategic options' are reversible and therefore allow companies to capture value upside due to uncertainty. McGrath (2019) refers to these types of reversible strategic options as 'Type 2 decisions'.

In reality, many strategic options face both endogenous and exogenous uncertainty and boards will have to decide when to commit and when to experiment and learn.

As part of the strategic planning process discussed earlier in this chapter, boards need to test whether the strategic options are *suitable* given the organisation's vision, purpose, and risk appetite; *feasible* given the organisation's resources, systems structure, and culture; and *acceptable* to a broad group of stakeholders (e.g., shareholders, customers and employees).

---

[26] See footnote 3.
[27] Rita McGrath, *Seeing Around Corners: How to Spot Inflection Points in Business Before They Happen*, Houghton Mifflin Harcourt, 2019.

6. The role of the board in developing strategy proposals

Until relatively recently, strategy used to be a management-driven process with the role of the board limited to providing oversight. This was driven by the fact that management must own the strategy and execute it.

These days, highly effective unified boards collectively develop strategy proposals then delegate their implementation to management and hold management accountable. John Nash, the founder of the US National Association of Corporate Directors (NACD), the equivalent of the UK Institute of Directors (IoD), refers to the relationship between directors and management as "noses in, fingers out". What John Nash means is that the board should be a sparring partner to executive management and provide oversight without intervening in the company's operations, which is management's responsibility.

Developing strategy proposals is increasingly a function where the role of the board overlaps with that of management. Despite this trend, the board should strive to maintain a distinct line between its role and the role of management, and focus on asking questions, advising, and reviewing and approving strategic business plans. Directors must become deeply knowledgeable about the company in order to provide adequate oversight of the large and complex topic of strategy, especially if the company is in an industry that is unfamiliar to the director.

These seven rules of thumb about the board's role in developing strategy proposals are important to consider:

- Clarity of responsibilities and roles between management and the board. The role of the board is to ensure that the strategy contributes to the sustainable long-term success of the organisation. Management's role, on the other hand, is to operationalise the strategy. It is often challenging for new directors to step into this new role and distance themselves from old hands-on behaviours. Therefore, this clarity of responsibilities and roles between management and the board is essential.

- The board as a sparring partner of executive management. Strategy permeates all aspects of the board, from assessing the merits of strategic options that are aligned with the organisation's risk appetite to setting objectives and monitoring performance against these objectives, and ensuring that strategy execution and executive compensation are aligned. Therefore, the board needs to develop a collaborative relationship with management based on mutual trust and respect.

- Continuously assess strategic options. Directors should not just contribute to board discussions based on their respective areas of expertise. Instead, they need to bring their background and expertise to the boardroom and be both a challenger and sparring partner to executive management. In doing so, they bring an outside-in perspective to strategy discussions. They can challenge assumptions and consider alternative strategic options that management may not have considered. But they need to do this continuously and not just during the strategic review session towards the end of the year. Since directors and boards have to make judgements in the face of uncertainty, assessing strategic options – to decide when to commit and when to experiment and learn – is an ongoing process.

- Monitor progress against objectives. Given that executive management needs to own the strategy and is ultimately responsible for its timely realisation, the board needs to set expectations about the strategic performance objectives and monitor its effective implementation. Dashboards can be useful tools to help monitor progress against objectives.

- Ensure diversity of thought at the board level, especially among the independent directors. Thought diversity at the board is a function of diversity in terms of gender, ethnicity, background, and age. Creary et al. (2019) argue that in order to improve the board decision-making process, boards should reflect both social diversity, such as gender age and ethnicity, and also professional diversity.[28] There is significant evidence that diverse boards make better decisions because board members bring fresh insights and are able to shift board culture and behaviour (see also Chapter 6 and 7 on board diversity).

---

[28] Stephanie Creary, Mary-Hunter McDonnell, Sakshi Ghai, and Jared Scruggs, "When and why diversity improves your board's performance," *Harvard Business Review*, March 2019.

- Align compensation with objectives and the risk appetite of the organisation. Another critical factor is to ensure that there is a cohesive link between strategic objectives and executive compensation. Not only will this motivate management, but it will also contribute to the right types of behaviours around strategy execution. Executive sessions and the strategic review typically conducted during the last quarter of the year provide a great opportunity for the board to meet with a broader group of management and assess the calibre and quality of executives. This can be particularly useful to identify potential candidates to succeed the CEO.

- Create value for all stakeholders, not just the shareholder. Without any doubt, the shareholder is the provider of risk capital and needs to be rewarded for it, but there are other stakeholders that are important for any organisation. In August 2019, the influential Business Roundtable redefined the purpose of an organisation and 181 CEOs pledged to create value for all stakeholders.[29] This is in stark contrast with the Friedman doctrine which advocates that the social responsibility of business is to increase its profits.[30] Indeed, we have come a long way with the purpose of an organisation increasingly focused on contributing to the company's sustainable long-term success.

7. Conclusion

The board's role in strategy has evolved over the years, and while different opinions continue to exist, the board is increasingly seen as a sparring partner to management in the development of strategy options, assessing the underlying risks of these options, and monitoring performance against objectives. It is increasingly important for companies to anticipate discontinuities in the external environment and develop strategic options that contribute to the sustainable long-term success of the company. Failure to do so makes it difficult for boards and individual directors to discharge their duties, especially their duty of skill and care.

---

[29] https://www.businessroundtable.org/business-roundtable-redefines-the-purpose-of-a-corporation-to-promote-an-economy-that-serves-all-americans (accessed 19 February 2021).

[30] Milton Friedman, "A Friedman Doctrine: The social responsibility of business is to increase its profits," *The New York Times Magazine*, September 1970.

Corporate Governance 3.0

CHAPTER 9. PROVIDING FINANCIAL STEWARDSHIP OF COMPANIES

Jean Pousson, Managing Director, Jean Pousson & Associates Limited and Founding Shareholder, Board Evaluation Limited

Introduction

That finance is a key capability for a board member is not new, as all decisions in business, whether strategic or operational, are bound to have some financial impact. Likewise, collectively, a board of directors needs to have the financial acumen and knowledge to discharge its legal and regulatory duties in line with what is expected of them. Directors owe it to themselves not to rely on these professionals with blind faith, but instead arm themselves with a sufficient level of knowledge to not just simply understand but also be able to contribute meaningfully to board meetings.

The role of finance, as spearheaded by the CFO, is often misunderstood. It is simply not just about stewardship or control; it is far more strategic than that.

1. Finance Strategy

As a preface it is worth noting that the corporate strategy drives the financial strategy, not the other way around. A typical finance strategy in an organisation would usually cover the following:

Shareholder value. Although shareholder primacy is being finessed to include contributing value to all stakeholders and to society as a whole, it nevertheless remains that board members need to promote the success of the organisation by ensuring that providers of capital (i.e. equity and other financiers) get a return in line with their expectations. For the business, this means understanding what is meant by the 'cost of capital,' often referred to as the weighted average cost of capital (WACC)[1] (or the discount rate or hurdle rate).[2]

Essentially, capital is not free; providers of capital expect a return. As boards allocate capital to pursue their chosen strategies, there needs to be an understanding and an awareness as to what is that cost of capital – how much does capital cost – because the results of strategic investments must exceed such costs. A question that boards should always be able to answer is this: Do we understand how our chosen strategies create shareholder value?

The financial impact of any chosen strategy should be clear and understood by board members. Likewise when evaluating the merits of a number of strategic options, a key metric has to be this financial impact.

Profitability. It goes without saying that businesses need to be profitable. In my experience, directors often know who is their biggest customer, but not necessarily who is their most profitable one. Board members need to understand their profit drivers, they need to be certain as to how costs are allocated across all products, services, even divisions.

Boards should also know their break-even point, i.e. at what revenue level

---

[1] For more information on how the WACC is calculated, see Tim Koller, Marc Goedhart, and David Wessels, *Valuation: Measuring and Managing the Value of Companies, 7th edition*, John Wiley & Sons, 2020.
[2] In most organisations, the hurdle rate is set at a higher level than the discount rate because they do not want to invest in projects with a net present value (NPV) equal to zero.

are all their costs covered exactly.[3] This understanding will also allow directors to be confident about the company's ability to fight a price war, at least from a financial point of view.

Liquidity. The "cash is king" saying has been around for decades: cash is a reality check, cash doesn't lie. Board members need to: 1) appreciate the cash drivers and the cash absorbers of their business, 2) be able to describe the company's liquidity position at any given time, and 3) understand the concept of free cash flow (FCF), i.e. the cash that is left after all non-discretionary activities have been taken into account (including debt repayment on existing obligations). And if the FCF is negative: why is it negative and when can the company expect that to change? A business cannot be cash negative forever.

Although used widely in business, directors should understand that earnings before interest taxes, depreciation and amortisation (EBITDA) is not cash. They should focus on an analysis of their company's FCF based on a sustainable normalised basis. Should the company be experiencing difficulties (e.g. a recession or a pandemic), the board should be able to answer these questions:

- What do the cash reserves look like?
- What is the timeline for survival before the need to raise additional capital or make drastic decisions?
- What is the extent of the cash burn?
- How long can the business keep going?

Capital structure. Funding is a natural point of discussion for all boards. For example, how should the company be financed? With debt, equity, or a bit of both? There are many considerations here as both types of finance have advantages and disadvantages.

Debt is cheaper on two fronts: the interest is tax deductible, and the return expected by shareholders is usually higher as they carry greater risk. Debt can also be more flexible as there are many banking products that can be

---

[3] Once during a client meeting, the break-even point was being discussed. However, neither the company's new CFO nor the board chair knew how it had been calculated; it had just been accepted for years.

configured to match the funding requirements. But debt has to be repaid and banks typically have many debt covenants in place that may restrict flexibility. Going all the way to an initial public offering (IPO) brings in capital and possibly access to future capital, but it also brings other considerations, including extra governance arrangements, different stakeholders, a need for complete transparency, and the risk of shareholder or activist interventions. The existing shareholders' control will inevitably be diluted.

Dividend strategies now become public. This is about balancing the company's need for cash to fund future strategies against the needs and expectations of shareholders.

Boards should always consider two key questions: 1) Do we have sufficient financial flexibility? 2) If we needed to raise additional capital (debt or equity) at short notice, could we do so?

Management reporting (the Board's Dashboard). Financial accounting is subject to numerous regulations and legislation, but the choice of the management accounting reporting regime is a matter of choice. The board, under the CFO's guidance, must agree on the form, the frequency, the level of detail, and ensure the right balance between financial and non-financial indicators. Key performance indicators (KPIs) need to be naturally aligned to the company's strategic objectives as well as its vision and mission.[4] A good way to approach a strategic review is to start with the KPIs as this will enable the board to get an early indication of what the strategy is all about.

Environmental, social and governance (ESG) impacts. ESG reporting is increasingly important for regulators and other stakeholders (e.g. investors) and has become mandatory in many countries as part of their business reporting requirements.[5] The articulation of the company's purpose and culture is also becoming more important to more stakeholders. Increasingly, stakeholders are demanding that big business take responsibilities for this in

---

[4] KPIs are metrics used to track, measure, and analyse a company's financial health (e.g. return on equity [ROE], working capital). See https://online.hbs.edu/blog/post/financial-performance-measures.

[5] See for example, Philipp Krueger, Zacharias Sautner, Dragon Yongjun Tang, and Rui Zhong, "The effects of mandatory ESG disclosure around the world", ECGI Finance Working Paper No. 754/2021, 2021, SSRN-id3832745.pdf.

their roles as responsible corporate citizens. Many countries (and stock exchanges) are now insisting on various forms of integrating reporting which will encompass all of the above.

In an age of advanced digital technologies (e.g. AI), there is no excuse for a CFO and the finance division to be late in producing financial information, especially the major financial statements – income statement, balance sheet, and cash flow statement – for internal or external stakeholders.

Corporation (and other) tax. Tax management is an area where significant financial savings can be made as many countries have very different tax regimes. Capital is a global commodity thus profits can be migrated to tax-friendly jurisdictions rather easily. Though, in line with stakeholder pressures mentioned above, intelligent tax schemes aimed at deferring or avoiding taxes altogether often backfire as society considers this unfair and that corporations should pay their fair share of taxes in line with their corporate responsibility duty.

A 2012 Reuters article, for example, revealed how Starbucks UK avoided paying millions in taxes over multiple years.[6] The company's first response was to say that no law was broken, they followed tax laws, they are a good employer etc. But faced with a public relations backlash (and declining customers) they promised to pay more UK tax by re-organising their tax affairs. Their (legal) practice of profit shifting is considered unethical by many as it contradicts their stated commitment to being a socially responsible company. This is an example of when business and ethics collide, and boards will often have that discussion about balancing the pure financial need against the needs of stakeholders.

Tax is a complex matter; the UK tax code well over 20,000 pages. No one single person can claim to be an expert. Thus, boards rely on their CFO to ensure that they are getting the best advice wherever possible. It is about finding specialists within specialists. And this applies to all types of professional advisers, especially on non-recurring transactions (e.g. an acquisition or disposal).

Risk and risk management. The topic of risk is not well covered in many

---

[6] https://www.reuters.com/article/us-britain-starbucks-tax-idUKBRE89E0EX20121015.

governance codes and regulations. Standards like ISO 31,000,[7] frameworks like COSO,[8] accepted practices like the Three Lines of Defence model, the Financial Reporting Council[9] and other sources do offer guidance to directors. Essentially, it is about risk appetite and embedding the risk approach into the culture, identifying principal risks, mitigation (or not) or transfer, keeping risk registers, having the right controls, terms of reference for the audit committee, training etc.

Risks should be monetised. While it is recommended to have heat maps, probability/impact analysis etc., what is often missing is an understanding of the impact on revenues, profitability, cash flow and potentially the share price should these risk events materialise. Guidelines need to be put in place (e.g. no one customer can contribute to more than X% of revenues).

Supply chains have become fragmented. Consequently, an organisation's points of frailties have increased as supplier risk has changed to supply chain risk. It is no longer simply about the counterparty but also about the counterparty's counterparties' risks.

New business models also bring about new risks. Boards should always ask themselves these questions:

– Where are the new and emerging risks?
– Looking back over the last 12 months or so, what has surprised us?
– Should we have been surprised?

Reverse stress testing. A 2010 volcanic eruption in Iceland spewed ash over parts of Western Europe resulting in airlines not being able to fly for several weeks (with all the personal/business disruptions that this entailed). This signalled to boards to consider some other 'what ifs':

– What if we cannot do what it is that we are supposed to do? (i.e., if we are an airline that can't fly for a day, a week, a month etc.?)
– What if we are prevented from doing the activity that brings us revenues?

---

[7] See www.iso.org.
[8] See www.coso.org.
[9] See www.frc.org.uk.

This mind-set was adopted by many boards who were much better prepared to weather the pandemic with revenues disappearing. For example, Uber, which saw an 80% drop in passenger-trip volumes in 2020, strengthened its Uber Eats service allowing Uber drivers to continue to earn a living while reducing the overall revenue impact caused by the pandemic. The message to boards is clear: when thinking about the worst-case scenario do indeed think about the REAL worst case and not one that you collectively feel comfortable about.

2. Directors duties and how to improve financial literacy

As mentioned, a (non-financial) director cannot hide behind the CFO. At the same time, a director cannot be expected to be as knowledgeable as the CFO or other financial specialists. However, a director is expected to be aware of the range of regulatory and legislative frameworks to turn to and ask questions like: Are we okay with local laws? Are we compliant with all accounting standards?

Nothing prevents a director asking the internal – or even the external – auditors to investigate an item, a transaction, or even a division in addition to the usual external audit. This request can be directed via the chair to the audit committee, or for smaller businesses directly to the external auditors (via the chair as a matter of professional courtesy).

Note that external auditors give you an opinion, nothing more. They are not forensic accountants; it is not their job to spot fraud (although sometimes they stumble on it). As a senior tax partner of one of the Big 4 accounting firms once said: "We give a true and fair view but not THE true and fair view of a company's affairs." A clean audit does not necessarily imply a clean bill of health, and auditors can provide false comfort.

Directors should be confident, and persistent, in their quest for clarification from both internal and external experts. If one director has not understood something, it is likely that other board members have also not understood. It is also important to ask a very simple question: Why are we doing this? Crisp answers like 'It's for tax reasons' deserve elaboration.

The relationship between the CFO/FD and the external auditors can range from cosy to combative. Directors should be wary of 'loophole talk' that suggests taking advantage of accounting or regulatory loopholes. In most countries, external auditors send a management letter to the company after an external audit. Directors should make sure that they have read it.

There are many training courses and technical coaching programmes on finance awareness that will enhance a director's skills. Getting a finance mentor and building professional connections with finance people also helps. Another developmental activity (especially for non-financial directors) is to offer to present the financial pack at the next board meeting.

3. Assessing financial health

Evaluating the financial health of a company is not an easy task. A director's questions might include:

- What is a good business?
- How would you go about deciding?
- Is there a formula for analysis?

It also depends on who is doing the analysis and why. For example, a bank looking to lend will focus on cash flow as they would want the debt repaid, an investor (depending on their investment preferences) would want a combination of growth and dividends, someone looking at a potential supplier would concentrate on solidity and solvency as they would not want supply chain interruptions. But all would go through a process of sorts.[10]

The process that most board members would go through looks something like this:

1. Why are we doing this? (Explained above.)

---

[10] For more information, see the methodologies of the three main debt rating agencies: Moody's (https://www.moodys.com/), S&P Global Ratings (https://www.spglobal.com/ratings/en/), and Fitch Ratings (https://www.fitchratings.com/).

2. Consider the non-financials: the industry, the sector, the company's strategy, the company's age, and all recent events that will go some way to explain the figures. For example a start-up business may well be loss making for a period and would rely on equity capital (from the founders and possibly other investors) for financing as debt finance could prove difficult. A well-established mature business, where there has been no change in strategy or major industry shake up, will show consistency in margins, a profit history, possibly dividends, a level of debt that is comfortable together with a sensible asset profile. The non-financial preview will inform and set expectations of what is to follow in the annual report.

3. Analyse at least three years' figures that are (reasonably) up to date.

4. Review the reports. The strategic and directors' reports can be quite instructive about the company's business model, strategy and risks.

5. Consider the external audit. Are there any cautions from the external auditors? Any recent change in external auditors? If so, why? Do the chosen accounting policies make sense? Have there been any recent changes? Any off-balance-sheet items (e.g. guarantees and other financial obligations) that may not be captured by the numbers? Also check the date of the year end as seasonal businesses will naturally choose a year end that will flatter their numbers.

6. Review the following statements, and any supporting notes, in this order:
   - Profit and loss (P&L)/Income statement (i.e. revenues, costs, and expenses)
   - Balance sheet/Statement of financial position (i.e. assets, liabilities, shareholder equity)
   - Financial ratios
   - Statement of cash flow

Going through the cash flow statement first without an understanding of what came before could easily lead to the wrong conclusions.

P&L/Income statement

Directors should begin with a thorough read of this statement (and all supporting notes). It records how and why the income and expenditures figures change. To better understand the income statement, directors should consider these questions (Table 9.1):

Table 9.1: P&L questions for boards

– Have sales increased? – Is the business profitable? – What about the overhead's growth? – Any exceptional items?
– Are the interest costs/finance costs in line with borrowings (check against total loans in the balance sheet)
– Does the corporation tax rate look about right? – Has that actually been paid?

Balance sheet

This statement tells directors what the company has (assets) and owes (liabilities) and should compare movements from the previous year(s). To better understand it, directors should consider se questions (Table 9.2).

There are four balance sheet items that do not reveal much at first glance: 1) receivables, 2) payables, 3) inventories, and 4) cash. The first three – receivables, payables and inventories – will probably increase in value from one year to the next. But that analysis alone is meaningless. The increase (if any) must be judged by the increase in revenues, and this is where financial ratios illuminate the analysis. The cash figure is the position on one day of the year and could disappear the next day. It is also the result of a year's activities taking into account what the business may have started the year with. In truth it does not tell you much.

Table 9.2: Balance sheets questions for boards

Fixed assets	– Do they look right for that type of business? – Are they investing? – Is the depreciation policy appropriate?
Intangible assets	– Do they constitute a large proportion of total assets? – If they were to be written off, could the balance sheet support that? – What exactly are they? – Could a value be easily placed on them? – Could that value be realised commercially?
Liabilities	– What are the short-term liabilities that need to be paid immediately (e.g. unpaid bills)? – What are the long-term liabilities (e.g. bank loans)?
Shareholder equity	– Have the owners got "skin in the game"? That is, have they invested heavily? – Or have they paid themselves rich dividends?

Financial ratios

While there are many financial ratios that can be calculated, it is important to realise what ratios will inform the analysis for any particular type of business. For example, calculating return on assets (ROA) for a business like Facebook is futile but crucial for a business like Boeing.

For some calculations the methodology is widely accepted, but on others there are very many variations. A director should be satisfied that the methodology is robust and that it does not change from year to year.

There are also many agencies that provide industry benchmarks, but a word of caution is necessary here. For instance, a five-star hotel would be grouped together with a low cost three-star establishment. While they are both hotels, they have such different business models that any comparison would be illogical if not dangerous. Wherever possible, comparisons should be made with similar businesses.

Any executive summary of a company's financial performance should concentrate on the dimensions[11] outlined below. Boards should know whether they are consistent from year to year – because they should be – and whether they are acceptable for that type of company. Margin ratios should also be consistent year on year since as overheads and cost of sales or production increase, these are usually passed along to the customers in the sales price. Boards should consider the following financial performance dimensions:[12]

1. Growth
   - Has the company grown? How?
   - Is that growth sustainable?
2. Profitability
   - Is the company profitable?
   - What do the margins look like?
     o Gross profit margin (how much of every revenue dollar is kept as gross profit).
     o Operating profit margin (how efficiently the company generates profit).
     o Net profit margin (how much net income is generated as a share of revenues)
3. 'Return on' ratios
   - Return on assets (ROA. How well is the company utilising its assets? This is often referred to as an efficiency measurement.
   - Return on equity (RoE). Are the shareholders getting a return commensurate with their expectations?
   - Return on capital employed (ROCE). What about the returns generated on all the capital at the company's disposal and simply the capital provided by shareholders? This is a more complete measurement about how the company is using its capital.

---

[11] Robert Higgins, *Analysis for Financial Management*, McGraw-Hill Higher Education, 2012.
[12] Ibid.

4. Efficiency ratios
   - How efficient is the company in utilising its assets? (see above)
5. Working capital
   - The different between current assets and current liabilities; this is the capital that some businesses require to fund their working cycle.
   - It is a measure of a company's liquidity, operational efficiency, and short-term financial health.[13]
6. Gearing ratio
   - A financial ratio that compares some form of owner equity (or capital) to funds borrowed by the company. That is, how much debt a company has. A highly geared (50% or above) company would mean a high level of debt versus shareholders equity.
   - How can the presence of debt be explained? For instance, is it to finance a loss, working capital or fixed asset replacements? Or to make an acquisition of pay dividends?
   - The board should understand that a lack of cash flow is not a reason to seek additional borrowings. A deteriorating cash flow is the result of something else. It is that result that needs to be understood.
7. Liquidity
   - Is the business cash generative or cash negative from its operations?

Statement of cash flow

This statement highlights the typical cash absorbers and cash drivers of a business. Directors should be comfortable with the cash cycles of their businesses. While this is year-on-year analysis, timing differences would naturally occur during the year and this is where the cash flow forecast and the monthly cash bank statements add the necessary details. All directors should be reasonably comfortable with the contents of this statement (Table 9.3).

---

[13] https://www.investopedia.com/terms/w/workingcapital.asp.

Table 9.3: Summary of cash flow statement for boards

Cash from operations (CFO)	– This reflects the cash flows associated with the main revenue-producing activities of a company, such as sales, purchases, and other expenses. – Adjusted profit
Cash flows from investing (CFI)	– This reflects the acquisition and disposal of non-current assets and other investments not included in cash equivalents. Directors should know what is included in cash and cash equivalents, for example. – Typically includes cash flows associated with buying or selling property, plants, and equipment (PP&E) – capital expenditures (CapEx) – other non-current assets (e.g. intellectual property, investments), and other financial assets.
Cash flows from financing (CFF)	– This reflects cash flows from financing activities that result in changes in the size and composition of a company's equity capital or borrowings. – Typically includes cash flows associated with new or repayment of debt (bank loans), new share equity, issuing/buying back shares (e.g. dividends paid). – Reflects increases/decreases in the cash position.

Directors should also understand these financial concepts:

– EBITDA (earnings before interest, taxes, depreciation, and amortisation) which is used in a number of ways (e.g. in bank loan covenants, as a valuation measure). Directors need to fully appreciate that while this measurement is a rough proxy for cash flow, EBITDA does not take into consideration working capital cash drains, interest on borrowings, corporation tax, CapEx, and debt repayment obligations on existing debt.

- Free cash flow (FCF) which is how much cash is left after all non-discretionary activities (e.g. taxes, debt repayments) have been taken care of.

These and other variables give an idea of how attractive (i.e. financially healthy) an investment is to existing or potential investors.[14]

4. Strategic Allocation of capital

Businesses raise capital from banks and financial institutions to do something with it. Directors often tell me they need finance to invest in the business. Whilst not incorrect as a statement, directors need to be more precise. A typical (profitable) business may have working capital requirements that need financing, a start-up business might well run at a loss for a while as it seeks to establish itself, this requires funding. From a strategic viewpoint, growth of a business will manifest itself in one of two ways, i.e. organically and/or by acquisition. (There may well be other avenues like joint ventures and alliances.)

Before deciding on a growth strategy, boards must be conscious, among other things, that growth ambitions necessitate some funding. Boards also need to appreciate that capital is not free. Providers expect a return on their investment based on the risk profile that they see in the business. Some businesses are very profitable and can generate the returns, and ultimately cash, to self-finance, but most require some form of external financing.

Capital comes in two broad forms, debt (i.e. from banks and financial institutions) and equity capital (from shareholders)

---

[14] These include earnings per share (EPS) or how much each share earned in post-tax profits; P/E ratio or how many years' profits are investors prepared to pay for this share. It is an indicator of value; total shareholder return that measures the total return to an investor over a time period; market to book/price to book which looks at the difference between the stock market value of a business (market capitalisation) and the shareholders' funds figure in the balance sheet. For more details, see, for instance Jean Pousson, "Financial analysis made easy" on YouTube:
https://www.youtube.com/watch?v=kRpfqzD4sNQ&t=180s.

Debt comes in many forms ranging from short-term loans (overdrafts in some countries) to bonds which can be traded on capital markets. Debt naturally has a cost. Banks will charge an interest rate, but in most jurisdictions this interest will be tax deductible as a legitimate business expense.[15]

A. Organic business growth

Organic business growth will necessitate investments in fixed/tangible assets, capital expenditures (CapEx). The methodologies to determine the viability of such investments need to be robust as these investments tend to consume a lot of capital They are also irreversible in nature.

Directors should seek to understand two valuation techniques often used in making capital budgeting decisions: the payback method and the discounted cash flow method.

1) Payback method: As the name implies – when do I get my money back? It does not measure profitability but only seeks to check the time horizon. Thus, it is usually used in conjunction with other measures. This method suffers from two additional critiques: it fails to consider both the time value of money (i.e. it makes no allowances for the timings of cash inflows) and cash flows after the payback period.

But it gives the board an indication of tenure and would assume more importance if the company had financial and strategic uncertainties and would not want to commit capital for any extended period(s).

2) Discounted Cash Flow (DCF) method: DCF helps determine the value of an investment based on its future cash flows. Future anticipated cash flows are converted (discounted[16]) to present value and compared against the present investment. The difference – cost vs future cash flows converted to today's worth – is the net present value (NPV). The NPV guides the 'accept or reject' decision. If positive then it is an investment to

---

[15] For examples of debt calculations, see source in Note 1.
[16] The WACC is often used as the discount rate because this is what capital costs and capital is being deployed here.

be considered, if negative then perhaps not, although there may be other variables (e.g. health and safety requirements) which force the investment. Another measure, the internal rate of return (IRR), considers timing differences of the cash inflows, and should exceed the WACC. The DCF analysis gets corrupted, however, where the inflows are exaggerated and the initial costs underestimated. Good practice suggests that several sensitivities be performed so that boards can make informed and sensible decisions.

B. Growth by acquisitions.

Another method to grow a business is to acquire other businesses. There are many reasons why boards choose an acquisition route. Here are some typical examples:

- Organic growth may have become challenging under difficult market conditions
- Access to new products, markets, countries, industries or technologies
- Product or cost synergies (centralised costs can be quickly eliminated for the new entity)
- Defensive moves (i.e. remove an existing/potential competitor)
- Acquire intellectual properties and/or patents, or buy brands
- Integrate vertically/horizontally
- Industry consolidations, especially where scale matters (e.g. pharmaceuticals)
- Ego of boards or CEO's (and that is not a frivolous point!)

History teaches us that acquisitions often fail to achieve the intended objectives in the intended time frames. Thus, boards may want to consider the following:

- Corporate strategy drives the acquisition strategy, not the other way around.

- Advisers are expensive and get paid on completion, not success. They will rarely suggest that you take a step back and re-evaluate.
- Implementation can be time and energy consuming.
- Directors who have never been involved in one should feel comfortable to consult advisers.
- There will be many side issues that even the most robust due diligence will miss —and these things tend to have a monetary impact – so plan for surprises.
- Market conditions at the time of the transaction are naturally also important.

C. Acquisition valuations.

The old adage that the value of anything is ultimately what someone is prepared to pay still holds true. The context of the acquisition will almost always affect the ultimate price paid (e.g. a family business may well accept a lower price if they feel that their business will be in safe hands and their legacy will be preserved).

Some typical methodologies include: net asset value (NAV);[17] price earnings (P/E)[18] multiple approach; enterprise value, which gives an accurate calculation of the overall current value of a business (i.e. market capitalisation plus debt);[19] equity value, which offers a snapshot of both current and potential future value (i.e. enterprise value plus redundant assets minus debt net of cash available).[20] Extensive resources are available for non-finance directors to better understand different valuation methods, including comparable company analysis (using P/E and EBITDA ratios and multiples), DCF, the football field chart method (which summarises the

---

[17] NAV is rarely used in practice but gives an indication of the intrinsic asset value of the business. This would be totally irrelevant for service-based businesses but more useful in asset-intensive businesses.
[18] The price earnings (P/E) ratio is a measure of value and is usually done on an historic and futuristic basis.
[19] https://www.investopedia.com/ask/answers/111414/what-difference-between-enterprise-value-and-equity-value.asp
[20] Ibid.

results of different valuation methods used to value a company), etc.[21]

5. Conclusion

Finance is not simply for finance professionals. Directors have financial responsibilities and boards and directors and need to constantly raise their levels of comprehension in this crucial area. Pleading ignorance in a court of law will not help. This chapter covered some of the key questions directors should be able to answer in order to discharge their duties. The journey to improved financial knowledge is a helpful and hopefully stimulating one.

---

[21] E.g. the IoD's 'Finance for Non-Finance Directors' training programme (www.iod.com/training/open-courses/finance-for-non-finance-directors), the Institute of Chartered Accountant in England and Wales (ICAEW, www.icaew.com/technical/corporate-finance), the Corporate Finance Institute (www.corporatefinanceinstitute.com), Investopedia (www.investopedia.com), etc.

Corporate Governance 3.0

CHAPTER 10. THE GOVERNANCE OF BIG TECH

Simon Osborne, Chartered Governance Consultant and Former Chief Executive, The Chartered Governance Institute UK & Ireland

Introduction

Technological innovation is transforming global society. We live in the age of artificial intelligence (AI), in which machines and computer systems simulate elements of human intelligence processes. It is the age of the fourth industrial revolution or 4IR,[1] which has been described as "a fusion of advances in artificial intelligence, robotics, the Internet of Things, genetic engineering, quantum computing, and more."[2] Simply, 4IR encompasses the changes flowing from modern technology, specifically internet technology, affecting how we live, work and learn.

---

[1] The person who labelled today's advances as a new revolution was Klaus Schwab, founder and executive chairman of the World Economic Forum and author of, *The Fourth Industrial Revolution* - Schwab, K. (2017), *The Fourth Industrial Revolution*, New York: Penguin.

[2] McGinnis, D. (2020), 'What is the Fourth Industrial Revolution?', *The 360 Blog*, available online: <https://www.salesforce.com/blog/what-is-the-fourth-industrial-revolution-4ir/> (accessed 7 July 2021).

AI can navigate many aspects of human interaction – verbal communication, recognising emotion in speech and images, driving vehicles, flying drones and mastering some medical diagnoses more accurately than doctors.[3] Smart data, the "secure and consented sharing of customer data with authorised third party providers…[who] use this data to provide innovative services for the consumer or business,"[4] is adding a layer of insight to everyday activities, enabling analysts to predict, incentivise and even change the way we shop, exercise – the list goes on.[5] Connectivity and automation have the potential to rewrite the rules of work, allowing people to collaborate with even greater flexibility and changing the nature of our roles altogether as robotics takes on routine tasks. Supply chain technology is developing so that "experts hope that [by 2050] traceability will be so refined that shoppers will be able … to scan a code and find the exact source of a product and all its constituent parts."[6] These changes are upon us and will only increase in speed and scope.

According to Deloitte's second 'State of the AI in the Enterprise' report, a survey conducted in Q3 of 2018, 42% of managers believed AI would be critical for their companies in the next two years.[7] Should we commiserate with the 58% who did not and who might suffer the consequences of ignoring a revolution? In PwC's 22nd Annual Global CEO Survey (2019), 42% of the CEOs surveyed agreed and 21% strongly agreed that AI will

---

[3] Newton-Rex, E. (2017), '59 impressive things artificial intelligence can do today', *Business Insider UK (7 March)*, available online: <https://www.businessinsider.com/artificial-intelligence-ai-most-impressive-achievements-2017-3?r=US&IR=T> (accessed 7 July 2021).

[4] BEIS. (2020), *Next steps for smart data: Putting consumers and SMEs in control of their data and enabling innovation*, available online:
<https://assets.publishing.service.gov.uk/government/uploads/system/uploads/attachment_data/file/915973/smart-data-consultation-response.pdf> (accessed 7 July), at 6.

[5] EY. (2016), *The Upside of Disruption: Megatrends Shaping 2016 and Beyond*, available online: <http://cdn.ey.com/echannel/gl/en/issues/business-environment/2016megatrends/001-056_EY_Megatrends_report.pdf> (accessed 7 July 2021), see Trends 2 and 4.

[6] Gross, A. (2019), 'Tech paves way for transparency in supply chains', *Financial Times (3 December)*, available online: <https://www.ft.com/content/033b9f2e-dfb5-11e9-b8e0-026e07cbe5b4> (accessed 7 July 2021).

[7] Deloitte. (2018), *State of AI in the Enterprise* (2nd ed.), available online: <https://www2.deloitte.com/content/dam/insights/us/articles/4780_State-of-AI-in-the-enterprise/DI_State-of-AI-in-the-enterprise-2nd-ed.pdf> (accessed 7 July 2021), at 7.

have a larger impact on the world than the internet.[8] Alphabet's CEO, Sundar Pichai, said in 2020 that AI will be more profound than fire or electricity.[9]

Business and other organisations are arguably at the heart of these changes:

1. As innovators – developing and implementing new technology.
2. As causalities, or even *casualties*, losing employees, market-share and reputational prestige to new or more advanced competitors.

That raises a big question about the implications of Big Tech and 4IR for good governance. How concerned should we be about this? There is so much fluidity in current developments that unequivocal answers are impossible. However, there are real causes for concern about the governance of Big Tech.

Since the financial crash of 2008, all types of business, not just financial services, have suffered a dramatic loss of public trust.[10] It behoves all types of organisations therefore, across all sectors, to be clear about their place and role in the societies in which they operate and their relationships with their different stakeholders. Boards need to be crystal clear about the business purpose of their organisation; to define with clarity the values by which they expect the management team to deliver that purpose; and to put a governance framework in place reflecting that business purpose and those values, which demonstrates an ability to adopt, and adapt with, technological innovations in an ethical way.

---

[8] Available online: <https://www.pwc.com/gx/en/ceo-survey/2019/report/pwc-22nd-annual-global-ceo-survey.pdf> (accessed 7 July 2021), at 35.
[9] Thomson, A. and Bodoni, S. (2020), 'Google CEO thinks AI will be more profound change than fire' *Bloomberg*, available online: <https://www.bloomberg.com/news/articles/2020-01-22/google-ceo-thinks-ai-is-more-profound-than-fire> (accessed 7 July 2021).
[10] Harrington, M. (2017), 'Survey: People's trust has declined in business, media, government, and NGOs', *Harvard Business Review*, available online: <https://hbr.org/2017/01/survey-peoples-trust-has-declined-in-business-media-government-and-ngos> (accessed 7 July 2021).

Expectations of what governance is for and can deliver have moved on considerably since the days of the Cadbury report published in 1992.[11] The definition of corporate governance in that report was commendably brief and understandable: "The system by which companies are directed and controlled."[12] Some 23 years later in 2015, the G20/OECD Principles of Corporate Governance set out an expanded purpose for corporate governance viz: "To help build an environment of trust, transparency and accountability necessary for fostering long-term investment, financial stability and business integrity, thereby supporting stronger growth and more inclusive societies."[13]

So how can organisations stay on the right side of such unprecedented change and the growing expectations of their stakeholders? How will these risks and opportunities shape the responsibilities of boards and the roles of executives and managers? Should the tech companies attempt or be permitted to regulate themselves and can they be trusted to do so? What role should governments and regulators play?

Boards and executives cannot be expected to get every strategic decision right – but having the right mind-set overall should help. How can boards, executives and managers support this evolution within organisations, teams and career journeys? What are the risks and challenges? There are questions ahead about human rights, data protection, consumer interests and the role of governments and regulators, lending an urgency to companies' need to prioritise learning about new technologies.

1. Having the right mind-set

Let us consider three important aspects: knowing your blind spots; being trustworthy; and believing in your ability to change.

---

[11] Cadbury, A. et al. (1992), *Report of The Committee on the Financial Aspects of Corporate Governance*, available online: <https://www.icaew.com/-/media/corporate/files/library/subjects/corporate-governance/financial-aspects-of-corporate-governance.ashx?la=en> (accessed 7 July 2021).
[12] Ibid at paragraph 2.5.
[13] Available online: <https://www.oecd-ilibrary.org/docserver/9789264236882-en.pdf?expires=1625667782&id=id&accname=guest&checksum=CCAE83772313B6324E4FE31AB08A70F4> (accessed 7 July 2021), at 7.

A. Knowing your blind spots

Disruptive innovation is not new. In 1997, Clayton Christensen famously explored the idea and spotted a particular cycle.[14] He noted that:

- New entrants come into a market offering a different way of addressing a particular challenge through new technology – often resulting in a cheaper, but inferior, product that attracts customers in the low-end of the market
- Established businesses do not recognise this as a threat – and may even be happy to leave the lower-end market and concentrate on high-value products
- Over time, the new entrants refine their technology and are able to move into higher-value products
- By then, it is too late for the established business to learn the new technology behind their competitor's advance – they end up being pushed out altogether.

Does that sound familiar? Think about IBM and Microsoft; Nokia and Apple; or LoveFilm and Netflix.

Success can make businesses and organisations complacent about the need to innovate. As the American consultant and writer, Jim Collins, wrote in his book *How the Mighty Fall: And Why Some Companies Never Give In*, the hubris born of success is the first of five stages of decline. In contrast, start-ups are looking at challenges from a fresh perspective and will often spot the blind spots.[15]

Leaders therefore need to recognise that they cannot see the whole picture and must find ways to include other voices in their decision-making. This may throw up challenges for the organisation's governance structure:

- Is there the right kind of tech expertise at board level?

---

[14] *The Innovator's Dilemma: When New Technologies Cause Great Firms to Fail*, Boston: Harvard Business School Press.
[15] (2009), *How the Mighty Fall: And Why Some Companies Never Give In*, London: Random House.

- Is the unitary board model with, say, just two executive directors, the CEO and the CFO, still fit for purpose?
- Should we re-think the dominance of accounting/finance backgrounds on company boards?
- Does there need to be a reappraisal of the hierarchical nature of leadership in the organisation – for example, by implementing programmes like reverse-mentoring to allow senior leaders to benefit from the insights of more junior colleagues?
- Are more polymaths, with broad experience of life, required?

Creating a more inclusive decision-making culture could unlock the loyalty and creativity of a whole generation of the workforce. The 2017 results from Deloitte's annual Millennial Survey of, on average, 8,000 millennials in 30 countries, indicated that millennials appreciate working in a collaborative and consensual environment.[16] Deloitte's 2016 survey showed high employee satisfaction in 76% of organisations taking a "liberal/relaxed" approach to management, compared to only 49% in more controlling, rules-based organisations.[17] Whatever route your organisation takes to listen, learn and innovate, the argument seems clear – someone will find a new way of doing what you do.

B. Being trustworthy

This second consideration is crucial and goes to the heart of this chapter. The flipside of creativity is responsibility. Like Mary Shelley's Frankenstein, there is a danger of bringing into being something which we do not fully understand and cannot control. Consider just three examples:

First, Twitter CEO Jack Dorsey admitted in 2018 that the social media company "didn't fully predict or understand the real-world negative

---

[16] Available online: <https://www2.deloitte.com/uk/en/pages/about-deloitte-uk/articles/millennial-survey.html> (accessed 7 July 2021), at 17.

[17] Available online: < https://www2.deloitte.com/al/en/pages/about-deloitte/articles/2016-millennialsurvey.html> (accessed 7 July 2021), at 23.

consequences of its platform" and had struggled to turn the tide.[18]

Secondly, public outrage and mistrust was directed at Facebook in 2018 after revelations that Cambridge Analytica was able improperly to access and misuse data from 50 million Facebook users to develop targeted political advertising,[19] with both US and UK regulators and politicians investigating the scandal.[20] Facebook was fined the maximum penalty of only GBP 500,000 by the UK Information Commissioner.[21] What might the turnover based penalty have been if Facebook's offence had taken place after new powers for the UK regulator came into force.

Thirdly, in 2019, Microsoft pulled from the internet its database of 10 million faces, which had been used to train facial recognition systems around the world. The database, known as MS Celeb, was published in 2016 and described by Microsoft as the largest publicly available facial recognition data set in the world, containing more than 10 million images of nearly 100,000 individuals, who were not asked for their consent. Their images were scraped off the web from search engines and videos under the terms of the creative commons licence that allows academic reuse of photos. According to a report in the *Financial Times* on 6 June 2019, Microsoft said: "The site was intended for academic purposes. It was run by an employee that is no longer with Microsoft and has since been removed."[22]

Other data sets have also been taken down since a special *Financial Times*

---

[18] Fagan, K. (2018), 'Twitter CEO Jack Dorsey says 'we aren't proud of how people have taken advantage of our service,' pledges big fixes', *Business Insider (2 March)*, available online: <https://www.businessinsider.in/twitter-ceo-jack-dorsey-says-we-arent-proud-of-how-people-have-taken-advantage-of-our-service-pledges-big-fixes/articleshow/63131559.cms

[19] The Verge. (2018), 'The Cambridge Analytica scandal: Understanding Facebook's data privacy debacle', available online: <https://www.theverge.com/2018/4/10/17165130/facebook-cambridge-analytica-scandal> (accessed 7 July 2021).

[20] Shieber, J. (2018), 'Regulators in the UK are also calling for more hearings into Facebook and Cambridge Analytica', *Techcrunch (18 March)*, available online: <tinyurl.com/wvh8xen4> (accessed 7 July 2021).

[21] (2015), 'ICO issues maximum £500,000 fine to Facebook for failing to protect users' personal information', *Information Commissioner's Office*, available online: <https://ico.org.uk/facebook-fine-20181025> (accessed 7 July 2021).

[22] Murgia, M. (2019), 'Microsoft quietly deletes largest public face recognition data set', *Financial Times* (6 June), available online: <https://www.ft.com/content/7d3e0d6a-87a0-11e9-a028-86cea8523dc2> (accessed 7 July 2021).

report[23] was published in April 2019, including, for example, a Stanford University data set called Brainwash. Footage of customers in a café called Brainwash, in San Francisco's Lower Haight district, was taken through a livestreaming camera. Stanford said it had removed the data set after a request by one of the authors of a study it was used for. A spokesperson said the university is 'committed to protecting the privacy of individuals at Stanford and in the larger community'.

Although MS Celeb has been deleted by Microsoft, it is still available to researchers and companies which had previously downloaded it. But as a researcher quoted in the *Financial Times* article on 6 June 2019 stated, *"You can't make a data set disappear. Once you post it, and people download it, it exists on hard drives all over the world. Now it is completely disassociated from any licensing, rules or controls that Microsoft previously had over it."*[24]

Transparency and accountability are twin considerations which need to be at the heart of new developments and their ongoing oversight. The Facebook/Cambridge Analytica scandal shows that what people find particularly upsetting is being kept in the dark about how their data is used – and research shows that this extends to wanting to be told if they are interacting with bots or AI.[25]

Adam Greenfield, a technology writer who was included in Microsoft's MS Celeb data set, commented, "… there is no way in which I have ceded my right to privacy"; and, rather tellingly, he added that "it's indicative of Microsoft's inability to hold their researchers to integrity and probity that this was not torpedoed before it left the building."[26]

Actually, it is arguable that Microsoft may have violated the EU's General Data Protection Regulation by continuing to distribute the MS Celeb data after the GDPR took effect on 25 May 2018 because there was no basis for

---

[23] Murgia, M. (2019), 'Who's using your face? The ugly truth about facial recognition', *Financial Times, FT Magazine Life and Arts* (19 April), available online: <https://www.ft.com/content/cf19b956-60a2-11e9-b285-3acd5d43599e> (accessed 7 July 2021).
[24] Note 22.
[25] Beckett, H. (2017), 'We have to keep the bots under control', *Raconteur (7 December)*, available online: <https://www.raconteur.net/technology/artificial-intelligence/we-have-to-keep-the-bots-under-control/> (accessed 7 July 2021).
[26] Note 22.

processing biometric data such as faces. Biometric data is special category data under the GDPR for which there are enhanced consent requirements.[27]

Understandably, experts and regulators are calling on organisations to do more to put ethics first, rather than allowing those considerations to play catch-up after the new technology has been developed.[28] The UK's Information Commissioner, Elizabeth Denham, spoke out in August 2019 following the disclosure that live facial recognition technology (LFR) was in use in the King's Cross area of London. She said in part: "Put simply, any organisations wanting to use facial recognition technology must comply with the law - and they must do so in a fair, transparent and accountable way. They must have documented how and why they believe their use of the technology is legal, proportionate and justified."[29] The EU Commission's Vice-President for Digital has opined that facial recognition technology is likely to breach GDPR, where its use cannot be justified by reference to public security concerns.[30]

At a London Business School event on 9 September 2019, the Secretary-General of the Organisation for Economic Co-Operation and Development (OECD), Ángel Gurría, speaking on the topic 'AI for Sustainable Development', said, "To realise the full potential of this promising technology, we need one critical ingredient. That critical ingredient is trust. And to build trust we need human-centred artificial intelligence that fosters sustainable development and inclusive human progress – and I stress the word inclusive."[31] See also chapter 18 for a

---

[27] 'What is special category data?' *Information Commissioner's Office*, available online: <https://ico.org.uk/for-organisations/guide-to-data-protection/guide-to-the-general-data-protection-regulation-gdpr/special-category-data/what-is-special-category-data/> (accessed 7 July 2021).

[28] Note 25, see reference to Professor Alan Winfield, Professor of Robot Ethics, UWE.

[29] (2019), 'Statement from Elizabeth Denham, Information Commissioner, on the use of live facial recognition technology in King's Cross, London', *Information Commissioner's Office*, available online: <tinyurl.com/4r2jkmc4> (accessed 7 July 2021).

[30] Valero, J. (2020), 'Vestager: Facial recognition tech breaches EU data protection rules', *Euractiv*, available online: <https://www.euractiv.com/section/digital/news/vestager-facial-recognition-tech-breaches-eu-data-protection-rules/> (accessed 7 July 2021).

[31] Laurance, B. (2019), 'AI: ethics must be the starting point – OECD', *London Business School website*, available online: <https://www.london.edu/think/iie-ai-significant-potential-but-ethics-must-be-the-starting-point-says-oecd> (accessed 7 July 2021).

discussion on sustainable (or inclusive) capitalism.

Factors which ethics codes should address include making sure new technology operates with intelligibility and fairness and is not used to diminish individuals; either through the direct power to harm or deceive people, or indirectly by violating rights to privacy. The wider context of new technology needs also to be considered; for example, making sure everyone has access to the education and opportunities needed to benefit from advances. OECD estimates that across its 36 member countries, over the next 10 to 15 years, technological changes threaten the existence of about 14% of today's jobs; and a further third of the workforce in those countries will suffer serious disruptions in their workplace.[32] Aggregate those two groups and practically half of the workforce in OECD countries will suffer some kind of consequence. However the low-skilled, who are particularly vulnerable to the impact of automation, have about 40% less chance of sharing in adult learning. That is why the development of AI must have an ethical dimension.[33]

New technology itself could be used to increase transparency and accountability. For example, although blockchain has mainly been used in relation to virtual currencies, there are features of the open source technology platform that could apply to other processes. A blockchain is essentially a ledger of digital events.[34] It can only be updated with the consensus of a majority of the participants in the system, and, once entered, information can never be erased. Incorporating this kind of technology into processes like online voting systems could make decision-making more secure, collective and accountable.[35] How though can blockchain be monetised if no one owns it – who will invest in it? Although there is much work being done in the AI world around creating machine learning tools which themselves are designed to increase the transparency of other machine learning models e.g. models which explain how other models

---

[32] Ibid.
[33] Ibid.
[34] Nakamoto, S. (2009), 'Bitcoin: A peer-to-peer electronic cash system', *Bitcoin.org*, available online:
<https://web.archive.org/web/20140320135003/https://bitcoin.org/bitcoin.pdf> (accessed 7 July 2021).
[35] Ibid.

work, there is a conceptual tension in making machines responsible for explaining how other machines operate!

Is there then a risk that AI may face a public backlash unless researchers and companies make more effort to engage society in this development? In September 2018, speaking to the *Financial Times* ahead of the British Science Festival in Hull, Professor Jim Al-Khalili, Professor of Physics at Surrey University and the then incoming President of the British Science Association, considered that AI was more important than all other big issues facing humanity including climate change, world poverty, terrorism, pandemic threats and antimicrobial resistance.[36] He warned that "it will dominate what will happen with all these other issues, for better or for worse."[37] There is an unprecedented level of interest, investment and technological progress in the field but he wondered if people may feel that this is happening too fast.

Although official bodies in the UK are issuing reports on the subject, Professor Al-Khalili opined that insufficient effort was being made to engage the wider public in a debate about the risks and benefits of AI. A particular concern was that this could leave the technology to proliferate, uncontrolled and unregulated, in the hands of a few increasingly powerful private technology companies at the expense of jobs, equality and transparency. He estimated that AI could add USD15 trillion a year to the global economy by 2030, more than the current output of China and India combined. However, this success would depend on "putting transparency and ethics at the heart of AI development and ensuring that regulations were in place."[38] While previous technological revolutions had not led to mass unemployment, despite gloomy predictions at the time, Professor Al-Khalili felt that there was no guarantee that AI would necessarily follow that historical precedent; a view which chimes with concerns expressed 12 months later on behalf of OECD.[39]

---

[36] Cookson, C. (2018), 'Artificial intelligence faces public backlash, warns scientist', *Financial Times (6 September)*, available online: <https://www.ft.com/content/0b301152-b0f8-11e8-99ca-68cf89602132> (accessed 7 July 2021).
[37] Ibid.
[38] Ibid.
[39] Note 31.

C. Believing in our ability to change

We must rise to the challenge of 4IR because it is not going away. We have to believe in our ability to adapt and change, remembering that there have been periods of significant upheaval in previous industrial revolutions.

The speed, scale and scope of current changes may all be new, but change itself is constant. So we have to cultivate a genuine belief that we are able to adapt and change; and to foster an ethical organisational culture which evidences that belief throughout the organisation from the apex at board level right to the bottom.

Nothing demonstrated that ability to change more dramatically than the impact of the COVID-19 pandemic on the lives of everyone in 2020-21. As recently as the first two weeks of March 2020, long hoped-for changes in attitudes towards, and usage of, technology were just that – a hope. The onset of lengthy periods of lockdown and other restrictions on freedom of movement necessitated a sea-change in the use of technology and the widespread adoption of new ways of working. What has been remarkable is that across all generations, from children attempting to continue their education at home to 'silver surfers' of advancing years, adoption of new ways of living, working and socialising have been embraced.

2. Impact on directors, executives and managers

If organisations need to be alert to gaps and opportunities, what does this mean for directors, executives and managers? Consider that question from the aspect of a company secretary, often referred to as the 'conscience' of an organisation, and the different ways in which that role of ethical guardianship is demonstrated.

Some tasks are more process-orientated, such as the overall management of meetings – formulating agendas, organising board packs, writing minutes and supervising voting procedures and monitoring compliance.

Other aspects call for distinctly human qualities, such as the emotional intelligence and sensitivity required to manage dominant personalities and defuse conflict; or the tact and judgment involved in providing inductions and training to senior leaders.

The current consensus is that the capabilities of AI can dramatically improve the handling of routine tasks – with algorithms regularly outperforming humans in both speed and accuracy, leading to increased productivity and transparency.[40]

For company secretaries, this could mean:[41]

- AI improving due diligence and research; for example, conflicts checks in the recruitment of new directors.
- Cyclical administrative tasks being largely or wholly automated by algorithms – such as lodging documents with regulatory bodies and completing filings; drafting meeting agendas and distributing board papers and minutes of meetings – any type of task that is routine, methodical and fact-based, where formats are repeated.
- Utilising blockchain to create transparent and secure depositaries of corporate records.

A report in January 2019 from the FRC Financial Reporting Lab looked at the impact of technology on corporate reporting, highlighting some of the key decisions and considerations boards and others need to consider.[42] Taking company data from across an organisation, aggregating it into a single communication and distributing it to an audience of investors and stakeholders, who want to analyse and combine it with other external information, is a complex process and typically involves large numbers of people at each stage. AI, and its related technologies, could provide opportunities to drive efficiencies and enhance effectiveness.

Developments like these would shift the emphasis of the company secretary's role, necessitating 'the rise of the adviser', with company

---

[40] Chartered Governance Institute Southern Africa. (2018), *CSSA Best Practice Guide: Artificial Intelligence and the Impact on the Company Secretary*, available online: <https://www.cgiglobal.org/media/mz3f0vfm/cssabestpracticeguide-ai-and-the-company-secretary.pdf> (accessed 7 July 2021).
[41] Ibid. at 6-7.
[42] Financial Reporting Lab (2019), 'Artificial intelligence and corporate reporting: How does it measure up?', *Financial Reporting Council*, available online: <https://www.frc.org.uk/getattachment/e213b335-927b-4750-90db-64139aee44f2/AI-and-Corporate-Reporting-Jan.pdf> (accessed 7 July 2021).

secretaries increasingly stepping into elements of the role that are more complex, and arguably much more fulfilling. This is a trajectory which will be mirrored across many roles – it has been referred to as the need for 'explorers'.[43] These 'explorers' – creative, ethical strategic and lateral thinkers with emotional intelligence and strong social skills – will be capable of identifying issues that go beyond the obvious. 'Explorers' will view the ethical and governance landscape more broadly; not just in areas where legislation already exists, but in emerging fields too.

For the company secretary, as the guardian of the organisation's conscience, those skills will come to the fore in identifying, and making the top executives aware of, risks and non-compliance issues which could threaten the organisation and lead perhaps to reputational damage, corporate liability and even director liability.[44]

3. What kinds of risks and non-compliance issues may arise?

Some of these emerging governance challenges will relate to the ethics involved in an organisation's use of technology. For example:

- **Monitoring capabilities**: Facial recognition technology makes it possible for organisations covertly to read moods. To which interactions should this be applied? Consumers – to check customer satisfaction and improve services? Employees – to ensure that desired behaviours such as courtesy and empathy are demonstrated in the workforce? Where does privacy fit into these considerations? If something is not unlawful and serves a legitimate objective for an organisation, does that necessarily make it right?

- **Employment screening:** Some organisations have been using third party AI software to review candidates' application forms or even to analyse their performance in interviews. What if the individual has a bad day? An AI system cannot display empathy like humans. How do we know the AI system's review of the application form or interview is reliable and non-discriminatory?

---

[43] Note 40 at 2; a quote from Vivienne Ming – Co-founder of Soccos.
[44] Note 42.

- **Task allocation**: The use of algorithms to give different types of work to employees based on their past performance might improve overall productivity by giving people jobs at which they are most efficient or giving more work to the best people.[45] Would an individual be perpetually disadvantaged by one bad day? What if there were extenuating circumstances – a family bereavement or personal health crisis? What about the satisfaction which comes from self-improvement or personal challenge? Board game AI has become so powerful that it is a challenge even to work out how it wins. That is fine for games but what about when it affects human lives and livelihoods?

- **Financial advice** – What about 'Putting the 'AI' into financial advice'?[46] That was the title of an article in the *Financial Times* in early November 2019 which asked, "Would you reveal your money wish list to a chatbot?" The article highlighted regulatory concerns "that the boundaries between regulated financial advice and DIY investment platforms – where the risk is on the individual – are becoming blurred, which would put consumers at risk."[47]

The strength of people's views about data usage should never be underestimated. In 2018/18, the first year after the GDPR took effect on 25 May 2018, the UK Information Commissioner's Office (ICO) received 13,840 personal data breach reports compared with 3,311 the year before.[48] Similar levels of complaint in that timeframe were recorded apparently in other jurisdictions. On 10 June 2019, it was reported in *The Times* of London that the Driver and Vehicle Licensing Agency had sold to bailiffs, private investigators and vehicle clamping firms the personal details of 23 million vehicle owners and the ICO was to conduct an inquiry.[49]

---

[45] Ibid – a feature, apparently, of certain platforms like Uber, Deliveroo and various delivery services.
[46] Fantato, D. (2019), 'Putting the 'AI' into financial advice: Would you reveal your money wishlist to a chatbot?', *Financial Times (8 November)*, available online: <https://www.ft.com/content/132365f0-ff1f-11e9-be59-e49b2a136b8d> (accessed 7 July 2021).
[47] Ibid.
[48] Law Society Gazette, 28 October 2019 p. 20 (accessed 8 July 2021)
[49] Paton, G. (2019), 'Personal details of 23m drivers given out by DVLA', *The Times (10 June)*, available online: <https://www.thetimes.co.uk/article/personal-details-of-23m-drivers-given-out-by-dvla-t9njvlzbz> (accessed 7 July 2021).

This is a timely reminder that data rights are human rights. Appearing before the UK Technology and Law Policy Commission, the English High Court judge, Mr. Justice Knowles, called for the development of an ethical and legal framework for AI: "AI is going to go deeper into people's lives than many things have before…[and] it is imperative that we take the opportunity for law and ethics to travel with [AI]".[50] In her statement about the use of live facial recognition in the London King's Cross area, the UK Information Commissioner concluded: "…new technologies and new uses of sensitive personal data must always be balanced against people's legal rights…"[51]

What about areas aside from technological changes? Emerging governance challenges which should be on an organisation's radar may come from other sources of change and development. They may be made increasingly relevant by the way that technological change intensifies the scrutiny faced by organisations. This could be something as simple as a 'Twitter-storm' brewing because of the way a stakeholder has been treated – perhaps employees have been harassed; or exploitation has been uncovered in a supply chain; or a product has caused environmental damage.

The speed and pervasiveness of social media means that public perception of an organisation's governance regime and conduct is as important as its actual compliance with laws and regulations. However, there is evidence that in some tech companies, growth may be being prioritised over governance. It has been said that "Facebook's prioritisation of growth over governance is egregious [but the]…crisis in corporate governance is bigger and deeper than one company alone."[52] Has Google, for example, established too large a market in the field of online education? Is too much power concentrated at the top of big tech companies which want to behave as if they are still small start-ups?[53] Is there sufficient investment in risk

---

[50] Cross, M. (2018), 'AI probe hears calls for ethics code', *Law Society Gazette (19 November)*, available online: <https://www.lawgazette.co.uk/news/ai-probe-hears-calls-for-ethics-code/5068358.article> (accessed 7 July 2021), at 4.
[51] Note 29.
[52] Faroohar, R. (2018), 'Facebook has put growth ahead of governance for too long', *Financial Times (23 December)*, available online: <https://www.ft.com/content/b9ef082e-052b-11e9-9d01-cd4d49afbbe3> (accessed 7 July 2021).
[53] In April 2021, US Supreme Court Justice Clarence Thomas said, "digital platforms provide avenues for historically unprecedented amounts of speech" and suggested that these

management? Facebook's early motto of 'move fast and break things' may have led executives to enter into data-sharing deals which, in truth, neither party really understood. Belatedly Facebook faced up to the challenge with some 35,000 human moderators watching over billions of daily posts and comments. Mark Zuckerberg was confident that AI would solve the problem but a solution still seems distant.[54]

In the meantime, on 4 June 2021 the UK Competition and Markets Authority announced it was investigating whether Facebook might be "abusing a dominant position in the social media or digital advertising markets through its collection and use of advertising data."[55] This came on top of ongoing CMA investigations into Apple, Facebook and Google launched this year.[56] Separately on 4 June, the European Commission opened a formal antitrust investigation to assess whether Facebook violated EU law "by using advertising data gathered in particular from advertisers in order to compete with them in markets where Facebook is active such as classified ads."[57] On 14 June, the UK's Financial Conduct Authority warned that it will take legal action against Google and social media companies if they continue to accept advertisements for online financial scams.[58]

---

platforms should be viewed as common carriers, such as telephone companies, and subject to similar regulation – see Mostert, F. (2021), 'Your day in court: social media needs a system of due process', *Financial Times (Special Report TechFT: Big Tech & Ethics, 17 May)*, available online: < https://www.ft.com/content/48c49453-9a8f-4125-85d7-94220497d13c> (accessed 7 July 2021).

[54] Murphy, H. and Murgia, M. (2019), 'Can Facebook really rely on artificial intelligence to spot abuse?', *Financial Times (8 November)*, available online: <https://www.ft.com/content/69869f3a-018a-11ea-b7bc-f3fa4e77dd47> (accessed 7 July 2021).

[55] Competition and Markets Authority. (2021), 'Investigation into Facebook's use of data', *gov.uk (4 June)*, available online: <https://www.gov.uk/cma-cases/investigation-into-facebooks-use-of-data> (accessed 7 July 2021).

[56] Competition and Markets Authority. (2021), 'CMA to scrutinise Apple and Google mobile ecosystems', *gov.uk (15 June)*, available online: <https://www.gov.uk/government/news/cma-to-scrutinise-apple-and-google-mobile-ecosystems> (accessed 7 July 2021).

[57] Available online: <https://ec.europa.eu/commission/presscorner/detail/en/IP_21_2848> (accessed 7 July 2021).

[58] Makortoff, K. (2021), 'UK regulator warns Google about accepting scam adverts', *The Guardian (14 June)*, available online: <https://www.theguardian.com/business/2021/jun/14/uk-regulator-warns-google-about-accepting-scam-adverts> (accessed 7 July 2021).

Belated recognition of the need for a new approach by tech companies to ethics, governance and human rights came in March 2021 from Miranda Sissons, the Human Rights Director of Facebook: "There is no question that we, and other social media and tech companies, have been slow to recognize and address their adverse human rights impacts." She went on, "To our observers and critics: Keep up the pressure. We need your insight. Share your scrutiny. Know that we're using the [UN Guiding Principles on Business and Human Rights] and other frameworks to send the message: rights matter."[59]

That message sounds good but only time will tell whether or not these are just warm words and how far tech companies are putting values ahead of value. One way of demonstrating values would be for social media companies to remove the option of anonymity so that users would have to own their posts.

Regrettably, a recent report suggests that business is not taking AI ethics seriously enough.[60] Quoting a McKinsey survey in 2020, only 24% of global organisations across sectors considered equity and fairness to be relevant (down from 26% in 2019), while only 39% rated personal/individual privacy as relevant (down from 45% in 2019). The outlook, with values losing out to value, is not encouraging.[61]

4. Challenges ahead

The *Financial Times* reported on 1 December 2019 that, according to leaked documents which it had obtained, Chinese technology companies are alleged to be shaping new facial recognition and surveillance standards at the United Nations, as they try to open up new markets in the developing world for their cutting-edge technologies.[62] Companies such as ZTE,

---

[59] Sissons, M. (2021), 'Facebook's commitment to human rights', *Opinio Juris (16 March)*, available online: <http://opiniojuris.org/2021/03/16/facebooks-commitment-to-human-rights/> (accessed 7 July 2021).
[60] (2021), AI for Business, *Raconteur: The Times*, available online: <https://www.raconteur.net/report/ai-business-2021/> (accessed 7 July 2021).
[61] Ibid.
[62] Gross, A., Murgia, M. and Yang, Y. (2019), 'Chinese tech groups shaping UN facial recognition standards', *Financial Times (1 December)*, available online:

Dahua and China Telecom are said to be among those proposing new international standards in the UN's International Telecommunication Union (ITU) specifically for facial recognition, video monitoring, city and vehicle surveillance. Standards ratified in the ITU, which comprises nearly 200 member states, are commonly adopted as policy by developing nations in Africa, the Middle East and Asia, where apparently the Chinese government has agreed to supply infrastructure and surveillance tech under its "Belt and Road Initiative."[63]

That story, whether true or not, demonstrates that standards writing gives companies a market edge by aligning global rules with the specifications of their own proprietary technology. There are not many human rights, consumer protection or data protection experts participating in ITU standards meetings, so many of the technologies that threaten privacy and freedom of expression may remain unchallenged.

5. The role of governments and regulators

The big unresolved question is who should legislate for digital technologies. Currently, it seems that private companies can adopt their own standards – Microsoft, for example, adopted GDPR privacy rights as its global standard.[64] Yet what authority do tech companies have to determine, for example, access to information or privacy protections? Is the Australian approach a way forward where, owing to the imbalance in bargaining power between Facebook and Google on the one hand and media companies on the other regarding payment for news content, the Australian Competition and Consumer Commission intervened and the federal government legislated to regulate the relationship? Will competition regulators in other jurisdictions follow suit?

During each industrial revolution, new technologies have led to increased concentrations of economic power, which governments have tended to address piecemeal, so perhaps governments need to intervene. However,

---

<https://www.ft.com/content/c3555a3c-0d3e-11ea-b2d6-9bf4d1957a67> (accessed 7 July 2021).
[63] Ibid.
[64] See <https://www.microsoft.com/en-gb/trust-center/privacy/gdpr-faqs>.

can governments be trusted always to act in the best interests of their citizens? At what point, for example, do human rights give way to security concerns about the encryption of digital messaging or the needs of medical research? What is lacking is a global framework of rules which put people's rights, safety and security in pole position.

The UK Department of Health is preparing to scrape the medical records of 55 million patients, including information on mental and sexual health, criminal records and abuse, into a database that will be shared with third parties.[65] The Clinical Director of NHS Digital stated that rapid access to patient data during COVID-19 was key to the Oxford University trial and that names, addresses and NHS numbers will not be shared, nor will data be sold or provided for insurance, marketing or promotional purposes.[66] There have been widespread calls, including threats of litigation, for the exercise to be rethought,[67] and implementation has been pushed back from 1 July to 1 September 2021;[68] but the mere fact that a government pursues such an initiative, with poor publicity and inadequate explanations of how patients' records will be protected, begs a question as to how far governments can be trusted to do the right thing.

Indicating possible ways forward, on 11 June 2021 it was announced that legislation to dismantle the dominance of Big Tech companies had been introduced in the United States Congress.[69] Then on 17 June it was announced that Professor Lina Khan of Columbia Law School had been appointed by President Biden to chair the Federal Trade Commission, the

---

[65] Murgia, M. (2021), 'England's NHS plans to share patient records with third parties', *Financial Times* (26 May), available online: <https://www.ft.com/content/9fee812f-6975-49ce-915c-aeb25d3dd748> (accessed 8 July 2021).
[66] Dhillon, A. (2021), 'Letter: Public shouldn't worry about NHS data sharing', *Financial Times (2 June 2021)*, available online: <https://www.ft.com/content/2e154302-0053-4454-99fe-1bbfc6bdc4b4> (accessed 8 July 2021).
[67] Note 65.
[68] News Desk. (2021), 'New NHS patient data store delayed by two months', *BBC News (8 June)*, available online: <https://www.bbc.co.uk/news/uk-politics-57400902> (accessed 8 July 2021).
[69] News Desk. (2021), 'Legislation to break up Big Tech introduced in US Congress', *The Week* (12 June 2021), available online: < https://www.theweek.in/news/sci-tech/2021/06/12/legislation-to-break-up-big-tech-introduced-in-us-congress.html> (accessed 8 July 2021).

principal US antitrust agency.[70] Professor Khan has been a leading critic of Big Tech companies so the way ahead for Big Tech may be lively, though a recent federal court decision in the US has shown that FTC litigators need to mount better arguments to win antitrust cases alleging market abuse.[71] It is early days so perhaps the old adage applies: nothing is certain till the cheque clears the bank.

6. Learning must be a priority!

As matters develop, and while boards, executives and managers ready themselves to embrace the potential of 4IR for good governance and otherwise, they must be vigilant and attuned to the potential real-world consequences of these new virtual realities; the risk of reputational risk and a keener focus on organisations' place in the societies in which they operate.

Many tasks which lend themselves to automation are the more administrative functions often carried out by junior team members. However, more senior colleagues may find the transition to unfamiliar technology and new ways of thinking about the remit of their role daunting. Intra-organisation support for challenges emerging from the shift towards roles complemented by technological developments *is* possible: the key lies in learning.

Learning has to become a priority. In the 'busy-ness' of doing the day job, taking time out to get to grips with new technologies could seem like an unaffordable luxury. Actually, it is a necessity for:

– **Safeguarding organisations**: Without the necessary insight and expertise, opportunities will be missed and risks will materialise with potentially catastrophic consequences. Increasingly, business decisions will be influenced by the use of AI and other new technologies. The presence of a specialist or two on the board does not absolve other directors of collective responsibility for decisions made in relation to, or

---

[70] Politi, J. and Lee, D. (2021), 'Big Tech critic Lina Khan to lead US competition regulator', *Financial Times (16 June)*, available online: <https://www.ft.com/content/bee1b959-b2aa-4ee1-8391-d5b5832ededd> (accessed 8 July 2021).
[71] Federal Trade Commission v. Facebook, Inc. 28 June 2021 [Civil Action No. 20-3590 (JEB)].

indeed by, the use of AI and other new technologies. It is imperative to have at least a fundamental understanding of the landscape in which your organisation is operating.

- **Career advancement**: Experts argue about the extent to which technological change will lead to job losses, but there is widespread agreement that within most roles, discrete tasks will be altered by automation and other developments. The ability to provide ethical oversight, and to contribute those qualities considered to be innately human, will be crucial to continued employment in fulfilling roles. Upskilling is essential.

- **The well-being of global society**: It is not far-fetched to say that the choices we make in our interactions with developing technology will shape the future course of humanity. Professor Jim Al-Khalili, despite his warnings referred to earlier,[72] proclaims himself an AI optimist: "AI is going to transform our lives in the coming decades even more than the internet has over the last few decades. Let's make sure we are ready for it."[73]

7. Conclusion

There will always be doomsayers and enthusiasts. The public, politicians, regulators, judiciary and media are having their say. Arguably the most influential players in this brave new world will be those organisations which quietly adopt sound and ethical policies and procedures, bringing new technologies into homes, schools and workplaces, integrating it into the fabric of daily life. Are boards and executives equipped to take the decisions that will need to be made as technological development races ahead?

The UK's Financial Conduct Authority addressed that question in a paper about AI in the boardroom, stating, "The advent of AI is not just a matter for the technicians, those at the very top of firms must take responsibility for the big issues' and 'boardrooms are going to have to learn to tackle some major issues emerging from AI – notably questions of ethics,

---

[72] Note 31.
[73] Ibid.

accountability, transparency and liability."[74]

According to a report published in December 2019, "The boardroom unicorn with a balance of digital, sector and governance skills is still a much sought-after beast. A quarter of respondents want to see more digital fluency in the boardroom."[75] The report goes on: "Being digital savvy at board level can be defined as having an understanding, developed through experience and education, of the impact that emerging technologies will have on businesses" success over the next decade.[76] Given that recent research by MIT Sloan shows that digitally savvy boards significantly outperformed others on key metrics, are boards as attuned to digital as they need to be?[77] The research highlighted that organisations with three or more digitally savvy directors had 17 per cent higher profit margins than those with two or fewer, 38 per cent higher revenue growth and 34 per cent higher return.[78]

Meanwhile the development of ethical, governance and legal standards is not keeping pace. Unforeseen consequences of the development of AI have affected many people in a negative way. Whether those consequences are the result of greed, lack of foresight or understanding, the absence of strong governance standards cannot have helped. So a robust, ethical and transparent approach to the governance of technological innovation must be the way forward. This is where we confront the battle of Value versus Values.

The boardroom and the C-suite are where many of those key decisions will be shaped; and those with an "explorer" mentality – the creative, ethical, strategic and lateral thinkers with emotional intelligence and strong social

---

[74] Falk, M. (2019), 'Artificial Intelligence in the boardroom', *FCA: Insight (1 August)*, available online: <https://www.fca.org.uk/insight/artificial-intelligence-boardroom> (accessed 8 July 2021).
[75] Harvey Nash and London Business School Leadership Institute. (2020), *Predicting the Unpredictable: The Alumni/Harvey Nash Board Report 2020*, London: Harvey Nash / LBS, at 20.
[76] Ibid at 20.
[77] Weill, P., Woerner, S. and Banner, J. (2019), 'Companies with a Digitally Savvy Board Perform Better', *MIT Center for Information Systems Research*, available online: <https://cisr.mit.edu/publication/2019_0101_DigitallySavvyBoards_WeillWoernerApelBanner> (accessed 8 July 2021).
[78] Ibid.

skills mentioned above – are really well-placed to influence and steer those conversations for the greater good of global society.[79] If they fail to do so, government intervention and regulation will be necessary.

---

[79] Note 43.

CHAPTER 11. THE GOVERNANCE OF LARGE PRIVATE COMPANIES

Kenneth Olisa, Founder and Chairman, Restoration Partners and Chairman, Interswitch

Introduction

Good corporate governance is not something which should only concern large, publicly traded companies. Organisations of all sizes and sectors need to be well-governed – and whether they are listed on a public exchange or privately held is irrelevant to their obligations to deliver sustainable long-term success.

In 2018, the UK government commissioned an expert group chaired by James Wates to develop a set of governance principles for large private companies. This was triggered by the recent collapse of several major unquoted UK companies including BHS and Monarch. Since January 1st, 2019, large private companies which either employ more than 2,000 employees or have a turnover and a balance sheet exceeding £200 million and £2 billion respectively are required to report on an apply and explain basis. The report must provide commentary on six principles: 1) purpose and leadership, 2) board composition, 3) board responsibilities, 4) opportunities and risk, 5) remuneration, and 6) stakeholder relationships and engagement.

This chapter explores the importance of sound corporate governance for large private companies and make the case why the 'apply and explain' philosophy is more appropriate than the traditional 'comply or explain'.

The publication in December 2018 of The Wates Corporate Governance Principles for Large Private Companies (Wates)[1] represented something of a revolutionary change in the otherwise evolutionary development of corporate governance from the publication of the Cadbury Report to the present day.[2]

The obvious break from the past is that, for the first time in the UK, the Financial Reporting Council (FRC) extended its reach from companies listed on public exchanges to encompass large entities owned by their founders, management or private investors. The stimulus was the collapse of two large private companies – BHS and Monarch – just as the stimulus for Cadbury was the death of two large public companies – Polly Peck and BCCI.

Putting these cosmetic similarities to one side, the more subtle change is that Wates compels the directors of companies that apply the principles to consider and explain the nature and application of their corporate strategy and, moreover, to do so in the context of the public good as required by the 2006 Companies Act.

This is not a matter of mere theology. It has been my experience that far too many organisations – not just businesses – lack what would pass as a strategy, or even a strategic objective beyond, perhaps, survival and a marginal growth in dividends.

---

[1] Financial Reporting Council (2018), The Wates Corporate Governance Principles for Large Private Companies, available online: <https://www.frc.org.uk/getattachment/31dfb844-6d4b-4093-9bfe-19cee2c29cda/Wates-Corporate-Governance-Principles-for-LPC-Dec-2018.pdf> (accessed 18 June 2021).

[2] Report of The Committee on the Financial Aspects of Corporate Governance, available online: <https://www.icaew.com/-/media/corporate/files/library/subjects/corporate-governance/financial-aspects-of-corporate-governance.ashx?la=en> (accessed 14 May 2021).

This revolutionary change is especially welcome because past experience tells us that the Wates Principles are likely to expand over time to include most privately held companies and their essence will eventually permeate the public sector.

To understand the import of this change and the likely direction of travel, it is necessary to start with a definition of 'governance' and then to appreciate its nature by studying its historical evolution.

1.   What is Governance?

Any businessperson worth their salt can answer that question. At least until they are asked!

'Governance' is one of those concepts – like 'rule of law' or 'personal hygiene' – that is so taken for granted that few people are able to articulate it in a form that would pass muster in even a GCSE Business Studies exam!

The dictionary is no use. The Oxford English Dictionary (OED) defines governance as "the action or manner of governing" and you will have to find a specialist site to get close to a useful meaning. Investopedia is quite helpful, stating that "Corporate governance is the structure of rules, practices, and processes used to direct and manage a company"; while the Financial Reporting Council (FRC) has a position which hasn't changed since Cadbury. It is "the system by which companies are directed and controlled".

What does that mean about those companies that fail – the public and private businesses which have led to the production of so many corporate governance reports over the decades? The logical conclusion is that either they had no corporate governance or it was inadequate.

Given the ever-increasing involvement of regulators, auditors and management consultants it is hard to imagine that there are many deviations from the norm in companies' direction and control systems. The explanation must lie elsewhere and I argue that it is the lack of strategy that leads to the downfall of so many establishments.

Let me therefore offer you my definition of corporate governance, starting with the answer to a different and more fundamental question than this chapter's – "what is a board of directors for?"

It is my position that there are only three things with which a board needs to concern itself, namely, to ensure that the organisation:

– Has a credible strategy;
– Is implementing that strategy to the best of its abilities; and
– Complies with all applicable laws and regulations.

Importantly, these objectives are equal imperatives and totally interdependent. That means that if there is no strategy, execution is impossible, while a brilliant strategy and flawed execution are fatal; and a market-beating strategy being brilliantly implemented, but illegally, will end in trouble!

The best way to comprehend these three objectives is as an equilateral triangle; or better still, as three independently operating but interconnected wheels controlled by a central differential gear which ensures that each is performing optimally (Figure 11.1).

Figure 11.1 Equilateral governance triangle – governance in context

This simple *Equilateral Governance Triangle* applies to organisations large and small, irrespective of whether they are commercial, not for profit or governmental and its three corners and interconnected gearing define where all of the elements of the "system by which companies are directed and controlled" can be placed in context. It is worth spending a moment to examine each in a little more detail.

Strategy: Much is written on strategy definition and development but a former serving RAF officer colleague of mine described it these simple terms: "Strategy is the bridge which will get you from where you are to where you want to be." Roger Martin, legendary former Dean of Toronto's Rotman School, distils strategy down to the answers to two simple questions:

− Where do you want to play? and
− How are you going to win?

A well-crafted strategy will contain all of the technical paraphernalia of budgets, departmental schemes and policies and the rest which define business as usual, along with plans to tackle the opportunities and risks which will inevitably present themselves along the way. In addition, an effective strategy is one which is believed in and owned by the leadership, a fact which militates against buying an off the peg strategy devised by a third party consultancy.

Execution: Monitoring and advising on performance against plan in accordance with the strategy should take up most of a board's time. Intelligent, value-adding contributions from directors require them to have a deep understanding of the business and its key stakeholders – especially customers and staff.

Compliance: Red tape, from the auditor's externally devised rules of engagement to local employment laws, must be respected and, as with the progress of the business, boards must assure themselves that all of the legal and regulatory 'i's are dotted and the 't's are crossed. It follows that a well-governed organisation is one for which the system of direction and control consistently deliver 10/10 for each of the three imperatives

Simple as the above may appear, I have lost count of the number of organisations which I have observed where an obsession with compliance blinds them to any meaningful examination of strategy or execution. Indeed, I would contend that the majority with which I have had a close association had no form of strategy beyond a financial budget for the next twelve months and a set of departmental priorities which lacked any real sense of joined up purpose.

2. A brief personal history of tragedy and resistance

My first job was at IBM in the 1970s. It was a superbly well-run company in an exciting market which seemed to have infinite capacity for growth. Those were seemingly stable times with the concept of entrepreneurialism in its infancy and the word 'start-up' was yet to be invented. On the rare occasions that a colleague left IBM to launch their own business, we would shake our heads and justify this act of tribal betrayal by reminding ourselves that X or Y had always been a bit of a spiv! So when Polly Peck and Coloroll went bust at the beginning of the 1990s, losing vast sums for their banks and shareholders, I and many others again shook our heads and discussed the foolhardiness of working for, or investing in, companies run by people like Asil Nadir[3] and John Ashcroft.[4] Having shaken our heads, we returned to the cosy security of our corporate lives.

By then I had joined another leading American computer company – Wang Laboratories – and was General Manager of their European business whose customers were stalwarts of the FTSE and Fortune 100s. Thus, when the Cadbury Committee published its preliminary report in May 1992, it hardly registered on my personal radar[5] for two reasons. First, as I have implied, my corporately confident cultural upbringing meant that I had no particular

---

[3] BBC News (2012), 'Asil Nadir jailed for 10 years for Polly Peck thefts', available online: <https://www.bbc.co.uk/news/uk-19352531> (accessed 18 June 2021).

[4] Durman, P. (1994), 'Pension Scandal: Coloroll chief ordered to compensate ex-colleagues: Ombudsman rules former company chairman abused his position', available online: <https://www.independent.co.uk/news/uk/pension-scandal-coloroll-chief-ordered-to-compensate-excolleagues-ombudsman-rules-former-company-chairman-abused-his-position-1368330.html> (accessed 18 June 2021).

[5] Note 2.

interest in the prevention of seemingly victimless crimes of bankrupted companies led by people with whom I would never do business in the first place. The second was rather more existential and is perfectly expressed in FE Smith's famous epigram – "there is nothing like the prospect of death for concentrating the mind".

In May 1992 the venerable Wang Laboratories whose eponymous founding genius, Dr Wang, had died two years earlier, was only three months away from going bust with the loss of all shareholder value and most jobs, including mine.

With my mind concentrated elsewhere, I paid scant attention to the furious backlash against the Cadbury recommendations as I set about recovering from the shock of seeing my employer disappear. My solution was to found my own company – an act which by the late 1990s was no longer considered dodgy, but rather a badge of courage! In truth, what little that I did observe of Cadbury sounded deeply esoteric and pretty Big Brotherish in my new capacity as start-up founder. That view was amplified by the cacophony of antipathy which greeted the report's recommendations.

Today, in the manner of someone who has one of their decade old social media posts dragged into public view, I am now embarrassed to admit that I felt the idea of laying down rules about how businesses should conduct themselves was insulting. Surely that was what the market was for? At this point, the pedant will point out that Cadbury was rooted in principles rather than rules, but I confess that the subtlety of that distinction went over my head as it appeared to do for most commentators and directors.

So confident was I in my view that even the collapse of BCCI and the Maxwell empire didn't shake it. Indeed, they reinforced my conviction that investors in businesses run by people like Abadi and Maxwell got what they deserved. Whatever had happened to caveat emptor? I didn't limit my disdain to mere commentary when a company, on whose board I served, proposed setting up a Governance Committee. Initially I opposed it and only agreed to support its formation on the condition that its members received no incremental remuneration.

Mea culpa! I cite youth and inexperience in my libertarian defence, coupled with a failure to analyse the deeper messages of the demise of those companies, not least of which was the one I had worked for – Wang Laboratories.

By now, the sharp-eyed reader will likely be wondering what this brief history of personal tragedy and resistance has to do with the governance of large private companies!

The answer lies in two aspects of my own salutary tale:

- Businesses' failure is far from victimless, whether the ultimate ownership is held publicly or privately;
- Distinctions between public and private are marginal at best in most regards and especially in the context of social responsibility and governance.

Polly Peck, Coloroll, BCCI, Maxwell and Wang were very different entities in terms of their purpose, industrial sectors, areas of operation and ownership models. However, in addition to their unseemly ends, they shared one other common factor – each was led by a mercurial leader whose word was law. This meant that their inevitably flimsy, governance mechanisms, though nominally intended to protect shareholders' interests, were designed more to implement their Dear Leaders' will than to provide checks or balances. Board members were more akin to courtiers than critical friends and were far removed from what we would recognise today as effective non-executive directors. In reality, the distinction between public and private is limited solely to the nature of the shareholders – it is pretty much just a technical matter. If an employee loses its job, or a supplier's invoice go unpaid, it matters not who owns the company's shares!

Those mercurial leaders from the convicted Asil Nadir to the irreproachable Dr Wang offered their stakeholders – especially customers, supply chains and employees – little or no effective engagement with the way the businesses were run. Yet everyone suffered when bankruptcy struck. Because those stakeholders had families and lived in communities, the toxic ripple effect of the companies' descent from hero to zero spread far and wide. Plus, of course, the losses experienced by the pension funds invested in these companies visited another blow on the public at large.

The more recent disappearances of BHS and Monarch, with their seismic impact on the lives and livelihoods of so many, merely serve to demonstrate why a civilised society has a right to set standards for the governance of <u>all</u> companies irrespective of their ownership models.

The obvious conclusion from the above is that insomuch as they are the natural descendants of Cadbury – born out of privately owned corporate collapses rather than their listed cousins – the Wates Principles were long overdue. That this is a truism possibly explains why they received a far better (or rather a far less bad) reaction from the business community.

Perhaps one further reason for the reaction to Wates is that the global interest in ESG is clear evidence that society in its widest sense is taking an increasing interest in, and engagement with, the conduct of business. As a result, it has become generally accepted that private companies depend on society for their success, so society has a right to set the operational parameters within which those entities must function.

3. From defence to offence

As I hope is becoming apparent, it is a mistake to view Wates as an uncontroversial extension of the regulatory governance boundary into the uncharted territory of businesses not listed on an exchange. It has far greater symbolic and substantive value.

Cadbury was essentially a defensive move. UK-listed businesses seemed to be falling like nine pins and examination of their entrails exposed governance misdemeanours which were as egregious as they were chronic, but which were only exposed to the light of day when the music stopped and denial was no longer an option. In a sense, that was unsurprising. What shocked the system was not that the signs had been present for a long time but that they had gone uncalibrated for years (consider the Bower[6] or Preston[7] biographies of Robert Maxwell for proof that the excesses were in plain sight).

---

[6] Bower, T. (1992), Maxwell: The Outsider, New York: Viking; see also (1995), Maxwell: The Final Verdict, London: HarperCollins.
[7] Preston, J. (2021), Fall: The Mystery of Robert Maxwell, New York: Viking.

Cadbury's genius was to avoid the natural, but flawed, temptation to codify a set of operating rules. Instead, it laid down a set of principles to which public companies were mandated to adhere. This philosophical approach was later bolstered by the Higgs' revisions to the UK Combined Code on Corporate Governance which introduced the novel concept of 'comply or explain'.[8] This contrasted with other jurisdictions which have adopted rules-based formulae – ranging from Sarbanes-Oxley in the USA[9] to the Nigerian FRC's 'apply and explain' dictum.[10] I have experience as a company director under all three regimes and can confirm that while no system has totally eliminated unacceptable governance practices, it is much harder to find a way round a principle than it is to circumvent a rule.

This rules/principles dichotomy is a critical one and is well illustrated by a small experiment in conduct with which I was personally involved – the MPs' Expenses scandal.[11] Over a torrid few months in 2009, as details of moats and duck houses raised the collective blood pressure, parliamentarians threw petrol on the fire by defending their innocence on the grounds that they couldn't have done anything wrong (by definition) because they "had followed the rules." I was an inaugural member of IPSA (Independent Parliamentary Standards Authority) charged with cleaning up the mess and can confirm that the courts shared the public's view that principles trumped rules and several Honourable Members went to jail for infringing the fundamental values by which they had sworn to abide; irrespective of whether or not they had discovered a clever way to interpret a poorly drafted rule to their advantage.

Because the trigger for Cadbury had been examples of gross financial misreporting, the report's objective was to restore Britain's reputation for probity by describing what good looked like and then requiring directors to report to their shareholders on how far they had complied with those standards. All with a principal focus in the areas of financial reporting.

---

[8] Financial Reporting Council (2003), The Combined Code on Corporate Governance, available online: <https://www.frc.org.uk/getattachment/edce667b-16ea-41f4-a6c7-9c30db75bb0c/Combined-Code-2003.pdf> (accessed 18 June 2021).

[9] See <https://sarbanes-oxley-act.com/>.

[10] See <https://www.financialreportingcouncil.gov.ng/faqs-on-nccg-2018-2/>.

[11] Maitlis, E. (2019), 'MPs' expenses: The scandal that changed Britain', available online: <https://www.bbc.co.uk/news/uk-47669589> (accessed 18 June 2021).

Section 1.2 of the introduction to the first report left no doubt about the report's target:

"The Committee's recommendations are focused on the control and reporting functions of boards, and on the role of auditors. This reflects the Committee's purpose, which was to review those aspects of corporate governance specifically related to financial reporting and accountability."[12]

To be fair, Cadbury believed that, rather than being important for its own sake, top quality and accountable financial management was good for business and the nation. Section 1.2 continued:

"Our proposals do, however, seek to contribute positively to the promotion of good corporate governance as a whole."

Since my ignominious departure from full-time employment all those years ago I have enjoyed the privilege of serving on many boards, both public and private and on both sides of the Atlantic. During those years, that privilege has allowed me to observe some of the best and the worst of board performances. It is a matter of great regret to me that despite the original Cadbury Code explicitly hoping to contribute positively to good corporate governance as a whole, too many directors saw the Code – and therefore governance – as narrowly focused on financial reporting and accountability; essentially a sort of unstructured textual approach to Sarbanes-Oxley's rigid spreadsheet methodology. A myopia which perpetuates the myth that rules can prevent bad behaviour. Unfortunately, this led to so many directors viewing governance with the same enthusiasm with which they probably viewed school rules, not as a repository of wisdom constructed for the benefit of all, but as a set of unwelcome constraints.

Put simply, 'governance' came to be considered as a synonym for 'compliance'. It isn't.

As I have laid out above, governance does include the management of a company's compliance obligations, but the scope of its mechanisms are far more extensive.

---

[12] Note 2.

Rather than being seen as an end in its own right, governance is the mechanism which regulates the conduct of the directors and those who report to them and facilitates the collective delivery of the three wheels of strategy, execution and compliance.

Wates is not the first attempt by governance gurus to promote thinking and action around strategy. Cadbury made passing reference to it and subsequent evolutions of the Code increased mention of strategy, but always as subordinate to structure and process. Indeed, the FRC currently mandates that a public entity's annual report should include a strategic report and provides guidance for its authors.[13]

Wates recognises the central importance of strategy i.e. that without one, the board can't monitor its execution – and subliminally acknowledges that a strategy's centrality to competitive advantage makes mandating the form of its explanation wholly inappropriate. Thus Wates' guidance pretty much limits its instruction to the requirement to have one.[14]

As mentioned above, Roger Martin has reduced strategy to two questions, of which the second, "how are we going to win?", is the more important. To Illustrate this, think of a football team's approach to success. If their captain adopts a defensive game plan with the strategic objective (aka purpose) of avoiding conceding any goals, the team is unlikely to win any matches. In soccer, winning entails racking up more goals than the other side. Therefore a plan that concentrates on avoiding goals rather than scoring them is unlikely to be a winner. Yet so much of the pre-Wates governance guidance has focused on how companies can avoid losing by conforming to a norm, rather than how they can achieve innovation and victory by following Schumpeter's dictum of 'creative destruction' [15].

By placing strategy front and centre, Wates gives boards permission to listen to the voices proposing expansion and change <u>as well as</u> heeding

---

[13] Financial Reporting Council (2018), Guidance on the Strategic Report, available online: <https://www.frc.org.uk/getattachment/fb05dd7b-c76c-424e-9daf-4293c9fa2d6a/Guidance-on-the-Strategic-Report-31-7-18.pdf> (accessed 18 June 2021), p. 12.
[14] Note 1.
[15] Schumpeter, J. (1942), Capitalism, Socialism and Democracy, London: Routledge.

those urging caution and stasis. Or, better put, Wates instructs the board of large private companies to tackle all three points of the *Equilateral Governance Triangle*.

4. Quo Vadis?

Early in my career I attended a training session on strategy. I had low expectations as, like so many young executives, I assumed that the topic would be a dry and theoretical waste of time when I could be getting on with the actions on my seemingly never-ending To Do list. The presenter shared my military colleague's definition of a strategy, defining how to get from where you are to where you want to go. He then won my life-long belief in the importance of knowing your destination with the following pithy aphorism:

> "There is only one advantage of not knowing where you're going – you can't get lost."

He went on to differentiate between a plan and a strategy – the latter contains lots of the former – and the need to understand the 'terrain' through which you intend to travel. That sage advice was enshrined in the step-change Companies Act 2006. In this probable world-first, section 172 codified directors' responsibility for a version of a destination and the terrain.

172 Duty to promote the success of the company

(1) A director of a company must act in the way he considers, in good faith, would be most likely to promote the success of the company for the benefit of its members as a whole, and in doing so have regard (amongst other matters) to

    (a) the likely consequences of any decision in the long term,

    (b) the interests of the company's employees,

    (b) the need to foster the company's business relationships with suppliers, customers and others,

    (c) the impact of the company's operations on the community and the environment,

(d) the desirability of the company maintaining a reputation for high standards of business conduct, and

(e) the need to act fairly as between members of the company.

At first view, the destination might seem a little woolly – "to promote the success of the company" – but when you add having regard to impacts on a range of stakeholders identified in a set of subsidiary provisions, it starts to have bite. Test its power by inserting the word "not" between "would" and "be" or by substituting "ignore" for "have regard for" and one sees how far the 2006 Act moved away from the narrow interests of shareholders or creditors.

Clear though this is, because these key points are principles open to wide interpretation of execution if not of purpose, the law leaves it to boards to decide how to discharge their duties. This makes total sense – business is a competitive sport. This means that as for any competitive activity it is entirely right that players are subject to rules but how they compete within them is a matter of seeking competitive advantage.

Perhaps surprisingly, it has been my experience that many boards struggle with that fundamental concept, placing survival as their only real objective. This is despite section 172 providing more than a clue or two that a board should consider its purpose to be rather more noble than merely not going bust! Read properly, this section offers a framework within which a board can set and give a meaningful explanation of its intentions to deliver competitive advantage and its beneficial impact on its employees, suppliers, customers, communities and the environment. Tragically, all too often, boards eschew this opportunity, resorting in their annual reports to a boilerplate declaration (often displaying the lack of sincerity evident in third party authorship) limited to cataloguing what activities they have undertaken under each sub-heading. Put another way, all too often the noble objective contained in section 172 is reduced to vicarious virtue signalling.

But all is not lost! Although Wates, like Cadbury, was born out of seismic corporate failures, it was able to move away from Cadbury's essentially defensive prescriptions focusing on financial management to cover a broader canvas much more in line with the Companies Act. To be fair to Cadbury, this was made easy for Wates because so much of the responsibility for setting and monitoring standards of financial management has been placed, entirely appropriately, on the shoulders of the accounting profession and, specifically, on those aristocrats of caution and defence, a company's auditors. This opened up the opportunity for Wates to adopt an offensive posture by laying out six forward-facing areas of governance which should be attended to by any large private company.

Flick through the pages of an average company report and the reader will be presented with volumes of information, most of which will be descriptions of past events. In one sense, that isn't a surprise – since they began, annual reports have been a record of the past twelve months. Unfortunately, this obsession with the past, all too often, infects boards and their perspectives. As my dear friend, the late Robert Bittlestone, founder of Metapraxis, was wont to point out, "It is entirely possible to drive a car solely by reference to the rear-view mirror. But it's far from efficient and fraught with danger." The 2006 Act opened up the opportunity for radical change. By presenting an unequivocal widening of stakeholder responsibility and ethical conduct, boards had the opportunity to do a metaphorical 180 handbrake turn and start to describe where they were going instead of where they were coming from.

Promoting the success of a company – public or private – doesn't happen by accident or by extrapolation of past performance. It can only result from the effective execution of a plan which takes into account the many forces which possess the power to impede or accelerate a company's journey.

Somewhere along the evolutionary route from Cadbury to the present day, the UK government began to appreciate what I call the Polly Peck/Wang effect; namely that the failure of companies has a wide societal impact reaching far beyond the damage done to creditors and/or shareholders. Moreover, they realised that the negative consequences of poor governance weren't confined to publicly listed entities, what might be called the BHS amendment to the Polly Peck/Wang effect.

5. The Wates principles

As a result, the then Secretary of State for Business, Greg Clark, initiated a consultation on the wisdom of extending the regulatory reach of the FRC to encompass the governance of large private companies.[16]

Clark set up a committee chaired by James Wates CBE of the eponymous privately-owned construction company and in 2018, the FRC published the *"The Wates Corporate Governance Principles for Large Private Companies"*.[17]

If the 2006 Act widened UK company directors' responsibilities, the six Wates principles architected a framework specifically designed to guide the boards of large privately held businesses either employing over 2,000 employees or with turnover exceeding £200 million coupled with a balance sheet of more than £2 billion.[18]

Wates defines the principles in these terms:

- **Purpose and leadership**: An effective board develops and promotes the purpose of a company, and ensures that its values, strategy and culture align with that purpose.

- **Board composition**: Effective board composition requires an effective chair and a balance of skills, backgrounds, experience and knowledge, with individual directors having sufficient capacity to make a valuable contribution. The size of a board should be guided by the scale and complexity of the company.

- **Director responsibilities**: The board and individual directors should have a clear understanding of their accountability and responsibilities. The board's policies and procedures should support effective decision-making and independent challenge.

- **Opportunity and risk**: A board should promote the long-term sustainable success of the company by identifying opportunities to create and preserve value, and establishing oversight for the identification and mitigation of risks.

---

[16] See <https://www.frc.org.uk/consultation-list/2018/consultation-the-wates-corporate-governance-princ>.
[17] Note 1.
[18] The Companies (Miscellaneous Reporting) Regulations 2018, Regulation 14.

- **Remuneration**: A board should promote executive remuneration structures aligned to the long-term sustainable success of a company, taking into account pay and conditions elsewhere in the company.
- **Stakeholder relationships and engagement**: Directors should foster effective stakeholder relationships aligned to the company's purpose. The board is responsible for overseeing meaningful engagement with stakeholders, including the workforce, and having regard to their views when taking decisions.[19]

The big exam question for directors of large private entities is "What do we do with Wates?"

To answer, it is helpful to break down the practice of governance into its two components – the 'Whys' and the 'Hows':

- Why should a company or director take a particular action; and
- How should that action be implemented?

The fundamental principles of good governance as described in the *Equilateral Governance Triangle* (the 'Whys') apply to the boards of all organisations, irrespective of size or purpose. The differences emerge between commercial and charity, public and private, large and small once one starts to contemplate the 'Hows'.

To make the obvious point, the resources available to a FTSE100 company permit it to build highly sophisticated internal mechanisms and relationships, while those available to a two-person start-up charity are obviously de minimis. However, irrespective of the depth or otherwise of the 'Hows', the principles (the 'Whys') remain the same.

Let me illustrate by examining two elements of the Wates Principles – board composition and stakeholder relationships. Both of these suffer from the danger of being seen as jobs for HR and Marketing at best and clichés at worst.

---

[19] Note 1.

The foundation for this analysis is the axiomatic premise that any organisation that doesn't empathise with its principal stakeholders – customers, supply chains, employees, recruitment pools, local communities and, if they have them, regulators, are at a competitive disadvantage when compared to businesses that do.

How does an organisation gain that empathy? Simple – by having people on their team whose lived experiences give them the visceral appreciation of those stakeholders' expectations and behaviours.

How does it attract employees with that depth of understanding? Simple again, by demonstrating that the organisation welcomes and nurtures people with the widest spread of relevant knowledge and backgrounds.

Where is the best place for people to be to be able to communicate that message? Answer, the board; hence the importance of ensuring that a board includes (or at least has easy access to) a spread of experiences and talents which supports its strategic ambitions.

But the point goes deeper. With an inclusive enterprise locked and loaded with the wherewithal to relate to its stakeholders, it follows naturally that for this asset to be effective, those stakeholders need to know what they are dealing with – and so stakeholder relations become a priority; not as a matter of compliance but as one of fundamental competitive advantage. This is true irrespective of the size, sector or purpose of the organisation.

6. Wates Applied

How a board chooses to interpret and apply the Wates Principles to their day-to-day operations is a matter for individual companies – that is the essence of competitive advantage – so there can be no formula or boilerplate to tell directors what to do (although there are legion management consultants who will willingly try!). Answering the big exam question calls for those in an organisation's cockpit – the leadership – to debate and decide on its purpose and then how to configure the various assets defined by the Wates Principles in ways which give the highest likelihood of playing to win – the 'Why' and the 'How'.

In the manner of solving all complex matters, cracking it requires a proven framework which can be deconstructed to expose its constituent elements and then to construct the solution. The *Equilateral Governance Triangle* can be used as just such a framework in order to produce the offensive equivalent of an organisation's defensive risk register. Each of the Wates Principles can be classified according to its relevance to one or more of the triangle's points.

In the hypothetical example below, the board have prioritised four of the Wates Principles as being of high importance to strategy and three of high importance to execution. By contrast, they have resolved that the six principles are of minor relevance to compliance which reflects the shift in governance emphasis achieved by the Wates Principles, namely that they are substantive contributors to strategy and only marginally associated with compliance (Figure 11.2).

Figure 11.2 Wates Principles prioritisation matrix
Source: The Corporate Governance Principles for Large Private Companies, 2018

	Strategy	Execution	Compliance
1. Purpose and leadership	High	Medium	None
2. Board composition	High	Medium	Low
3. Director responsibilities	Low	Medium	Low
4. Opportunity and risk	High	High	None
5. Remuneration	Low	High	Low
6. Stakeholder relationships	High	High	Low

Key Importance/Relevance	High ●	Medium ◐	Low ◔	None ○

A board which achieves consensus on its Wates priorities as illustrated above can then proceed to assure itself that their plans, implementation and compliance are assigned the detail and priority demanded by the collective weighting. The danger with all strategy exercises is that they have a short half-life and a long shelf life. A board's version of the above table provides a handy 'pledge card' to help ensure that the organisation retains its commitments and attends to them according to the agreed prioritisation. In this way, Wates becomes a living mechanism and not an annual review.

7. Conclusion

Businesses are part of society, so it is reasonable for their conduct to be subject to democratic constraints. In addition to obvious responsibilities such as paying taxes and complying with health and safety requirements, the prevention of destructive collapses of businesses has, since Cadbury, been a policy imperative in many jurisdictions around the world. In the UK, the Companies Act 2006 made the seminal shift of enshrining wide societal obligations in law. This compares with the Polly Peck and BCCI era when thriving businesses owed their principal fealty to shareholders in times of plenty and to creditors in times of distress. Those legally ascribed duties were underpinned by an evergreen set of principles which evolved from Cadbury into the UK Corporate Governance Code. The Code's original over-riding purpose was to avoid future accounting frauds in order to protect the public, shareholders and creditors which naturally limited its scope to listed companies. The failure of a set of private businesses crystallised the realisation that societal impact necessitated an extension of the regulatory reach to embrace all business types.

But Wates goes further. Its contribution to the body of thinking on good governance practices goes far beyond the elimination of an artificial border between the parallel public and private universes. That accolade belongs to the combination of two other innovations. The first is the shift from defensive conformance to the liberating offensive focus on strategy. So important is this that Wates explicitly labels the company's purpose – its strategic raison d'etre – as its 'North Star' – the ever-present point of reference which directs all movement. The second is the need to communicate with the widest community of stakeholders, as defined in the 2006 Act. The clarity of this latter obligation is assured by the new requirement to "apply and explain".

This upgraded commandment replaces its libertarian forebear to "comply or explain" and compels businesses, not only to do the right thing as defined in the Act, but to explain to those to whom they are beholden – in good times and bad – how precisely, they are doing the right thing.

There couldn't be a clearer recognition that large businesses are an integral part of society and that their leadership must now view the state and its institutions with the respect they deserve.

Corporate Governance 3.0

CHAPTER 12. AN AUSTRALIAN PERSPECTIVE

Julie Garland-McLellan, CEO, The Director's Dilemma

Introduction

"Corporate structures, it is said, depend in part on the structures a country had in earlier times, in particular the structures with which the economy started."[1] In Australia, corporate governance emerged from a framework of legal rules, stock market expectations and soft law, which refers to principles and agreements that are not legally binding. That framework largely dates back to its colonial past. Unlike governance of many Commonwealth nations, Australian corporate governance predates the 1992 Cadbury Report and therefore Australia can be considered as one of forerunners in the field of corporate governance.

This chapter will review the historical development of corporate governance in Australia and provide a critical analysis of its strengths and benefits to provide guidance to company boards to promote the long-term success of companies.

---

[1] Farrer, J. (1999), 'A brief thematic history of corporate governance', *Bond Law Review*, vol. 11, no. 2, 259, available online: < http://www.austlii.edu.au/au/journals/BondLawRw/1999/17.html > (accessed 11 July 2021).

1. A Governance Forerunner

Many of the early businesses in Australia were branches or subsidiaries of UK companies. The larger local banks were mostly owned by, or affiliated with, UK banks. The economy was outward-looking from its inception and the distant owners of the companies within it were keen to hold management to high standards of accountability.

The law and the economy depended to a large extent on the UK and most statutes, including the corporations and companies laws, were derived from their UK counterparts. This derived system worked well while the interests of the UK coincided with Australia. Over time, as interests diverged and independence grew, there were difficulties and a growing support for purpose-written Australian legislation. The introduction of the no liability company in 1871 was driven by the requirements of the local gold mining industry.[2] As other industries developed, the accretion of laws written to serve the national interests created a steady divergence from the British laws that had previously been only slightly adapted to suit local conditions and requirements.

This trend came to a head when the UK joined the European Union in 1973.[3]

Australia increasingly looked to North America and its own business and legal communities for ideas about how to design and develop legislation that was fit for the growing nation.

As companies grew and needed capital to finance their growth, they began to list, either on the domestic stock exchanges, or overseas.

Again, the need to ensure fair treatment of investors, especially when far distant from the operations of the companies in which they owned shares, led to development of legislation specifically conceived for the circumstances. This need to balance local interests with a stock market that

---

[2] Lipton, P. (2007), 'A history of company law in colonial Australia: Economic development and legal evolution', *Melbourne University Law Review*, vol. 31, no. 1, 805, available online: <https://law.unimelb.edu.au/__data/assets/pdf_file/0008/1707803/31_3_4.pdf > (accessed 11 July 2021).
[3] Note 1.

was internationally competitive is possibly the powerhouse that fuelled the early development of legislation to protect the rights of shareholders and establish reasonable levels of management accountability.

2. National Corporations' Legislation

Australia is divided into six states and two territories. Each has the power to create its own legislation. The Federal Government had no powers to legislate the formation, operation or winding up of companies. During and after World War II, the Federal Government invoked its defence powers to regulate some aspects of companies, including the formation and transfer of shares. However, there was a political reluctance to extend this into a permanent uniform Commonwealth legislation to protect investors or regulate companies.[4]

Different states and territories passed different legislation that reflected their different ethoses and economies. For companies that operated across state and territory borders, this created a burdensome complexity leading to calls for a uniform company law. This uniform law was passed in 1961, but continued unilateral actions by states and territories caused the 'uniform' law to vary across borders until its uniformity was in name only.

In 1987 all the states and the Commonwealth (Federal) government agreed to coordinate companies' legislation.[5] The first part of the plan was for the Commonwealth to pass comprehensive companies legislation [the Corporations Act 1989 (Cth)]. The next stage was the states to pass a law that 'automatically' adopted the Commonwealth Act. The aim was to have states' companies legislation operate as if under a national statute without the constitutional (and political) problems of a truly national scheme. It was effective for a while.

---

[4] Ford, H. (1962), 'Uniform companies legislation: Its effect in Victoria', *Melbourne University Law Review*, vol. 3, no. 2, 461.
[5] Senate Standing Committee on Constitutional and Legal Affairs. (1987), *The Role of Parliament in Relation to The National Companies Scheme*, Fyshwick: Canberra Publishing and Printing, available online:
<https://www.takeovers.gov.au/content/Resources/parliamentary_reports/downloads/national_companies_scheme.pdf> (accessed 11 July 2021).

In 1990 the states and Commonwealth entered into a new agreement. This was similar to the 1987 approach and also established the Australian Securities and Investments Commission (ASIC) as a national corporations regulator. A High Court challenge in 1999 ruled that state legislation that purported to confer jurisdiction on the Federal Court to hear matters arising under the Corporations Law was invalid.[6]

In 2001, the states and Northern Territory referred their own constitutional law-making powers over corporations to the Commonwealth. This empowered the Commonwealth to pass the Corporations Act 2001. Australia finally had a single jurisdiction for corporations law; inefficiencies and bureaucracy were reduced and business confidence increased.

A. Directors' Duties under the Corporations Act 2001

The Corporations Act is a relatively modern piece of legislation and incorporates modern thinking about the role of boards and the purpose of governance. The role of a company director in Australia is now held to be a responsible and complex one involving personal liability, public accountability, and a high expectation of diligence and care[7].

Directors' duties under the Corporations Act are outlined in sections 180 – 184. This is supplemented by other legislation, common law, and various other standards and requirements. In addition, directors are expected to fulfil a fiduciary duty that is constantly evolving to meet community expectations.

Section 180 states that a director or other officer of a corporation must exercise their powers and discharge their duties with the degree of care and diligence that a reasonable person would exercise if they were

---

[6] Longo, J. (2000), 'Constitutional challenges facing ASIC: An overview', *Paper Presented at the Corporate Law Teachers Association Conference: The Future of Corporate Regulation: Hughes and Wakim and the Referral of Powers*, available online:
<https://law.unimelb.edu.au/__data/assets/pdf_file/0005/1710167/133-longo1.pdf> (accessed 11 July 2021).

[7] Ramsay, I. (1997), *Corporate Governance and the Duties of Company Directors*, Melbourne: The Centre for Corporate Law and Securities Regulation, available online:
<https://law.unimelb.edu.au/__data/assets/
pdf_file/0004/1721173/7-Ian-Ramsay-1997.pdf> (accessed 11 July 2021).

a director or officer of a corporation in the corporation's circumstances; and occupied the office held by, and had the same responsibilities within the corporation as, the director or officer. This is often referred to as the 'reasonable person test'. It is an extremely difficult test to pass as it is never invoked until there has been a disaster, after which hindsight renders the level of diligence required in proportion to the level of the disaster.

Section 180 has been extended with a business judgment rule: A director who makes a business judgment is taken to meet the requirements outlined above, and their equivalent duties at common law and in equity, in respect of the judgment if they make the judgment in good faith for a proper purpose; do not have a material personal interest in the subject matter of the judgment; inform themselves about the subject matter of the judgment to the extent they reasonably believe to be appropriate; and rationally believe that the judgment is in the best interests of the corporation. Note that all of these must apply, not just one or some.

The director's or officer's belief that a judgment is in the best interests of the corporation is a rational one unless the belief is one that no reasonable person in their position would hold. The duty to 'be informed' is often the one that will render the reasonable person test unpassable. Not knowing is no excuse if people, with hindsight, believe that you should have known.

Section 181 holds that a director or other officer of a corporation must exercise their powers and discharge their duties in good faith in the best interests of the corporation and for a proper purpose.

Section 182 states that a director, secretary, other officer or employee of a corporation must not improperly use their position to gain an advantage for themselves or someone else or cause detriment to the corporation.

A person who obtains information because they are, or have been, a director or other officer or employee of a corporation must not improperly use the information to gain an advantage for themselves or someone else or cause detriment to the corporation.

A director or other officer of a corporation commits an offence if they are reckless or are dishonest; and fail to exercise their powers and discharge their duties in good faith in the best interests of the corporation or for a proper purpose.

B. ASIC – The Corporate Regulator

ASIC is Australia's integrated corporate, markets, financial services and consumer credit regulator. ASIC is an independent Australian Government body. It was incorporated under, and administers, the Australian Securities and Investments Commission Act 2001 (ASIC Act), and undertakes most of its work under the Corporations Act. ASIC's role is to:

- maintain, facilitate and improve the performance of the financial system and entities in it
- promote confident and informed participation by investors and consumers in the financial system
- administer the law effectively and with minimal procedural requirements
- receive, process and store, efficiently and quickly, information received
- make information about companies and other bodies available to the public as soon as practicable
- take whatever action it deems necessary, to enforce and give effect to the law.[8]

In recent years there has been significant debate about ASIC's role. This has moved from a pragmatic stance of working with companies to improve governance using compliance orders and agreements to a more aggressive stance of asking 'why not litigate?' in every instance of reported or suspected wrongdoing.

---

[8] Australian Securities and Investments Commission, see: <https://asic.gov.au/about-asic/what-we-do/our-role/> (accessed 16 May 2021).

C. Director Titles and Types

Australians often use the title 'director' imprecisely. This leads to some confusion. Many job titles include the word 'director' but do not confer director's duties or powers on the incumbent. Under the Corporations Act a director is:

- any person who is validly appointed to a board
- any person who acts in the role even if their appointment is not valid
- any person on whose wishes or orders a board is accustomed to act.

This is important because anyone who acts as a director will be held liable at law for those actions even if they have not been appointed or if their appointment was invalid. This is a particularly vexing issue for multinational corporations with a subsidiary in Australia where the line management may provide orders that local management and board members are expected to act upon.

To further complicate matters, there are several different terms that are applied to directors:

- Executive director – a person who is on the board and also employed by the company, for example the Managing Director
- Non-Executive Director (NED) – a person who is on the board but is not employed by the company
- Independent director – a person who is not employed by the company, not a significant shareholder of the company, not a significant supplier or customer of the company, and not a close relative of any of these. Furthermore, they should not have come within any of these categories for at least two years.
- Shadow Director (uninsured director) – a person who is the 'power behind the throne' and controls or significantly exerts influence on the board's decisions. The Corporations Act will find these people to be directors even if, as above, they have never been appointed to the board.

This confusion is not only visible among the uniformed public; in a recent commission of inquiry[9] a hitherto respected director with a track record of board and CEO roles was unable to answer a question about the nature of the role of an independent director without referring to notes (which is not allowed under the rules of the commission). In addition, many directors when pressed will suggest that it is not 'reasonable' for them to act against the wishes of a major or controlling shareholder, even if they are clearly identified to other shareholders as 'independent'.

3. Other Statutory Governance Requirements

The Corporations Act is not the only piece of legislation that imposes duties and standards upon company directors. There are numerous statutes imposing duties on directors, many of which prescribe personal penalties for directors as well as penalties for the company. It is often claimed that Australia has the toughest legal regime for company directors because of the complex and interlocking nature of the laws and the duties they impose.[10]

Some key laws are discussed below. This is not an exhaustive list.

A. ACCC and Consumer Protection

The Australian Competition and Consumer Commission (ACCC) is an independent Commonwealth statutory authority whose role is to enforce the *Competition and Consumer Act 2010* and a range of additional legislation, promoting competition, fair trading and regulating national infrastructure for the benefit of all Australians. It can impact virtually every business in Australia. The ACCC's current priorities are:

– Cartel actions
– Financial services

---

[9] The Honourable P A Bergin SC. (1992), *Inquiry under section 143 of the Casino* Control Act 1992 (NSW).
[10] Colvin, J. and Hord, B. (2020), 'Criminal director liability: A bridge now too far?', *Australian Journal of Corporate Law*, vol. 35, no. 2, 187-207.

- Customer loyalty schemes
- Franchise issues
- Unfair contracts

The Act requires directors and senior officers to fully understand the operations of their company and the relevant legislative provisions. It places an obligation on directors to be concerned with the existence and effectiveness of internal procedures to secure compliance with the Act. Potential penalties are severe. Directors should ask:

- Are management in a position to assure the board that the internal controls against violations of the Trade Practices Act are based on a considered review of the basic elements of liability control?
- Are controls monitored and enforced?
- Can the board provide a convincing and documented demonstration of the adequacy of compliance controls should they be attacked in court or elsewhere?

Interlocking directorships

Interlocking directorships occur where directors of two or more companies that are in competition with each other share a common interest in another board. While there is nothing in Australian law which prohibits this, interlocking directorships have the potential for raising concerns in a trade practices context. They may also give rise to conflicts of interest which may breach a fiduciary duty.

When competitors have directors on a board, there is *the appearance of the potential for a breach* of the *Competition and Consumer Act 2010*. Interlocking directorships *are unlikely* to raise concerns under the competition provisions of the Act unless it can be demonstrated that it is being used, directly or indirectly, as a conduit for information or other anti-competitive purposes.

Australian directors should be aware of their broad obligations under the Trade Practices Act.

- Part IV deals with anti-competitive practices by seeking to prevent behaviour that has the purpose or effect of substantially lessening competition in a market.

- Part V of the Act contains a range of provisions aimed at protecting consumers, and businesses that qualify as consumers.

- Section 52 of the Act is an all-encompassing provision that states: A corporation shall not, in trade or commerce, engage in conduct that is misleading or deceptive or is likely to mislead or deceive.

B. ACNC Governance Standards

The economic contribution of charities to the Australian economy was estimated at $129 billion in 2017. This comprised a $71.8 billion direct contribution and a further $57 billion flow-on contribution. The sector directly employs 840,500 full time equivalent (FTE) paid workers, and its upstream activities result in a further 471,700 FTE workers being indirectly employed. Collectively, the sector is roughly equivalent in size to the Australian retail sector, education and training, or the public administration and safety sector[11]. This is a massive contribution to the wealth and well-being of the nation, yet many of the companies involved in making this contribution are run by unpaid volunteer boards with little formal governance education.

The Australian Charities and Not-for-profits Commission (ACNC) is the national regulator of charities and not for profit organisations. The ACNC was established in December 2012 to achieve the following objects:

- maintain, protect and enhance public trust and confidence in the Australian not-for-profit sector

- support and sustain a robust, vibrant, independent and innovative not-for-profit sector

---

[11] Deloitte. (2017), *Economic Contribution of the Australian Charity Sector: Australian Charities and Not-for-profits Commission*, Deloitte Access Economics, available online:
<https://www.acnc.gov.au/sites/default/
files/Download%20the%20report%20for%20Economic%20contribution%20of%20the%20
Australian%20charity%20sector%20%5BPDF%202MB%5D.pdf> (accessed 11 July 2021).

- promote the reduction of unnecessary regulatory obligations on the sector.

The ACNC Governance Standards are a set of <u>minimum</u> standards that deal with how charities (and other NFP organisations) are run, including their processes, activities and relationships. They have the force of law. Many directors in the sector are not aware of them and fail to monitor compliance with them.

The standards require charities to remain charitable, operate lawfully, and be run in an accountable and responsible way. They help charities remain trusted by the public and continue to do their work. Because the standards are a set of high-level principles, not precise rules, directors must decide how to comply with them.

Directors must be able to demonstrate that the steps taken to comply are appropriate (considering factors such as its size, purpose and activities). For example, a larger charity or one with vulnerable beneficiaries may need to take extra steps to comply with the Standards.

The standards are:

- Standard 1: Purposes and not-for-profit nature - Charities must be not-for-profit and work towards their charitable purpose. They must be able to demonstrate this and provide information about their purposes to the public.
- Standard 2: Accountability to members - Charities that have members must take reasonable steps to be accountable to their members and provide them with adequate opportunity to raise concerns about how the charity is governed.
- Standard 3: Compliance with Australian laws - Charities must not commit a serious offence (such as fraud) under any Australian law or breach a law that may result in a penalty of 60 penalty units (equivalent to $12,600 as at December 2018) or more.
- Standard 4: Suitability of Responsible Persons - Charities must take reasonable steps to be satisfied that Responsible Persons (such as board members) are not disqualified from managing a corporation under the Corporations Act 2001 (Cth) or disqualified from being a

Responsible Person of a registered charity by the ACNC Commissioner, and remove any Responsible Person who does not meet these requirements.

- Standard 5: Duties of Responsible Persons - Charities must take reasonable steps to make sure that Responsible Persons are subject to, understand and carry out the duties set out in this Standard.

- Standard 6: Maintaining and Enhancing Public Trust and Confidence in the Australian Not-For-Profit Sector - a registered charity to take reasonable steps to become a participating non-government institution if the charity is, or is likely to be, identified as being involved in the abuse of a person under the National Redress Scheme for Institutional Child Sexual Abuse.

The ACNC expects most charities will be meeting the Governance Standards and the ACNC enforcement actions focus on charities that have seriously or deliberately breached the Governance Standards by (for example):

- diverting money to non-charitable purposes
- not disclosing serious conflicts of interest, or
- being grossly negligent with their finances.

The ACNC has a range of formal penalties and powers it can use in regulating charities. If any of these formal powers is used the ACNC must publish it on the Charity Register. Publication is a strong deterrent in a country of only 25 million people where the director community are likely to know each other. The ACNC can apply penalties if a charity makes false or misleading statements or fails to lodge documents in time. Information about penalties will not be published. The powers include:

- revocation of charitable status
- enforceable undertakings
- dismissal of boards

Since its inception, the ACNC has not dismissed a board and there have been few court tests of the regulator's powers and the way that these overlap with the powers of the corporate regulator, ASIC. They have entered into enforceable undertakings with a range of companies including Construction Charitable Works, RSL NSW and RSL Lifecare, Australian Federation of Islamic Councils, and Yipirinya School Council; they have also deregistered over 100 organisations, issued directions and warnings, and entered into compliance agreements[12].

C. Fair Work Australia

This Commission is Australia's national workplace relations tribunal. It was established by the Fair Work Act 2009 (Fair Work Act) and is responsible for administering its provisions. The Commission's powers and functions include dealing with unfair dismissal, anti-bullying and unlawful termination claims; setting the national minimum wage and minimum wages in modern awards, making, reviewing and varying modern awards; assisting bargaining for enterprise agreements; managing enterprise agreements; making orders to stop or suspend industrial action; dealing with disputes brought to the Commission under the dispute resolution procedures of modern awards and enterprise agreements; and promoting cooperative and productive workplace relations and preventing disputes.

Directors have a duty to provide a workplace that is free from bullying and harassment, as well as safe (which includes mental and emotional safety considerations). They also have a duty to ensure that payments are made in line with awards and that terms and conditions of employment are reasonable. Failure to meet the Fair Work Commission's standards attracts penalties against directors as well as against the company itself.

The Commission and General Manager also have responsibilities in relation to the registration, amalgamation and cancellation of registered organisations and the making and alteration of their rules under the Fair Work (Registered Organisations) Act 2009.

---

[12] See <https://www.acnc.gov.au/raise-concern/regulating-charities/action-taken-against-charities> (accessed 11 July 2021).

D. Workplace Health and Safety

Safe Work Australia is an Australian government statutory body established in 2008 to develop national policy relating to workplace health and safety and workers' compensation. Safe Work Australia is jointly funded by the Commonwealth, state and territory governments through an Intergovernmental Agreement. It works to plans which are agreed annually by Ministers for Work Health and Safety (WHS) to drive national policy development on WHS and workers' compensation matters. The aim is to:

- develop and evaluate national policy and strategies,
- develop and evaluate the model WHS legislative framework,
- undertake research, and
- collect, analyse and report data.

As a national policy body, Safe Work Australia does not regulate WHS laws. The Commonwealth, states and territories retain responsibility for regulating and enforcing WHS laws in their jurisdictions. This leads to a range of different standards in different states and territories. Most WHS legislation provides a personal duty on directors to ensure that workplaces are safe. Some contain a reverse onus of proof, whereby a director is automatically presumed guilty of an offense if the company has breached the legislation.

Directors can be fined, jailed, or both and the regulator's website provides information on recent actions that should be salutary reading for directors.

E. Environment Protection

Each state and territory has an Environmental Protection Act (or equivalent) which makes directors personally liable for breaches by their corporations. Every organisation which has a physical presence (office, factory, warehouse) must comply with environmental protection laws. Broadly, the laws require organisations to obtain any relevant licence or government approval, comply with legal requirements and notify the relevant regulatory authority if unlawful or serious environmental harm occurs.

Every level of government (federal, state and local) has its own unique laws. In many cases, environmental laws make directors personally liable for breaches by their organisations. These laws are characterised by wide coverage (noise, air, water, land, waste, hazardous materials), penalties for both organisations and directors, and limited defence of due diligence. It is a commonly attempted defence in all the environmental protection cases where a director can show that he or she exercised 'due diligence' or 'took all reasonable steps to ensure the corporation complied with' those laws. 'Due diligence' can usually only be shown if there is a compliant environment management system in place and the board took steps to monitor the application of the system.

F. Tax

Australian taxation laws are complex and constantly changing. If a company breaches the taxation laws, directors can be deemed to have committed the breach. Company directors have an obligation to ensure that the company meets its pay as you go ('PAYG') withholding payment obligations. The director of a company which fails to pay a PAYG withholding amount on or before the due date can become personally liable for a penalty equal to the unpaid amount.

The Australian Taxation Office may issue a director penalty notice which can adversely affect the director's ability to remain on that board and others. The director penalty notice regime also applies to a director where a company does not meet its superannuation guarantee obligations. Each state and territory has taxes such as payroll tax, stamp duties or land tax which differ across borders.

In every state and territory, there is a Taxation Administration Act which allows for the recovery from directors where taxation obligations are not met by a corporation or makes directors liable for breaches by their corporations.

4. Voluntary, sectoral, and industry codes

There are state and territory laws regulating a broad range of professions, commercial activities, and industries[13] whereby directors can be held liable for breaches by their companies. In addition, there are numerous codes that directors are expected or exhorted to embrace and implement. Some of the most important ones are discussed below.

A. ASX Corporate Governance Principles

The Australian Stock Exchange (ASX) Corporate Governance Council develops and issues principles-based recommendations on the corporate governance practices to be adopted by ASX listed entities[14]. Adoption is on an 'if not, why not' basis so companies are free to make their own practices, that differ from the recommended practice, as long as they explain why their practice is better for the company in its current circumstances.

The recommendations are intended to promote investor confidence and to assist listed entities to meet stakeholder expectations in relation to their governance. However, many governance advisors and influencers exhort or coerce companies into adopting the recommendations rather than developing their own, fit for purpose, practices.

There are eight principles:

1. Lay solid foundations for management and oversight: A listed entity should clearly delineate the respective roles and responsibilities of its board and management and regularly review their performance.

2. Structure the board to be effective and add value: The board of a listed entity should be of an appropriate size and collectively have the skills,

---

[13] For example, architecture, building and building work, casinos, commercial fishing, electrical work and sales, explosives, gaming machines, liquor sales, lotteries, art unions, mining, pawnbrokers and second-hand dealers, pharmacies, private health facilities, real estate agents, retirement villages, security, tow truck, travel agents, veterinary practice.

[14] ASX Corporate Governance Council. (2019), *Corporate Governance Principles and Recommendations*, available online: <https://www.asx.com.au/documents/asx-compliance/cgc-principles-and-recommendations-fourth-edn.pdf> (accessed 11 July 2021).

commitment and knowledge of the entity and the industry in which it operates, to enable it to discharge its duties effectively and to add value.

3. Instil a culture of acting lawfully, ethically and responsibly: A listed entity should instil and continually reinforce a culture across the organisation of acting lawfully, ethically and responsibly.

4. Safeguard the integrity of corporate reports: A listed entity should have appropriate processes to verify the integrity of its corporate reports.

5. Make timely and balanced disclosure: A listed entity should make timely and balanced disclosure of all matters concerning it that a reasonable person would expect to have a material effect on the price or value of its securities.

6. Respect the rights of security holders: A listed entity should provide its security holders with appropriate information and facilities to allow them to exercise their rights as owners effectively.

7. Recognise and manage risk: A listed entity should establish a sound risk management framework and periodically review the effectiveness of that framework.

8. Remunerate fairly and responsibly: A listed entity should pay director remuneration sufficient to attract and retain high quality directors and design its executive remuneration to attract, retain and motivate high quality senior executives and to align their interests with the creation of value for security holders and with the entity's values and risk appetite.

The principles are supported by 35 specific recommendations of general application intended to give effect to these principles, as well as 3 additional recommendations that only apply in certain limited cases.

Although they are designed to apply only to listed companies (which are compelled to apply the principles under the ASX listing rules) these principles have been adapted and adopted across many other sectors.

B. Gender diversity initiatives

The Workplace Gender Equality Act aims to:

- to promote and improve gender equality (including equal remuneration) in employment and in the workplace,
- support employers to remove barriers to the full and equal participation of women in the workforce, in recognition of the disadvantaged position of women in relation to employment matters,
- promote, amongst employers, the elimination of discrimination on the basis of gender in relation to employment matters (including in relation to family and caring responsibilities),
- to foster workplace consultation between employers and employees on issues concerning gender equality in employment and in the workplace,
- improve the productivity and competitiveness of Australian business through the advancement of gender equality in employment and in the workplace.

The Act requires relevant employers to report a range of indicators to the Workplace Equality Agency.

The ASX Corporate Governance Principles and Recommendations recommend listed companies have and disclose a diversity policy. They further recommend that the board, or a committee of the board, set measurable objectives for achieving gender diversity in the composition of its board, senior executives and workforce generally and disclose in relation to each reporting period the measurable objectives set for that period to achieve gender diversity; the entity's progress towards achieving those objectives; and either the respective proportions of men and women on the board, in senior executive positions and across the whole workforce (including how the entity has defined "senior executive" for these purposes) or, if the entity is a "relevant employer" under the Workplace Gender Equality Act, the entity's most recent "Gender Equality Indicators", as defined in and published under that Act.

If the entity was in the S&P/ASX 300 Index at the commencement of the reporting period, the measurable objective for achieving gender diversity in the composition of its board should be to have not less than 30% of its directors of each gender within a specified period.

Many government entities support the aims of this initiative to improve gender equality in the workplace by preferencing grants and contracts to companies, listed or unlisted, that act in accord with the ASX recommended targets.

C. AICD NFP Governance Principles

The Not-for-Profit (NFP) Governance Principles[15] have been developed by the Australian Institute of Company Directors (AICD) to promote good governance in the NFP sector.

The principles are voluntary. They go beyond what may be considered a minimum standard of governance and encourage organisations to strive for and achieve good governance. The principles are complementary to, and build on, the Australian Charities and Not-for-profits Commission Governance Standards.

The principles are:

1. Purpose and strategy: The organisation has a clear purpose and a strategy which aligns its activities to its purpose.
2. Roles and responsibilities: There is clarity about the roles, responsibilities and relationships of the board.
3. Board composition: The board's structure and composition enable it to fulfil its role effectively.
4. Board effectiveness: The board is run effectively and its performance is periodically evaluated.
5. Risk management: Board decision making is informed by an understanding of risk and how it is managed.
6. Performance: The organisation uses its resources appropriately and evaluates its performance.

---

[15] Australian Institute of Company Directors. (2019), *The Not-for-Profit Governance Principles*, available online: <https://aicd.companydirectors.com.au/-/media/cd2/resources/director-resources/not-for-profit-resources/nfp-principles/pdf/06911-4-adv-nfp-governance-principles-report-a4-v11.ashx> (accessed 11 July 2021).

7. Accountability and transparency: The board demonstrates accountability by providing information to stakeholders about the organisation and its performance.
8. Stakeholder engagement: There is meaningful engagement of stakeholders and their interests are understood and considered by the board.
9. Conduct and compliance: The expectations of behaviour for the people involved in the organisation are clear and understood.
10. Culture: The board models and works to instil a culture that supports the organisation's purpose and strategy.

The principles are clarified and extended by 47 supporting practices.

D. UN sustainable development goals

Australians are great proponents of, and believers in, soft law. One of the more popular 'soft law' agreements in use in Australia is the UN Sustainable Development Goals. These are a universal call to action to end poverty, protect the planet and improve the lives and prospects of everyone, everywhere. The goals were adopted by all UN Member States in 2015, as part of the 2030 Agenda for Sustainable Development which set out a 15-year plan to achieve the Goals. These goals are increasingly referenced by Australian companies and boards, especially in the government and entrepreneurial sectors.

The 17 goals are:

1. No poverty
2. Zero hunger
3. Good health and well-being
4. Quality education
5. Gender equality
6. Clean water and sanitation
7. Affordable and clean energy
8. Decent work and economic growth
9. Industry, innovation, and infrastructure

10. Reduced inequalities
11. Sustainable cities and communities
12. Responsible consumption and production
13. Climate action
14. Life below water
15. Life on land
16. Peace, justice, and strong institutions
17. Partnerships

Precedent and public opinion

Australia extends its statutory framework with case law or precedent, where cases resolved in court are relied upon to refine the operation and understanding of the law and are used to resolve subsequent cases more rapidly. Of course, even judges make mistakes, and every case depends on its unique circumstances and pleading. However, the outcomes of preceding cases are often a strong indicator of the likely outcome of prospective cases.

Australia also makes use of public processes, such as commissions of inquiry, senate estimates, etc. to establish governance ideals and expectations. These have proven successful and, after every relevant inquiry, the governance and other professional institutions propagate recommended practices and checklists for boards. The larger listed and government-owned boards are quick to adopt these tools and they slowly percolate through the economy. They also impact public opinion and provide a feedback loop to the expectations of a 'reasonable person' about the standards of duty and care to be exercised by a properly diligent director.

5. Education and Performance Review

Australia is a leader in director education and has been a pioneer in board performance evaluation. This achievement is supported by a diverse ecosystem of education bodies, including an Institute of Company Directors and a Governance Institute, both of which provide recognised and respected education in governance and directorship. There is, however, no general requirement for directors to hold any specific qualification, even on the boards of large, listed companies that have the potential to significantly impact the national economy.

The ASX guidelines recommend that review conduct and process be disclosed and that a regular externally facilitated review be undertaken at least once every three years. Many boards undertake a 'tick the box' review but the frequency of deep reviews, followed by education, development and changes to processes, does appear to be increasing as the director community becomes comfortable with being held to account and confident that these activities will lead to better governance performance in future.

Given the complex system, in which the law is interpreted by judges as new cases are brought to the courts, this process of review and education is a fundamental part of the director landscape.

6. Conclusion

The existence of a nuanced (albeit complex and often confusing) statute law regime, reinforced by established practices, a culture of compliance, and constant revision of standards through public processes, has contributed to a well-respected governance regime. It is reinforced by a director liability regime that is a strong deterrent to egregious breaches.

An active and engaged institutional framework supports and promulgates governance ideals. Director education, while not compulsory outside a few highly regulated sectors[16], adds to the ability of Australia to provide a robust framework of governance that underpins an economy that attracts foreign investments.

---

[16] For example, the Registered Clubs Sector in NSW where directors must complete mandatory training in financial oversight and legal frameworks.

CHAPTER 13. A CENTRAL ASIAN PERSPECTIVE[1]

Kairat Kelimbetov, Governor, Astana International Financial Centre and Chairman of the Agency of Strategic Planning and Reforms

Alexander Van de Putte, Professor of Strategic Foresight, IE Business School and Chairman of Corporate Governance & Stewardship, AIFC

Introduction

According to a 2017 European Bank for Reconstruction and Development (EBRD) report, corporate governance in Kazakhstan is weak in its implementation, despite the fact that a code on corporate governance was adopted in 2005 and amended in 2007.[2] The report made recommendations in five different areas: 1) structure and functioning of the board, 2) transparency and disclosure, 3) internal control, 4) rights of shareholders, and 5) stakeholders and institutions.

---

[1] A book entitled "Scaling Sound Corporate Governance at the AIFC and Kazakhstan" is planned by the same authors and Simon Osborne for late 2021/early 2022.
[2] Financial Institutions' Association of Kazakhstan, Code on Corporate Governance, Almaty 2007. Available from https://ecgi.global/content/codes.

As a response, the Astana International Financial Centre (AIFC) began the development of the AIFC corporate governance principles. TheCityUK organised a number of working group meetings funded by the UK government under the aegis of the Kazakhstan–UK Inter-Governmental Commission. Alexander Van de Putte oversaw the development of the principles and its guidance document and the AIFC team was advised by board performance expert Simon Osborne. The principles are now being implemented throughout the AIFC on an 'apply and explain' basis. The objective is to branch out to other parts of the economy, a process that has already started.

This chapter starts with providing an overview of different approaches to corporate governance, including: 1) 'rules-based' versus 'principles-based' approaches, 2) 'comply or explain' versus 'apply and explain' approaches, 3) unitary versus dual-tier board structures, and 4) stakeholder versus shareholder orientation. It further describes the history of corporate governance in Kazakhstan and Central Asia and lays out a roadmap to gradually change the capabilities and mind-sets of boards and individual directors to provide sound corporate governance, board leadership and strategic direction to the company.

1. Corporate governance is at a crossroads in Kazakhstan

In 2017 the EBRD, assisted by Nestor Advisors, published a report on 'Corporate Governance in Transition Economies: Kazakhstan Country Report.'[3] The report concluded that for joint stock companies (JSCs),[4] corporate governance in Kazakhstan is weak in its implementation, even though a code on corporate governance was adopted in 2005 and amended in 2007. Led by Gian Piero Cigna of the EBRD, the team assessed and made recommendations in five different areas: 1) structure and functioning of the board, 2) transparency and disclosure, 3) internal control, 4) rights of shareholders, and 5) stakeholders and institutions. These five areas were

---

[3] Gian Piero Cigna, Yaryna Kobel, and Alina Sigheartau, "Corporate Governance in Transition Economies: Kazakhstan Country Report", European Bank for Reconstruction and Development, 2017.

[4] Joint stock companies are the dominant form of business organisation in Kazakhstan. JSCs require a minimum charter capital of about £300,000 and the liability of shareholders is limited to the charter capital.

further divided in sections. Table 13.1 summarises the different areas and sections assessed.

Table 13.1 Areas and sections assessed
Source: EBRD[5]

Structure and functioning of the board	Transparency and disclosure	Internal control	Rights of shareholders	Stakeholders and institutions
– Board composition – Gender diversity at the board – Independent directors – Board effectiveness – Responsibilities of the board	– Non-financial information disclosure – Financial information disclosure – Reporting to the market and to shareholders – Disclosure on the external audit	– Quality of the internal control framework – Quality of internal and external audit – Functioning and independences of the audit committee – Control over related party transactions and conflict of interests	– General shareholders' meeting – Protection against insider trading and self-dealing – Minority shareholders protection and shareholders' access to information – Registration of shareholders	– Corporate governance structure and institutions – Corporate governance code – Institutional environment

Each of the five areas qualitatively assessed and the various sections were rated on a scale from 1 to 5, as follows:

– Very weak (rating 1): Corporate governance practices of companies present significant risks, and the area and underlying factors need significant reform;

– Weak (rating 2): Corporate governance practices of companies present are acceptable in some areas, but need overall reform;

– Fair (rating 3): Corporate governance practices show some elements of good practice. However, some critical issues should be addressed to improve its effectiveness.

– Moderately strong (rating 4): Corporate governance practices are mostly fit-for-purpose. However, further reform is needed to make them world-class.

---

[5] See footnote 3.

– Strong to very strong (rating 5): Corporate governance practices are fit-for-purpose and world-class.

Figure 13.1 provides a summary of the assessment of corporate governance practices in Kazakhstan based on the five aforementioned areas.

Figure 13.1 Assessment of corporate governance practices in Kazakhstan
Source: EBRD[6]

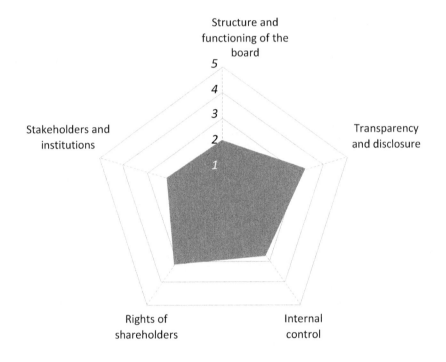

1. **Structuring and function of the board (weak):** Boards in Kazakhstan are unitary boards, but the CEO is the only executive director allowed to serve on the board, and cannot function as board chair or any of its committees. Independent directors are required to chair committees, but a majority of independent directors for key committees is not required. The code does not refer to key functions of the board, such as oversight of management, budget approval and risk

---

[6] See footnote 2.

management. A major area of concern is that shareholders can overturn board decisions at the general shareholders' meeting.

2. **Transparency and disclosure (fair):** Disclosure of financial information is in line with International Financial Reporting Standards (IFRS). However, companies are not required to disclose non-financial information in their annual report, and disclosure on the activities of the board and committees is very limited. Probably the biggest issue with transparency and disclosure is that listed companies do not disclose their compliance with the Kazakh corporate governance code.

3. **Internal control (fair):** Only financial institutions are required to have an internal audit function, but they do not necessarily report to the board and may not be independent. On the other hand, listed companies are required to have an audit committee chaired by an independent director. A major shortcoming is that external auditors are allowed to perform non-audit services which may impair external auditors' independence. To avoid potential conflicts of interests, it is advisable for audit committees to establish formal policies about which non-audit services the external auditors are allowed to perform.

4. **Rights of shareholders (moderately strong):** Basic shareholder rights are appropriately regulated in the law. Important changes in the company's structure and shareholding require a supermajority at the annual shareholders' meeting to take effect. Shareholders have the right to access corporate documentation. However, non-financial information disclosure, such as key deliberations during board meetings, is not required by law and lacks quality. A key issue is that directors are not required to disclose any dealings in the company shares. To avoid potential conflicts of interests, it advisable to clarify the disclosure requirement expected by directors of dealings in the company shares and when directors can buy and sell shares in their companies.

5. **Stakeholders and institutions (fair):** There is a lack in promotion of good governance and in monitoring companies' practices by the Kazakhstan Stock Exchange (KASE) and the regulator. The Kazakh corporate governance code is outdated and lacks proper implementation mechanisms. All listed companies in Kazakhstan are required to develop their own corporate governance codes in line with

the 2005 Code on Corporate Governance. However, only about 50% of the largest listed companies in Kazakhstan comply with this requirement.

Since publication of the EBRD's report on corporate governance in Kazakhstan in 2017, Kazakh companies have worked hard to address the challenges related to corporate governance. Especially, Sovereign Wealth Fund Samruk-Kazyna, and National Management Holding company Baiterek have made major progress in meeting international corporate governance standards.

2. Different approaches to corporate governance

Before starting the development of the AIFC corporate governance principles, we wanted to understand the various approaches to corporate governance that exist around the world and their relative benefits to the AIFC and Kazakhstan.

The AIFC was envisioned in 2015 and officially launched under the patronage of Nursultan Nazarbayev, the first president of Kazakhstan. The AIFC's mission is to contribute to the sustainable economic development of Kazakhstan and the region by fostering innovative financial products and services.[7] The AIFC wants to achieve its mission by bringing together the best practices and opportunities from around the globe. Its goal is to support Kazakhstan's policy of modernisation and growth; make the business environment friendlier; attract capital to accelerate development; and provide companies with the most advanced, secure and effective investment instruments.

The AIFC has its own independent judicial system and jurisdiction based on a combination of English common law and international good practice. Access to an independent judicial system is critical to attract investors.

---

[7] Sustainability is defined as "balancing and growing all capital stocks simultaneously – natural, manufactured, human, social, and financial", and is aligned with UN Sustainability Development Goals of which Kazakhstan is a signatory. See, for example, *Capitalism as if the World Matters* (Porritt, 2005) and *The Perfect Storm: Navigating the Sustainable Energy Transition* (Van de Putte, Kelimbetov & Holder, 2017).

Equally important is the development of the AIFC corporate governance principles (hereafter referred to as "the Principles"), which are based on international good practices and standards. They apply to the AIFC Authority and its 100%-owned subsidiaries on an 'opt-in' basis and are aimed at promoting transparency and integrity in business. They complement existing mandatory corporate governance rules which apply to entities listed on the Astana International Exchange (AIX). International best practices leveraged in the AIFC Principles are:

A. Aligned with the principal tenets of corporate governance

The 2015 G20/OECD Principles of Corporate Governance consider the principal tenets of corporate governance to be: 1) accountability, 2) fairness, 3) transparency and 4) responsibility.[8] The Association of Chartered Certified Accountants (ACCA) argues that in addition "… an organisation should be governed with a view to its long-term prosperity, which is interconnected with that of the society within which it operates."[9] Therefore, in addition to those tenets, the Principles emphasise the importance of contributing to the long-term success of the company.[10]

B. Principles rather than rules

Most Commonwealth countries have adopted corporate governance codes based on the 'comply or explain' model. This means that companies must comply with the principles and guidelines contained in the code, or explain their non-compliance. A principles-based approach to corporate governance implies that company directors adhere to the spirit rather than the letter of the code. In the UK, the notion of a principles-based approach to corporate governance was formally established by the Cadbury Committee. This has a number of advantages:

---

[8] Organisation for Economic Co-operation and Development, G20/OECD Principles of Corporate Governance, OCED Publishing, 2015.
[9] The Association of Chartered Certified Accountants (ACCA), Tenets of good corporate governance, May 2018.
[10] The Principles may also be applied to other forms of entity, such as joint ventures.

- The underlying key relationship is between the company and the providers of risk capital, i.e. the shareholders. Excessive regulation could hinder the timely realisation of shareholder value and an open spirit of effective communication between the shareholders and the company.

- There is strong evidence that a principles-based approach to corporate governance helps to reduce the cost of conducting business while stimulating innovation and the overall competitiveness of companies.[11]

- A principles-based code can be applied to a diverse set of situations and companies, thus providing flexibility as to how a company's board organises itself and discharges its duties.

- A rules-based approach to corporate governance may encourage companies and their advisers to focus on strict compliance with the rules rather than complying with the underlying spirit of the regime, thereby undermining the credibility of the corporate governance framework.

- PricewaterhouseCoopers, in its Corporate Governance: Best Practice Reporting, January 2010, recommends that: "A proper governance framework should be principles rather than rules-based", and that "The 'comply or explain' mechanism is effective provided that there is active and challenging engagement between investors and companies."

C. Stakeholder orientation needs to be reflected

In English common law jurisdictions, corporate governance was historically shareholder focussed, whereas in countries such as Germany and Japan a broader stakeholder focus was adopted. In the UK, the interests of key stakeholders are increasingly considered in addition to the interest of shareholders. In a break with tradition, 181 CEOs of some of the most influential companies in the US signed a one-page declaration that they

---

[11] https://www.accaglobal.com/content/dam/acca/global/PDF-students/acca/p1/exampapers/p1sgp/p1sgp-2013-dec-a.pdf

would commit value to all stakeholders. There is a clear trend that corporate governance codes are increasingly balancing the diverse interests of stakeholders versus the sole emphasis of maximising shareholder value (see also Chapter 18 for a broader coverage of stakeholder capitalism).

D. Unitary versus two-tiered boards

Two-tiered board structures prevail in countries such as Germany, Switzerland and China. In Germany, the management board is entirely made up of executive directors, while the supervisory board is entirely composed of non-executive directors. Two-tier board structures are increasingly being scrutinized because the non-executive directors tend not to have a good understanding about what is going on within the organisation. Unified board structures are the norm in Commonwealth countries and also in the US. The greater interaction between the executive and non-executive directors typically results in better strategy, performance, communication with stakeholders, and overall a better balance between conformance and performance. It is recommended that the AIFC corporate governance code adopts unitary over two-tiered board structures.

E. The need to promote sustainable business growth

Boards are increasingly being encouraged by institutional investors to focus on sustainable business growth, and Mazars recently conducted, in partnership with INSEAD and the European Confederation of Directors Associations (EcoDA), a study on embedding sustainability in corporate governance. Given the ratification of the UN Sustainable Development Goals and the Paris Agreement, of which Kazakhstan is a signatory, and given the AIFC's mission, the AIFC corporate governance code should include provisions to help promote sustainable business growth.

F. The need to balance conformance and performance

Currently, there is too much emphasis in Kazakhstan on compliance. This was one of the key findings of the 2017 EBRD study on corporate governance in Kazakhstan. According to the IoD's Role of the Director & Board Handbook (2019): "One of the challenges facing boards is ensuring there is a proper balance between performance and conformance. There can be a tendency in larger organisations – particularly those where the board consists mainly of non-executive directors – to focus on conformance issues, with performance activities mainly delegated to management. As a result, boards may increasingly see their jobs as ensuring compliance with law, regulation and corporate governance codes". The AIFC corporate governance code therefore needs to reflect the need for proper balance between performance and conformance and this also needs to be reflected in the articulation of the director duties.

G. The need to have a diverse working group

There is a tendency for corporate governance codes to be written by lawyers. Lawyers tend to focus too much on the compliance aspects of corporate governance. While lawyers should be involved in the process, a better way to reflect the needs of the AIFC's constituents is to involve a diverse group of international and local experts, including lawyers familiar with English common law, accountants, business leaders, policymakers and even civil society. This ensures that the AIFC corporate governance principles reflect the diverse interests of the AIFC's key stakeholders.

H. Tailored to the specific needs of the AIFC and its constituents

As mentioned, most Commonwealth countries have adopted corporate governance codes based on the 'comply or explain' model. This, however, does not mean that countries have copy-pasted their codes from each other. Instead, various countries have tailored their respective corporate governance codes to their own specific needs and circumstances. Singapore's economy, for example, is largely composed of family-owned businesses (see also Chapter 16). This is in stark contrast with the UK, where larger companies, often multinationals, dominate the corporate landscape.

I. Principles rather than a code

Virtually all countries, especially those with a stock exchange, have developed corporate governance codes, often based on the OECD Principles of Corporate Governance, first issued in 1999 and further revised in 2004.[12] Corporate governance codes are typically applicable to listed companies with the objective to encourage high standards of corporate governance. Nicolas Price argues that: *"The principle behind the Corporate Governance Code is to demonstrate to shareholders and stakeholders how the corporation applied the main principles of the code. In addition, corporations that are subject to the code must confirm that they've fully complied with the provisions of the code. Companies that can't or won't comply with the code's provisions must provide a reasonable explanation of why they haven't complied with the code"*.[13]

Corporate governance codes are typically not applicable to non-listed companies and given that the AIFC is not a listed entity, and currently has a single shareholder, we thought that a set of Principles, instead of a code, would make more sense at least for now. After all, we want to promote sound corporate governance throughout the AIFC and the Principles are designed for any company of any size.

3. The AIFC organisational structure

To help address the challenges of sustainable economic development, the Astana International Financial Centre (AIFC) was created by Presidential Decree in 2015. The AIFC traces its founding to Kazakhstan's "100 Concrete Steps" National Plan announced in 2015. Subsequently, the AIFC Management Council laid out a development strategy that gave the AIFC its initial focus on developing capital markets, Islamic finance, fintech services, asset management, and private banking.

The AIFC was formally launched in 2018 with the goal of developing financial services and spurring global investments into Kazakhstan and putting the country on a steeper and more sustainable and resilient growth

---

[12] Organisation for Economic Co-operation and Development, OECD Principles of Corporate Governance, OCED Publishing, 1999.
[13] https://insights.diligent.com/corporate-governance/what-is-the-corporate-governance-code

trajectory. As the first institution of its kind in the region, the AIFC offers a comprehensive platform to facilitate and protect investments. With over 70 experts and advisors from 35 countries currently part of AIFC, the Centre has been able to adopt a range of best practices from similar institutions across the globe — from New York City and London to Dubai, Hong Kong, and Singapore. The AIFC established its unique legal regime for its successful operation and its statutory legislation is based on principles, legislation and precedents of the law of England and Wales (i.e. English common law) and the standards of leading global financial centres. Figure 13.2 shows the AIFC's organisational structure.

Figure 13.2 The AIFC organisational structure
Source: AIFC

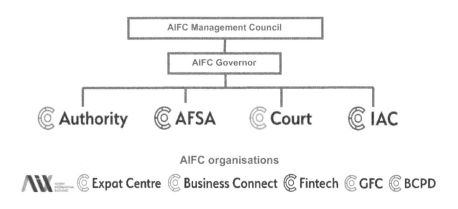

The AIFC Management Council is a permanent collegial body chaired by the president of Kazakhstan and is the AIFC's highest governing body. The Council determines strategic directions for the AIFC and fosters the development of favourable conditions for establishing the AIFC as a leading international financial centre. The Council is authorised to adopt AIFC Acts, determine the structure of the AIFC bodies, the composition of the AIFC Court and the basis for the establishment of the IAC, as well as approve annual reports on the activities of the AIFC.

The AIFC Governor is an official of the AIFC with special administrative and leadership functions as well as regulatory powers for the purpose of coordinating the functioning of AIFC bodies, including their interaction with the state bodies of Kazakhstan, international organisations, institutions, legal entities and individuals, and other entities.

The AIFC is composed of four bodies: 1) the AIFC Authority, which is responsible for formulating the centre's development strategy and drafting acts on matters not related to the regulation of financial matters; 2) the Astana Financial Services Authority (AFSA), the integrated regulator of all market activities, ancillary service providers, and companies within the AIFC; 3) the AIFC Court for civil and commercial dispute resolution within the AIFC and based on English Common Law; and 4) the International Arbitration Centre (IAC), which provides an independent alternative to court litigation.

In addition, there are several 100% or partially owned subsidiaries of the AIFC Authority, which facilitate business development. These include: 1) the Astana International Exchange (AIX), created as a platform to finance the growth of private businesses and the economy as a whole; 2) AIFC Business Connect provides investors and the international business community with fully structured information and the close support they need to access and invest in opportunities available in Kazakhstan; 3) the AIFC Bureau for Continuing Professional Development (BCPD) provides a portfolio of training programmes to help prepare candidates to become internationally certified; 4) the AIFC Fintech Hub seeks to utilise the latest financial technologies to future-proof the AIFC's key business pillars and to develop a vibrant multi-stakeholder fintech ecosystem; 5) the AIFC Expat Centre acts a one-stop shop for foreign investors and expats, assisting them in obtaining government and non-government services (e.g. visa and migration-related services); and 6) the Green Finance Centre offers strategic solutions to governments, financial institutions and enterprises, and facilitates the use of green and sustainable finance instruments.

4. The AIFC corporate governance principles

The AIFC recognises that good corporate governance practices are critical to the long-term success sustainable success of companies. To follow best practices in corporate governance, the AIFC has taken a range of measures to improve the corporate governance practices.

In 2020, the AIFC has adopted the AIFC Ethics Code and principles for corporate governance for AIFC bodies and AIFC organisations.[14]

Within the process of adopting the best global practice in investor stewardship and strengthening sustainable development, the AIFC in partnership with TheCityUK prepared a report on the proposals for the development of a Kazakh Stewardship Code[15] to assist the successful promotion of the AIFC in global markets. This commitment of the AIFC to the principles of sound stewardship enhanced its ability to attract global investors and companies.

To comply with international best practices and corporate governance standards, the AIFC began to develop its own corporate governance principles in July 2019. As mentioned, the AIFC developed its Principles in partnership with TheCityUK and funded by the UK government.[16] Prof. Alexander Van de Putte led the development of the Principles and the team was advised by Simon Osborne FCG, the former CEO of the Chartered Governance Institute. As a result of this joint effort of international and AIFC working group members, the Principles and its Guidance document were finalised in March 2020. The Principles are voluntary and are designed to improve the capabilities and mind-sets of boards (and individual directors) and contribute to the sustainable long-term success of companies. The AIFC Governor and Management Council have approved the Principles for adoption by the AIFC Authority and its 100%-owned subsidiaries.

At the end of 2020, the AIFC Corporate Governance Institute (ACGI) was created at the BCPD. The ACGI is aimed to promote and maintain the Principles, as well as offer training to the AIFC community, other quasi-government entities, and private businesses in Kazakhstan. A working

---

[14] The AIFC Ethics Code has been developed in consultation with the London-based Institute for Business Ethics (https://aifc.kz/ethics-code).
[15] https://www.thecityuk.com/research/responsible-shareholder-engagement-a-kazakh-stewardship-code
[16] UK-Kazakhstan-corporate-governance-working-group-report.pdf (thecityuk.com)

group under the ACGI has started to work with boards of the AIFC Authority, through their company secretaries, to determine the applicability of the Principles to their specific circumstances. This effort is expected to be completed by December 2021.

The BCPD has become an official training partner of the UK-based Chartered Governance Institute (CGI) to offer the CGI Qualifying Programme that leads to the Chartered Governance Professional qualification and CGI Fellowship.[17] In 2021 two modules of the CGI Qualifying Programme will be offered to eligible legal practitioners and chartered accountants in Kazakhstan and the Central Asia region. We believe that this is a unique programme in the CIS to promote corporate governance and corporate secretarial practice. The BCPD has publicly offered five full-day training programmes and several additional training programmes are scheduled in 2021, including a Certificate in Corporate Governance in partnership with the Academy of Law of the BCPD.

A. The Principles

The AIFC corporate governance principles consist of 13 high-level principles that are intended to contribute to sustainable long-term business growth, while reflecting the principal tenets of corporate governance. The 13 Principles (see Appendix A) were articulated and are logically grouped under 7 sections: 1) company purpose and board leadership, 2) division of responsibilities between executive management and non-executive directors, 3) board structure, composition and skills, 4) audit, risk, internal control and reporting, 5) risk governance, 6) evaluation of board and individual directors' performance, and 7) remuneration of directors.

In addition, a guidance document with 47 guidance provisions was developed to facilitate their adoption.

---

[17] The Chartered Governance Institute was founded in 1891 as the Institute of Secretaries to represent the interests of the emerging profession of company secretaries. The Institute was granted a Royal Charter in 1902 and in 2019 became the Chartered Governance Institute (www.cgi.org.uk).

B. Applicability

The Principles and its Guidance are applicable and on an 'opt-in' basis (in full or in part) to the AIFC Authority and its 100%-owned subsidiaries. As noted above, the Principles are being applied on an 'apply and explain' basis.

In other words, the AIFC Authority and its 100%-owned subsidiaries will be expected to apply those Principles they have opted-into, and to explain how they have been implemented and their impact on the performance of the company. It is believed that the combination of 'opt-in' with 'apply and explain' will provide maximum flexibility to the diverse set of the AIFC 100%-owned subsidiaries.

Appendix B illustrates how the combination of 'opt-in' and 'apply and explain' could work in practice for a hypothetical entity, 'X'.

C. Adoption of sound corporate governance practices at the AIFC

Since the approval of the Principles by the AIFC Management Council and AIFC Authority Board in July 2020, bi-weekly workshops have taken place with the company secretaries of the 100%-owned subsidiaries of the AIFC Authority and AFSA. The objective of these workshops is twofold: 1) to explore which provisions the various subsidiaries would opt-into (in part or in full), and 2) share experience and cross-fertilise ideas across the various subsidiaries. Most of the 47 provisions were opted-in, at least in part, with a clear timeline to cover all the provisions over time. The AIFC Authority and AFSA, both with large boards composed of international independent non-executive directors, are currently the most advanced in the adoption of sound corporate governance practices. Also, their company secretaries have contributed significantly to the professional development of the subsidiary companies' secretaries.

D. Further steps in scaling sound corporate governance at the AIFC and beyond

The major focus of the AIFC corporate governance framework is scaling sound corporate governance at the AIFC and beyond based on a philosophy of 'incubate and branch out'. The objective is that best-in-class international standards and corporate practices become the norm in Kazakhstan. To achieve that, the development of the Principles and branching them to the organisations and subsidiaries, tenants, and participants of the AIFC is on the Centre's corporate governance agenda:

- Scale sound corporate governance beyond the AIFC based on a philosophy of 'incubate and branch out' with the objective that best-in-class international standards and corporate practices become the norm in Kazakhstan.

- Dramatically scale corporate governance training through the BCPD that includes preparation for the (above-mentioned) CGI Qualifying Programme, a corporate governance certification programme, and a specialised company secretaries certification programme.

- Establish a branch of the Institute of Directors (IoD) in Kazakhstan to organise local activities and networking events for members and professionals interested in promoting sound corporate governance.

- Create a company secretaries forum at the BCPD to promote the profession and support board effectiveness by monitoring that board policy and procedures are followed. We are convinced that the company secretary, as the only full-time governance professional in an organisation, plays a pivotal role to ensure that sound corporate governance is promoted and practiced (See also Chapter 5).

- Organise quarterly conferences on current issues of corporate governance that are relevant to the AIFC and companies based in Kazakhstan. This will be done in collaboration with our partners internally, including the Institute of Directors, the Chartered Governance Institute, and the Chartered Institute for Securities & Investments.

- Promote the AIFC's work on corporate governance at international conferences to help enhance our reputation and brand recognition.

- Publish a chapter on sound corporate governance at the AIFC and Kazakhstan in a book to be published by The Governance Forum (UK).
- Publish a book on scaling sound corporate governance at the AIFC in 2022. This book is based on the work of the AIFC working group and will be co-authored by the AIFC Governor Kelimbetov, Prof. Van de Putte and board evaluation expert Simon Osborne.

5. Conclusion

Sound corporate provides the foundation to build trust and a relative degree of predictability, hence generating comfort among the investor community and a broad stakeholder group. Over time this will build the competitiveness of businesses operating in Kazakhstan and the Central Asian region. 'Rome was not built in a day' is a proverb attesting to the need for time to achieve great things. The same holds true for scaling sound corporate governance at the AIFC and in Kazakhstan. And similar to the UK since the influential 1992 Cadbury Report,[18] it will be an evolutionary process. However, with the adoption of the AIFC Corporate Governance Principles by an increasingly number of internal and external entities, we are well on our way to achieving this.

---

[18] https://www.frc.org.uk/getattachment/9c19ea6f-bcc7-434c-b481-f2e29c1c271a/The-Financial-Aspects-of-Corporate-Governance-(the-Cadbury-Code).pdf

Appendix A: The AIFC Corporate Governance Principles

1. Companies should be led by a board that promotes the long-term success of the company, generating value for its shareholders, acting responsibly towards key stakeholders, and in the case of companies operating in Kazakhstan, also contributing to the sustainable economic development.

2. Companies should have an effective board which is collectively accountable for ensuring that the company is managed prudently and effectively.

3. The board should establish the company's mission, purpose, values and strategy, and satisfy itself that these and its culture are aligned.

4. The board should set, and its members should comply with, high standards of ethical behaviour, and hold management accountable for delivering these standards throughout the organisation.

5. The board should ensure that there is a clear division of responsibilities between the non-executive directors and executive management, and that no one individual has unfettered powers of decision-making.

6. Boards should be large enough to accommodate all necessary skills and competences, but still be small enough to promote cohesion, flexibility and effective participation. "The optimum size for a board is within the range of 8–12 people. When boards are composed of more than 12 people a number of psychological phenomena, namely, span of attention, the ability to deal with complexity, the ability to maintain effective interpersonal relationships and motivation are compromised."[19]

7. The board, and its committees, should have an appropriate balance of skills, experience, independence and knowledge of the company's business, and adequate resources, including access to expertise as required and timely and comprehensive information relating to the affairs of the company.

---

[19] A review of corporate governance in UK banks and other financial industry entities: Final Recommendations, 2009.

8. The board should ensure that the company's financial and other reports present an accurate, balanced[20] and understandable assessment of the company's financial position and prospects by ensuring that there are effective internal risk control and reporting requirements.

9. The board should be responsible for setting the risk appetite of the company. Risk appetite refers to the amount of risk that a board is willing to take on in order to achieve its strategic objectives.

10. The board should ensure that the company has a risk management, internal control and compliance framework which is effective, well-defined and well-integrated.

11. The board should ensure that there is a formal and rigorous annual performance evaluation of the board, its committees and individual directors. Annual evaluation of the board should include composition, diversity and effectiveness. Individual director evaluation should determine whether directors are contributing effectively to the work of the board and its committees.

12. The board should have a formal and transparent procedure for developing policies on director and executive remuneration. No director should be involved in deciding his or her own remuneration.

13. The board should ensure that the remuneration policies and practices are designed to support strategy and are aligned with the long-term interests of the company.

---

[20] A balanced assessment of a company's financial position requires several alternative perspectives – this typically includes analysis of a company's operating, investing and financial performance, and funding structure.

Appendix B: How the combination of 'opt-in' and 'apply and explain' could work in practice

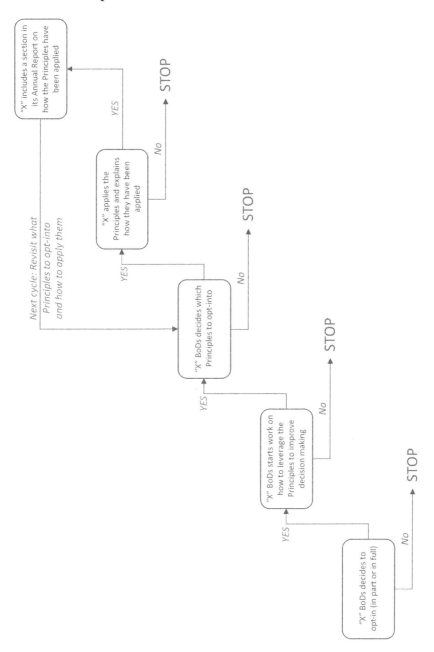

Corporate Governance 3.0

CHAPTER 14. A MENA PERSPECTIVE

Ashraf Gamal El Din, Professor of Management, Cairo University and CEO of Hawkamah

Introduction

When the Middle East is mentioned, what might come to your mind is conflicts and desert. What you may not know is that the Middle East is home for many large and quite successful companies, a few of them are even global ones. Examples include DP World, Aramex, Saudi Aramco, and ORASCOM, just to name a few. These companies were established on strong governance foundations, even though governance itself may not be that mature in the region.

The Sultanate of Oman was the first Arab country to issue an official code of corporate governance in 2002, then other countries in the Middle East and North Africa region (MENA) followed. Most of these governance codes are based on the guidelines of the Organisation for Economic Co-operation and Development (OECD) . Fundamentals of governance, however, existed in many MENA countries in their company laws, many of which describe roles and responsibilities of boards and AGMs in a detailed manner. But it was probably not until the early 2000s that MENA countries started to take governance more seriously.

Corporate governance in the MENA region is driven almost entirely by regulators. Codes of corporate governance are used for awareness creation and getting the buy-in from companies, directors and even regulators sometimes. Hawkamah, the Institute for Corporate Governance (Hawkamah) has been operating from the Dubai International Financial Center (DIFC) since 2006, serving the cause of governance in the region in different ways.

There ae many challenges facing the adoption and application of good governance in the region. Most governance regulations focus on listed companies, which represent a small percentage of companies operating in the region. State owned enterprises and family-owned businesses represent the dominant types of companies in almost all MENA economies. These companies either have no sound governance systems or are not strictly regulated at all.

This chapter aims to explain the governance landscape in the MENA region, highlighting main issues and key challenges facing the region and giving an overview of the expected future of good governance in the region. The chapter will also highlight the efforts that Hawkamah – the corporate governance institute – has been exerting to improve governance landscape and practices in the MENA region. It is an important read for those who plan to do business or invest in the region.

1. Background

The MENA region is considered an emerging market in which corporate governance is seen as a relatively new concept. Indeed, it was only in 2002 that an Arabic word for 'governance'- "Hawkamah" - has emerged from the Arabic Language Supreme Council in Egypt. Despite its relative infancy in the region, corporate governance has made significant headways. Although it is still difficult to assess the outcomes of the "Arab Spring" that started in 2011, and continues till now in some countries, it has highlighted some pressing demographic, political, governance and socioeconomic challenges, which, if properly addressed, should lead to further corporate governance reforms. The COVID-19 crisis has forced new realities onto businesses and economies of the region, which are pushing for even more reforms.

2. The MENA region's corporate governance journey: the past 14 years

Hawkamah celebrated its fourteenth anniversary in 2020. The institute was set up with the grand vision of "bridging the corporate governance gap" between the developed markets and the MENA region. Thus, Hawkamah's activities have ranged from awareness-raising to research, from policy work to standard setting and from capacity building of board directors to providing advisory services to companies, regulators, and governments of the region. Hawkamah's range of activities reflects the rapid development of corporate governance in the region.

In 2008, a joint study by Hawkamah and the World Bank's International Finance Corporation (IFC) revealed that while companies recognized corporate governance to be important, few could credibly claim to have undertaken broad scale governance reforms. The study also found that only 3% of the surveyed companies could be rated as following "good practice" and none following "best practice".

Disclosure practices by listed companies were extremely poor. Prior to 2009 it was difficult to obtain any publicly disclosed information of listed companies beyond the names of the board members and basic financials. Hawkamah's joint study with the *National Investor* in 2008 found that the contact details of investor relations officers were available for only a handful of Gulf Cooperation Council (GCC) listed companies; only 3% of them held analyst calls; 90% of them did not pre-announce their results publication dates; and it was not unusual to come across instances of interim financial results which were handwritten, often illegibly.

Boardrooms were largely populated by insiders, with appointments based on trust. Board members were often sitting on many other boards, and conflicts of interest were common. Boards were mainly "trophy" boards; hence, expectations placed on them were unclear and little regard was paid to issues such as independence and time commitment. During that time, board evaluations were unheard of and even unthinkable.

Discussions on corporate governance were often centered on why governance mattered, or indeed, was needed at all. The term itself was often misunderstood to mean corporate social responsibility or even corporate management, as our 2008 joint study with the IFC indicated.

The governance landscape has changed drastically in the last 14 years. Corporate governance codes have been issued by regulators across the region, mostly for listed companies and financial institutions. Many codes have been revised and improved a few times. Some countries have issued codes other than those issued for financial institutions and listed companies. These include codes for state-owned companies, government boards. Numerous frameworks and guidelines were issued for family-owned businesses, Islamic financial institutions and even SMEs. Discussions on corporate governance are now focused on governance structures and how to best implement good governance and get closer to international good practices.

One practical way to visualize the governance evolution in the region is to pick up a 2006 annual report of a regional listed company and compare it to its 2020 annual report. Today, the average annual report issued by a listed company in the region is well over 100 pages in length and this is increasingly supplemented by information disclosed on the company's website and even in a separate sustainability report, some even using the GRI framework.

Regulators in several countries of the region reformed the overall governance frameworks, covering subjects that were not covered before. United Arab Emirates (UAE), Saudi Arabia, Oman, Egypt, and Qatar, for example, have either revised or issued totally new company laws that address governance at a higher regulatory level. The role of boards has received much attention from regulators, and companies, alike. Delegation of authority matrixes are widely in place, detailing the range of decisions boards need to take and approve. Various board committees became mandatory, with detailed description of their roles and responsibilities.

A MENA Perspective

Board evaluations are becoming mandatory, accepted, and practiced even in countries where they are not mandatory. Board evaluations are now mandatory in many countries of the region such as Oman, Kuwait, Bahrain, and the UAE; and it is still a guiding principle in Saudi Arabia. Furthermore, Oman's code of governance requires new directors to undertake corporate governance training. The UAE new code mandates 20% female representation on boards of listed companies, UAE federal government boards and owned entities. The UAE recently issued corporate governance regulations that allow for the dual-board structure and that provide a comprehensive list of key processes – ranging from strategy to risk management, from internal controls to stakeholder management – which the board needs to be proactively overseeing.

While the region should be proud of these developments, it is yet too early to celebrate. Governance frameworks are now largely in place and companies have taken significant steps in governance implementation; but there is no room for complacency. In many ways, the region has accomplished the easy part, but the next challenges will be far harder to overcome. What we have achieved so far has been largely focused on forms and structures; now it is time to focus on the substance. For example, it is far easier to set up an audit committee than it is to ensure that the audit committee works effectively.

What this requires is leadership and self-awareness, i.e., soft skills. For the region to move to the next level, we need to change our approach to corporate governance. There is certain eagerness in the region, most notably in the GCC, to utilize international good practices, to seek certification against various international standards and to use international benchmarks as guides. Companies often tend to follow the same logic when looking to adopt corporate governance practices, but this logic is unlikely to yield desirable results in the MENA context.

Firstly, many of the international theories on corporate governance stem from the UK and other markets, such as Australia, with similar characteristics. The UK Corporate Governance Code represents an extremely well thought out set of governance principles, which have evolved and been revised numerous times since 1992. However, the UK Code addresses the governance issues arising in the UK ecosystem where there is a prevalence of fragmented ownership. It is a market where shareholding of 3% is considered significant. The nature of the ownership structure means that the relative power rests with the board and the management, as opposed to the shareholders. A typical governance issue in the UK relates to excessive executive remuneration, which is a logical outcome of that power dynamic.

The MENA markets are markedly different, where companies are controlled by block holders. In this power dynamic, the power rests squarely with the majority shareholder, usually related to the government one way or another. This situation raises several potential governance issues such as conflicts of interest, related party transactions, lack of independence and scrutiny mechanisms, protection of minority shareholders, etc. - problems that are not that common in the UK.

Secondly, the international-certification mindset often misses an important point about governance. Governance, like strategy, should be uniquely tailored to the company's business, circumstances, and vision. What we need is to empower boards and board members to reflect on the purpose of their companies and steer them accordingly within a relevant control and stewardship framework. Boards should formulate the overall vision and identify the key values for the business, while linking these with stakeholders and their needs and rights. The optimal governance framework for a company is derived from going through this process. This also forms the basis on which the board, in partnership with the management, develops the company's strategy and risk appetite. Deriving from these, the company should set objectives, embed these in the incentive structures and control practices and keep them under regular review. Boards need to shift their focus from merely providing financial oversight of the business to becoming actively engaged in how the company and its business are being directed by the executive leadership team. This means that it is the boardroom that should be driving corporate governance practices if the region is to continue its progress on the governance journey. This approach might be different from practices in other regions. However, our regional experience shows that management is focusing most of its attention on achieving targets and handling daily challenges. Management hence cannot be entrusted with takin the lead in establishing good governance in their companies. MENA companies that enjoy high levels of good governance are usually characterized by strong, non-executive boards stressing the need for good governance and putting pressure on the management to achieve it.

3. The need for a regional institute

Early on in the MENA region journey towards good governance, it became clear that international good practices and experiences are relevant and needed, but governance experts and practitioners must possess the regional knowledge of the specifics and the local culture if they are to move forward and achieve meaningful results. The Hawkamah Institute for Corporate Governance was therefore set up in 2006 to help bridge the corporate governance gap in the region. It was founded in partnership with international organisations including the OECD, the IFC, the World Bank's Global Corporate Governance Forum and regional organisations including the Union of Arab Banks and the DIFC Authority. It combined international good practice with regional knowledge. This has brought Hawkamah closer to the region, its regulators and a variety of institutions.

Hawkamah's primary goal was to establish corporate governance as a topic on the agendas of MENA policy makers by providing regulators, companies and various institutions, with practical tools on how to improve corporate governance. Its work involves engaging governments, industry, and regulators by means of surveys and studies and creating regional benchmarks, which often act as catalysts for reform in different countries of the region.

In its early years, Hawkamah's calls for corporate governance reform were very much like voices in the wilderness. Although the need for better corporate governance was recognized, the prevailing opinion was that the region was not ready for reform. Illustrative of the then state of corporate governance is the finding of the 2007 benchmark Hawkamah-IFC survey that only 3% of listed companies and banks in the MENA followed good corporate governance practices, with none complying with international "best" practices[1].

4. Drivers of corporate governance in the MENA

Corporate governance reform in the MENA region has not been investor driven. Many reforms stem from a combination of factors such as the ownership structures of MENA companies, the availability of liquidity and financing from regional banks and the relatively underdeveloped capital markets that are dominated by retail investors. The region is also generally overlooked by global long-term investors, largely because of its poor track record in transparency, disclosure and non-financial corporate reporting. Regional asset managers such as the sovereign wealth funds have not exhibited governance vigor in their local investment processes and have mainly invested outside the region to diversify away from local and regional risks. Therefore, the benefits of good corporate governance have been seen by companies typically in terms of better strategic decision-making and regulatory compliance, rather than being associated with better and cheaper access to credit and capital or improved valuation of companies, as is usually the case in developed markets.

5. S&P/Hawkamah ESG Indexes

One of the key influencers for improving governance practices is to place companies under scrutiny and exposure. To that end, Hawkamah has collaborated with Standard and Poor's (S&P) in creating two indices in the region; one that covers the entire MENA region, launched in 2011 and one that covers the UAE capital markets, launched in 2020.

---

[1] Hawkamah and the International Finance Corporation. (2007), *A Corporate Governance Survey of Listed Companies and Banks Across the Middle East & North Africa*, available online: <https://www.ifc.org/wps/wcm/connect/topics_ext_content/ifc_external_corporate_site/ifc+cg/resources/guidelines_reviews+and+case+studies/a+corporate+governance+survey+of+listed+companies+and+banks+across+the+middle+east+and+north+africa> (accessed 11 July 2021).

6. S&P/Hawkamah ESG Pan-Arab Index

This was the first, and remains the only, MENA-wide ESG index in the region. To launch this index, Hawkamah has partnered with S&P and the IFC. The index tracks and ranks the transparency and disclosure of regional listed companies on a spectrum of ESG issues. The constituents of the index are derived from 11 Arab equity markets. The purpose of the index is to identify the MENA companies that go the extra mile in ESG reporting and policy implementation, mostly not yet required by the regulators. The index is a tool available for international and regional investors who may not have the expert knowledge of MENA companies or of applying corporate governance principles to their investment processes.

The index is not only a tool for investors, but also for companies. Inclusion in the index provides public recognition for local companies on their ESG practices, but the index is more than just a badge of honour. As the socially responsible investment movement spreads across the region, capital will start flowing towards companies with better ESG reporting, thereby improving their access to external capital. A trend that is expected to flourish faster due to the COVID-19 pandemic and its aftermath.

7. Regional investors and banks

Regional investors typically have not formally incorporated corporate governance criteria in their investment decision-making processes. The index is being used to raise awareness among the region's sovereign wealth funds on the impact good corporate governance can have on the bottom line and the index has outperformed the market benchmark by a significant margin. One of the region's sovereign wealth funds has invested in the index and hopefully others will follow.

Given the size and growing importance[2] of MENA top 10 sovereign wealth

---

[2] Nine of which belong to GCC governments – see Amlôt, M. (2019) 'Here are the top 10 sovereign wealth funds in the Arab world', *Al Arabiya English (29 August)*, available online: <https://english.alarabiya.net/business/economy/2019/08/28/Here-are-the-top-10-sovereign-wealth-funds-in-the-Arab-world> (accessed 11 July 2021).

funds (SWFs) (they manage over US$ 3 trillion in assets), encouraging SWFs to adopt a more active role in promoting good corporate governance would not only be a welcome step for the development of the MENA capital markets, but also across the world in the markets and companies in which they invest.

But in a region which is dominated by non-listed, government and family-owned enterprises and/or small and medium sized companies that typically look to banks to finance their expansion through loans, it is the banks that are in the prime seat to drive governance reform. Indeed, bank intermediated finance represents some 60% of the overall financial structure in MENA, while debt finance is underdeveloped at 10% of the total.[3] Hawkamah, in partnership with the OECD and the UAE, have issued a Policy Brief on improving the corporate governance of banks in MENA.[4] Although the Policy Brief is primarily focused on addressing the governance challenges faced by the sector and the regulators/ central banks, one of its recommendations is for banks to incorporate corporate governance criteria into their overall lending criteria. The excessive liquidity that banks have, however, does not help. Banks need to give more credit to use their liquidity, hence they are willing to lower their standards, including governance, to achieve their targets.

A. The UAE S&P/Hawkamah ESG Index

In recognition of the importance of good environmental, social, and governance practices for companies, shareholders, and markets at large, the UAE government approved the development of an ESG index for its markets; namely Abu Dhabi (ADX) and Dubai (DFM). The Ministry of Economy, Securities and Commodities Authority (SCA) decided to follow the same structure and methodology of the S&P/ Hawkamah ESG Pan

---

[3] International Monetary Fund. (2011), *Global Financial Stability Report Statistical Appendix, April 2011*, available online:
<http://www.imf.org/external/pubs/ft/gfsr/2011/01/pdf/statappx.pdf> (accessed 11 July 2021).

[4] Hawkamah. (n.d.), *ARCG Task Force on Corporate Governance of Banks*, available online: <https://www.hawkamah.org/
uploads/Banks-English.pdf> (accessed 11 July 2021).

Arab Index. The new index was launched January 2020. The effects of the index are yet to be assessed. Launching the index, however, shows the commitment of the UAE government and regulators to ESG and their willingness to encourage companies to adhere to good practices to attract foreign investments.

B. Challenges to Good Governance

As mentioned earlier, corporate governance codes are mostly in place in almost all countries of the MENA region. The challenge is now in their implementation. Given the market dynamics, in which there is an absence of institutional investors scrutinizing the governance arrangements of companies, the burden of ensuring implementation falls on the regulators. Some countries have started taking significant steps in this regard. The regulators in Saudi Arabia (for listed companies and for financial institutions) are imposing hefty fines on companies and banks violating their governance rules. These rules have been updated few times over the last years in order to reflect international good practices. Moreover, Saudi Arabia has mandated its listed companies to use International Financial Reporting Standards (IFRS) in their financial reporting. Financial institutions in the UAE are now subject to two sets of rules: governance regulations of the UAE Central Bank, and governance rules set by SCA for listed companies.

The focus on regulators for enforcing compliance does not of itself assure success. In fact there are some economic and social features of the MENA region which make it impossible for regulators alone to be able to take governance forward. These include, in particular:

- **Non-listed companies:** Numerous companies in the MENA region are not listed and in many cases are the biggest in size and in economic substance. An OECD report, for example, mentions that in countries such as Bahrain, Lebanon, Egypt, Kuwait, Morocco, Oman, Saudi Arabia and the United Arab Emirates, the largest 20 or so companies (in each country) are not listed on the stock exchange.[5]

---

[5] (n.d.), 'Ownership structures in MENA countries: Listed companies, state-owned, family enterprises and some policy implications', *OECD.org*, available online: <https://www.oecd.org/mena/competitiveness/35402110.pdf> (accessed 11 July 2021).

- **State Owned Enterprises (SOE):** Almost all key economic sectors in the region are controlled by SOE, including infrastructure, oil and gas, mining, telecommunications, transportation, construction, and financial services. These companies are either non-listed, so they are not subject to listing rules, or they are listed but they are part of the government 'ecosystem' and enjoy special protection and treatment. One can observe the typical challenges that the OECD mentions in various publications: combining regulation and service provision under the same 'roof', the political use of SOE, loosely regulated monopolies, conflicts of interest and poor governance structures.

  SOE in the GCC countries are in fact a good example of what governments can do to establish good governance in their own companies. For example, while 32 of the top 100 listed companies in the MENA region are state-owned enterprises, 29 are based in the GCC. To the extent that successful listings represent a vote of confidence in majority state-owned companies, GCC companies appear further ahead in the game in the region[6].

- **Family-Owned Businesses (FOB):** The other dominant form of ownership in the MENA region is family ownership, which is particularly common in the GCC countries; much more so than other MENA countries. PwC concluded in a 2016 report that family businesses in the region constitute up to 90% of all companies, employ 80% of the workforce, and contribute up to 60 % of the region's GDP.[7] FOB operate in different fields, but usually take the holding company structure where many non-related business activities are grouped under one holding company. These companies are typically under the "company law", with minimum, if any, level of governance required. The UAE is the only country in the region that issued a law for FOB in 2020 wishing, rather than imposing, more governance

---

[6] Hertog, S. (2012), 'How the GCC did it: Formal and informal governance of successful public enterprise in the Gulf Co-operation Council countries' in Amico, A. (ed.), *Towards New Arrangements for State Ownership in the Middle East and North Africa*, London: OECD, 71-92, available online: <http://eprints.lse.ac.uk/46744/1/How%20the%20GCC%20did%20it%20%28lsero%29.pdf> (accessed 11 July 2021).

[7] *Middle East Family Business Survey 2019*, available online: < https://www.pwc.com/m1/en/publications/documents/family-business-survey-2019.pdf> (accessed 11 July 2021), 3.

requirements on them. However, as that law is neither mandatory "comply or explain", it remains doubtful whether families or FOB will embrace that law at all.

- **Board Information and Gender Diversity**: A survey conducted in 2020 about board practices and challenges concluded that, despite the improvements in board practices over the previous three years, many boards lacked know-how about governance reform and the quality of information presented in board packs which needed to improve. The study also concluded that gender diversity remained a challenge for regional boards.[8] Gender diversity in boards in MENA countries is well below that in more developed markets. On average, women occupy 2.5% of board seats in listed companies. However, countries do vary considerably as regards this metric. While Egypt has close to 10% female board members on its listed companies, Saudi Arabia has less than 1%. The UAE has doubled the percentage of women on boards of listed companies from 1.9% in 2017 to 4% in 2020.[9]

8. Overcoming the Challenges

To overcome the challenges that ownership structure poses to good governance, different kinds of effort are needed. While some might think of regulation as the key requirement, other efforts might be more relevant to the region, such as self-awareness and capacity building. Company owners, whether families or the state, need to be aware of the value of good governance and how it can benefit them. Based on our interaction with families in the region, one can easily sense that they are worried from disclosure, families do not wish to reveal too much about their wealth and assets. They need to be convinced that the value of good governance and the opportunities it brings far outweigh their fears. Governments, on the other hand, do not practice good governance in relation to their companies

---

[8] Hawkamah and Diligent Corporation. (2019), *Board Best Practices in the Middle East*, available online: <https://info.diligent.com/wp-content/uploads/2020/09/Digital_Hawkamah_Board-Best-Practices_Report_15122019.pdf> (accessed 11 July 2021).

[9] Hawkamah and Diligent Corporation (2020), *Gender Diversity in the GCC: Developments, Approaches and Best Practices*, available online: <https://www.hawkamah.org/files/shares/Gender-diversity-in-the-GCC-report.pdf> (accessed 11 July 2021).

either because they do not know that much about it or because they benefit from the lack of governance. In both cases, the lack of qualified board members, governance professionals and advisers also plays a key role in the lack of awareness and the inability to embed good governance in companies.

Hence, awareness creation and capacity building play an important role in facilitating the introduction of good governance to FOB and SOE. Regulation also plays an important role, but regulation alone cannot be enough. If company owners are not convinced of the need for good governance, regulation will turn into a box-ticking exercise where governance is only a facade with no underlying substance.

The challenge of gender diversity requires the demonstration of tangible good examples because reform cannot be achieved without proper regulation, a quota system, capacity building and awareness creation. A quota system would help break the glass ceiling; capacity building would make sure that we had board-ready females of the right calibre who could serve on boards; while awareness would educate current board members about the value that women bring to boards and companies.

9. The 'Arab Spring' and Governance

The turmoil in the Arab world that began with the self-immolation in Tunisia of Mohamed Bouazizi in mid-December 2010 now signals changes in the political, social, and economic geography of the region. The movement spread to many other MENA countries and more unrest occurred in the decade that followed. The region is far from being stable, but governance can surely play a positive role there. The two themes that emerge from the 'Arab Spring' are job-creation, employment and accountability, which directly relate to the need for private sector growth and reform of the SOE.

For the private sector to grow, a mechanism must be established to facilitate the process through which companies could tap into the equity markets. The regional capital markets are tailored for large companies, whereas a stock exchange should be created to meet the needs and ambitions of private companies. *A second-tier equity market* for young and growth companies might become a key driver in the development of a liquid capital market and diversification of economic activities as well as provide long-term capital for the growth of the dynamic entrepreneurial segment of the region's economies. It would also facilitate the introduction of corporate governance into this important segment of the economy and thereby become a key driver for the adoption of good governance. So far this has taken place in Egypt and the UAE. Second-tier markets need to be established in other countries of the MENA region with more relevant governance requirements to attract entrepreneurs and SMEs and help them attract more funding, secure more success and create more jobs.

10. What are we advising boards during the challenging times of COVID-19?

One of the features of MENA boards is that most of their seats are occupied by "people of status", VIPs, successful businessmen, government officials, and people with busy schedules. Hawkamah has therefore designed a board briefing to identify topics that matter. This includes their roles and responsibilities, interacting with the management, effective boards, etc. This service became more popular with the pandemic and we had to go virtual with it. Dubai has shown again its leadership in governance reform by mandating "board briefings" to its listed companies, at least once every two years. However, many other companies are using the service due to its value and the short period which needs to be spent on it.

During 2020, we focused on the role of the board in risk, strategy, culture and conducting effective virtual meetings. In our discussions with various boards, we covered several key topics which we advised boards to discuss with their management teams. The topics mentioned below overlap to some degree and should be considered together, not in isolation:

1. **Strategy and business model**: Boards need to discuss with the management the testing of current strategy for assurance that it is still relevant. This includes vision, mission and long-term objectives. The discussion must also include the company's business model; the way in which goals are achieved. It is very much expected that such

discussions will result in considerable changes to the strategy and business model.

2. The second topic on the table should be **technology**: The current crisis showed that technology can make or break a business. It can be a key source of competitiveness and the way to conduct business and run operations for years to come. The discussion will include topics such as how to make the best of technology and readiness for it? What changes and upgrades are needed? Does the organisational structure need updating? Are changes needed to policies and procedures? What are the risks associated with the extensive use of technology? How can they be mitigated?

3. The third topic concerns **stakeholders**. The crisis had a serious impact on three key stakeholder groups: employees, suppliers, and customers. The board needs to fully understand what the effects of the crisis on each were of those categories. What are the expectations of each group? How can employees be protected yet kept productive? What do customers need and how can the company deliver and cater for their needs? What is the best way to manage the supply chain? How are supply disruptions to be avoided? Should the supplier network be re-engineered to cover for contingencies? What is the impact of all this on costs, prices and profits?

4. Another key item on the agenda for each meeting between the board and management should be the **financials**. A major risk now facing organisations is insolvency. If companies do not manage their cashflows carefully, the consequences may be grave. Boards must feel comfortable about the way in which management is handling liquidity and need to understand as early as possible if more cash will be needed to assure survival of the company. If cash is needed, then when, how much and for how long; and what would be the best sources, not only in terms of the cost but also in terms of risk?

5. Finally, **corporate culture**: Boards are responsible for ensuring that the senior management team is fostering and embedding the right culture in the organisation. This can be done using different tools such as KPIs, incentive structure, training courses, and board-management sessions. Boards need to discuss with their management, do we have the right culture? Are we using the right KPIs and incentive schemes or

do we need to change them? It is common in times of crisis and business down-turn for employees and management to take short cuts to achieve targets and justify bonuses. Boards need assurance that this will not be the case. Employees will need assurance too from the board that they will not be sacrificed and be the victims of the crisis. Boards should figure out the measures they can take to protect employees without putting companies at risk of bankruptcy.

11. Conclusion

The MENA region has been striving to improve governance standards and much has been achieved in a relatively short period. Codes for listed companies and financial institutions have been issued and updated by most MENA countries. The challenge now is about implementation of those codes, particularly in the areas of transparency and disclosure, risk management, board composition and practices. Much of the burden of ensuring the adherence to good governance falls on the regulators. Investors, particularly institutional investors, are yet to play a more pro-active role.

The current challenges for the region involve addressing the governance shortcomings of SOE and FOB. Countries of the region need also to facilitate private sector growth, both of which require the willing adoption of good corporate governance practices. While these are sizable challenges, if the political response to the 'Arab Spring' leads to greater accountability and transparency in governance, the opportunities are greater and the promise of a 'New Age' for the Arab world can become a reality. The COVID crisis created many risks for companies in the region, but also offers opportunities. Only time will tell who can make the best of this global crisis and who will be the losers.

Corporate Governance 3.0

CHAPTER 15. A SOUTH AFRICAN PERSPECTIVE

Sharon Constançon, CEO, Genius Boards and Chair of the South African Chamber of Commerce in the UK

Simon Osborne, Chartered Governance Consultant and Former Chief Executive, The Chartered Governance Institute UK & Ireland

Introduction

"Action without vision is only passing time, vision without action is merely day dreaming, but vision with action can change the world." - Nelson Mandela

"Explanation also helps to encourage organisations to see corporate governance not as an act of mindful compliance, but something that will yield results if it is approached mindfully, with due consideration of the organisation's circumstances" - Foreword to the King IV Governance Report, by Mervyn E. King SC, chair of the King Committee[1]

---

[1] Institute of Directors South Africa. (2016), *King IV Report on Corporate Governance for South Africa 2016*, Johannesburg: IoDSA, available online:
<https://cdn.ymaws.com/www.iodsa.co.za/resource/collection/684B68A7-B768-465C-8214-E3A007F15A5A/IoDSA_King_IV_Report_-_WebVersion.pdf> (accessed 11 July 2021).

Governance in South Africa revolves around the King IV Report on Corporate Governance; King IV or simply the 'code', as it is known.

In the view of Deloitte, this incarnation of the King Code is 'bolder than ever before.'[2] It will be appreciated therefore that any consideration of Corporate Governance 3.0 in relation to South Africa necessarily involves a review of this remarkable report and its code. As the report states, "King IV ... sets out the philosophy, principles, practices and outcomes which serve as the benchmark for corporate governance in South Africa."[3]

1. Some Background

In 1992 the Institute of Directors in Southern Africa (IoDSA) asked retired Supreme Court of South Africa judge, Mervyn E. King SC, to chair a committee on corporate governance. He viewed this project as an opportunity to educate the newly democratic South African republic on the working of a free economy.[4]

The first three King Reports on Corporate Governance were published in 1994, 2002 and 2009 and provided guidance for governance structures and operations of companies. King IV was published in 2016. It has gone further than its predecessors and applies to all organisations across all sectors - private and public, large and small and for-profit and not-for-profit. The code refers to 'organisations' and 'governing bodies', which correlate to 'companies' and 'boards'.

King IV acknowledges that organisations do not operate in a vacuum, are integral to society and therefore accountable towards current and future stakeholders. It aims to establish a balance between conformance and performance. It is non-legislative, is based on principles and practices and,

---

[2] (2016), *King IV: Bolder Than Ever*, Johannesburg: Deloitte Touche Tohmatsu Limited, available for download at <https://www2.deloitte.com/za/en/pages/africa-centre-for-corporate-governance/articles/kingiv-report-on-corporate-governance.html> (accessed 11 July 2021).

[3] Note 1 at 20 – given the emphasis on King IV, further references will be limited to direct quotations.

[4] Stewart, N. (2010), 'An audience with the GRI's Mervyn King', *Inside Investor Relations (9 September)*, available online: https://web.archive.org/web/20110113123908/http://www.insideinvestorrelations.com/articles/16371/audience-mervyn-king/> (accessed 11 July 2021).

in its latest robust outcomes-based version, has adopted an 'apply and explain' approach to disclosure.

The philosophy of the King IV code is derived from the three key elements of leadership, sustainability and good corporate citizenship. Good governance involves effective, ethical leadership and looks to leaders to direct their organisation so as to achieve sustainable economic, social and environmental performance.

The code views sustainability as the primary moral and economic imperative of this century. This view of corporate citizenship flows from an organisation's standing as a juristic person under the South African constitution, so it should operate in a sustainable manner.

Application of all the principles is assumed and companies should explain the practices that have been implemented to give effect to each principle. Explanation should be provided in the form of a narrative account, with reference to practices that demonstrate application of the principles. All disclosures should be updated annually at least, approved by the governing body, and published on accessible media and communication platforms.

2. Global Influences on King IV

As noted in the foreword to King IV, various global factors have influenced the development of this code. Diverse realities which are testing organisational leadership include globalisation, social tensions and inequalities, population growth, climate change, geopolitical tensions, financial crises, rapid technological and scientific advances, together with ever-growing demands for greater transparency.

The foreword goes on to highlight seven concepts that form the foundation stones of King IV: ethical leadership, the organisation in society, corporate citizenship, sustainable development, stakeholder inclusivity, integrated thinking and integrated reporting. These concepts are described as relevant to three paradigm shifts in the corporate world viz. from financial capitalism to inclusive capitalism; from short-term capital markets to long-term, sustainable capital markets; and from siloed reporting to integrated reporting. King IV takes account of these shifts and goes on to outline how leading organisations, in response to these shifts, have started to change the way they operate in the areas of stakeholder management, technology and strategy.

Space in this publication does not permit a more detailed elaboration and discussion of these realities, paradigm shifts and tensions but readers are encouraged to study Dr. King's foreword to King IV, the better to appreciate what underpins the world leading approach to good governance mandated in the report.

3. Objectives of King IV

One cannot improve on the clarity of the statement of objectives of King IV, as they are set out in the report. They speak eloquently for themselves:

"King IV's objectives are to:

- Promote corporate governance as integral to running an organisation and delivering governance outcomes such as an ethical culture, good performance, effective control and legitimacy
- Broaden the acceptance of King IV by making it accessible and fit for implementation across a variety of sectors and organisational types
- Reinforce corporate governance as a holistic and interrelated set of arrangements to be understood and implemented in an integrated manner
- Encourage transparent and meaningful reporting to stakeholders
- Present corporate governance as concerned with not only structure and process, but also with an ethical consciousness and conduct."[5]

4. Definition of Corporate Governance

King IV sets out a unique definition of corporate governance:

"Corporate governance, for the purposes of King IV, is defined as the exercise of ethical and effective leadership by the governing body towards the achievement of the

---

[5] Note 1, 22.

following governance outcomes:

— *Ethical culture*

— *Good performance*

— *Effective control*

— *Legitimacy*

Ethical and effective leadership should complement each other."[6]

Extensive definitions of ethical and effective leadership are then provided. The former "is exemplified by integrity, competence, responsibility, accountability, fairness and transparency. It involves the anticipation and prevention, or otherwise amelioration, of the negative consequences of the organisation's activities and outputs on the economy, society and the environment and the capitals it uses and affects."[7] Effective leadership is defined as "results driven. It is about achieving strategic objectives and positive outcomes. Effective leadership includes, but goes beyond, an internal focus on effective and efficient execution."[8]

It is interesting to compare this definition of corporate governance, and the subsidiary definitions of ethical culture and effective leadership, with the well-known and memorably succinct definition of corporate governance found in the Cadbury Report viz. "The system by which companies are directed and controlled." [9] While this definition is a fair starting point, does it go far enough to explain what good governance should be seeking to achieve in the 21st century?

In 2004, the OECD Principles of Corporate Governance defined good corporate governance in this way: "[It] should provide proper incentives for the board and management to pursue objectives that are in the interests of the company and its shareholders and should facilitate effective

---

[6] Ibid, 20.
[7] Ibid.
[8] Ibid.
[9] Cadbury, A. et al. (1992), *Report of The Committee on the Financial Aspects of Corporate Governance*, available online: <https://www.icaew.com/-/media/corporate/files/library/subjects/corporate-governance/financial-aspects-of-corporate-governance.ashx?la=en> (accessed 11 July 2021), paragraph 2.5.

monitoring."[10] However, like the Cadbury definition, the 2004 definition from OECD addresses neither the question of legitimacy nor the vital interests of stakeholders.

Some 11 years later, the G20/OECD Principles of Corporate Governance 2015 expanded on that definition by describing the purpose of governance thus:

> *"To help build an environment of trust, transparency and accountability necessary for fostering long-term investment, financial stability and business integrity, thereby supporting stronger growth and more inclusive societies."*[11]

That expanded definition, particularly the aspirational reference to "more inclusive societies", requires all organisations – not just for-profit businesses – to reflect on their role in society at large and to conduct their activities in a way which demonstrates the genuine realisation that they should not conduct their activities in a vacuum. Implicit in that definition is the need to address the interests of the various stakeholders in each type of organisation.

While the definition in the OECD Principles of Corporate Governance 2015 is not so far apart from the King IV definition, the focus of the latter is on ethical culture and effective leadership (the first of which, in particular, seems to be in increasingly short supply across the world of business); and on the governance outcome of legitimacy which plays back directly to the legitimate interests and voices of each stakeholder body.[12]

That emphasis on ethical and effective leadership is expressed in Principle 1 of the King IV Code: "The governing body should lead ethically and effectively."[13]

---

[10] Available online:
<https://www.oecd.org/corporate/ca/corporategovernanceprinciples/31557724.pdf> (accessed 11 July 2021), 11.
[11] Available online: <https://www.oecd-ilibrary.org/docserver/9789264236882-en.pdf> (accessed 11 July 2021), at 7.
[12] Note 6.
[13] Note 1, 40.

5. Structure and Status of King IV

King IV is structured as a report that includes a code. There are 17 principles, including one for institutional investors, which are a consolidation of the previous 75 principles and 214 recommended practices found in King III. Five sector supplements for small and medium enterprises (SMEs), non-profit organisations (NPOs), state-owned entities, municipalities and retirement funds, guide these different types of organisation on how to apply King IV within their particular context. These supplements contain guidance on the interpretation of specific principles considered most relevant, and possibly challenging, to each of these sectors.

The legal status of King IV is that of a set of voluntary principles and good practices. If there is a conflict between legislation and King IV, the law prevails. King IV mandates an 'apply and explain' approach to disclosure, meaning that application of the principles is assumed and that a cogent explanation is provided on the practices which have been adopted and implemented and how these support the application of the associated governance principle.

Adherence to King IV is looked for in all organisations, including companies listed on the Johannesburg Stock Exchange, unlisted companies, trusts and NGOs. Whilst adoption of King IV is voluntary (unless prescribed by law or a stock exchange listing requirement), it is designed to be adopted by all organisations, irrespective of their form or manner of incorporation. Therefore, King IV is more far-reaching in its scope than other globally recognised codes such as the UK Corporate Governance Code.[14]

The UK regulator, the Financial Reporting Council (FRC), is responsible for the review and promulgation of the UK code, which has become the bedrock for other codes in the UK and many other Commonwealth jurisdictions. However, because the UK code is specifically applied to quoted companies, the way has been open for other organisations to develop their own sector specific governance codes.

---

[14] Financial Reporting Council. (2018), *UK Corporate Governance Code*, available online: <https://www.frc.org.uk/getattachment/88bd8c45-50ea-4841-95b0-d2f4f48069a2/2018-UK-Corporate-Governance-Code-FINAL.PDF> (accessed 11 July 2021).

For example, following the high profile insolvency of the UK companies BHS and Carillion, the FRC itself promulgated in 2018 a bespoke set of governance principles for large private companies (the Wates Principles);[15] and the Quoted Companies Alliance – the membership organisation for small and mid-size quoted companies in the UK – has published its own code for smaller quoted companies.[16] Meanwhile, the charitable sector has its own code as do the assorted emanations of the National Health Service in the UK.

One wonders whether the various codes which have been spawned could have been obviated by a more inclusive approach such as has been shown by the King IV Committee. Perhaps the difference flows from the King Committee having come into existence, and continuing to function, under the auspices of a professional body, The Institute Of Directors in South Africa (IoDSA), rather than at the initiative of a more narrowly focused sector regulator.

The King IV principles of good governance are presumed to apply on a 'proportionality' basis depending on the nature, size and complexity of the organisation.[17] King IV declares that good governance is beneficial for stakeholders as a well governed organisation will inspire the confidence of its stakeholders and lower its cost of capital.

The foundations of King IV, of inclusive and integrated governance that aspires to sustainability, are considered good for wider society, the economy and South Africa generally. The ambitious King IV principles will likely become the criteria by which the required standard of care and appropriate standards of conduct of the governing body and its members are measured – as Deloitte put it, "Our clients often debate the aspirational nature of corporate governance in South Africa taking into consideration the relative

---

[15] (2018), *The Wates Corporate Governance Principles for Large Private Companies*, available online: <https://www.frc.org.uk/getattachment/31dfb844-6d4b-4093-9bfe-19cee2c29cda/Wates-Corporate Governance-Principles-for-LPC-Dec 2018.pdf> (accessed 11 July 2021).

[16] (2018), 'New QCA Corporate Governance Code released', *QCA (25 April)*, available online: <https://www.theqca.com/news/briefs/143736/new-qca-corporate-governance-codereleased.thtml> (accessed 11 July 2021).

[17] (2016), *King IV Summary Guide*, KPMG Services Proprietary Limited, available online: <home.kpmg/za/en/home/insights/2016/10/king-iv-summary-guide.html> (accessed 11 July 2021).

stage of development of our economy and the cost burden that progressive governance brings."[18]

6. Some Key Features of King IV

There is no substitute for studying the full King IV report and code but here is a brief overview of some of the key features and of associated improvements in governance practice:

Ethical leadership, attitude, mindset and behaviour: In the words of the IoDSA, "Because it is not trying to be a law, and because it recognises that ethical behaviour is ultimately a matter of choice, King is a *voluntary* code.' King IV's 'apply and explain' approach reflects this ethos and prompts the governing body to apply its mind to achieving the principles, rather than blindly following a set of rules."[19]

It seems too that those companies which had embraced and embedded the governance principles of King IV by the end of 2019 have, from the limited research carried out, been more effective at dealing with the COVID-19 pandemic.[20] In the context of risk management, given the high level of uncertainty, unknown factors and lack of predictability regarding the future, it seems that organisations with more mature and better embedded risk governance and management frameworks will have fared better through the pandemic.

Stakeholder Engagement: King IV emphasises the critical role of stakeholders in the governance process. Not only must the governing body consider the legitimate and reasonable needs, interests and expectations of stakeholders, but the responsibilities of stakeholders are specifically recognised. Active stakeholders are required to hold the organisation and governing body accountable for their actions and disclosures.

Considering the interests of all stakeholders is essential so managing the stresses of and internal focus on survival, while still complying ethically with

---

[18] Note 2, 18.
[19] (2018), 'Understanding King IV and what it is intended to achieve', *The Institute of Directors in South Africa NPC (6 March)*, available online:
<https://www.iodsa.co.za/news/news.asp?id=389613> (accessed 11 July 2021).
[20] Foster R. (2020), 'Critical insights into Covid-19's impact on organisations through the lens of the King IV Report', *The Corporate Report*, vol. 10, no. 1, 7-19.

good governance standards and behaving as a good corporate citizen will be crucial. This will be challenging in cases where actions fall short of stakeholders' expectations.

Foster articulates that stakeholders, such as regulators, funders, employees, customers and suppliers, need to understand the dynamics of the organisation they are dealing with, particularly in uncertain times.[21] Conditions before COVID-19 should be explained therefore, as well as the continuing and associated impacts in 2020, and the annual report should carefully describe the organisation's prospects, after considering possible scenarios.

It is advisable for governing bodies to consider extending this dialogue to all key stakeholders of the company. Shareholder engagement is recommended where there is a 25% or higher advisory vote against the adoption of either the remuneration policy or the implementation report.

Overall, the level of stakeholder expectation has been further increased by calls such as that at the World Economic Forum 2020 in Davos for the adoption of a stakeholder-driven view of business.[22]

IT Governance: A greater level of IT risk awareness is demanded at director level, in line with the trend of IT becoming pervasive in all aspects of the operations of organisations. Responding to 4IR (the Fourth Industrial Revolution), King IV has deliberately separated technology and information, recognising information in isolation as a corporate asset that is part of the company's stock of intellectual capital and confirmed the need for governance structures to protect and enhance this asset.

It is anticipated that some strategic initiatives may need to be reprioritised or put on hold in favour of investment more heavily and rapidly in digitisation initiatives and intellectual capital. This will not be an easy strategic initiative, given the time and the financial, intellectual and people-

---

[21] Ibid.
[22] (2020), *Measuring Stakeholder Capitalism Towards Common Metrics and Consistent Reporting of Sustainable Value Creation*, World Economic Forum Report, available online: <https://www.weforum.org/reports/measuring-stakeholder-capitalism-towards-common-metrics-and-consistent-reporting-of-sustainable-value-creation> (accessed 11 July 2021).

resource utilisation, and the risk therefore of any initiative being seen as a net cost to the organisation. It has been pointed out that "governing bodies face a delicate balancing act. They are aware of the need to secure business assets, yet cannot afford to relinquish opportunities in doing so. We think the King IV principles are broad enough to focus on both protection and growth."[23]

Ethics & Social and Ethics Committee (SEC): The focus in King IV is on achieving specifically identified outcomes, including ethical culture, good performance, effective control and legitimacy.

King IV recommends the establishment of a governing body committee, the social and ethics committee (SEC), as a prescribed governing body committee with a role going beyond the functions listed in the South African Companies Act to include matters pertaining to ethical behaviour and ethics management. It proposes greater integration between the role and function of the SEC and other committees. The SEC's responsibilities include oversight of, and reporting on, organisational ethics, responsible corporate citizenship, sustainable development and stakeholder relationships (or allocating those responsibilities).

Remuneration: In line with international developments, remuneration receives far greater prominence in King IV than in earlier iterations of the code. It requires a three part disclosure relating to remuneration including the remuneration background statement, policy and implementation and recommends that both the remuneration policy and the implementation report (stipulating the various aspects of remuneration together with a link to performance), should be tabled for a non-binding advisory vote by shareholders.

The implementation report should provide evidence of pro-active engagement with shareholders to address their concerns and the governing body is tasked with ensuring fair and responsible executive remuneration practices, considering overall employee remuneration.

---

[23] PricewaterhouseCoopers (2016), *King IV: An Outcomes-based Corporate Governance Code Fit for a Changing World*, available online: <https://www.pwc.co.za/en/assets/pdf/king-iv-steering-point.pdf> (accessed 11 July 2021), 9 – quote from Sidriaan de Villiers S. (PwC Africa Cybersecurity Leader.

King IV recommends that the governing body should use remuneration as a tool to ensure that the business creates value in a sustainable manner within the economic, social and environmental context in which the organisation operates. The governing body should establish a remuneration committee, which will assess, and then recommend to the governing body, a fair and responsible company-wide remuneration policy which promotes the creation of value in a sustainable manner.

The need for transparency on remuneration in 2020-21 will have been challenging owing to the importance of remaining, and being seen to be, fair to all stakeholders. Companies will need to have considered responsible remuneration in relation to an organisation's financial position and affordability. These considerations have taken on a new meaning given the level of uncertainty about the future faced by many organisations.

Risk and Opportunity Management: King IV places a strong focus on opportunity management in addition to risk management and tasks the risk committee with the identification of opportunities linked to risks. In particular, it requires the governing body to pay specific attention to opportunities in the process of strategic planning.

Significantly, the code recommends the overlap of membership of the risk and audit committees, where these function as separate committees, for better coordination. If it is a single committee, the audit and risk committee should satisfy itself that it dedicates sufficient time to risk and opportunity management.

Auditors: King IV acknowledges the need to assess and confirm the external auditor's independence but, unlike UK governance requirements, does not specifically address audit firm rotation. It suggests that the audit committee oversees auditor independence, considering the impact of non-audit services, audit firm tenure and audit partner rotation.

King IV proposes several specific disclosures which may be included in the audit committee report, including any significant audit matters considered and how the committee addressed them.

Combined Assurance Model: King IV has refined the concept and requirements of combined assurance by no longer prescribing the three lines of defence model.[24] The combined assurance model is to be designed and implemented to cover adequately the organisation's significant risks and material matters. This is to be achieved through a combination of several assurance services and functions, including the organisation's line functions, which own and manage risks, and specialist functions, which facilitate and oversee risk management and compliance; internal auditors; internal forensic fraud examiners and auditors; safety and process assessors; statutory actuaries; independent external assurance service providers such as external auditors; and other external assurance providers.

Independence Assessment: The concept of independence has evolved from a tick box style list of disqualifications to a more practical approach which focuses on the perception of independence by an informed third party.

Independence is deemed to be predominantly a state of mind which is both a moral characteristic and a legal duty of all directors, whether executive or non-executive. In the code it is defined thus:

> *"Independence generally means the exercise of objective, unfettered judgement. When used as the measure by which to judge the appearance of independence, or to categorise a non-executive member of the governing body or its committees as independent, it means the absence of an interest, position, association or relationship which, when judged from the perspective of a reasonable and informed third party, is likely to influence unduly or cause bias in decision-making."*[25]

One of the key principles in King IV is the establishment of a unitary governing body which reflects a balance of power and to ensure that no one individual, or group of individuals, wields unfettered power on or in relation to the governing body.

King IV mandates the appointment of independent non-executive directors

---

[24] The Chartered Institute of Internal Auditors published a global position paper in 2013, titled: *The Three Lines of Defence in Effective Risk Management and Control* (available online: <https://na.theiia.org/standards-guidance/Public%20Documents/PP%20The%20Three%20Lines%20of%20Defense%20in%20Effective%20Risk%20Management%20and%20Control.pdf> (accessed 11 July 2021)). It is a valuable framework that **outlines internal audit's role in assuring the effective management of risk**. However, applying the three lines of defence model in an organisation is not a silver bullet for achieving effective internal audit.

[25] Note 1, 13.

who are required, in common with other directors, to apply an independent state of mind and objective judgment. Related to this, all directors are required always to act in the best interests of the company, which can only be achieved if directors set aside their personal interests.

Mandating Ethical Leadership and Culture: King IV requires the embedding of an ethical culture, ethical leadership and the governance of ethics throughout each organisation. Good corporate governance is essentially about effective ethical leadership. While leadership starts with each individual director, it finds its expression through the governing body as a collective, setting the appropriate example and tone which is referred to as 'ethical governance'.

King IV explains the governance of ethics as the role of the governing body in ensuring that the ethical culture within the organisation is aligned to the tone set by the governing body through the implementation of appropriate policies and practices. The governing body is to set the tone of leading by example, by being ethical and effective, and to ensure that the organisation's ethics is managed effectively.

The governing body must oversee the effectiveness of management's response to non-adherence or contraventions of ethical standards and proposes disclosure of effective ethics management and its outcomes. Specifically, King IV requires that the governing body ensures that the relevant codes of conduct and policies are incorporated, by reference or otherwise, in supply and employee contracts. In essence, this should result in a situation where all employees and suppliers agree contractually to adhere to the ethics and values of the company.

The disclosure requirement ensures that the governing body remains accountable to stakeholders, including with respect to the company's performance on embedding values, ethics and culture.

Diversity in the Governing Body: In Principle 7 of the code, which deals with the composition of the governing body, the recommended practices emphasise the need for the governing body to comprise the appropriate balance of knowledge, skill, experience, diversity and independence for it to discharge its governance role and responsibilities objectively and effectively.

Diversities which are highlighted include age, culture, race, gender and expertise. Targets are proposed to address race and gender representation.

Corporate Citizenship: Under Principles 3 and 17, stakeholders have an obligation to ensure that the company acts as a responsible corporate citizen and as such they should exercise their rights as well as their legitimate and reasonable needs, interests and expectations in a responsible manner towards the creation of value in the context within which the company operates.

Embraced focus on transparency: COVID-19 led rapidly to a new raft of regulations so that sub-optimal compliance and non-integrated risk management systems will fail to meet transparency requirements for disclosures to stakeholders. A fundamental precept in King IV is that there should be a responsible and transparent tax policy which is compliant with the applicable laws; and which is also congruent with responsible corporate citizenship and takes account of reputational repercussions. Tax collections in South Africa are vastly improved, demonstrating that King IV has supported a changed mindset with tangible outcomes.

7. A Practitioner Viewpoint

It will be helpful for readers to consider the sobering conclusions of Jill Parratt, the group secretary of Liberty Holdings Limited and a member of the Southern Africa Division of The Chartered Governance Institute, on some of the realities of governance as practised in South Africa:

It is clear that in the listed company sector, there is almost full compliance with King IV. Much of this is due to the fact that the ongoing JSE Listings Requirements mandates compliance with King IV and if there is no compliance with one or more of the principles, such as the role of the chief executive and chairman being separate, an application needs to be made to the JSE for condonement. A sound argument for non-compliance needs to be provided before receiving the condonement and continual reporting provided on progress made in rectifying the lack of compliance.

In addition, the asset managers who invest in listed companies are uncomfortable investing in companies where there is poor compliance with King IV and would need robust engagement and a sound explanation before they would consider investing, if they ever did invest. Another area where listed companies are impacted by not applying King IV in its entirety is the voting at the annual general meeting. For instance, shareholders are starting to vote against the re-election of a director who has served on a governing body for more than nine years. This is despite the governing body reviewing the independence of the director in question and resolving that the director still acts independently, and despite the years of service.

Insurance companies and banks are closely regulated by the Prudential Authority and sound governance is very much top of mind. There would be serious ramifications if King IV were not applied.

However, there have recently been two spectacular corporate failures, viz. Steinhoff Limited and African Bank Limited. The interesting point to note in these two cases is that King IV was applied, there was appropriate and sound reporting on governance and reputable audit companies signed off on the financials. So what went wrong? In the case of Steinhoff, it appeared to be the strong and charismatic personality of the chief executive, and a chairman who was financially invested in the company. The audit committee members were influenced by the chief executive and the chairman and did not dig deeply enough into the financials. Audit committees can now be held liable by the JSE in instances like this. African Bank Limited was properly governed by the JSE and the Prudential Authority but had poor lending practices. Savvy asset managers were concerned and advised against investing in African Bank, but when the bank collapsed many people lost their money. In both cases, class actions have been instituted by shareholders and investors.

Of great concern in South Africa is the performance of state-owned enterprises (SoEs). Under the previous government, governing bodies of SoEs used to be constituted by the heavy hitters of the private sector. The trend now is to appoint people with no business or public profile; with little or no business experience; often with soft qualifications such as human resources, management diplomas, etc. Often these governing body members have also been implicated in misuse of money cases, conflicts of interest, falsifying qualifications and tender fraud. Tender fraud in respect of personal protection equipment was particularly prevalent in South Africa during COVID-19.

In 2010, during President Jacob Zuma's budget vote in Parliament, he announced the establishment of the Presidential Review Committee ("PRC") on SoEs. In its comprehensive review, the PRC ascertained that while SoEs have an important role to play, they are faced with significant weaknesses and threats that may become impediments to their optimum contribution. The governance, ownership policy, and oversight systems were found to be inadequate. The quality of the governing body and executives' recruitment was found to be lacking. There was no clarity on the role of the executive authority, governing bodies and the chief executive in the governance and operational management of SoEs. Lending practices were irregular and not in line with the Companies Act. The was a lack of proper record keeping and the governing body of directors did not take effective steps to prevent irregular, fruitless and wasteful expenditure. Proper control systems to safeguard and maintain assets were not implemented. Nothing was done about this and most certainly King IV was not applied. When considering the state capture that followed, one must ponder whether the presidency ever had any intention to rectify the problem.

In 2016, Carol Paton, a reporter from the *Business Day*, commented that an SoE was a sole shareholder at odds with itself.[26] The worst governance traits all came together: weak skills and capacity; cronyism; corruption; poor governance; and unchecked presidential power. The appointment of the governing body and the chief executive was muddled within government departments. There was no concept of a nominations committee made up of independent directors. Government was making all the governing body appointments and government was the shareholder. Some governing body appointments were made directly by the President, and during the state capture years, governing body appointments were made by the Gupta family. This has all come to light through the Zondo Commission.

---

[26] (2016), Chartered Governance Institute of Southern Africa Conference, see: <https://www.chartsec.co.za/index.php?option=com_content&view=article&id=550&Itemid=268>.

Carol Paton prophesised that it would get worse before it got better. She was right. There is no accountability in SoEs and municipalities in South Africa. There is no real concept of a conflict of interest, ineptitude is growing worse, corruption is still rife and despite the Zondo Commission investigations and arrests, the problem continues. It shows mankind at its worst, driven by greed and self-interest. Certainly lip-service is paid to King IV but without the intention to actually live by its principles."[27]

8. Conclusion

At the launch of King IV in 2016 it was considered the most innovative and effective governance code globally. Today, and notwithstanding Jill Parratt's reflections on standards of governance in SoEs in South Africa, this far-reaching code continues to stand tall internationally.

In a country which has suffered high levels of corruption and state capture, this influential code should support organisations to influence change in business ethics and empower effective influence on government governance.

The King IV principles and practices foster ethical leadership, transparency, corporate citizenship, integrated thinking and reporting, risk management and stakeholder engagement, and set out consequences for non-conformance, together providing a powerful foundation for high quality corporate governance. So too do the embracing of data as an asset, the requirement for digital enhancement and the ability to challenge transformation at governing body level.

Richard Foster considers a black swan event such as the advent of COVID-19 as a catalyst which shines a spotlight on how organisations are governed and managed, revealing the quality of the leadership. He warns however, that "key decisions taken by governing bodies will be judged by the various key stakeholders and, in many instances, by the general public – particularly with the surge of information, often out of context, on social media – factual or fictitious."

---

[27] Personal communication with the author.

Global organisations could beneficially adopt provisions from the King IV code that are not embraced in their national code, thereby seeking to empower their governing body to lead ethically, to pursue high levels of transparency in their stakeholder engagement and to focus on risk effectively.

Ethical leadership needs to be delivered visibly, embedded into the organisation and its policies and behaviours, and become part of the ethical DNA that will attract talent, investors and customers. As PwC has stated, "[King IV is] an outcomes-based corporate governance code fit for a changing world."[28]

---

[28] Note 23.

Corporate Governance 3.0

CHAPTER 16. THE GOVERNANCE OF ASIAN FAMILY BUSINESSES – THE SECOND GENERATION GROWTH AND SUSTAINABILITY IMPERATIVES[1]

Ser-Keng Ang, Principal Lecturer of Finance and the Academic Director for the EMBA and MBA programs, Singapore Management University

Alexander Van de Putte, Professor of Strategic Foresight, IE Business School and Chairman of Corporate Governance & Stewardship, AIFC

Introduction

Family businesses are the most prevalent form of business organisations in the world. According to White (2017), family businesses account for 70% of global GDP and 60% of global employment.[2] Alshaikh argues that family businesses account for 80% to 90% of the world's companies.[3] Besides

---

[1] A book with the same title is planned for by the same authors in 2022.
[2] https://knowledge.insead.edu/family-business/what-family-firms-need-to-ensure-longevity-7751 (accessed 21 January 2020).
[3] Alaa Alshaikh, "Solving succession problems in family-owned businesses", Gallup, April 2019.

their significant contributions to the growth of economies across different parts of the world, they are also among the main drivers of innovation and entrepreneurship. This is no different in Asia, where family businesses are thriving. Although family businesses remain a strong force in developed economies, the largest listed companies in the UK, the US, and Japan tend to have a dispersed mix of shareholders. In emerging Asia, on the other hand, the trend of family businesses dominating 80–90% of large companies continues to this day.

There is currently no consensus on what constitutes a family business. For the purpose of this chapter, the European Union's definition of a family business will be used throughout this book:[4]

1. The majority of decision-making rights, direct or indirect, are in the possession of the natural person(s) who established the business, or those who have acquired the share capital of the firm, or their family members.

2. At least one representative of the family or kin is formally involved in the governance of the business.

3. A listed company meets the definition of a family business if the family possesses 25% of the decision-making rights mandated by their share capital.

This chapter aims to provide a good understanding of the importance of the following:

- Corporate governance issues in the Asian context.

- The dilemma of an Asian founder-successor in shaping and scaling a family business while preserving the legacy of their founder parents.

- Examples of family businesses that have made significant inroads in this respect.

- Showcasing the mechanisms and structures that are used by Asian family businesses in maintaining control over the family business, while at the same time sustaining and securing its growth and development.

---

[4] http://www.europeanfamilybusinesses.eu/family-businesses/definition (accessed 21 January 2020).

Asian firms have several distinct characteristics compared to their counterparts in developed markets. Firstly, the national economies in most parts of Asia are dominated by family businesses, particularly the overseas Chinese.[5] Morck, Wolfenzon and Yeung report that the output of the top 15 family-controlled firms account for 84% of gross domestic product (GDP) in Hong Kong, 76% in Malaysia, 48% in Singapore, 46% in the Philippines, and 39% in Thailand.[6] Secondly, the strong presence of a controlling blockholder, which could be a family or government, is common across Asian markets.[7] However, the average blockholder ownership varies from country to country – from 37% in South Korea to 73% in Thailand.[8] In addition to block ownership, the blockholder can control a firm even without being a majority shareholder – such as via pyramid structures or cross-holdings.

1. Corporate governance in Asia

A brief background on the evolution of corporate governance in Asia provides some context. Singapore has been regarded by many as a trailblazer of corporate governance, not only in Asia but also around the world. Driven by a strong vision to develop rapidly, yet sustainably, Singapore's Companies Act came into force in 1967;[9] three years later, the Singaporean Parliament passed the Monetary Authority of Singapore (MAS) Act with the objective of having MAS regulate the financial services sector in Singapore.[10]

Several Asian countries also started to draft their first corporate governance codes. In Hong Kong, the Hong Stock Exchange developed a high-level

---

[5] Steven Globerman, Mike Peng, and Daniel Shapiro, "Corporate governance and Asian companies", *Asia Pacific Journal of Management* 28: 1–14, 2011.
[6] Randall Morck, Daniel Wolfenzon, and Bernard Yeung, "Corporate governance, economic entrenchment, and growth", *Journal of Economic Literature* 43(3): 655–720, 2005.
[7] Michael Lemmon and Karl Lins, "Ownership structure, corporate governance, and firm value: Evidence from the East Asian financial crisis", *Journal of Finance* 58(4): 1445–1468, 2003.
[8] Clifford Holderness, "The myth of diffuse ownership in the United States", *The Review of Financial Studies* 22(4): 1377-1408, 2009.
[9] https://sso.agc.gov.sg/Act/CoA1967 (accessed 17 February 2021).
[10] https://www.mas.gov.sg/who-we-are/Our-History (accessed 17 February 2021).

Code of Best Practices in January 1999,[11] but it was not until late 2004 when a full-fledged code begun to emerge. In Singapore, the Corporate Governance Committee (CGC), published its Code of Corporate Governance in March 2001, a few years after the Asian Financial Crisis.[12]

In both Hong Kong and Singapore, similar to most other Commonwealth nations, principles-based codes were adopted based on the 'comply or explain' approach to corporate governance.

Given the differences in the practice of corporate governance across Asia, several factors drive the standard of corporate governance in Asia:

– Family businesses operate in an environment where government (via government companies) shape the standards of corporate governance, such as in Singapore.
– Family businesses operate in a financial hub, which attracts foreign investors who expect a high standard of governance. Major financial hubs in Asia ex-Japan are Hong Kong and Singapore. The focus on corporate governance in Asia heightened in response to the 1997 Asian Financial Crisis (AFC), which led to massive outflows of capital from foreign investors. The AFC led to a severe liquidity crunch in the domestic capital markets resulting from a sudden and intense capital flight from the markets in Asia. This in turn severely damaged the real economy as a result of insufficient capital and investor apprehensions. However, the importance of, and hence the imperative to, developing high standards of corporate governance varies across Asia, largely due to the relative importance of the stock markets to their respective economies. The stock market capitalization to GDP ratio varies across Asia: Hong Kong (1,768.8%), Singapore (191.9%), Malaysia (129.7), Thailand (108.2%), and the Philippines (75.5%).[13] In contrast, the ratios for the US and the UK are 137.1% and 152.2%, respectively. In addition, the level of corporate governance and practices differ across Asia as countries in the region are very diverse in terms of their stage of

---

[11] https://ecgi.global/code/code-best-practice (accessed 17 February 2021).
[12] https://www.mas.gov.sg/regulation/codes/code-of-corporate-governance (accessed 17 February 2021). On 1 September 2007, the Code of Good Governance became the responsibility of the MAS and the Singapore Exchange Limited (SGX).
[13] https://knoema.com/atlas/topics/Economy/Financial-Sector-Capital-markets/Market-capitalization-percent-of-GDP (accessed 21 June 2021).

economic development and institutional setup.[14] The standard of corporate governance continues to evolve in some of the emerging markets in Southeast Asia, such as Cambodia, Laos, Myanmar and Vietnam.

- Family businesses that are listed on foreign exchanges with stringent standards regarding corporate governance.

2. The challenges facing family businesses in Asia

Despite the importance of family businesses, they face important challenges as well. Longevity is apparently the biggest challenge with less than one-third of global family businesses surviving beyond the founder and only 12% surviving to the third generation.[15] The low survival rates among family firms are well documented in the literature.

For example, Ward's[16] seminal study on family firm succession shows that 30% of firms survive through the second generation, 13% survive the third generation, and only 3% survive beyond that. Chu and MacMurray[17] and Weidenbaum[18] observe that most overseas Chinese family firms are unable to last beyond the second generation. It is with such widespread findings that led to the proverb: 'From shirt sleeves to shirt sleeves in three generations', or as they say in Chinese "富不过三代 ('Wealth does not survive beyond three generations'). Some go further by saying that the first generation earns the wealth, the second generation enjoys the wealth, and the third generation squanders it. There are, however, notable exceptions, which we will illustrate at the end of this chapter.

The following factors are believed to contribute to these challenges:

- Honouring the founder's mission and legacy.

---

[14] Stijn Claessens, Simeon Djankov, and Larry Lang, "The separation of ownership and control in East Asian corporations", *Journal of Financial Economics* 58(1–2): 81–112, 2000.
[15] See Note 3.
[16] John Ward, *Keeping the Family and the Business Healthy*, Jossey-Bass, 1987.
[17] T.C. Chu and Trevor MacMurray, "The road ahead for Asia's leading conglomerates", *The McKinsey Quarterly* 3: 117, 1993.
[18] Murray Weidenbaum, "The Chinese family business enterprise", *California Management Review* 38(4): 141–56, 1996.

- Founders' fear of losing control of the firm they built and life-long achievements.
- Allocating resources in an increasingly sustainability focused environment.
- Changing intergenerational capabilities and ambitions.
- A disruptive global business environment.
- Inadequate (and not timely) succession planning. Both Handler[19] and Kets de Vries[20] argue that the high mortality rate of family firms is due to the lack of succession planning.
- Balancing the need for family control, driving growth, and expectations of external stakeholders.
- Disagreements amongst the new generations on the direction of and control over their family business.

The issue of trans-generation wealth transfer is of huge relevance in Asia at least in the next decade. In recent years, Asia has been experiencing rapid wealth transfer from the family patriarchs to their offspring.[21] Given that family wealth and corporate matters are inextricably linked in family firms in Asia, the transfer of control over family wealth also translates to the transfer of control with respect to the family business. Founder succession is the most critical event in the history of any firm[22], particularly for founder-led family businesses.

While those in the US, Europe and the UK have undergone successions over several generations, the Asian family firms have only recently begun encountering founder-succession. This is largely due to the age of family businesses in developed markets. While there are some exceptions, many family patriarchs are past retirement age, so the path to founder-succession

---

[19] Wendy Handler, "Succession in family firms: A mutual role adjustment between entrepreneur and next-generation family members", *Entrepreneurship Theory and Practice* 15(1): 37–52, 1990.
[20] Manfred Kets de Vries, "The dynamics of family controlled firms: The good and the bad news", *Organizational Dynamics* 21(3): 59–71, 1993.
[21] Ser-Keng Ang, 'A qualitative study on the challenges of private banking in Asia", *The Journal of Wealth Management* 12(4): 68–77, 2010.
[22] Charles Hofer, "Turnaround strategies", *Journal of Business Strategy* 1(1): 19–31, 1980.

is likely to continue in the foreseeable future. A study by Singapore Management University (SMU) and Deloitte in 2013 on Asian business succession finds that Asian founders tend to relinquish the CEO role in family business in their 70s.[23] In addition, founders tend to continue to stay on with the business to offer strategic advice after succession, sometimes as the board chair.[24] This presents a unique opportunity to study corporate succession occurring for the first time. Together with the prevalence of controlling shareholding, founders may wish to leave their firms in the hands of their family successors, as their legacy, rather than handing them to unrelated external successors.[25] Regardless of the circumstances, succession in emerging markets usually involves handing both management and ownership to family members.[26] Founder-succession in family firms puts them at the crossroads, in terms of how the new generation of business leaders shape their family businesses. One potential source of conflict in the smooth journey to success is that many family successors are educated abroad. As such, they are exposed to different ideas of management, largely in Western markets. Unless they embrace changes in the traditional governance structure, the sustainability of the family firm may be jeopardised.

The importance and persistent effects of founders underlie the study by Dobrev and Barnett,[27] who found that the identity of the founder is more tightly linked to the firm than that of any subsequent successors. This makes founder-succession more important than any subsequent successions, as failure to manage this process may rob the firm of vital organisational asset. Therefore, a good outcome for founder-succession can determine a firm's long-term survival and success.

---

[23] Annie Koh, Elaine Tan, and Jeandra Ejercito, *Asian Business Families Succession: Going the Distance with the Next Generation*, Singapore Management University and Deloitte, 2013.
[24] Noam Wasserman, "Founder-CEO succession and the paradox of entrepreneurial success", *Organization Science* 14(2): 149-172, 2003.
[25] Ronald Anderson and David Reeb, "Founding-family ownership and firm performance: Evidence from the S&P 500", *The Journal of Finance* 58(3): 1301-1328, 2003.
[26] Mike Burkart, Fausto Panunzi, and Andrei Shleifer, "Family firms", *The Journal of Finance* 58(5): 2167–2201, 2003.
[27] Stanislav Dobrev and William Barnett, "Organizational roles and transition to entrepreneurship, *Academy of Management Journal* 48(3): 433–449, 2005.

3. Improving the odds of sustaining the family business beyond the third generation

Knowing that family successions are fraught with difficulties, we believe that the new generation of business leaders needs to consider the following factors that could improve the chances of sustaining the family business beyond the third generation:

- Taking an interest in the preservation of the mission and legacy of the founder in the founder-succession journey.
- Actively managing the family business' progress to professionalization.
- Considering different models of family constitution and control and adopting one that is suitable for the family.
- Honing the ability to respond quickly to a more disruptive global business environment.

A. Honouring the founder's mission and legacy.

For succession to be smooth, family successors must be sensitive to the founder's mission and to preserve the legacy of the founder. It is natural that founders are more emotionally attached to the family business. After all, it is often said that the family business is the founder's baby. Any changes made to the family business would inevitably be met with resistance from the founder. This is also the source of many conflicts between the founder and family successors – the transition stage between generations. Seemingly trivial changes from the perspective of the successors may be regarded as highly significant to the founder. Examples of such changes include refreshing the logo or brand image of the company's product. As such, successors should take affirmative steps to sustain the family business to avoid unnecessary clashes with the founder who may see well-intentioned changes as a mark of disrespect to his/her efforts in building the family business.

Both US and Europe have a long history of family businesses, and the more successful ones – those that endured over many decades and generations – have always been able to preserve and honour the founder's mission.

In the US, for example, Biltmore estate (located in Asheville, North Carolina) has been a key asset of the Vanderbilt family for more than 125 years and is currently owned and operated by the fourth generation. The current generation has always honoured the founder's mission which was articulated as: 'The preservation of Biltmore as a privately owned, profitable, working estate'.[28] In addition, the estate was envisioned by George Vanderbilt to be fully self-sustaining and has since embraced circular economy principles.

In Europe, family-owned Pollet, a cleaning products firm founded in 1763, is another example where the founder's mission has been preserved until today. Pollet is the oldest family business still operating in Belgium. In 2013, Pollet joined Henokiens, the global association of family companies that have been in continuous operation for over 200 years.[29] Although the company has evolved tremendously over the years, it has always remained faithful to its founder's mission which is based on strong moral values and a stakeholder, rather than a shareholder, orientation to growing the business. Pollet was founded as a salts, soap, and oil trading company. During World War I, glycerine was a key ingredient in the manufacture of soap and also explosives. Instead of letting glycerine fall into the wrong hands, Mr Pollet closed the factory until after the war but kept his employees on the payroll. It comes as no surprise that this created a very loyal workforce with multigenerational employees as a result. This further strengthens the current generation's commitment to remain a family business and to remain true to the founder's mission and values.

A final example is Pictet, the Geneva-based asset manager. Pictet was founded in 1805 in Geneva, Switzerland, often referred to as 'the capital of private banking'. Pictet's mission and the Calvinist principles of discipline, living a sober life, and hard work are intrinsically intertwined. Pictet is now one of the largest European family-owned wealth and asset managers. At the beginning of 2021, it had CHF 609 billion ($689 billion) of assets under management and employed almost 5,000 people worldwide. There are several fundamental reasons why Pictet has been able to honour the

---

[28] https://www.biltmore.com/our-story/our-mission (accessed 19 February 2021).
[29] https://www.henokiens.com (accessed 19 February 2021). The association's oldest member is Japanese hotel Hoshi Ryokan, founded in 717.

founder's mission over several centuries:[30] 1) it operates as a partnership, where the majority of partners come from a very small circle of the Geneva society; 2) key decisions are made jointly by the seven 'senior' partners based on a consensus-driven process; 3) an apprenticeship model is used to develop people (not dissimilar from McKinsey's development model, for instance), 4) Pictet is known for its deeply embedded and shared values that are a guide to action throughout the organisation and around the world.[31]

B. Professionalisation of a family business

Scholars on family business argue that Chinese family enterprises do not usually last beyond three generations because Chinese patriarchs fail to embrace the concept of professionalization of their family business. Instead, they simply pass the helm of the business to family members regardless of capabilities. One interesting exception of this practice in the West is the Dupont family which has over 170 years of history. The offspring in the Dupont family lineage are all evaluated based on their competencies. If they are found to be unsuitable or less capable than non-family managers, they will be managed out of the family business. There are similar examples of Asian families who have successfully institutionalized professionalization of the family business: Quek Kai Tak's family (Hong Leong Group), the Lee family (OCBC), and the Yeo family (Yeo's food and beverage company).

In the backdrop of the new global economy, emerging tech firms in Asia have moved away from family-business styled operations, even if they are founded by individuals. In contrast, they are usually led by professional managers. In these firms, checks and balances are provided by co-founders, employees, and private equity firms. Several interesting observations: tech firms that have undergone many rounds of funding would be conditioned by private equity investors on the importance of good corporate

---

[30] Torsten Groth and Fritz Simon, "The Pictet model: A company that continuously reinvents its family ownerhip", Witten Institute for Family Business, July 2019.

[31] These values are driven by the partners with the objective to constantly improve the Pictet Group, remain true to its mission, and to pass the company to the next generation in a better situation. As wealth custodians, their philosophy is that wealth is passed on to the next generation and that the business cannot be sold to company outsiders.

governance practices. In addition, in order to attract tech talents these tech firms also have to provide stock options to employees. As such, employees become an important part of the governance structure of these firms. The emergence of such industries and practices may drive changes in the management of family businesses, particularly when it comes to the succession of these firms going forward.

Traditionally, in addition to close shareholder control, family firms, particularly those controlled by overseas Chinese families,[32] engage in traditional business practices which Ahlstrom, Young et al. (2004) describe as 'excluding outsiders from management and the board, maintaining secrecy and tight control of information, and eschewing transparency'.[33] Even though they are the minorities in other parts of Asia, overseas Chinese wield significant, if not dominant, economic influence in their respective jurisdictions. As an illustration, overseas Chinese account for 1% of the population in the Philippines but control 60% of the wealth in that country (Chua, 2004).[34] Similarly, these migrants account for 10% of the population in Thailand but control 80% of the market capitalization of listed firms in Thailand.

To provide some context about Chinese family-controlled businesses, consider the following:

- Large Asian Chinese businesses tend to generate a strategic divide between the professionalization of management and the preservation of family control.
- The extent of family control differs in response to the market situations and regulatory factors as well as the willingness and capability of the family successors to harness the strengths of the family enterprise.

The limited use of professional managers is a common characteristic of the

---

[32] Overseas Chinese are those with Chinese ancestry that have migrated from the People's Republic of China.
[33] David Ahlstrom, Michael Young, Eunice Chan, and Garry Bruton, "Facing constraints to growth? Overseas Chinese entrepreneurs and traditional business practices in East Asia", *Asia Pacific Journal of Management 21*(3): 263-285, 2004.
[34] Christian Chua, "Defining Indonesian Chineseness under the new order", *Journal of Contemporary Asia* 34(4): 465-479, 2004.

Asian family businesses. One can attribute this phenomenon to the strong overlap between the identity of the family in control and the top echelon of the Asian family business. Also, many listed Asian companies do not have the formal position of CEO. Instead, the board chair fulfils the role of directing the firm's strategy.[35] This is detrimental for several reasons:

- This restricts the talent pool from which founders can choose successors from.
- It self-imposes a glass ceiling for non-blood-related professionals. Not being able to progress to top management makes working for such firms less desirable, and also prevents the firm from having the best qualified person for the job.

The strong evidence in finance research on family ownership and control suggesting that a predominance of family management and control weakens overall performance only further substantiates these arguments.

In essence, one of the key challenges for Asia's next generation of business leaders is to switch from 'family-ruled and family-managed' to becoming 'professionally managed and family-ruled' businesses. There are two family businesses in Singapore, Yeo Hiap Seng and OCBC Bank, that have successfully accomplished the switch. This switch is critical because financial markets increasingly demand greater transparency. Increased transparency can, in itself, create value for the family owners since it brings about the reduction in the overall cost of capital for the family business. Furthermore, good governance practices also lead to access to fresh capital necessary for the family business to grow, without having to commit additional financial resources from the family. This in turn allows the family business to achieve diversification in the family wealth. Then, the relevant question becomes how can the founder's family continue to maintain control over the family business despite the increased injection of fresh capital by outside investors?

There are several interpretations of professionalization in literature. At one end of the spectrum, professionalization involves hiring a set of senior professional managers from outside of the firm to lead the firm. Another

---

[35] See note 34.

interpretation of professionalization involves the adoption of a systematic and formal process to induct family members into formal positions in the family business. This may include specifying that family members must continue to meet minimum performance standards in order to remain in the position, for example. Additionally, the professionalization of the family business can be supplemented by the appointment of more non-executive independent directors. This is consistent with best practices in corporate governance in Asia: that firms have diverse boards that include more independent directors.

If professional managers run the family business, then an appropriate system of corporate governance must be introduced to ensure that these managers act in the interest of the family as opposed to serving their own interest – the classic agency problem extensively documented in finance literature. A key advantage of family managers is that they are not bound by limited tenure, unlike non-family managers. In addition, family managers are immune to the pressures arising from variabilities of the stock price of the family business, which may force non-family managers to adopt short-term solutions to address the situation. However, these differences also mean that family managers will not have good career prospects if they are not exceptional in their capabilities, do not demonstrate loyalty, lack well-thought-out long-term visions, or do not have the family's long-term interest at heart.

C. Adoption of a suitable model for family constitution

One of the root causes for wealth not passing beyond three generations is the failure to consider complications resulting from future successions. As the family grows with the passage of generations, it is inevitable that family members start to have divergent views on their own involvement in the family business, as well as who is going to lead the family firm in the future. This may be driven by the fact that the emotional attachment to the family business dwindles over time, and further compounded by the dilution of ownership with each subsequent generation of successors.

To illustrate this point, consider an example: Let's say a founder owns 100% of the firm and has four children. Assuming an equal share in succession, each child will obtain 25% ownership of the family firm. In the following generation, assuming each successor has four children each, then each of their children will get 6.25% ownership of the family business. If we imagine the family business running into the sixth generation, which is what most European family businesses are in, the level of ownership would become less and less significant and dispersed even within the family.

To this end, some families introduce a 'family constitution' (or 'family charter'). This serves to establish a framework that guides a family in making joint decisions as a whole. In essence, it relates to how the family itself is governed. It will typically address the mission, vision and values of the founder as well as how disagreements and conflicts are handled. In addition, it will likely provide clarity on the respective roles and responsibilities for each family member, and outline the boundaries between family, ownership and family enterprise. Very often, the family constitution also provides for the role of family elders.

It is perhaps useful to illustrate the importance of family constitution by highlighting one of such cases involving a European family, the Dumas family. In October 2010, LVMH, the world's biggest luxury goods company by sales, bought a 17.1% stake of Hermès International, famed for silk scarves and Birkin bags. LVMH already owns Dom Pérignon champagne, Louis Vuitton bags and Tag Heuer watches. The deal put LVMH in the pole position to take control of what is widely considered the world's most desirable luxury brand, should the family owners wish to sell. The deal involved the acquisition of 15m Hermès shares (14.2% stake). Hermès is tightly controlled by the Dumas family, with 40-50 members controlling 72% of the shares. In order to preserve the values and culture at Hermès, the family decided to form a holding company in December 2010, called H51, which aggregated 50.2% of the shareholding, thereby safeguarding the family's control over the century-old brand.

As this example illustrates, for the family to continue to maintain control over the family firm, it is critical for them to adopt an appropriate model of family constitution. A family constitution that will govern the conduct of family members with respect to their involvement and engagement in the family business. While it is not possible to pre-empt every situation wherein things go wrong in the relationships between family members, lessons can be learned from cases involving other families where family rifts occur due to politics, mixed family-styled management, and sudden alterations of power. These lessons can help existing and future family businesses to prepare accordingly.

A more elaborate governance structure for the family can include an assembly, a family council, an ownership council, a board of directors, and an advisory council. Figure 16.1 below depicts this structure:

Figure 16.1 Family Governance Structure
Source: Bork, Jeffe, Lane, Daschew and Heisle (1995)[36]

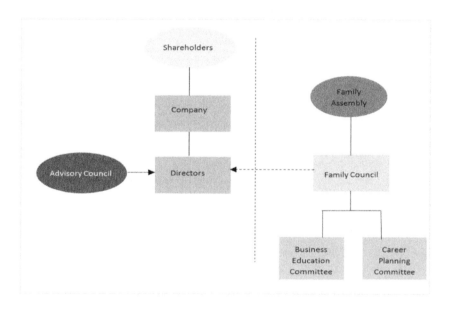

Alternatively, the family can adopt a family board model. This model is relevant to some Asian families following the death or incapacity of the family patriarch. In a nutshell, a family board refers to a holding company structure with respect to decision-making. If the family adopts the family board model, then it would mean the members of the family will start to view their commonly-owned businesses as a portfolio of assets being collectively controlled by their own family board. However, this also

---

[36] David Bork, Dennis Jeffe, Same Lane, Leslie Daschew and Quentin Heisler, *Working with Family Businesses: A Guide for Professionals*, Jossey-Bass, 1995

assumes that each member of the family has the ability to transition from a position where they are not accountable to anyone to an alternate position where they:

- collaborate via power sharing at the ownership level;
- perceive themselves as being accountable to the family board;
- discern between ownership level and operational decisions; and
- acknowledge and respect the boundaries between ownership and management.

D. Preparing to respond quickly to a more disruptive global business environment

We currently operate in a volatile, uncertain, complex, and ambiguous (VUCA) world.[37] Although the concept is not new, it is becoming even more urgent to address this, given that market and technological clockspeed is accelerating[38] driven by the emergence of the fourth industrial revolution (4IR). World Economic Forum founder Klaus Schwab characterises the 4IR as 'a fusion of technologies that is blurring the lines between the physical, digital, and biological spheres.'[39]

In addition, COVID-19 has illustrated that global value chains lack sustainability, inclusiveness, and resilience. In other words, traditional capitalism has its limitations, and a stakeholder capitalistic approach may be more effective to contribute to the long-term sustainable success of a company. Under a stakeholder capitalistic philosophy (see also Chapter 18), boards aim at balancing and growing all five capital stocks simultaneously – natural, manufactured, social, human, and financial.[40] Fortunately, most family businesses have a stakeholder rather than a pure shareholder

---

[37] https://www.forbes.com/sites/jeroenkraaijenbrink/2018/12/19/what-does-vuca-really-mean/?sh=72f1825417d6 (accessed 2 March 2021).
[38] The term 'clockspeed' was coined by MIT professor Charles Fine in his book: *Clockspeed: Winning industry control in the age of temporary advantage*, Perseus Books, 1998.
[39] https://www.weforum.org/agenda/2016/01/the-fourth-industrial-revolution-what-it-means-and-how-to-respond (accessed 2 March 2021).
[40] Alexander Van de Putte, Kairat Kelimbetov, and Ann Holder, *The Perfect Storm: Navigating the Sustainable Energy Transition*, Sustainable Foresight Institute, 2017.

orientation to corporate governance, something that Dr Fung, chairman of the Li & Fung Group of companies, confirmed during the Astana Finance Days conference in July 2019.

This increasingly disruptive and sustainability focused environment implies that companies can be disrupted from the outside, even for companies that operate in capital-intensive industries. Family businesses are not immune from these phenomena and it implies that retained earnings alone may be insufficient to finance the growth of the family business. At some point, a family business may have no choice but to opt for a partial initial offering. In a partial initial offering, the family retains a controlling share of the business, and gains access to growth capital to finance innovation projects at the edges of its markets. Stock exchanges require that family businesses add independent directors to the board to ensure that all shareholders' interests are well represented. When searching for independent directors, the family business needs to consider the following:

1. Candidates should be identified based on merit and objective criteria and should promote diversity of gender, ethnic background, cognitive and personal strengths, and age (see also Chapters 4 and 6).
2. Candidates need to have demonstrated a high level of authenticity and should be able to align their purpose with that of the organisation.
3. Candidates should be independent in terms of character and judgment.
4. Candidates should bring unique perspectives about the key trends and potential discontinuities that the industry faces to the board.
5. Candidates should bring expertise to the board that is currently not available among the family members that serve on the board.
6. Candidates should leverage their network and mentor family members, especially the upcoming younger generation, to groom them for future leadership of the business.

These characteristics are crucial to ensure that there is a strong cultural fit among the various board members, while at the same time contributing to the long-term sustainable success of the family business.

4. Successful succession stories

The following examples illustrate Asian family businesses that have undergone generations of succession.

A. OCBC Bank (Singapore)

OCBC is one of the major banks in Singapore. It was founded by Dr Lee Kong Chian, a leading businessman and philanthropist. The family set up the Lee Foundation as the vehicle with which it conducts charitable and philanthropy activities. While many of the later generations of the Lee family were educated in Western countries, the values and culture of the family and the family enterprise have still been kept intact. This can be illustrated by a point raised by Lee Seng Gee, the eldest son of Lee Kong Chian: 'We didn't believe in importing wholesale Western methods. Ours is still a Chinese company based on traditional Chinese values but improved by adding Western ideas that would help to improve the whole structure.'

Through an appropriate level of involvement, the Lee family has maintained family control while recognising the need for outside talents serving as professional management. The Lee family has cultivated and nurtured trusted and highly competent non-family managers who work closely with family professional managers. Family members are continually sent for professional education and remain expected to start out as managers in various departments within the family enterprise. This enables the next generation of business leaders to build strong rapport with non-family professional managers, with whom they will need to rely on when their time comes to take over the helm of the family business.

B. YTL Group (Malaysia)

YTL is a major diversified conglomerate in Malaysia. It was founded in 1955 and named after its founder, Yeoh Tiong Lay. YTL started as a modest contracting business and has advanced into a high-profile multinational firm with interests in various industries including cement manufacturing, water, hospitality, construction and real estate, and communications.

YTL has successful managed several generations of successions; the family is currently in its fourth generation of successors, and has a total of 27 members. The conduct of both the family and the family enterprises are based on Christian values.

The family constitution states the desired type of leaders the company wants. It specifically states that the family 'want to preserve unity and this Godly purpose of steward', as they believe that the wealth they produce is never their own, and that should adhere to the stewardship principle. As such, the family constitution states very clearly the need to build trust with all stakeholders as well as to be a responsible corporate citizen.

C. Li & Fung (Hong Kong)

Li & Fung has its origins in Guangzhou in China since 1906. The families moved the business to Hong Kong because of political uncertainty in China in the early years. To date, Li & Fung has transformed itself into a leading player in the global supply chain arena. They have also been very successful in leadership succession, having successfully passed down the family business over four generations, despite facing various crises in their earlier years.

Li & Fung handled family conflicts and differences by way of listing and delisting the family enterprise. This is a unique and highly interesting approach that deserves to be looked at more closely. In the 1970s the family business was listed on the flourishing Hong Kong stock exchange to tackle internal family conflict and management inefficiencies. Listing itself provided several catalysts for changes. Firstly, it opened up the business to public scrutiny, thus necessitating high levels of managerial efficiency. Secondly, listing itself brought about access to fresh capital, which was used to fuel expansion through multiple projects. Expansion brought many opportunities for everyone in the family. In effect, there was ample to go around, and there was no need to squabble.

However, in 1989, when Hong Kong's socio-political atmosphere was at its all-time low as a result of tensions with China, the share price of Li & Fung plummeted. Internally a bigger crisis was looming: Fung Hon-chu, the successor to one of the co-founders of Li & Fung, was approaching 80 years-old and in poor health. The third-generation successors, Victor and William Fung, proposed the delisting of Li & Fung. The proposed move resulted in deep divisions in the family that threatened to disintegrate the family. The Fungs convened a family meeting in Boston to discuss shareholding issues. There were family members who objected violently to the proposed delisting of the family business. The meeting resolved the conflict with some members of the family selling their shares to other members so that the other family members could proceed to delist the company. Ultimately, despite their disagreements, the family culture enabled them to amicably resolve their conflicts.

There are perhaps several key reasons why these three family businesses has been able to transition well across generations. The first is the role of education, which is considered as a key human capital that helps to sustain family status, as well as drive the expansion of the family business. Education is an important barometer of professional status and earning power. Younger generations of the Fung families have all attended top universities for their education. Some of them even hold several master's degrees from these institutions. Going abroad also helped them to build important social networks and connections that the family regards as important resources for their family business. The second reason is the importance of succession planning. Once the children return from their overseas education, they are dispatched to work in internationally renowned multinational firms for several years to gather work experience, as well as connections that will help them when they take over the family business. As such, it seems that family members cannot join the family business unless they have worked for some time at an external organisation. When they return to the family business, they usually start out at relatively low positions in a subsidiary or holding company of the family business to get bottom-up training. They are promoted gradually over time to be head of a subsidiary. Only when the family elders feel that they are ready for the challenges ahead are they granted full empowerment and independence. Another advantage of the bottom-up training is that they will help to build internal networks and credibility among key employees, some of whom they will be managing later in their career.

5. Conclusion

Family businesses dominate as a form of business organisation anywhere in the world. Family businesses have characteristics that are different from other non-family related organisations. The nuances existing in family businesses present challenges in the application and practice of corporate governance, particularly in Asia where family businesses are more prevalent.

It is often said that family wealth does not pass over three generations. There are many plausible reasons why this may be so. Many of these are succession related and family relationship focused. Hence, successful trans-generational transfer of corporate control and family wealth will be greatly enhanced if these issues are addressed at an early stage. It is timely for Asian families to tackle these issues because founder succession in Asia is happening swiftly but quietly.

There are four key areas in succession and family relationships that can improve the sustenance of the family business across multiple generations. Firstly, the next generation family owners must take an interest in the preservation of the mission and the legacy of the founder in the founder succession journey. Secondly, there should be a conscious effort to professionalize the family business. Only then will the family business be able to maximize the use of the top talents from inside and outside the family. The indiscriminate use of family members regardless of capabilities will invariably lead to an inability to hire top non-family talents from the wider labour market. Thirdly, the family should consider adopting a suitable model of family constitution and control. This document is important as it will govern the conduct of relationships between family and the family enterprise as well as between family members. The family constitution will include guides to conflict resolution and the management of deadlocks. Finally, the next generation of family business leaders are likely to be leading the family business that will operate in a more disruptive global business environment. How they prepare their family businesses to face different challenges will determine their success in sustaining the family business.

To challenge the conventional wisdom that family wealth does not pass beyond three generations, we provided several examples of Asian families that have successfully sustained their family business through different generations – OCBC in Singapore, YTL in Malaysia, and Li & Fung in Hong Kong. These families have been successful in sustaining their wealth transfer because they actively managed the process and prepared their subsequent generations to sustain the family business in an increasingly uncertain world.

'Improving the odds of sustaining the family business beyond the third generation', explored potential recommendations pertaining to the second-generation growth and sustainability imperatives.

CHAPTER 17. THE DYNAMICS OF CORPORATE REPORTING

George Littlejohn, Senior Advisor, Chartered Institute for Securities & Investment.

Alexander Van de Putte, Professor of Strategic Foresight, IE Business School and Chairman of Corporate Governance & Stewardship, AIFC.

Introduction

For much of the latter half of the 20th century, academia ruled the roost when it came to innovation and thought leadership in accounting and financial reporting. David Flint, in a long career at the University of Glasgow, for instance, was a leading light and an exemplar during those decades. He brought the same thirst for knowledge and desire to empower young change-makers as his eminent predecessor Adam Smith had done at the same university some 200 years earlier. By the end of the 20th century, though, much of the intellectual firepower had been wooed to finance, with much higher salaries and greater resources. By then, most corporate boards of any significance were beholden in some ways or many to banks and asset managers.

Driven by people like Professor Flint's son Douglas (now Sir Douglas), then finance director of HSBC (and en route to becoming group chairman from 2011 to 2017), banks and asset managers were wooing the best thinkers in the field into their halls.

In the two decades since then, another seismic shift has taken place. In 2000, the market data arm of the mighty Reuters news agency was a lowly outpost of that empire. Twenty years later, now branded Refinitiv and custodian of colossal amounts of data – the lifeblood of today's business and finance – that former Cinderella of a business was bought by London Stock Exchange Group (LSEG) in January 2021 for $27 billion. (The acquisition fees alone touched $1 billion). Power had shifted; the demand for much-improved data and analysis of governance-related issues was a major driver of that sea change. The quality and reliability of environmental, social and governance (ESG) data for company boards, investors and banks is the stand-out issue.

Leon Saunders Calvert, head of research and portfolio management at LSEG (and Refinitiv's former head of sustainable finance) is one of the field's leading actors, not least because he is open about his doubts around some of the data that drives board and investment decisions. In April 2021, Mr Saunders Calvert remarked:[1] "The filmmaker, Stanley Kubrick, once said that, 'If you can talk brilliantly about a problem, it can create the consoling illusion that it has been mastered.'" He then, while disowning the idea that he was speaking 'brilliantly,' launched what he called "an attempt to try and mature the conversation about ESG scores/ratings and identifying the inherent complexities therein and why, amongst other things, they are not comparable to a credit score." By pulling apart the various component parts that might constitute how the business and financial worlds think about ESG he aimed to make "a small contribution to articulating the problem statement with slightly better clarity than the dialogue I typically see on the subject."[2]

Apart from providing a historical account of the changing reporting landscape, this chapter explores how ESG and sustainability reporting helps build bridges between corporations, investors and data providers.

---

[1] Leon Saunders Calvert, LinkedIn post, 7 April 2021 (accessed 2 May 2021).
[2] Details of his report follow later in this chapter.

1. Board characteristics driving climate challenge responses

A recent (and ongoing) research project at the University of Cambridge with a varied and experienced team of practitioners from business and finance working towards master's degrees in sustainability management considered what board of director characteristics are driving the climate change response of firms in the finance sector.[3]

The importance of the topic, the researchers say, is reflected in the growing awareness of the risks posed by climate change to society, the environment and the economy which is generating demand from regulators, investors and other stakeholders for organisations to demonstrate they take climate change into account in their decision-making.[4] At a global level, the Paris Agreement[5] saw nations reach an agreement on climate goals and the United Nations (UN) 2030 Agenda[6] articulates how nations and organisations must take action on climate change. Furthermore, the World Bank states that the private sector is crucial to delivering the UN Sustainable Development Goals (including climate change). This is supported in the European Union by the EU Commission Action Plan to Finance Sustainable Growth which stresses the importance of the finance sector in relation to "sustainable economic growth, […] more transparency and long-termism in the economy".[7]

---

[3] Richard Burrett, Sam Anthony, Beate von Loo-Born, David Jones, Clare Nickson-Havens, Veronica Palmgren, and Nawaz Peerbocus, "Understanding what board characteristics are driving the climate change response of firms in the finance sector", University of Cambridge https://www.cisi.org/cisiweb2/docs/default-source/sir/rfm-q1-2021--boards-and-climate-challenge.pdf?sfvrsn=f8a0ff4d_0 (accessed 20 May 2021)

[4] Alastair Marsh, "Barclay's shareholders vote to support UK bank's climate plan", Bloomberg, 2020. https://www.bloomberg.com/news/articles/2020-05-07/barclaysshareholders-vote-to-support-u-k-bank-s-climate-plan (accessed 4 July 2020).

[5] United Nations, "Paris Agreement of the United Nations Framework Convention on Climate Change", 2015. https://unfccc.int/process-and-meetings/the-parisagreement/the-paris-agreement (accessed 4 July 2020).

[6] Institute of International Finance (IIF), *IIF Sustainable Finance Working Group Report - The case for simplifying sustainable investment terminology*, 2019. https://www.iif.com/Publications/ID/3633/The-Case-for-Simplifying-SustainableInvestment-Terminology (accessed 4 July 2020).

[7] European Commission, "Action plan on sustainable finance", 2018. https://ec.europa.eu/info/publications/sustainable-finance-renewed-strategy_en (accessed 4 July 2020).

Finance leaders such as Mark Carney, former Bank of England governor and now UN special envoy for climate action and finance, and Larry Fink, board chair and CEO of the world's largest asset manager, BlackRock, have articulated the importance of the finance sector in the transition to a low-carbon economy.[8] The finance sector, as a gatekeeper to the world's private and public capital, has the potential to direct capital towards climate change solutions. This could include leading the transition to renewable technologies (i.e. directing capital away from fossil fuels) and offering investment products that address climate change. If the finance sector's response to climate change were to be enhanced, this could accelerate capital flow to investments that support global climate goals, increasing the probability they are achieved.

For individual firms within the finance sector, climate change is developing from a reputational or financial risk to becoming a strategic risk.[9] While regulators have introduced financial and non-financial reporting requirements[10] and have set standards for sustainable investments,[11] guidance on how financial firms should plan for or manage their climate response has only recently begun to emerge, such as the Task Force on Climate-related Financial Disclosures (TCFD).[12]

---

[8] Damian Carrington, "Firms ignoring climate will go bankrupt, says Mark Carney", The Guardian, 2019. https://www.theguardian.com/environment/2019/oct/13/firms-ignoring-climatecrisis-bankrupt-mark-carney-bank-england-governor (accessed 4 July 2020); Larry Fink, "A fundamental reshaping of finance", 2019. https://www.blackrock.com/uk/individual/larry-fink-ceo-letter (accessed 12 June 2020).

[9] University of Cambridge Institute for Sustainability Leadership, *Bank 2030: Accelerating the Transition to a Low Carbon Economy*, 2020. https://www.cisl.cam.ac.uk/resources/publication-pdfs/bank-2030.pdf (accessed 4 July 2020).

[10] European Commission, "Proposal for a regulation on disclosures relating to sustainable investments and sustainability risks and amending Directive (EU) 2016/2341", 2018. https://ec.europa.eu/info/publications/180524proposal-sustainable-finance_en (accessed 4 July 2020). European Commission, Regulation (EU) 2019/2088 of the European Parliament and of the Council on sustainability-related disclosures in the financial services sector. https://eurlex.europa.eu/eli/reg/2019/2088/oj (accessed 4 July 2020).

[11] European Commission, "Sustainable finance: TEG final report on the EU taxonomy", 2020. https://knowledge4policy.ec.europa.eu/publication/sustainable-finance-teg-final-report-eu-taxonomy_en (accessed 4 July 2020); US Securities and Exchange Commission, 2020 Examination priorities. https://www.sec.gov/about/offices/ocie/national-examination-program-priorities-2020.pdf (accessed 4 July 2020).

[12] TCFD, "Final Report – Recommendations of the Task Force on Climate-related Financial Disclosures", 2017. https://www.fsb-tcfd.org/wp-

Best practice corporate governance, for example the UK Corporate Governance Code, requires the board of directors to oversee the stewardship of the firm.[13] To achieve its fiduciary and regulatory duty regarding climate response, the board needs to ensure governance structures and processes are in place.[14] Therefore, it is the board's responsibility to provide strategic direction on the firm's climate response and to oversee implementation by management.

The Cambridge University research project therefore seeks to understand this question: what board characteristics are driving the climate change response of firms in the finance sector?

In their paper, "board characteristics" are variables which individually or in combination influence the quality of governance. The term "climate response" is defined as a board's governance and management of climate change within the firm. In assessing literature on the topic, ESG factors are often used as a proxy for climate response, given climate's significance within environmental factors. The paper does not attempt to quantify climate response, but rather assesses the qualitative relationship between board characteristics and a firm's climate response. The lack of standardised assessment methodologies makes comparisons of firms' climate responses challenging; the ratings agencies which measure climate change variables report widely divergent scores.[15] The study focuses on financial firms in Australia, Finland, Switzerland and the UK. Ultimately, gaining a better understanding of which board characteristics are driving the climate change response of financial firms is essential in ensuring the finance sector provides capital for the transition to a low-carbon world.

---

content/uploads/2017/06/FINALTCFD-Report-062817.pdf (accessed 4 July 2020).

[13] Financial Reporting Council (FRC), *UK Corporate Governance Code*, 2018. https://www.frc.org.uk/directors/corporate-governance-and-stewardship/uk-corporate-governance-code (accessed 4 July 2020).

[14] World Economic Forum, "How to set up effective governance on corporate boards. Guiding principles and questions", 2019. https://www.weforum.org/whitepapers/how-to-set-up-effective-climate-governance-on-corporate-boards-guiding-principles-and-questions (accessed 4 July 2020).

[15] Florian Berg, Julian Koebel, and Roberto Rigobon, "Aggregate confusion: The divergence of ESG ratings", *SSRN Electronic Journal*, 2019. https://doi.org/10.2139/ssrn.3438533 (accessed 5 July 2021).

A. Interim research results

Under its fiduciary duty, the board is responsible for overseeing and ensuring the long-term success and strategic direction of the firm and is therefore in a crucial position to impact a firm's climate response. Three overarching themes emerged from the literature review on board characteristics driving a firm's climate response: board structure; board diversity and mindset; and board processes. These themes were investigated for underpinning characteristics, to respond to the research question.

The literature review revealed that drivers of climate response are not well defined, which means that establishing causation between board characteristics and financial firms' climate response is challenging. Board structure appeared to be of low importance, with separation of CEO and chair roles the only characteristic found to positively influence climate response. Board processes are necessary to enable boards to meet their fiduciary duty, but there was no consensus on characteristics necessary to achieve this. However, both the literature review and the primary research provided evidence that board diversity, including gender, age, and expertise, positively contributes to a firm's climate response, as does a sustainability mindset. Furthermore, research found that aspects of diversity such as gender and age are associated with a sustainability mindset (see also Chapters 6, 8, and 18).

The research also highlights the importance of the chair in driving the firm's climate response. When the chair possesses a sustainability mindset, this has an impact on whether climate is included on the board agenda and ultimately in the firm's climate response. However, even a climate-literate chair with a sustainability mindset still needs to bring other directors along on the journey. These findings make a useful contribution to the existing knowledge regarding board characteristics positively impacting climate response.

The implications of the research findings could be relevant to nominations committees when seeking to recruit board directors, and climate should be included in both board and director skills evaluation. Interviews with banking chief executives and chairs of banks highlighted that there is an opportunity to educate board recruitment firms on the importance of sustainability mindset as an attribute for board appointees. Although the definition of sustainability mindset is subjective, literature includes dimensions such as creative thinking, inclusive thinking, connection with nature and partnering as well as a good level of climate knowledge; these features can be targeted in the recruitment process.

The relative immaturity of climate as a systematically integrated board topic opens research opportunities into how a sustainability mindset can be fostered at board level. The research team recommends it be pursued through education and awareness, targeted recruitment, or by enhancing the board's gender and age diversity. Given the board's fiduciary duty to the firm's stewardship and that regulators have indicated that financial firms' climate-related disclosures will continue to increase, they recommend further research on the connection between sustainability mindset, board diversity and climate response to contribute to the body of knowledge on effective climate governance and management in financial firms.

Although financial firms are a subset of the business world, the information their boards need to govern properly is both the same if not significantly greater in volume than that required by boards of non-financial firms. An understanding of the information required and being used in the financial sector is of vital importance to all but the very best-capitalised privately-held firms. So, the views on data held by the financial markets – such as London Stock Exchange through its data subsidiary Refinitiv – are critical.

2. Pinpointing what is actually being measured in ESG

In his April 2021 analysis referred to above,[16] LSEG's Mr Saunders Calvert explains: "While [ESG] scores are increasingly debated in the financial industry, pinpointing what they actually measure can be less clear. The layperson may legitimately expect that an ESG score provides an overview or rating on how ethical a company or its products are. This is not necessarily the case. Refinitiv ESG scores, for example, reflect a relative performance based on fundamental ESG attributes which are publicly

---

[16] https://www.refinitiv.com/perspectives/future-of-investing-trading/understanding-how-esg-scores-are-measured-their-usefulness-and-how-they-will-evolve/ (accessed 2 May 2021).

disclosed and auditable. It is in this context that we continue to call for ESG data to be treated as objective and fundamental data, not categorised as merely alternative data or dependent on subjective opinion. In shaping the debate, we need to examine the key definitions.

1. ESG is an aggregate term that covers a range of thematic issues and measures which are non-financial, although they may be financially material. They do not necessarily correlate with one another. For example, a company's carbon footprint does not necessarily correlate with its diversity and inclusion practices, its employee rights principles or its resource usage. A single ESG score cannot capture this complexity.

2. ESG data and the disclosures that companies make have mostly focused on a company's operations rather than its products and services or its supply chain. This is necessarily the case. It is much harder to expect companies to be able to report on the social impact of their products and services in an objective and measurable way. However, this approach can lead to counter-intuitive outcomes unless the focus of ESG data is clearly understood (consider the example of Tesla scoring relatively poorly on ESG criteria).

3. We may assume that ESG scores can measure the ESG risks a company faces, the risks a company poses to the environment and society or the correlations on long-term performance of a company. Although we may want an ESG score to measure all these areas, they are not the same, and a single score cannot represent all of them."

Commenting on Mr Saunders Calvert's views, Neil Brown, chief risk officer at Earth Capital, a sustainable asset manager, commented:[17] "[A] clear explanation of the strengths and weaknesses of the ESG process today. Standardisation/credit Rating 'status' is not an objective in itself – transparency and usable information is the objective. Standards evolve from making the important measurable, not the measurable important."

---

[17] Neil Brown, LinkedIn 7 April 2021 (accessed 9 May 2021).

3. The $100 trillion-plus playbook

Why is this distinction important? In April 2021, the Association for Financial Markets Europe (AFME) published, with law firm Latham & Watkins, an extensive and farsighted report: "ESG Disclosure Landscape for Banks and Capital Markets in Europe."[18] European regulation in this field, affecting both listed and private concerns and their financial backers, has mushroomed in recent years, affecting board conduct on both sides of the financing divide. Even in the teeth of the Covid pandemic, corporate reliance on ESG-related funding is soaring. In 2020 ESG bond and loan issuance increased by almost 60% to €398 billion.[19]

In the report's foreword, Michael Cole-Fontayn, chair of AFME and also of the Chartered Institute for Securities & Investment, said: "While a lot has been achieved, the scale of what will be needed to meet the objectives of the Paris Agreement and the Sustainable Development Goals cannot be understated. According to a recent report by the Global Financial Markets Association and Boston Consulting Group, investment needs will amount to $100–$150 trillion over the next three decades, to fund the transition to a low-carbon economy.[20] This translates to at least $3–$5 trillion of investment per year – an increase of five to eight times from current levels. The United Nations has estimated that for the complementary ambition of reaching the Sustainable Development Goals, the annual funding gap is $2.5 trillion per year."[21]

Paola Bergamaschi Broyd has some 30 years' experience of capital markets in the City of London, at Goldman Sachs, Credit Suisse, and State Street. She is currently a non-executive director on several boards, including BNY Mellon International and Wells Fargo Securities International. In a May 2021 analysis for *The International Banker*, the journal of the Worshipful

---

[18] https://www.afme.eu/publications/reports/details/ESG-Disclosure-Landscape-for-Banks-and-Capital-Markets-in-Europe (accessed 15 May 2021).
[19] https://www.afme.eu/Publications/Data-Research/Details/AFME-European-ESG-Finance-Quarterly-Data-Report-Q4-2020 (accessed 15 May 2021).
[20] https://www.sifma.org/wp-content/uploads/2020/12/Climate-Finance-Markets-and-the-Real-Economy.pdf.
[21] https://www.un.org/press/en/2019/dsgsm1340.doc.htm (accessed 15 May 2021)

Company of International Bankers (WCIB), [22,23] she provided an overview of the importance of the sector in the investment world, focusing on seven key types of responsible investment strategies: negative or exclusionary screening, ESG integration, corporate engagement, norms-based screening, positive screening, sustainability-themed investing, and impact investing.

"In 2016," she writes, "negative screening represented 66% of responsible assets under management, while ESG integration accounted for 45%. But asset managers are currently opting for more sophisticated strategies that couple exclusions of controversial industries with ESG integration and a positive or best-in-class screening approach (the latter is estimated at only 2-3% of the total at this point). It is very important to understand that positive screening is what drives really better behavior at the corporate level given the granularity of the research attached to the investment decision … With positive screening, you're selecting stocks within, say, the oil industry, but you're selecting the best-in-class within the oil industry."[24]

Active strategies, she adds, represent most ESG-related assets under management (75% in the US and 82% in Europe). "However, passive ESG strategies and ESG indexes captured about 60% of new asset inflows in the US in 2019 and the trend is not weakening. The wall of liquidity and savings generated by the everlasting low interest rate environment has been exacerbated by the Covid pandemic and it is boosting the ESG passive alternatives as the cheapest and quickest way to participate in responsible investing."

With investment products increasingly characterised by so many different "shades of grey," all under the same banner of 'ESG', how can the saver … obtain transparency and avoid 'greenwashing'.…" One urgent problem to solve, she believes, is agreeing on a unified set of criteria, standards and rules that would parallel the work done by the Financial Accounting Standards Board (FASB) on corporate accounts "eons ago."

---

[22] Paola Bergamaschi Broyd, "ESG: If it cannot be measured it cannot be managed", *The International Banker*, Spring 2021. https://internationalbankers.org.uk/magazine (accessed 20 May 2021).
[23] WCIB is one of the City of London's 100+ livery companies that comprise London's ancient and modern trade bodies.
[24] See Note 22.

4. Accountability in financial reporting

Accountability and transparency are two of the principal tenets of corporate governance and this chapter looks at how these principles work in practice through the disclosure companies make.

Historically, disclosure made by companies focussed on financial performance reporting. Over the years, corporate governance codes required that companies make disclosures on non-financial matters such as corporate social responsibility and on narrative reporting. In 2010, the International Integrated Reporting Council (IIRC) was launched by the Prince of Wales and several partners, including the Big Four accounting firms, to report on how the company's strategy and operations impact the six capital stocks – natural, manufactured, human, social, intellectual and financial – with an objective to understand a company's financial and sustainability performance. Although voluntary, integrated reporting has been widely adopted, at least in part, by many multinationals.

Although climate-risk disclosures recommended by the Taskforce on Climate-Related Financial Disclosures (TCFD) are voluntary, the UK government has proposed mandatory reporting in line with TCFD starting in 2022 for listed companies. Other countries are also exploring the introduction of mandatory TCFD disclosures in the near future, including Australia, Singapore, Hong Kong, Japan, and the Philippines. The alignment of mandatory TCFD disclosures will mean greater transparency across identifying the risks and opportunities of climate change.

B. Ground-breaking steps towards global climate reporting standards

"Changes in climate policies, new technologies and growing physical risks will prompt reassessments of the values of virtually every financial asset," says Dr Mark Carney.[25] In 2020, he reminded us of the risks and

---

[25] https://www.bankofengland.co.uk/-/media/boe/files/speech/2019/tcfd-strengthening-the-foundations-of-sustainable-finance-speech-by-mark-carney.pdf?la=en&hash=D28F6D67BC4B97DDCCDE91AF8111283A39950563 (accessed 1 July 2021).

opportunities of climate change for companies and financial institutions: "Achieving net zero will require a whole economy transition – every company, every bank, every insurer and investor will have to adjust their business models. This could turn an existential risk into the greatest commercial opportunity of our time."[26]

Now, as we see exponential increases in sustainable investing, sustainability disclosure has become increasingly critical, both for investors, as they seek to make robust economic decisions, and regulators, as they look at the overall stability and efficiency of financial markets.

Veronica Poole, corporate reporting leader and transparency advocate at Deloitte, made the case plain in *The International Banker* in late 2020 as the campaign for a more coordinated approach gathered force:[27] "Investors are clear in their expectations that climate-related information, including on governance, strategy, risks and performance, should be included by companies both in the narrative in annual reports and in the assumptions and forecasts used in the financial statements. Financial institutions are increasingly required to measure and disclose carbon exposure in their portfolios – including assets and lending."

As a result of this pressure, there has been a surge in calls from capital market participants, regulators, and other stakeholders in support of transparent measurement and disclosure of information about sustainability performance. "Investors and other stakeholders want to understand how the risks and opportunities faced by business translate into long-term value creation and profitability and how, in turn, these relate to shorter-term financial performance," says Ms Poole.

The duties of directors, as described elsewhere in this book, includes considering stakeholders and the environment while promoting the long-term success of the company. The success of a business is inextricably

---

[26] https://www.bankofengland.co.uk/-/media/boe/files/speech/2020/the-road-to-glasgow-speech-by-mark-carney.pdf?la=en&hash=DCA8689207770DCBBB179CBADBE3296F7982FDF5 (accessed 1 July 2021).

[27] Veronica Poole, "Ground-breaking steps towards global climate reporting standards", *The International Banker*, Autumn 2020. https://internationalbankers.org.uk/magazine (accessed 1 July 2021).

linked to its impacts on people, planet and the economy, and how its purpose translates into positive outcomes in relation to the UN Sustainable Development Goals (SDGs). Information on these topics is therefore also of greater importance than ever before.

However, there is now a large proliferation of voluntary standards, codes, tools and methodologies, all developed with a genuine desire to provide solutions as to how business works in the context of people and planet. But the number of competing offerings is hindering comparability between reporting organisations, and that has led to complexity in reporting, and "greenwashing" in the system.

By early 2020 the international reporting community formed a resolve, under leaders such as Ms Poole, to work on the best of what is already available in terms of reporting standards, and gather round one flag of global sustainability standards (just as the global community had done with financial reporting). Moving to standards allows consensus to be achieved among market participants – companies, investors, policymakers, regulators and civil society. It will also ensure that information on people, planet and prosperity that is relevant to understanding how enterprises create value can be of the same quality as information on profit, backed by the right rigour of governance and controls to enhance the quality and verifiability of reported information.

During the latter part of 2020, three significant moves took the world a stage nearer standardised sustainability reporting:

- In September 2020, the Trustees of the International Financial Reporting Standards Foundation (IFRSF) issued a ground-breaking public consultation that set out possible ways the organisation might build on its experience in international standard-setting, its well-established due processes and its governance structure to develop global sustainability standards. This would include the introduction of a new Sustainability Standards Board (SSB), alongside the existing financial reporting board, the International Accounting Standards Board (IASB).[28]

---

[28] consultation-paper-on-sustainability-reporting.pdf (accessed 1 July 2021).

- In order to meet the urgent needs of climate change and the SDGs, the board argued, there is simply no time to start the technical content from scratch. So the IFRSF Trustees stressed the importance of building on the existing work of the leading international sustainability standards and frameworks – the Climate Disclosure Project (CDP),[29] the Climate Disclosure Standards Board (CDSB),[30] the Global Reporting Initiative (GRI)[31] the International Integrated Reporting Council (IIRC),[32] and the Sustainability Accounting Standards Board (SASB).[33] These organisations have issued a statement of intent[34] that sets out a vision for a coherent and comprehensive corporate reporting system. They make a joint commitment to work together and collaborate with the IFRSF and other key stakeholders to drive towards this goal.

- A further accelerator was the work of the IOSCO Task Force on Sustainable Finance.[35] The chair of the task force, Erik Thedéen, has publicly said that he expects these parallel initiatives to come together, to lead to the foundation of a structure that can deliver a more coherent and comprehensive corporate reporting system. He has set out a vision for a system that meets the information needs of capital markets, operates with a governance model that serves the public interest and can potentially be integrated with existing regulatory frameworks across IOSCO member jurisdictions.

- "These are very exciting developments," argues Ms Poole, whose firm (alongside the other accounting majors) has laid much of the groundwork to enable this process. "The IFRSF is extremely well positioned to take on the global sustainability standard-setting role, having demonstrated a successful track record with financial reporting by operating an effective model of private sector, independent and high-quality standard-setting, overseen by public authorities. Connectivity to financial reporting, under the oversight of the IFRSF, is

---

[29] https://www.cdp.net/en.
[30] https://www.cdsb.net.
[31] https://www.globalreporting.org.
[32] https://integratedreporting.org.
[33] https://www.sasb.org.
[34] Statement-of-Intent-to-Work-Together-Towards-Comprehensive-Corporate-Reporting.pdf (accessed 1 July 2021).
[35] IOSCO is the International Organization of Securities Commissions.

critical to achieve the much-needed alignment between business model and sustainability disclosures, and assertions that underpin information in the financial statements."

C. The Taskforce on Climate-Related Financial Disclosures (TCFD)

During the key 2015 climate negotiations in Paris, Mark Carney, then Bank of England governor, and Michael Bloomberg, former New York City mayor, announced the creation of a new task force, to help investors understand their financial exposures to climate risk and help companies disclose this information in a clearer and more consistent way.

Users of financial information (e.g. investors, lenders and insurers) have had limited clarity until recently on which companies will prosper or indeed survive as our environment changes, regulations evolve, new technologies develop, and customer behaviour shifts. A lack of consistent information hinders investors and others from considering climate-related issues in their asset valuation and allocation processes.

In 2015 the Financial Stability Board (FSB) established the Task Force on Climate-related Financial Disclosures (TCFD) to develop recommendations for more effective climate-related disclosures that could promote more informed financial decisions in investment, credit, and insurance underwriting. In 2017, the TCFD produced climate-related financial disclosure recommendations designed to help companies provide better information to support informed capital allocation and risk management decisions.

According to Mark Carney, the TCFD's work has become the go-to standard for consistent, comparable and efficient information.[36] "Most importantly", he said, "it represents the best views of the private sector of what is decision useful, capturing the opinions of both the companies that must access finance and of the providers of capital from across the financial

---

[36] Remarks made by Dr Carney in a keynote address in London's Guildhall in February 2021 on the start of his "Road to COP26" – the UN climate change summit in November 2021 on which he is the UK's climate adviser.

system." This will help ensure that every financial decision takes climate change into account, by putting the information into the management process that will transform climate risk management and move everyone closer to a point where investing for a net zero world will go mainstream.

Investors worldwide are demanding more and better disclosures from corporate preparers of annual reports; so too are borrowers and portfolio companies. This will quickly build the availability and quality of data that investors need to integrate sustainable finance into their investment processes. Larry Fink, CEO of BlackRock, made exactly the same point in his 2020 annual letter to CEOs; that sustainability will be at the centre of the firm's investment approach. By the end of 2020, BlackRock expects clients to report in line with both the TCFD and the US-based SASB. The changes afoot in the reporting world are all part of this wider movement. And this means that boards will be scrutinised more by the regulator, market participants and a broader group of stakeholder whether company reporting meet the TCFD and SASB standards.

Consistent categorisation of climate-related risks and opportunities is inevitably an important part of this process, and the TCFD splits climate-related risks into two major categories: (1) risks related to the transition to a lower-carbon economy and (2) risks related to the physical impacts of climate change (Table 17.1).

These disclosure recommendations have been structured around four thematic areas that represent the key core elements of how organisations operate, namely: governance, strategy, risk management, and metrics and targets.

Governance disclosures

Professional users of climate-related financial disclosures (collectively referred to in TCFD as "investors and other stakeholders") need to understand the role an organisation's board plays in overseeing climate-related issues as well as management's role in assessing and managing those issues. Such information supports evaluations of whether climate-related issues receive appropriate board and management attention.

Table 17.1 TCFD climate-related risks impacts[37]
Source: TCFD recommendations report

	Risk Type	Example Risks	Example Financial Impacts
Physical Risks	**Acute**	– Increased severity of extreme weather events such as cyclones and floods	– Reduced revenue from decreased production capacity (e.g. transport difficulties, supply chain interruptions)
	Chronic	– Changes in precipitation patterns and extreme variability in weather patterns	– Increased capital costs (e.g. damage to facilities)
		– Rising sea levels	– Cost of replacing assets in high-risk locations and/or increased insurance premiums and potential for reduced availability of insurance
Transition Risks	**Policy and legal**	– Increased pricing of greenhouse gas emissions	– Increased operating costs
		– Exposure to litigation	– Increased costs and/or reduced demand for products and services resulting from fines and judgments (in – extremis, certain products and services may be banned)
	Technology	– Substitution of existing products and services with lower-emissions options	– Write-offs and early retirement of existing assets
		– Costs to transition to lower emissions technology	– Costs to adopt/deploy new practices and processes
	Market	– Changing customer behaviour	– Reduced demand for goods and services due to shift in consumer preferences
		– Changing market valuations	– Re-pricing of assets (e.g. fossil fuel reserves, land valuations, securities valuations)

---

[37] https://ww.fsb-tcfd.org/recommendations (accessed 2 July 2021).

		– Stigmatisation of high-carbon sectors	– Lower revenues and higher costs from combination of reduced customer demand and negative impacts on workforce management and planning (e.g. employee attraction and retention)
	Reputation	– Increased stakeholder concern of investing in high- carbon sectors	– Reduction in capital availability

Strategy disclosures

Likewise, those professionals need to understand how climate-related issues may affect an organisation's businesses, strategy, and financial planning over the short, medium, and long term. This information is critical in informing expectations about the future performance of an organisation.

Risk management disclosures

Investors and other stakeholders further need to understand how an organisation's climate-related risks are identified, measured and managed, and whether those processes are integrated into existing risk management processes. This information helps recipients of climate-related financial disclosures evaluate the organisation's overall risk profile and risk management activities.

Metrics and targets disclosures

Measurement is critical to much of this process. Investors and other stakeholders need to understand how an organisation measures and monitors its climate-related risks and opportunities. Access to the metrics and targets used by an organisation allows stakeholders to better assess the organisation's potential risk-adjusted returns, ability to meet financial obligations, general exposure to climate-related issues, and progress in managing or adapting to those issues. They also provide a basis on which investors and other stakeholders can compare organisations within a sector or industry, and across sectors.

At the time of writing, some 1,500 organisations globally – including almost 1,400 companies with a market capitalisation of some $13 trillion, and financial institutions responsible for assets of $150 trillion – have adopted the *principles* of TCFD reporting. However, implementation of the recommendations has not been as fast as many, such as the TCFD itself, other policymakers, and investors would like. As a result, local regulators (as in the UK) are beginning to move towards mandatory disclosure.

5. The pivotal importance of materiality, and focus

In September 2020, a key "summary of alignment discussions among leading sustainability and integrated reporting organisations" set the stage for a radical shake-up of climate-related disclosures. Five key framework- and standard-setting institutions from the alphabet soup which makes up this world – CDP, CDSB, GRI, IIRC and SASB – had decided on a radical shake-up. The process had been facilitated by the Impact Management Project, World Economic Forum and Deloitte.

At a high level, this group sees itself as a "nested eco-system":

1. The GRI Standards are developed in the public interest and enable companies to report sustainability information that describes their significant impacts on the economy, environment or people, and hence their contributions – positive or negative – towards sustainable development, and can also be used to describe impacts on the company.

2. The SASB Standards and CDSB Framework focus exclusively on enabling companies to identify the sub-set of sustainability information that is material for enterprise value creation, and therefore relevant for users making economic decisions. Whereas CDSB's Framework is industry agnostic and designed to facilitate effective disclosure of a company's natural capital, environmental and climate-related risks and opportunities, the industry-specific SASB Standards aid companies in preparing disclosures on five dimensions of sustainability, including the environment, social capital, human capital, business model and innovation, and leadership and governance.

3. The Framework connects reporting of sustainability information to reporting on financial and other capitals.

4. Finally, all the organisations acknowledge the crucial role of technology in reporting. This includes the importance of enabling access for all stakeholders to corporate performance on sustainability topics, as CDP's platform does today for climate, water and forests.

6. Conclusion

Historically, disclosures made by companies focussed on financial performance reporting. Over the years, corporate governance codes required that companies make disclosures on non-financial matters such as corporate social responsibility and on narrative reporting.

It is clear that a new era of corporate reporting is emerging where companies need to report on how the company's strategy and operations impact the six capital stocks – natural, manufactured, human, social, intellectual and financial – with an objective to understand a company's financial and sustainability performance.

CHAPTER 18. IS CORPORATE GOVERNANCE 4.0 EMERGING?[1]

Alexander Van de Putte, Professor of Strategic Foresight, IE Business School and Chairman of Corporate Governance & Stewardship, AIFC

Introduction

In 2015 and 2016, respectively, countries from around the world ratified the UN Sustainable Development Goals and the Paris Agreement. This implies that countries have made commitments to mobilise $100 billion a year in climate finance until 2025 under the Paris Agreement.

An analysis conducted by Amundi, one of Europe's largest asset managers, shows that ESG compliant investments between 2014 and 2017 resulted in annualised excess returns of 3.3% in North America, and a remarkable 6.6% in Europe, compared to non-ESG compliant investments. In addition to Amundi, other global asset managers – including Blackrock, BNP Paribas, Vanguard, and Fidelity Investments – have launched ESG funds.

---

[1] Karl George, Simon Osborne, and Alexander Van de Putte (eds). Corporate Governance 3.0. The Governance Forum, 2021

In a departure from history, in August 2019 the prominent US Business Roundtable announced that 181 CEOs of the most influential global companies committed to the redefinition of the purpose of the corporation. The CEOs pledged to commit to deliver value to all stakeholders, for the future success of companies, communities and country. There seems to be a clear trend emerging that sustainable investment practices are increasingly considered by both institutional investors and in the boardroom of multinational corporations.

This chapter will make the case that corporate governance 4.0 is emerging where company directors will have to consider building inclusive, sustainable and more resilient businesses for the benefit of humanity, not just the shareholder and in the short term.

1. Capitalism as we know it

The economist Milton Friedman, winner of the 1976 Nobel Memorial Prize in Economic Sciences, in 1970 famously wrote in the *New York Times* that 'There is one and only one social responsibility of business, and that is to increase its profits'. He further argued that executives who claim that companies have 'responsibilities for providing employment, eliminating discrimination, avoiding pollution and whatever else are undermining the basis of a free society.'

The resulting Friedman doctrine influenced corporate governance laws in the US and corporate governance practices in other Anglo-Saxon countries and resulted in short-termism, compliance-driven and a shareholder-centric focus of the board. The unintended consequences of the Friedman doctrine and the resulting shareholder orientation of corporate governance are both profound and lasting. Indeed, shareholder capitalism has led to global climate change, inequality, and lack of economic resiliency.

Global climate change is indeed one of those externalities that needs to be internalised by a company in order to contribute to the sustainable long-term success of the company. When Lord Nicholas Stern released *The Economics of Climate Change: The Stern Review* in 2006, the cost of global climate change was estimated to be $500 billion or slightly less than 1% of global GDP.[2] He further argued that although the cost of stabilising global climate change is significant, that there is still time to prevent the worst impacts from happening. Today, 15 years later, the cost of global climate change is $16 trillion (almost 19% of global GDP), a compounded annual growth rate of 26%. In October 2019, then Bank of England governor Mark Carney said: 'Firms ignoring the climate crisis will go bankrupt'.[3]

Thomas Piketty in *Capital in the Twenty-First Century* demonstrates that market capitalism has shown some important flaws.[4] According to Piketty, market capitalism had quite a good outcome during the 20th century – purchasing power rose, inequalities receded. However, based on analysis of data starting from the First Industrial Revolution during the late 18th and early 19th centuries, he arrives at a different set of conclusions: the second half of the 20th century was an outlier, the rich are getting richer, and the poor are getting poorer. Thus, although market capitalism has shown that it can be effective in mobilising and allocating capital, and thus can provide a powerful basis for growth, it is less effective at distributing wealth.

In addition to lacking sustainability, the Fukushima nuclear disaster[5,6] and COVID-19 made it apparent that our global value chains are far from being resilient. The recent blockage of the Suez Canal further attests to a lack of resiliency of our global physical trading – a single container ship brought 12% of global trade to a standstill and it took more than 1 month for it to be cleared. Therefore, it is important to focus not only on the sustainability but also on the resiliency of global trade networks. Unfortunately, executives and policy leaders alike tend to revert to the old way of doing business after the crisis has waned.

---

[2] https://www.lse.ac.uk/granthaminstitute/publication/the-economics-of-climate-change-the-stern-review (accessed 12 May 2021).
[3] https://www.theguardian.com/environment/2019/oct/13/firms-ignoring-climate-crisis-bankrupt-mark-carney-bank-england-governor (accessed 13 May 2021).
[4] Thomas Piketty, *Capital in the Twenty-First Century*, Belknap Press, 2014.
[5] Caused by the 2011 magnitude 9.0–9.1 Tohoku offshore earthquake and resulting tsunami which knocked out the cooling systems of the Daiichi Nuclear Power Plant in Okuma, Fukushima Prefecture in Japan. This resulted in the meltdown of three of the four reactors. The impact on global supply chains, especially the automotive and consumer electrics, was severe and prolonged.
[6] https://hbswk.hbs.edu/item/japan-disaster-shakes-up-supply-chain-strategies (accessed 11 June 2021).

In conclusion, shareholder capitalism has led to growth, but its growth is not sustainable or inclusive, and is far from being resilient. What is needed is sustainable capitalism or stakeholder capitalism, a form of capitalism that aims to simultaneously balance and grow or maintain all five capital stocks.[7] This is similar to the argument made by Jonathon Porritt in his book *Capitalism as if the World Matters*.[8]

2. A new philosophy is emerging

Government and businesses both increasingly consider that the climate crisis poses an existential threat to companies and countries alike, because markets are increasingly internalising the cost of global climate change. Many governments around the world have announced sweeping reforms to decarbonise. For example, over the next 10 years, the US wants to reduce emissions by 50–52% from 2005 levels,[9] the EU by 55%,[10] and the UK by 78% compared to 1990 levels over the next 15-year period.[11]

Similarly, governments around the world have taken action to reduce inequality. In its 2015 report on income equality, the Organisation for Economic Co-operation and Development, argued that not everyone in society benefits from economic growth and that those groups in society that have lower-level skills and have not committed to life-long learning suffer most, not just economically but also health wise, including mental health.[12] There are some relatively straightforward solutions to help address inequality – mass tertiary and technical vocational education, basic

---

[7] Prof. Mervyn King SC noted that he prefers to refer to stakeholder capitalism as 'inclusive capitalism' during a panel entitled 'Is Corporate Governance 4.0 Emerging?' at the Astana Finance Days conference on 2 July 2021. Panelists also included Simon Osborne FCG, George Littlejohn, and me as moderator.

[8] Jonathon Porritt, *Capitalism as if the World Matters*, Routledge, 2007.

[9] https://www.whitehouse.gov/briefing-room/statements-releases/2021/04/22/fact-sheet-president-biden-sets-2030-greenhouse-gas-pollution-reduction-target-aimed-at-creating-good-paying-union-jobs-and-securing-u-s-leadership-on-clean-energy-technologies (accessed 5 June 2021).

[10] https://ec.europa.eu/clima/policies/strategies/2030_en (accessed 5 June 2021).

[11] https://www.gov.uk/government/news/uk-enshrines-new-target-in-law-to-slash-emissions-by-78-by-2035 (accessed 5 June 2021).

[12] https://www.oecd-ilibrary.org/docserver/9789264246010-7-en.pdf?expires=1624714024&id=id&accname=guest&checksum=97888F1D43969B4DADE134D14CB6939F (accessed 5 June 2021).

healthcare for all and social security. Business can also play an important role by offering better pay to workers and providing workers and staff with educational opportunities. Recently, Amazon announced that it will raise wages for more than 500,000 workers by $3 per hour. At $15 per hour, workers would earn more than twice the $7.25 per hour US federal minimum wage.[13] Most German multinationals have their own vocational training schools. For example, Siemens one of the world's largest industrial companies has around 14,000 of its staff enrolled in training and reskilling programmes for its current and future staff. Siemens argues that both staff and the company benefit from its training programmes – the employees develop more relevant skills that result in higher pay, healthier jobs and social promotion, while Siemens benefits from motivated staff, higher productivity and increased competitiveness.

Addressing sustainability, inequality and resiliency often go hand in hand and McKinsey argues that that investments in climate-resilient infrastructure and the transition to a lower-carbon future can drive significant near-term job creation while increasing economic and environmental resiliency.[14]

In addition, both shareholder and stakeholder activism are on the rise largely because of the passive behaviour of company executives in addressing ESG issues. Consider the case of oil giant Shell, for example. Royal Dutch Shell Plc was ordered on 26 May 2021 by a Dutch court to reduce emissions by 45% by 2030 compared to 2019 levels,[15] after Friends of the Earth, six other NGOs and 17,000 Dutch citizens filed a court case. Although Shell's initial reaction was to appeal the court's ruling, Ben van Beurden, Shell's chief executive, announced on 9 June 2021 that it is determined to rise to the challenge.[16]

---

[13] https://www.cnbc.com/2021/04/28/amazon-to-hike-wages-for-over-500000-workers-to-up-to-3-an-hour.html (accessed 5 June 2021).
[14] https://www.mckinsey.com/business-functions/sustainability/our-insights/sustainability-blog/accelerating-economic-recovery-and-investing-to-make-the-global-economy-both-cleaner-and-more-resilient (accessed 18 June 2021).
[15] https://www.bloomberg.com/news/articles/2021-05-26/shell-loses-climate-case-that-may-set-precedent-for-oil-industry (accessed 18 June 2021).
[16] https://www.shell.com/media/speeches-and-articles/articles-by-date/the-spirit-of-shell-will-rise-to-the-challenge.html (accessed 18 June 2021).

Both ExxonMobil and Chevron have been reluctant to articulate and communicate their strategy for a low-carbon future and navigate the sustainable energy transition. Earlier this year Engine No. 1, a hedge fund manager, forced ExxonMobil to replace two of its board members with more sustainability focussed directors.[17] Similarly, a significant majority of Chevron shareholders forced the group to reduce its carbon emissions, following a campaign spearheaded by Follow This, a Dutch activist NGO.[18]

Why are we then observing this different type of shareholder activism? One reason may be the fact that ESG compliant investments outperform unsustainable investments as previously mentioned.

Another reason may be BlackRock CEO Larry Fink's letters to shareholders. Ever since 2016, Fink has urged company CEOs to invest for the long term and for the benefit of society. This is quite remarkable given that BlackRock is by far the world's largest asset manager with $8.7 trillion under management.[19] CEOs around the world (e.g. 181 US Business Roundtable chief executives) are moving, or being moved by various shareholders, towards a different type of capitalism, a different way of defining how a company delivers value, who receives it and how is that value defined.

This new philosophy is increasingly driven by stakeholder or sustainable capitalism. In his 2021 book, Klaus Schwab, the executive chairman of the World Economic Forum, defines stakeholder capitalism as: "A model where companies seek long-term value creation instead of short-term profits; governments cooperate to create the greatest possible prosperity for their people, and civil society and international organizations complete the stakeholder dialogue, helping balance the interests of people and the planet".[20]

---

[17] https://www.theguardian.com/business/2021/may/26/exxonmobil-and-chevron-braced-for-showdown-over-climate (accessed 18 June 2021).
[18] https://www.theguardian.com/business/2021/may/20/climate-activist-shareholders-to-target-us-oil-giant-chevron (accessed 18 June 2021).
[19] https://www.blackrock.com/corporate/investor-relations/larry-fink-chairmans-letter (accessed 18 June 2021).
[20] Klaus Schwab and Peter Vanham, *Stakeholder Capitalism: A Global Economy that Works for Progress, People and Planet*, John Wiley & Sons, 2021.

Economist Joseph Stiglitz, winner of the 2001 Nobel Memorial Prize in Economic Sciences, argues that stakeholder capitalism should replace shareholder primacy as the principle of corporate governance.[21] Stiglitz views corporations as shared enterprises, which are made up of people, including employees, investors, and managers. At the centre of this perspective is to whom is the board accountable? In the United States accountability is to the shareholders, who are considered the owners of the company, while in the UK and other commonwealth nations, accountability is to the company.[22] Here, the shareholders own shares in the company but are not considered the owners of the company because there are other parties that hold claims against the company. Fox and Lorsch (2012) argue along the same lines by stating that: "In legal terms, shareholders don't own the corporation – they own securities that given them a less-than-well defined claim on its earnings".[23]

Whether stakeholder capitalism will ultimately prevail remains to be seen. What is clear is that the mindsets of shareholders, regulators and other stakeholders, including civil society, is changing rapidly and is increasingly embracing the idea that stakeholder capitalism is superior to shareholder supremacy.

3. The evolution of corporate governance

Although some form of corporate governance has been around since the formation of the East India Company (1600), the Hudson's Bay Company (1670) and other chartered companies, a type of company created by the British Crown, modern era corporate governance started in the United States[24] during the hostile takeover movement of the early 1980s.[25]

---

[21] https://www.project-syndicate.org/commentary/how-sincere-is-business-roundtable-embrace-of-stakeholder-capitalism-by-joseph-e-stiglitz-2019-08 (accessed 19 June 2021).

[22] Shareholders are always stakeholders in a corporation, but stakeholders are not always shareholders. Shareholders own part of a public company through shares of stock, while a stakeholder has an interest in the performance of a company for reasons other than stock performance or appreciation.

[23] Justin Fox and Jay Lorsch, "What Good are Shareholders?" *Harvard Business Review*, July–August 2012.

[24] In the US the term 'corporate governance' was first introduced by the Securities and Exchange Commission in 1976 (Sommer, 1977).

Corporate Governance 1.0 was effectively designed to fence off undesirable takeover bids and many corporate boards introduced protective practices.[26] These practices were, however, seen as acting against the interests of some shareholders. The emergence of institutional investors (e.g. pension funds), which are considered to be more active in company affairs compared to retail investors, shifted the balance of power away from management towards the shareholders.[27,28]

Corporate Governance 2.0 emerged following corporate scandals and failures across the Atlantic – Enron and WorldCom in the US, Polly Peck and Coloroll in the UK, Parmalat in Italy, and Ahold in the Netherlands. This resulted in growing public distrust of the corporation and various committees were formed to articulate proposals about how to largely reduce the possibility of corporate scandals and failures. In the UK, The Committee on the Financial Aspects of Corporate Governance, chaired by Sir Adrian Cadbury, issued the 1992 Cadbury Report that sets out recommendations to help prevent future corporate failures, including the separation of the roles of the Chief Executive and the Chair, the requirement to have a minimum of three independent non-executive directors, and the creation of an audit committee.[29] Similarly, in the US the 2002 Sarbanes-Oxley Act (SOX) required public company boards to have audit committees that are entirely composed on independent non-executive directors. SOX also required that the board meeting minutes reflect deliberations of material issues accurately.[30]

Following the 2008 global financial and economic crisis (GF&EC), it became clear that corporate boards are too short-term focussed and are not skilled at peripheral vision. The GF&EC was anticipated by various

---

[25] John Armour, and Brian Cheffins, "The Origins of the Market for Corporate Control", European Corporate Governance Institute (ECGI) – Law Working Paper No. 226/2013.
[26] A popular anti-takeover practice was the introduction of anti-takeover charter amendments (ATCAs), which restricts the partial takeover by corporate raiders through changes in the company's constitution. Poison pills, another anti-takeover defence tool, are permissible under Delaware law to protect the company's assets.
[27] John Pound, "The rise of the political model of corporate governance and control", *New York University Law Review* 68(5): 1003, 1993.
[28] John Pound, "Beyond takeovers: Politics comes to corporate control", *Harvard Business Review*, March–April, 1992.
[29] http://cadbury.cjbs.archios.info/report (accessed 21 June 2021).
[30] https://www.soxlaw.com (accessed 21 June 2021).

economists, yet bank executives failed to act. The result was catastrophic for both the financial sector and the world economy. The market capitalisation of global banks shrank by more than 75% between 2007 and 2009, and Lehman Brothers collapsed. The ripple effect on the global economy was even more pronounced, resulting in a deep V-shaped global recession.[31] With new Dodd-Frank and Walker affecting especially financial sector players – the 2009 Walker Report[32] and the 2010 Dodd-Frank Wall Street Reform and Consumer Protection Act[33] – **Corporate Governance 3.0** effectively became a reality. Both regulations made specific recommendations to strengthen risk management in financial institutions, through the creation of a separate forward-looking risk committee.[34]

Although the economy recovery was swift, many of the economic, social and environmental imbalances remained unaddressed.[35] Also, both the Walker Report and Dodd-Frank Act fell short in recommending that multinational corporations should also establish forward-looking risk committees in addition to the typically backward-looking audit committee. With global climate change reaching a tipping point, the United Nations developed both the Sustainable Development Goals (SDGs) and the Paris Agreement. Both were ratified in 2015 and 2016 respectively. The SDGs are a call for action by all countries to promote prosperity while protecting the planet,[36] while the Paris Agreement is a legally binding international treaty to foster climate resilience and to limit global warming to below 2°C, preferably to 1.5°C, compared to pre-industrial levels.[37] **Corporate Governance 4.0** was spearheaded in South Africa with the King IV Code in

---

[31] https://en.wikipedia.org/wiki/Recession_shapes (accessed 21 June 2021).
[32] https://the-walker-report.com (accessed 21 June 2021).
[33] https://www.cftc.gov/LawRegulation/DoddFrankAct/index.htm (accessed 21 June 2021).
[34] Historically, risk management is overseen by the audit committee. The creation of a separate risk committee would effectively split the risk oversight roles of the two committees. The audit committee would continue to oversee financial reporting risks and those compliance-related risks that have financial reporting implications, while the risk committee would oversee forward-looking risks and assess their implications for company strategy.
[35] https://blogs.imf.org/2018/10/03/lasting-effects-the-global-economic-recovery-10-years-after-the-crisis (accessed 21 June 2021).
[36] https://sdgs.un.org/goals (accessed 21 June 2021).
[37] https://unfccc.int/sites/default/files/english_paris_agreement.pdf (accessed 21 June 2021).

2016, which lays out a set of principles and practices to achieve desired outcomes, where businesses adopt a philosophy of accountability to current and future stakeholders for the benefits of society.[38] Similarly, one of the key objectives of the Dutch Corporate Governance Code is to promote long-term value creation and sustainable business growth.[39] There are two key differences between the two codes: 1) The King IV Code has adopted an 'apply and explain' philosophy, while the Dutch code remains with the more traditional 'comply or explain', and 2) The South Africa code mandates the use of integrated reporting, while the Dutch code promotes sustainable busines growth but does not mandate integrated reporting. Table 18.1 provides an overview of the four generations of corporate governance, what triggered it, and its underlying philosophy.

Table 18.1 Four Generations of Corporate Governance
Source: Sustainable Foresight Institute, 2016

Corporate Governance 1.0	Corporate Governance 2.0	Corporate Governance 3.0	Corporate Governance 4.0
– Defensive-driven governance – 1980s	– Compliance-driven governance – 1990s	– Foresight-driven governance – Since 2008	– Outcomes-driven governance – Emerging since 2015
– Triggered by undesirable corporate takeover bids	– Triggered by corporate scandals and failures	– Triggered by the global financial and economic crisis	– Following the 2015 SDGs and the 2016 Paris Agreement
– Anti-takeover charter amendments (ATCAs)	– Sarbanes-Oxley (US) – The Cadbury Report (UK)	– Dodd-Frank (US) – The Walker Report (UK)	– King IV Code (SA) – The Dutch Code (NL)
Focus on hostile takeover defences	**Focus on preventing fraudulent failure**	**Focus on balancing conformance and performance**	**Focus on the sustainable long-term success of companies**

---

[38] https://www.pwc.co.za/en/publications/king4.html (accessed 21 June 2021).
[39] https://ec.europa.eu/info/law/better-regulation/have-your-say/initiatives/12548-Sustainable-corporate-governance/F583943_en (accessed 21 June 2021).

Is Corporate Governance 4.0 Emerging?

The emergence of Corporate Governance 4.0 coincides with the emergence of the Fourth Industrial Revolution.

The First Industrial Revolution started in Britain in the 18th and 19th centuries and was driven by the invention of the steam engine and the development of the iron and textile industries. Europe gradually overtook China and India as the engines of global growth.

The Second Industrial Revolution, which started around 1870, witnessed the emergence of steel, oil and electricity, the development of modern forms of transportation of goods (e.g. shipping and rail), and the transition from coal to oil. Rapid industrial development in Britain, Germany, France, Italy, Japan and the US followed. This is often referred to as the era of mass production and vertical integration.

The Third Industrial Revolution, also referred to as the information age, was driven by the mass diffusion of technologies, such as the personal computer and the Internet. This is in turn led to the globalisation of companies and the rise of emerging markets, especially China, which became the world's manufacturing hub, and the emergence of the commodities super cycle. During the first 15 years of this century, China consumed about 50% of the world's commodities, compared to 10% during the last 15 years of 20th century.

In 2007, Alexander Van de Putte and Ged Davis at the World Economic Forum oversaw the development of the medium-term scenarios on the emergence of the digital eco-system,[40] or the convergence of the physical and digital worlds, and the pre-cursor of the fourth industrial revolution (4IR) described by Klaus Schwab in his 2016 book *The Fourth Industrial Revolution*. In it, Schwab argued that we stand on the brink of a technological revolution that will fundamentally alter the way we live, work, and relate to one other. He defines the 4IR as: "… a range of new technologies that are fusing the physical, digital and biological worlds, impacting all disciplines, economies and industries, and even challenging

---

[40] https://www.weforum.org/reports/digital-ecosystem-convergence-between-it-telecoms-media-and-entertainment-scenarios-2015 (accessed 13 June 2021).

ideas about what it means to be human."[41] Although the 4IR has the potential to contribute to more sustainable, inclusive, and resilient business growth, this is not guaranteed; boards play an even more important role in this fast-paced environment in contributing to the sustainable long-term success of the company.

4. Corporate governance and boards need to adapt quickly

In corporate finance a fundamental relationship exists between risk and return, and this provides the basis for the 'time value of money' concept. Another concept is becoming increasingly important: the 'time value of time' concept.

The velocity of change has dramatically accelerated, and given the emergence of the Fourth Industrial Revolution, this trend will continue. To remain competitive, organisations need to change at least as fast as the environment in which they operate to remain relevant.

The boardroom is these days a more challenging environment and therefore boards have many more areas to oversee compared to during Corporate Governance 3.0, ranging from company culture, climate issues, social issues (including employee welfare), cybersecurity and technology disruption. What should always be on the mind of directors is how can we disrupt ourselves before we are disrupted by a competitor, including future competitors. For example, Airbnb, a start-up at the time, disrupted the hotel industry, resulting in increased room availability, reduced prices for customers, and therefore has made it much more difficult for large hotel groups such as Marriott International and Hilton Worldwide Holdings to remain competitive.

To remain relevant, Corporate Governance 4.0 companies and their boards increasingly need to reflect several characteristics:

---

[41] https://www.weforum.org/about/the-fourth-industrial-revolution-by-klaus-schwab (accessed 13 June 2021).

A. They are purpose driven.

Based on a survey conducted by the Sustainable Foresight Institute, annually since 2008, five factors drive the longevity of companies.[42] One of these factors only emerged in the 2016 survey: long-lived companies are being increasingly purpose driven. Purpose-driven organisations recognise the need to create value for all stakeholders, including society at large.

Stakeholder governance considers the diverse interests of all stakeholders and sees the shareholders as owners of shares in the company not as the owners of the business. For stakeholder governance to be effective, a company needs to articulate a purpose about how it aims to create value for all its stakeholders and then needs to report – in a transparent, ethical and accountable way – how the company has contributed to this and thus the sustainable long-term success of the company.

Benefit corporations (B corps) have been designed to deliver value to all their stakeholders, not just the shareholders. C corporations (C corps) are typically designed to maximise shareholder value and be shareholder centric. However, as argued by law professors Jill Fish and Steven Davidoff Solomon, C corps "…have a purpose to do anything they can under the law."[43] Based on the views of former Delaware (US) Chief Justice Leo Strine, this view of corporate purpose does not seem so clear-cut.[44]

Given that directors of C corps may take other stakeholders into account when discharging their duties, constituency statutes passed in the wake of anti-takeover defences in the 1980s state that there is no obligation that they must under law. Although there are differences between the California Benefit Corporation and the Delaware Public Benefit Corporation, for instance, all types of B corps make it mandatory for directors to take into consideration the diverse interests of other stakeholders in all their deliberations and decisions.

---

[42] Annual survey, 2008-2020, "What drives corporate longevity", Sustainable Foresight Institute.

[43] Jill Fish, and Steven Davidoff Solomon, "Should corporations have a purpose?," European Corporate Governance Institute (ECGI) – Law Working Paper No. 510/2020.

[44] Leo Strine, "The dangers of denial: The need for a clear-eyed understanding of the power and accountability structure established by the Delaware General Corporation Law", University of Pennsylvania Institute for Law and Economics, Research Paper No. 15-08, 2015.

Even though C corps do not have an obligation to create value to all stakeholders, it is really the company charter that gives the corporation the license to operate. Therefore, C corps that have company charters that reflect a clear purpose and objectives to create value to all stakeholders can contribute to more sustainable and inclusive business growth as well as B corps. For example, Paul Polman changed the purpose of Unilever during his 10-year tenure as chief executive. Despite his ousting in 2019 following a shareholder rebellion, Unilever's purpose to make sustainable living commonplace prevails today.

Although a strong case in favour of stakeholder governance and benefit corporations to achieve this can be made, the future will likely see a combination of B corps and C corps with amended company charters to move us all towards stakeholder governance.

B. They are skilled at spotting discontinuities in the external environment.

A second factor identified during the survey conducted by the Sustainable Foresight Institute annually since 2008[45] is that long-lived companies are skilled at peripheral vision.

Corporate Governance 4.0 boards continuously scan the periphery in search of discontinuities in the external environment. As discussed in Chapter 9, not everything can be accurately anticipated, but that does not mean that organisations should not try to identify discontinuities in the external environment. Boards need to provide oversight to spot discontinuities in the external environment, including black swans, grey rhinos, and white elephants (Figure 18.1).

Black swans or wildcards (or the unknown unknowns) were specified as a phenomenon by Herman Khan (1960s) and Pierre Wack (1970s). It was, however, former options trader Nassim Taleb who popularised the term 'black swan', which he describes as having three characteristics: 1) low probability, 2) big impact, and 3) can only be logically explained after the

---

[45] Annual survey, 2008-2020, "What drives corporate longevity", Sustainable Foresight Institute.

facts.[46] Taleb's definition is incomplete, though, and has been developed from the perspective of a mathematician, who approaches future events from a purely probabilistic perspective.

Figure 18.1 Black Swans, Grey Rhinos and White Elephants
Source: Sustainable Foresight Institute, 2004[47]

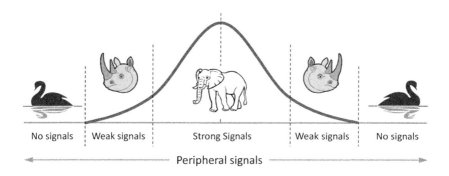

A key characteristic of a black swan is that the event in question cannot be anticipated, either in time or in space.[48] In addition, black swans emerge suddenly, without any early warning. Thus examples of black swans are COVID-19, the Fukushima triple disaster (i.e., earthquake, tsunami, and nuclear meltdown), and the 2010 BP Macondo oil spill. None of these events were anticipated, by anybody, either in time, or in space.

Niall Ferguson (2021) puts it as follows: *"Disasters are inherently hard to predict. Pandemics, like earthquakes, and wars, are not normally distributed; there is no cycle of history to help us anticipate the next catastrophe. But when catastrophe strikes, we ought to be better prepared than the Romans were when Vesuvius erupted or medieval Italians when the Black Death struck."*[49]

---

[46] Nassim Taleb, *The Black Swan: The impact of the highly improbable*, Random House, 2010.
[47] Taken from a report that I wrote when transitioning from Shell International to the World Economic Forum. Alexander Van de Putte, "Actionable foresight – Identifying disruptive forces that shape companies, industries, countries and the future of competition", Sustainable Foresight Institute, 2004
[48] Alexander Van de Putte, "The evolution of scenario planning: A perspective from a capital intensive, slow clock-speed industry", unpublished PhD thesis, University of Cambridge, 2012.
[49] Niall Ferguson, *Doom: The Politics of Catastrophe*, Penguin, 2021.

Grey rhinos (or the known unknowns) are different in that they are driven by an event or a combination of events that can be reasonably anticipated based on cause and effect. They also tend to emerge gradually and therefore weak signals provide early indications of what is about to unfold. [7,50] Examples of grey rhinos include the global financial crisis, the use of blockchain to make global value chains more resilient, and the emergence of driverless vehicles.

Finally, white elephants (or the known knowns) pose potential existential risks to the company. A well-documented example of a white elephant is that although Kodak invented digital photography, the board was unwilling to cannibalise its existing chemical photography business until it was too late. Other examples of white elephants include, global climate change and cyber security.

C. They internalise externalities.

Another factor identified during the survey conducted by the Sustainable Foresight Institute annually since 2008[51] is that long-lived companies have an experimental mindset at the fringes of their market. Therefore, it is not sufficient to continuously scan the periphery in search of discontinuities in the external environment. Corporate Governance 4.0 boards need to make judgements in the face of uncertainty to contribute to the sustainable long-term success of the company.

Although black swans cannot be anticipated either in time, or in space, it is still important for boards to try to anticipate 'possible' future black swans as part of their risk practices. The benefit for companies to anticipate possible future black swans is to be operationally ready to mitigate an event, should disaster strike. Thus, it would be possible for companies to mitigate most of the severe consequences of black swan events.

Scenario planning – plausible, divergent and internal consistent views of the

---

[50] Michele Wucker, *The Gray Rhino: How to Recognize and Act on the Obvious Dangers We Ignore*, St. Martin's Press, 2016.
[51] Annual survey, 2008-2020, "What drives corporate longevity", Sustainable Foresight Institute.

future – is a useful tool to anticipate how the future could unfold. And when combined with strategic options thinking and strategic early warning, it helps companies remain competitive in a changing, complex and uncertain environment.[7] The benefit of anticipating grey rhinos is to avoid being blindsided because of the changes in the external environment or by changes in the strategy of both current and future competitors.

Table 18.2 Various foresight tools and their use
Source: Sustainable Foresight Institute, 2004[52]

	Black Swans "unknown unknowns"	Grey Rhinos "known unknowns"	White Elephants "known knowns"
Characteristics	– Cannot be accurately anticipated nor in time nor in space	– An event or series of events that can be reasonably anticipated based on cause and effect	– The writing is on the wall
Manifestation	– Abruptly (no early warning)	– Gradually (early warning signs)	– Already omnipresent – Strong signals
Examples	– Pandemics, natural disasters	– Financial crises	– Complacency, lack of vision & risk taking
Mitigation tool	– Contingency planning	– Scenario planning driven peripheral vision	– Internal peripheral vision
Objective	– Operational readiness & rapid response	– Avoid being blindsided or being disrupted	– Avoid becoming obsolete

Proper succession planning and board diversity are ways to avoid complacency from ignoring white elephants.[53] White elephants, when

---

[52] See footnote 47.
[53] Succession planning and board diversity are discussed in Chapters x and y, respectively.

ignored, pose a potential existential threat to the company. Consider the cost of cybersecurity, which is expected to inflict damage in the amount of $6 trillion in 2021,[54] or 7% of global GDP. Ignoring cybersecurity or not providing appropriate board oversight of cybersecurity could lead to significant financial and reputational losses and even bankruptcy. The US National Association of Corporate Directors (NACD) argues that cybersecurity is an enterprise-wide risk management issue, not just an IT issue, and should thus be dealt with by the board.[55]

Table 18.2 summarises the various strategic foresight concepts and their potential strategic response.

D. They are outcomes driven (as opposed to compliance driven).

A company's longevity is intrinsically linked to how seriously the board addresses ESG risks. Given that corporate governance is concerned with contributing to the sustainable long-term success of the company, it could be argued that tying executive compensation to ESG targets and outcomes will significantly contribute to achieving this objective.

There are several benefits of tying executive compensation to how ESG risks are managed:

1. It sends a strong message to the investor community and other stakeholders that ESG risks are taken seriously by the board and top management. This may lower the underlying cost of capital and improve a company's stock price. It may also make the company more attractive to customers, suppliers, and employees – in general, it makes it easier for a company to conduct its business.

2. It demonstrates that ESG risks are inherent to the company's strategy and are part of its culture and values system.

---

[54] https://cybersecurityventures.com/hackerpocalypse-cybercrime-report-2016 (accessed 25 June 2021).
[55] NACD Director's Handbook on Cyber-Risk Oversight. www.nacdonline.org (accessed 25 June 2021).

3. The general perception is that what is good for society is not good for the shareholder. Linking executive compensation to ESG targets, and how ESG risks are managed, pushes management to think differently about ESG and explore joint gains.

4. Compensation provides an important incentive for executives to do the right thing and manage the company for the benefit of all its stakeholders, including society at large.

There are other ways to achieve this, but linking executive compensation to desired ESG targets and outcomes, will incentivise company executives to balance and grow all five capital stocks – natural, manufactured, human, social and financial.

E. They are truly diverse.[56]

Board diversity needs to be seriously considered in succession planning. Diverse boards, when well designed, are better at risk oversight, including ESG oversight. Although diversity comes in many forms, typically the following four are considered: gender, ethnic, experience and age diversity.

Boards need to make judgements with the objective to contribute to the sustainable long-term success of the company. During the era of the 4IR, a critical aspect for the board while discharging its duties is to provide risk oversight, including oversight of the potential unintentional consequences that AI may have on exacerbating racial and gender inequity.

Cognitive biases often impair a leader's ability to make rational and informed decisions. The risk of unconscious bias – the potential prejudice against a particular group or decision – is largely reduced in more diverse boards where the various issues, risks, and societal perspectives are constructively debated before a decision is made. Similarly, more diverse boards tend to suffer less from over-confidence and confirmation bias.

Several studies illustrate that gender diversity leads to improved business performance, less extreme risk-taking, and enhanced governance. Ethnic

---

[56] See also Chapter 3: Board leadership; Chapter 6: Board Diversity – A Historical Perspective; and Chapter 7: The Gen 3.0 Broader Context of Board Diversity.

diversity at the board level has contributed to more consideration of the wider societal aspects in and the implications of strategic decisions. Similarly, younger board members tend to challenge decisions that would adversely affect future generations, therefore ensuring that risk-taking is better aligned with the company's risk appetite. This in turn contributes to improved long-term performance.

Companies should promote truly diverse boards in terms of gender, ethnicity, thought, age, and even neurodiversity, to contribute to the company's sustainable long-term and ensure that critical risk, such as AI, does not exacerbate racial and gender inequity.

F. They are increasingly assisted by artificial intelligence.

The UK 2006 Companies Act states that at least one board member needs to be a natural person. This gives company boards the opportunity to appoint directors that are not natural persons, such as an artificial intelligence (AI) powered robot.[57] At its most basic level, this could be an expert system, a basic form of AI, that helps directors make better judgments in the same way that physicians have used expert systems to arrive at more accurate diagnoses and even suggest treatments. Typically, an expert system performs well in its area of expertise, which is usually very narrow. More advanced AI-powered decision support systems, commonly referred to as knowledge-based systems, use an algorithm to develop explicit knowledge of a problem, such as strategy of finance. The system is then used to arrive at a better recommendation faster. Even more advanced AI-powered systems such as DeepMind have the ability to solve very complex problems without being taught how to do it.[58]

The emergence of the 4IR, big data and accelerating velocity of change, the amount of data that needs to be processed by boards increasingly exceeds human processing capabilities.

AI is unlikely to replace the human director. But if well used, it could help individual directors and the board make better decisions. The combination

---

[57] https://www.legislation.gov.uk/ukpga/2006/46/contents (accessed 29 June 2021).
[58] DeepMind, a UK-based AI company, was acquired by Google in 2014.

of AI algorithms – to gather, augment and analyse vast amounts of data – with the human experience is potentially a very powerful one that could lead to competitive advantage.

G. They monitor organisational culture.

A third factor identified by the Sustainable Foresight Institute's surveys[59] is that long-lived companies have a set of deeply ingrained and shared values that are a guide to action. Values are the beliefs, the guiding principles and philosophies that drive behaviour in an organisation. In essence, values drive organisational culture.

Companies with healthy cultures have a risk-aware culture. The characteristics of a risk-aware culture include risk management devolved to the workplace, participative management style, utilisation of knowledge and skills of employees at all levels of the organisation, good communication and teamwork. Organisations with healthy cultures are therefore better able to demonstrate the relationship between culture, strategy, risk and outcomes.

Weak organisational cultures come in many forms and very often lead to devasting outcomes. Consider Enron, whose board twice suspended its ethics code before its demise in 2001. While this is an extreme case of organisational failure because of the absence of deeply ingrained and shared values that are a guide to action, the importance of a healthy organisational culture cannot be underestimated.

EY articulates five ways to enhance board oversight of culture:[60]

1. Boards oversee how culture is defined and how culture and strategy are aligned;
2. Boards create accountability for how culture is communicated and lived – internally and to key external stakeholders;

---

[59] Annual survey, 2008-2020, "What drives corporate longevity", Sustainable Foresight Institute.
[60] https://www.ey.com/en_gl/board-matters/five-ways-to-enhance-board-oversight-of-culture (accessed 27 June 2021).

3. Boards monitor how culture and talent metrics are measured to keep a pulse on how culture is evolving;
4. Boards provide oversight of intentional culture shifts to stay in step with strategy shifts;
5. Boards challenge the board's culture.

The importance of organisational culture cannot be underestimated. After all, management theorist Peter Drucker famously said: 'Culture eats strategy for breakfast'. With this quote, Drucker implied that a healthy organisational culture leads to better outcomes.

H. They adopt an integrated reporting approach.[61]

In 2010, the International Integrated Reporting Council (IIRC) was launched several partners including the Big Four accounting firms to report on how the company's strategy and operations impact the six capital stocks – natural, manufactured, human, social, intellectual and financial – with an objective to understand a company's financial and sustainability performance. Although voluntary, Integrated Reporting has been widely adopted, at least in part, by many multinationals.

In principle, a voluntary over mandatory disclosure should be favoured because it is difficult to develop a disclosure framework that works for companies in different industries and of different sizes and levels of complexity. However, given that failure to identify and mitigate material ESG risks poses a potential existential threat to the company, it can be argued that mandatory disclosure of ESG information is warranted. Considered the ESG disclosure requirements imposed by the US Securities and Exchange Commission (SEC).[62]

It is important though to highlight that, to date, the SEC only mandates the disclosure of ESG information that is financially material as seen by the

---

[61] See also Chapter 17: The Dynamics of Corporate Reporting.
[62] https://corpgov.law.harvard.edu/2021/05/28/sec-regulation-of-esg-disclosures (accessed 27 June 2021).

investor. In other words, any ESG related information that would significantly alter the mix of information available to investors.

These days, not disclosing any material information about ESG risk is simply not an option for companies. By requiring mandatory disclosure, the SEC provides guidance as to what to disclose, therefore helping companies to paint a fair and transparent picture to investors about the ESG risks and what the company is doing about them. This has several benefits: 1) it creates trust among investors, especially institutional ones, 2) it reduces the volatility of cash flows, and 3) it avoids potential future litigation from investors who may feel that they have been misled by the company.

Arguably, by requiring mandatory disclosure, the SEC provides a service to companies: the risk of lawsuits resulting from a false or misleading company statement perceived to have misled investors is thus drastically reduced.

5. Conclusion

It can be argued that corporate governance 4.0 is emerging and that many stakeholders, from shareholder to regulators and civil society, are increasingly welcoming this needed change in the way that boards provide stewardship to contribute to the sustainable long-term success of the company for the benefit of society. Building inclusive, sustainable and more resilient businesses for the benefit of humanity – and not just the shareholder and in the short term – is a corporate director's emerging duty.

Corporate Governance 3.0

ABOUT THE AUTHORS

Lead Authors/Editors Biographies

Dr Karl George MBE, FCG, FCCA

Karl George is a thought leader, author and internationally established consultant in governance. He is managing director of the governance forum (tgf), creator of The Governance Framework and the Effective Board Member programmes, the "Board Game" and The Diversity in the Board Room Pledge. An experienced board member himself, he works with boards and senior executives in the private, public and voluntary sectors and has over 25 years' combined experience in accountancy, business and strategic development. Karl is a Fellow of both the global accounting body, ACCA, and of the international body for governance practitioners, The Chartered Governance Institute.

His consultancy and support work extends to his role in academia as an Honorary Doctor and visiting professor at Birmingham City University, Karl demonstrates his ability to adapt and share his passion, expertise and proficiency in governance. The delivery of governance in the academic world is combined with his skills as researcher, conference speaker and author, resulting in the development of The Governance Framework and quality mark for governance. The framework assists those working in governance in every sector to effectively manage their governance processes and was endorsed by the late Sir Adrian Cadbury.

Karl is the author of The tgf Governance Code – principles of governance for organisations of all sizes, sectors and geographical jurisdictions, The Effective Board Member – What Every Board Member Should Know and, more recently The RACE Equality Code 2020.

Simon Osborne FCG, Solicitor

Simon Osborne is a board evaluation specialist, governance consultant and trainer. He stepped down as chief executive of ICSA: The Chartered Governance Institute UK & Ireland (CGI) on 30 June 2019, having held the role since 1 October 2011. That appointment followed eight years as

Joint Head of ICSA Board Evaluation, a consultancy role to which he has since returned.

Simon is a Fellow of the global CGI, having qualified first as a solicitor in 1973. He worked as in-house counsel for 30 years in the railway industry, latterly as company secretary and general counsel and then as a main board executive director of the former Railtrack Group PLC. Simon is now an Executive Fellow with the London Business School Leadership Institute. In addition to his board evaluation practice, he delivers training programmes for company directors. Simon is a member of the International Corporate Governance Network (he is immediate past chair of ICGN's Bylaws & Procedures Committee and was a founder member of its Business Ethics Committee). He is a vice-president of a charity, the Railway Benefit Fund of which he was previously the deputy chair. In 2019/2020, Simon served as the Principal Advisor to develop the AIFC Corporate Governance Principles and its Guidance.

He has served also as a NED of a boutique media and events company; as chair of the ICSA Company Secretaries Forum; as a member and chair of the audit committee of The Law Society of England and Wales; as a member of the audit committee of a major City of London law firm; as a member of the former police authority for the British Transport Police; and as a member of the Committee of Inquiry into UK Vote Execution.

Professor Alexander Van de Putte, PhD, FCG, CDir FIoD, NACD Board Leadership Fellow

Professor Alexander Van de Putte is Chairman of Corporate Governance & Stewardship of the Astana International Financial Centre (AIFC), Chairman of the Board of the AIFC Bureau for CPD, Chief Strategy Officer of the AIFC Governor's Council, Chairman of the AIFC Academic Council and Chairman of the AIFC Academy of Law Academic Council, the Founding Director & Chairman of the Sustainable Foresight Institute. At IE Business School, Alexander is a Professor of Strategy and Strategic Foresight. At the AIFC, he recently oversaw the development of the AIFC Corporate Governance Principles and its Guidance.

Previously, Professor Van de Putte was a Member of the Board of the National Investment Corporation of the National Bank of Kazakhstan, a

Managing Director with the Kazakhstan Development Bank, Senior Director and Head of Global Practices with the World Economic Forum. At Shell, Alexander was the Senior Strategy and Portfolio Advisor to the Committee of Managing Directors. Prior to Shell, Alexander was Director and co-leader of the shareholder value practice at PricewaterhouseCoopers. At McKinsey, Alexander was a core team member of the European Corporate Finance and Strategy Practice.

Alexander is a decision scientist and engineer by training. He holds advanced degrees in Management and Decision Sciences from Boston University, was a BAEF Fellow at Harvard Business School, holds a PhD in Applied Economics (Strategy & Finance) from the University of London, a Doctorate in International Relations from the Geneva School of Diplomacy, and an MSt in Sustainability Leadership and PhD in Engineering (Complex Adaptive Systems) from Cambridge University. Alexander is a NACD Board Leadership Fellow, a Chartered Governance Professional and Fellow (FCG) with The Chartered Governance Institute, a Chartered Director (CDir) and Fellow (FIoD) of the Institute of Directors, an Academic Member of the European Corporate Governance Institute, and a Member of the Singapore Institute of Directors from where he holds the Executive Certificate in Directorship.

Alexander is a Fellow and Visiting Professor of Scenario Planning and Disruptive Risks at Energy Delta Institute (The Netherlands). From 2006 to 2007, he was a Visiting Professor of scenario planning at INSEAD and from 2001 to 2004, he was (part-time, full) Professor of Strategy & Finance and Dean of the Grande Ecole Programme at the Rouen School of Management (France) and a Teaching Fellow at the University of London. He has taught at IMD, Wharton, and Solvay Business School.

Chapter Author Biographies

Dr Ser-Keng Ang

Dr. Ser-Keng Ang is a Principal Lecturer of Finance and the Academic Director for the EMBA and MBA programs at the Singapore Management University (SMU). He has been actively teaching, undergraduate, post graduate and executive programs since 2003. In addition to his teaching appointment, Dr. Ang serves as the member of the board of governors and director for the UOB-SMU Asia Enterprise Institute, which works closely with SMEs across Southeast Asia. One of his research interests, and one he has been engaged in for years, is founder succession in Asia.

Prior to his academic career at SMU, Dr. Ang was an investment banker. He spent nine years in London, Hong Kong and Singapore, where he was involved in the origination and execution of a number of cross-border transactions in Asia Pacific at international banks, such as Deutsche Bank, ABN AMRO and Flemings. At Deutsche Bank, Dr. Ang was responsible for an acquisition in the US, amounting to US$5.5 billion, for a Japanese MNC. As a Senior Vice President at ABN AMRO, he was responsible for cross-selling a broader range of products, to corporate clients. He also served at Arthur Andersen and Credit Suisse First Boston.

Dr. Ang received his Ph.D. in Finance from UNSW Business School, MBA from London Business School, Master in Business Research from the University of Western Australia, and Bachelor of Accountancy (BAcc) from the National University of Singapore (NUS). He is also a certified executive coach. In 2016, Dr. Ang was conferred the Commendation Medal for his contributions to the education in Singapore.

Sharon Constançon FCIS

Sharon is the CEO of Genius Methods - a company that offers tailored robust, behaviour focused board evaluation services to many industries, listed entities and regulated businesses including FTSE, SME, Family, Investment Trusts, Insurance, Financial Services, Regulated, Health Services, Charities and the Housing Sector. She has a well attested reputation for providing confidential, straightforward, honest and effective

Board Evaluations which have very successfully enabled Boards to improve performance.

Sharon has extensive experience in director mentoring and is regularly invited to address industry audiences, run workshops and chair round-table debates or panels. She has stories of her own and those from her role as Board Evaluator which she successfully uses to help others learn and understand the role of the Board and of being a NED.

She is a Chartered Director, Chartered Secretary and has an MBA. She is Chairman of the South African Chamber of Commerce, Non-Executive Director for Transact SA, International Committee member for CISI and Membership Committee Member for WCCSA and CEO of Valufin, a forex advisory firm. Previous roles include NED and Chairman of Conduct and Culture Committee for Buckinghamshire Building Society.

Dr Ashraf Gamal El Din

Dr. Ashraf Gamal El Din is a Professor of Management at Cairo University where he authored many research papers on governance. He is also the CEO of Hawkamah, the Corporate Governance Institute owned by the Dubai government that advises governments and companies in the region on good governance. Dr. Ashraf was the founder and first head of the Egyptian Corporate Responsibility Center and the Egyptian Institute of Directors. He served as a board member, head of audit committee and committee member of different types of companies in the MENA region, including listed companies, state owned enterprises and family owned companies.

Professor Simon Haslam CDir FIoD

Professor Simon Haslam is the Director and co-owner of a strategy research and consulting firm FMR Research Ltd and of the Consulting Mastered Ltd online platform. Simon is also the Programme Lead for Strategy at the Institute of Directors and a Chartered Director. He has been part of the IoD team since 2004, where he looks after the strategy aspect of the Chartered Director Programme and runs leadership programmes for directors. In addition, he is the non-executive Chairman of a transport business. Simon has worked in the consulting sector internationally for 20 years. His firm has clients across the private, public and third sectors from SMEs to global brands.

Simon has an MBA from Durham University Business School and a PhD from Strathclyde Business School. He is a Visiting Professor at Durham where he leads the Strategic Management module of its Global MBA programme. He also has a visiting faculty role at Strathclyde Business School where is leads on post-graduate programmes around Corporate Governance. His book, Strategic Decision Making: A Discovery-Led Approach to Critical Choices in Turbulent Times, co-written with Dr Ben Shenoy, was published by Kogan Page in 2018. He is founding editor of the Management Consulting Journal and chairs the Academic Fellows community for the International Council of Management Consulting Institutes.

Julie Garlan McLellan

Julie Garland McLellan is a boardroom expert. She has personal board experience ranging from Australia's largest and most respected boards to little-known government-sector, not for profit, and start-up boards.

Julie trains directors with practical skills that will enhance their abilities and performance immediately.

Julie is one of Australia's leading governance consultants. She is also a professional non-executive director with experience on a range of boards within government and other sectors. She has served the boards of Bounty Mining, Oldfields Holdings, Melbourne Water Corporation, Victorian Energy Networks Corporations, City West Water, Victorian Minerals and Energy Council, Melbourne University Engineering Foundation, Kimbriki Environmental Enterprises, Hats Holdings, Wind Hydrogen, Tamar Gold, Kyoto Energy Park, and Hassall & Associates.

She is the author of:

- The Director's Dilemma
- Presenting to Boards; Practical Skills for Corporate Presentations,
- All Above Board: Great Governance for the Government Sector,
- Dilemmas, Dilemmas; practical case studies for company directors,

- Dilemmas, Dilemmas II; More Practical Case Studies for Company Directors, and
- Not-For-Profit Board Dilemmas; Practical Case Studies for Directors in the Non-Profit Sector.

Julie has an Executive MBA, a diploma and advanced diploma of company directorship, a graduate diploma in Finance and Investment, and is a Fellow and former Councillor of The Australian Institute of company Directors.

Helen Higginbotham FCG

Helen is a corporate solicitor at Harrison Clark Rickerbys Limited, where she works as Head of the Due Diligence Team advising clients on areas of risk when buying or investing in a company or business. Helen provides detailed analysis of company filings and statutory records, and works closely with specialist teams at the firm to provide commercial solutions to issues identified. Helen provides training on company law and company secretarial matters. Helen is co-Chair of the Chartered Governance Institute West Midlands Branch Committee, a Fellow of the Chartered Governance Institute (chartered company secretary) and a Governor of the West Midlands Ambulance Service University NHS Foundation Trust.

Ann Holder

Ann Holder is the chief editor at the Sustainable Foresight Institute. As a research writer/editor, her project work has included helping develop scenario narratives for organisations including the World Economic Forum, the US National Intelligence Council, and ARPEL, the regional association for the energy sector in Latin America and the Caribbean. Previously, she worked in marketing research for the pharmaceutical division of Warner-Lambert (now part of Pfizer) then moved to NYC-based not-for-profit the New York Foundation for the Arts to develop arts education programming in schools and cultural organisations throughout New York State.

Ann holds an AB from Princeton University, an ALM from Harvard University, and has completed doctoral-level studies in applied economics at the Catholic University of Leuven (KUL) in Belgium. She is a passionate lifelong learner.

Dr Kairat Kelimbetov MIoD

Kairat Kelimbetov is Chairman of the Agency of Strategic Planning & Reforms and Governor of the Astana International Financial Centre (AIFC). Previously, he was the governor of the National Bank of Kazakhstan, deputy prime minister of Kazakhstan, CEO of Kazakhstan's sovereign wealth fund, Samruk-Kazyna, head of the administration of the President of the Republic of Kazakhstan, and Kazakhstan's minister of economy and budget planning.

He is a graduate of Moscow State University, attended the Market Institute of the Kazakh State Academy of Management and the National School of Public Administration of Kazakhstan, and holds a doctorate in economic sciences from the Diplomatic Academy of the Ministry of Foreign Affairs of the Russian Federation. Kairat completed the Pew Economic Freedom Fellows Program at the Edmund A. Walsh School of Foreign Service at Georgetown University and the master in sustainability leadership at University of Cambridge and is also a life-member of the Institute of Directors (UK).

George Littlejohn MCSI, FCA

George Littlejohn qualified as a chartered accountant with PwC in London before becoming editor of Accountancy Age, then the world's leading magazine on accounting and financial reporting, with a weekly circulation of some 80,000. He then became a journalist with The Economist, specialising in financial and economic matters. He is now Senior Adviser at the Chartered Institute for Securities & Investment, a global professional body with more than 50,000 members that was formerly part of London Stock Exchange. In that role, and working for asset management firms and development banks, he has conducted extensive advisory work with financial organisations across Europe, the Middle East and Asia over recent years.

His specific interests focus on the opportunities and challenges facing the financial sector in trying to meet the UN's Sustainable Development Goals, initially on the climate and biodiversity challenges, but bringing in also issues relating to the finance around agriculture, education, health, renewables, and transportation, and is one of the leaders of a global project to bring the brainpower of the best and brightest young financial professionals, in their 20s, to bear on these key themes.

He is a graduate of the University of Edinburgh, with a master's in development economics, and the author of a number of works on risk management in finance. He is a Governor and Vice Chair of Rose Bruford College, a performing arts school in London, and of Black Mountains College, a new university focusing on sustainability being formed in the Brecon Beacons National Park in Wales.

Sir Kenneth Olisa

Ken is Founder and Chairman of Restoration Partners, the boutique technology merchant bank and architects of Inogesis formerly known as The Virtual Technology Cluster model. Ken's technology career spans over 30 years commencing with IBM from whom he won a scholarship while at Fitzwilliam College, University of Cambridge. In 1992, after twelve years as a senior executive at Wang Labs in the US and Europe, Ken founded Interregnum, the technology merchant bank. He was elected as a Fellow of the British Computer Society in 2006.

He is currently Chairman of Interswitch (Africa's largest e-payments company).

Ken is a Freeman of the City of London, Liveryman and Past Master of the Worshipful Company of Information Technologists, Patron of Thames Reach (for which he received an OBE in 2010), and Chairman of charity Shaw Trust. He is the Founder and Chairman of the Aleto Foundation. He is a past Sunday Times Not for Profit Non-Executive Director of the year and was named Number 1 in the 2016 Powerlist's roster of the UK's most influential black people. In 2013 Ken and his wife, Julia, endowed the Olisa Library at his alma mater Fitzwilliam College, Cambridge. In 2015, Her Majesty the Queen appointed Ken as Her Majesty's Lord-Lieutenant for Greater London and he was knighted in the 2018 New Year's Honours List for services to business and philanthropy. In September 2018 Ken was appointed as the director on the board of Huawei a Chinese multinational networking, telecommunications equipment and Services Company.

Jean Pousson

Jean Pousson is an experienced company director and management consultant, who has conducted training and consultancy assignments in well over 30 countries over a 30 year period. Originally from Mauritius, his formative career was with Barclays Bank in South Africa in retail and corporate banking, where assessing risk in businesses was a capability that he nurtured. A spell followed in the City of London before he joined the then TSB Banking Group where his last appointment was Director of Studies, responsible for academic leadership within the Group.

His two consulting businesses have kept him active and with Board Evaluation Limited, he has carried out numerous Board performance reviews across a good spectrum of Boards. This is complemented with his board positions.

He is a senior consultant with the Academy for Board Excellence, the only accredited supplier of the UK Institute of Directors, and has been a regular contributor to their programmes leading to the prestigious Chartered Director qualification. In 2019 he was voted "Lecturer of the Year" for UK Finance, the professional body that oversees the Asset Finance Industry in the UK.

A keen sportsman he has run over 30 marathons including two ultra marathons and is now a keen cyclist having already completed a few 100 milers.

Tom Proverbs-Garbett FCG

Tom is a corporate lawyer at Pinsent Masons LLP and a Fellow of the Chartered Governance Institute (chartered company secretary). Having been an M&A lawyer for 10 years, his practice now focusses on corporate governance matters and issues surrounding directors' duties. Tom leads the firm's company secretarial function. He writes on governance matters and corporate law and provides training for boards and individual directors, with a particular interest in conflicts of interest and subsidiary governance. Tom trained in the City and, after completing his MBA, worked in-house with Jaguar Land Rover, leading on their commercial research relationships and assisting with company secretarial matters.

Professor Jeffrey Ridley FCG

Jeffrey Ridley is a visiting professor at three universities in the United Kingdom London South Bank University*, University of Lincoln" and Birmingham City University – teaching and researching auditing, sustainability assurance and governance. He currently also supervises doctorate students at the London South Bank University where he took up his chair in 1991. Before that he worked in two major US global manufacturing and distribution companies as a senior internal auditor and manager, following working for ten years as a Colonial Audit Officer in Nigeria, West Africa.

In 1975 he was elected the first President of the U.K. Chapter of The Institute of Internal Auditors in the United States, now the Chartered Institute of Internal Auditors. In 2010 he was honoured with its Distinguished Service Award. Since his retirement from full-time employment in 1993 he has lived in Lincolnshire with his family but continued his academic career part-time. He is a Fellow of The Chartered Governance Institute (CGI), Fellow of the Chartered Institute of Internal Auditors (CIIA) and a Certified Internal Auditor.

He was a practicing auditor for many years, and is now a consultant on all aspects of corporate governance, a researcher with published papers, has published three books on auditing and since 1975 many articles on auditing, governance quality management, environmental, social and sustainability issues. His latest articles are on quality in good governance, published in 2017 in the Journals of the Chartered Quality Institute, United Kingdom and The Institute of Internal Auditors in the United States: A Civil Future (2019) and Project Zero (2020) were published by the Chartered Institute of Internal Auditors in the United Kingdom.

ENDORSEMENTS

Corporate Governance 3.0 provides a timely analysis of the history and latest developments in global corporate governance. From the Cadbury Report in 1992, to the increasing dependence on computers and IT in the 1990s and 21st century, to the move from the primacy of the shareholder approach to the focus on value creation that is sustainable, this book usefully advocates an inclusive rather than exclusive approach to corporate governance based on trust, integrity and openness and collective business judgment by boards, enabling dynamic solutions to current business and wider society challenges. The book is easy to read and expertly edited.

Chris Campbell-Holt
Registrar and Chief Executive
AIFC Court and International Arbitration Centre

This rich volume offers a wealth of varied governance perspectives. Having travelled the world for twenty years at researching best in class governance, I still found many refreshing views across chapters. The classification of governance evolution differs from the usual regulatory evolution. The base for a values-based governance system, governance 4.0, is already manifest amongst the most influential asset owners. The strength of governance transformation has become a key driver of performance. No sole principle or regional practice defines today's governance excellence. Each of us, investor or corporate, needs to define the appropriate form to our purpose. This volume will inspire further reflexion with truly current information.

Professor Didier Cossin,
Founder and Director of the IMD Global Board Center,
President of the Stewardship Institute, Chaired Professor of Governance.
IMD

Corporate Governance 3.0 perfectly succeeds in analysing all the essential aspects of its subject matter in a clear, easily understandable and exhaustive way, adding a lot to its readers' knowledge and comprehension....and hopefully, to the support of many boards for much needed, rapid action. As a career diplomat and financial sector governance professional, I am impressed by this set of chapters that offers powerful arguments to all those who engaged in trying to solve, both at the public and at the private level, the urgent sustainability, inclusiveness and resiliency issues of today's company boards.

Dr Guy de Muyser
Honorary Ambassador, Luxembourg

Dr Karl George, Simon Osborne and Professor Alexander Van de Putte take readers into this changing corporate world and they deal with the question of trust, integrity and openness and propose an alternative approach to corporate governance that is more sustainable, inclusive and resilient. This pioneering book is to be welcomed at a time when there is significant change in the corporate reporting world. It acts as a great go-to guide for corporate leaders who want to excel as strategic global leaders and stewards.

Professor José Esteves
Associate Dean for MBA & TECHMBA Programs
IE Business School

Governance and the work of the Board is much more than compliance. As the expectations on boards evolve, directors must be very thoughtful about their role and the broad range of issues that they need to consider in carrying it out. This book will be invaluable to directors, and those who advise and train them, as it sets the development of 3.0 Governance in context, provides clear methods for addressing the challenges which Boards are now facing and gives directors much on which to base their thinking.

David Jackson
Company Secretary
BP plc 2003-2018

For those who are keen to understand the core issues of governance but without getting bogged down by theories and technical details of compliance and rules, this book is recommended. It provides the generational perspectives for understanding how the core and unchanging principles of governance are supplanted by changing environment, changing expectations of stakeholders and the unintended consequences of technology and data. This book addresses not only the need for leadership role of the board in overall management of the company, but ventures into uncovering the goings on in the board otherwise known as the ' black -box'. Board members, company secretaries, governance professionals, and those interacting with boards whether in public or private companies, will find the relevant topics on board dynamics interesting and insightful.

Professor Syed Abdul Hamid Aljunid
International Centre for Education in Islamic Finance
Kuala Lumpur, Malaysia

Another corporate governance book?! The authors are well aware that corporate governance has gotten bogged down numerous times in bureaucratic application of over-prescriptive lists. It is always time for a rethink, and they reassert the need to redevelop four basic areas - board effectiveness, culture, stakeholder engagement, and integrated assurance. Above all though, corporate governance is ineffective if it is not adaptable. This book challenges us to reinvent and apply fresh approaches to corporate governance at all times. Never succumb to thinking governance is 'done and dusted'.

Professor Michael Mainelli
Executive Chairman
Z/Yen Group

Corporate Governance 3.0 provides critical insights into all facets that contribute to an effective corporate governance framework. The chapters are arranged to allow for easy referencing which is useful given the need to adapt to rapidly changing paradigms. This book offers macro and micro perspectives and addresses the need for introspection and continuous self-development. The authors examine emerging trends/issues that will invariably impact tomorrow's Boards - including ESG, diversity and cultural shifts. Many of these topics are also focal points for regulators in their oversight of licensees and the necessary, increased scrutiny of corporate governance. A 'must read'!

Simone Martin
Deputy Director
Anguilla Financial Services Commission

This useful history of governance charts the progress and change in attitudes within company boards and stakeholders over what is a relatively short timeframe. The authors are all experienced professionals in their areas. Their examples help us understand the evolution of governance, while encouraging us to consider the need for the next layer of change. Certainly, the role of the Board, consideration of the interests and expectations of all stakeholders and the importance for companies to demonstrate how they act as responsible entities has never been more vital, especially in a post-pandemic and climate-challenged world. This book is relevant to directors, company secretaries and the wider stakeholder community and highlights the role we can all play in enhancing board effectiveness, corporate governance and global reporting standards. Gen 4.0 has much to do!

Amanda Mellor
Group Company Secretary
Standard Chartered Bank

What a wonderful roller coaster of a governance ride!!!! This integrated, pragmatic, and innovative book takes you through the history of corporate governance, starting before the Cadbury report, known as the paper age, and then going into detail about the computer age. An account of the digital age follows, where the disruption of incumbents became the norm. This book provides a new blueprint for sustainable corporate governance in which regulations and personal values mutually reinforce each other, taking into account the resource constraints of planet earth and accepting that in making decisions in the best interests of the company there will invariably be trade-offs between the various stakeholder groupings. This book is a must-read for all governance professionals at a time when there are so many changes and the world, and indeed life, seem so fragile and unsustainable.

Jill Parratt, FCG
Group Company Secretary
Liberty Holdings Limited, South Africa

Corporate Governance 3.0 is a timely gift to those who have a deep interest in understanding the history and related lessons of the 3 generations of corporate governance models that have been practiced over the last 50 years. The book also captures a fountain of wisdom on critical topics that both new and experienced directors will find refreshing. Three standout topics include the need for boards to include digitally conversant directors in an increasingly digital world, all board members to achieve a basic level of financial literacy and sustainability as a catalyst for driving more sustainable business growth.

Bruce Scott
Partner & Risk Assurance Leader
PwC Jamaica, PwC in the Caribbean

To map the evolution of corporate governance and then evaluate it in the context of today's environment is not an easy task but Corporate Governance 3.0 does just that. Corporate Governance 3.0 starts at the beginning but distinguishes itself when it takes the reader across jurisdictions and across all levels of an organisation. It critiques the evolution of governance in meeting today's challenges such as more intensive shareholder engagement or the importance of board behavioural dynamics. It looks at the role of all the participants in the governance matrix, including the often over-looked company secretary. I highly recommend Corporate Governance 3.0.

Tim Sheehy FCG
Director General
The Chartered Governance Institute

Good governance has evolved to more than just a tick-the-box compliance process to a narrow array of stakeholders. In a constantly changing and unsure environment, it is critical to learn from the past while focusing on a more sustainable future for an ever-expanding, diverse range of stakeholders. This impressive body of work is essential reading at a time when corporate structures are continually developing, where stewardship in most organizational structures is questioned, where we are starting to value inclusivity and where accountability is beginning to matter.

Connie Smith
Managing Director
Tricor Caribbean Limited

Dive into the historical drama of corporate governance, appreciate its criticality, explore the timeless principles practised by corporate leaders, and indulge in the collective wisdom of the past, present, and future. The authors challenge us to see corporate governance through a global lens, augmented by the unique regional perspectives. I discovered deep insights after every chapter and even re-visited some to expand my insights further. I am sure that every reader will enjoy the immense knowledge, practical applications, and personal reflections from the book as much as I did.

Dr Noel Yeo
Chief Operating Officer
IHH Healthcare Singapore

Printed in Great Britain
by Amazon